University of

MARKETING SKILLS

P165 Novel segmentation

P163 sorts of differences
at three different
leverage points

key
MARKETING
SKILLS

a complete action kit
of strategies, tools & techniques for marketing success

peter cheverton

KOGAN
PAGE

First published in 2000
Reprinted 2001

Kogan Page Limited
120 Pentonville Road
London N1 9JN
UK

Kogan Page
22 Broad Street,
Milford CT 06460
USA

© Peter Cheverton, 2000

British Library Cataloguing in Publication Data

A CIP record for this book is available from the British Library.

ISBN 0 7494 3355 8

Typeset by Jean Cussons Typesetting, Diss, Norfolk
Printed and bound in Great Britain by Bell & Bain Ltd, Glasgow

Contents

Foreword

Why does the world need another book on the principles and practice of marketing?

Well, for one thing, marketing by its very nature must keep pace with the changing business practices of the real world, and perhaps it is now, more than at any other time in the last thirty years, that these changes promise to alter the shape of the marketer's vision. That is the upside. But, if misunderstood, these new practices also threaten to disrupt the poorly informed marketer's equilibrium, sending them back into the dark age of a secondary support function.

What are these changes? They include the so-called 'new economy' heralded by the *e-revolution* – does it change the rules of marketing? Another is the increasing focus on *Key Account Management* – does that move the responsibility for marketing elsewhere? And a third, looking beyond the hype that most threatens to engulf and suffocate, is *Customer Relationship Management* – is there genuine value for the marketer?

In answering these questions, this book shows how the marketer's vision can indeed be reshaped. But perhaps the more important contribution to the practice of marketing lies in the stress given to the continued importance of a disciplined approach, without hyperbole or false expectations. The sad truth behind many of today's marketing failures is the false belief that fundamentals such as understanding the market, segmentation, positioning, marketing planning and management of the marketing mix are no longer relevant.

Twenty years ago, companies were too often guilty of investing millions in advertising campaigns with little or no understanding of their true impact, or sometimes even of their purpose. This book certainly shows how to avoid such mistakes, and lays down the warning not to repeat the malpractice with today's 'new toys'.

The fundamentals still apply, but it isn't just about 'sticking to your knitting'. The new concepts provide opportunities for these fundamental tools of marketing to be used and envisioned in radically different ways. The Internet certainly changes the face of the marketing mix: Customer Relationship Management offers approaches to segmentation that would previously have been extremely difficult or expensive, whilst Key Account Management provides the opportunity to build barriers to entry and achieve sustainable competitive advantage through integrated relationships.

The second reason that this book is needed (and any marketer knows that needs are what drive the market) is that professional marketers are crying out for help with the practical application of marketing tools and concepts. This book's approach throughout is a practical one. Written by a practitioner, for practitioners, it uses real case studies in abundance to illustrate what could otherwise sometimes seem rather abstract concepts. As such, the book is a mine of inspiration, and of timely warnings.

Case studies, particularly those that are still running their course, are always dangerous territory for an author. This author chooses his with an eye first and foremost on whether they instruct and illuminate. If posterity sees some of them turn the 'wrong way' then so be it – the emphasis here is on learning, not prediction.

My third reason for welcoming this new book to the distinguished list of marketing texts is perhaps a more depressing one. The role of marketing in guiding and directing business strategy is a vital and fundamental one, yet for many companies it is still their 'weak link'. All too often marketing is seen as the promotional arm of an organization rather than the function that informs all other functions what their contribution should be to creating customer value.

This book is intended to help raise the profile of marketing as a crucial element of corporate strategy. It offers help to experienced marketers through a disciplined focus on what the activity really means. By stripping away some of the trees we have a welcome re-sighting of the wood. Newcomers will benefit from the hugely efficient explanation of key tools and concepts, while those from the so-called 'non-marketing functions' will appreciate the wealth of cases that bring the activity to life, rather than shrouding it in abstruse and academic models.

If you are interested in marketing, whether in pursuit of a professional qualification, or in order to make an effective contribution to your own company's marketing activity, or simply to better understand and work with your marketing colleagues, please be assured that reading this book will be a rewarding experience.

Professor Malcolm McDonald
September 2000

Preface

This book is designed as a practical guide to the skills, disciplines and *application* of professional marketing practice. As well as discussing the concepts, the book and the accompanying CD ROM will help professional marketers to apply those concepts in their own businesses and markets. The tools and processes provided are equally applicable to consumer, industrial, business-to-business or service environments.

A SHORT COMMENT ON THE EXAMPLES AND CASE STUDIES USED

Wherever possible I have used real examples, often as up to date as the moment of writing. The advantage of this is a topicality and immediacy that I hope are welcomed, but the downsides are obvious and potentially embarrassing! I trust that not too many of my 'success stories' have gone bust by the time the book reaches the bookstore or that events have not so long overtaken any questions or predictions as to render them the mutterings of an imbecile. As I write, a crop of e-retailers appear ready to fall out of the sky while another bunch of new dotcoms are still racing up the equity charts –

which ones to quote? The moral might be to invent fictitious companies, but in the end I take another moral from the story – times change and so do fortunes, and such is marketing's challenge.

Acknowledgements

My thanks as ever to my colleagues in INSIGHT Marketing and People whose knowledge and experiences have added greatly to the relevance and practicality of this book. In particular my thanks to Irene and Barbara for coping with the *many* revisions to the text over the last year, and to Kate for her hard work in putting the CD ROM together.

Professor Malcolm McDonald of Cranfield University School of Management, and Chairman of INSIGHT, has been his usual generous self in providing encouragement for my ideas as well as allowing me to use a number of his own.

Peter Cheverton
September 2000

Part I

Getting Started – Purpose And Process

Good marketing

How might you measure good marketing? If, as claimed by many practitioners, marketing is a profession, then surely there will be professional standards, as there are for doctors, lawyers and architects.

But what makes a good doctor – the number of ill patients made better? Observers might look at more than that. What about doctors' role in preventative medicine? What about their bedside manner? And what makes a good lawyer – the number of clients vindicated? Many observers would be swayed as much by the way they spoke in court, or the ingenuity of their arguments. Judging a good architect has always been a tough one – is it the number of buildings still standing and in use after 100 years? What about architects' influence on building development? Is it just a matter of taste?

It can be much the same with marketers. Whilst you might expect some hard measures and seek a close correlation between a successful business and good marketing – the equivalent of the healthy patient, the victorious case, the long-standing building – some onlookers might make other judgements that can obscure the real task of marketing. Marketing has its own versions of bedside manner, ingenious argument and questions of taste.

Like award-winning buildings that start to crumble after only three years and are pulled down after 10, advertising awards often go to adverts that make only minimal impact on the product's sales. Rewarding creativity and top production is one thing, but don't mistake it for rewarding marketing effectiveness. The casual observer of marketing activity often cares more for the surface than the substance – good marketing being synonymous with a 'clever' advertising campaign or a 'novel' product launch, almost regardless of business success. 'This is the age of the train' was a 'clever' slogan, as was 'That's the wonder of Woolies', but who believed them, and who acted on them? The launch of Clive Sinclair's now infamous C5 'car-cum-oversized roller-skate' was impressively high-profile and the product was certainly novel, but few were ever sold. Focusing only on the surface appearance of such marketing activity would be rather like admiring a doctor's bedside manner while forgiving them the death of the patient.

Good marketing doesn't have to be flashy, it doesn't need the backing of huge advertising budgets and it doesn't even have to be novel. Some of the best marketing is routine and repetitive – but it is never stupid.

Perhaps it is easier to describe bad marketing, that is marketing that comes from ignorance and above all else from arrogance (a particular sin of many large businesses). When Mr Dyson invented his bag-less vacuum cleaner based on the cyclone system, he took it first to Hoover. They rejected it. What attraction could such an invention have for them when such a large proportion of their income and profits came from selling bags? So Dyson launched it himself and redefined the whole market within a year. His offer was appropriate to the needs of consumers because he understood their predicament – poor suction as bags filled and messy disposal once they were full. He knew his offer would work, but Hoover couldn't, or wouldn't, see it – they were of course the number one brand, big, successful and very superior.

The tale of how IBM missed, ignored, or wilfully denied the opportunity to develop the market for personal computers is so often told as to need no retelling, other than to point out the danger of being the biggest, the most successful, the most complacent and the least observant.

READING THE SIGNALS

The old stories are often the best and there is still a wonderful debate to be had over one of the oldest in the marketing textbooks – the shoe salesman in darkest Africa (it is an old story, so salespeople are still men and Africa is still dark). Picture the scene as the salesman steps off the plane at some remote airport, surrounded by the noises of the jungle, and looks, as is his instinct, at the feet of those come to greet him – no shoes.

What is the response of the good marketer? Get on the next flight home, or regard this as the single biggest opportunity of his life? Either could be true, or made to be true, but assumptions and arrogance will surely blind us to the truth, whichever the case. Is the second choice that of the stereotypical salesperson – equating lack of something with a need for that thing? Stereotypical indeed, and no more a sin of selling than of marketing. But the former option, to give up without enquiry, isn't that just how to waste a travel budget?

There is no right answer without more information, starting perhaps with 'Why no shoes?' Obvious, of course, but so often there is something that makes us resist asking such questions, an arrogance that comes with being big and successful or, worse, with feeling superior.

Carrying on the theme, consider the first world's response to Third-World famine over the last 100 years. At first the answer was a coin in a collection box, or a food parcel. But as crops were seen to fail time after time the 'clever' answer slowly became 'Give them a fish' – get them to change their diet. But what if they didn't like fish, couldn't cook fish, had problems digesting fish? Nobody asked such questions and the generosity of the West turned to frustration as the fish rotted at food depots. Then came the wisest idea yet: let's not send them fish; let's teach them how to fish instead. For many this is still the wisdom of Third-World aid.

All very worthy, but why do we not stop to wonder why they hadn't turned to fishing before, on their own initiative? Perhaps there were no fish, or maybe they were inedible? Despite the very best intentions – we want to help, they're bound to like it, we like it, and it's a damn good idea – ignorance and arrogance can conspire to defeat us.

What does this have to do with marketing? For aid to succeed it must be accepted and used; it must be appropriate, and that means that the givers of aid must understand the context of the need and the applicability of their offer. This is not such a bad starting-point for good marketing – matching need and applicability – but so often the simplicity of this concept is forgotten by the big, the successful and the superior.

SOME FIRST RULES

So we are led to some first rules of good marketing – rather general, you might think, certainly simple, but no less important as a consequence:

● Never take anything for granted.
● Always ask questions – 'why?' is a good one – and listen to the answers, however uncomfortable.
● Seek to understand before trying to persuade. This is a maxim for persuaders, managers and coaches, and one that applies equally well to marketers.
● The bigger and more successful you are, the more you should be watchful for signs of arrogance – learn to doubt a little your own certainties.
● Novelty and cleverness are in the eye of the beholder, not of the creator.

This requirement to deal with uncertainty yet seek answers on which to base your activities is what makes marketing the challenge that it most certainly is, and accounts for the 'fun' that many get from its practice. The day-to-day application of good marketing can sometimes be mundane and repetitive, but it is carried out in an environment of continual change and intellectual challenge.

The best tip I was given when I took on my first marketing role for an fmcg (fast-moving consumer goods) company was: think like our customers, read the newspapers they read, watch the television programmes they watch, and talk to them whenever you can. And make sure that whatever you do it is relevant to them and their needs. 'Oh, and of course,' said my adviser, 'make sure you're always one step ahead of them.'

2

What is marketing?

Put yourself in the shoes of each of the following three customers and ask yourself, 'Why might I be doing this?'.

1. You are the buyer for a large building firm and one of your regular orders is for paint, thousands of litres at a time. You always use the same supplier and the sales reps from rival manufacturers have a problem getting appointments with you even though you know you are paying as much as a 5 per cent premium and there is no appreciable difference in quality.

2. You are doing the weekly supermarket shop and more out of interest than economy you are comparing prices of products that make it into your trolley. It intrigues you to note that you are paying more for a small (but attractive) glass bottle of still mineral water with a *twist* of peach (or was it a *hint* of loganberry?) than for a plastic bottle of orange squash that will make 20 pints at home with good old-fashioned tap water. Intriguing, but it doesn't bother you; in fact, you think about putting the bottle of squash back on the shelf.

3. You are the marketing manager of a small software house based in Cheltenham, small in turnover but big in ambition. You are hiring a company to deliver marketing training to all staff in your business, and you have a choice between a large London-

based company with an impressive client list and a long track record, and a smaller local company just making its way in the business. Cost is not the issue – the London firm has a surprisingly low price as they have put a junior partner on the job and the local company is at its top whack because you're getting the MD. You choose the smaller company.

Three situations, the first from a *business-to-business* environment, the second an *fmcg* situation and the third an example from the *service* industry. Assuming that in each case customers have a good and convincing reason for their behaviour, what might it be?

What is it that makes us choose one product or supplier over another? Is it marketing? In each of these cases, having assumed that the customer is behaving with good reason, and we also assume that the successful supplier knows what it is doing rather than just getting lucky, then the answer to that question is – yes, it's marketing.

Customers seek value for money – a phrase that can mean a hundred and one things from the cheapest to the longest lasting, the most convenient to the most fitting for the purpose. It all depends on the customer. Perhaps marketing is about finding the customers who regard your particular offer as good value for their money?

1. The building company put more store by speed of delivery than anything else. They reckon that if they can have a delivery within 24 hours rather than the industry-standard 72 hours (and their favoured supplier manages 24 every time), then that is worth the premium. They have very little storage space and the little that they have they prefer to use for things that can take months to deliver. Fast delivery means low stocks and that equals value for money.

2. As you push your trolley around the aisles you remind yourself that money isn't a big issue with you, but time and convenience count for a lot. You work hard and when it comes to relaxing you want to treat yourself. Novelty is always fun and it helps you feel that all your hard work is worth it. The mineral-water company has had your aspirations in its sights for some time. The problem with squash is that with the water in your area it's sometimes more like rust than orange, and you always have to run the tap for three minutes before it starts to come out even remotely cool.

3. The trouble with big companies, it seems to you as you consider the ideal training supplier, is that they speak big-company language. That's OK if your staff are wielding advertising budgets of millions and are launching new products in global markets, but if your biggest concern is satisfying local customers for whose needs you can design bespoke packages, then maybe a company that speaks your language and shares your challenges might be more appropriate – better value for money.

So, is marketing success simply about finding the customers who regard your offer as value for money? In part, but that is still less than half the story. The company that first makes the product and then seeks a market is chancing its arm, and sooner or later it will come unstuck. Good marketing is about understanding the customer's expectations of value for money, and then meeting them. Very good marketing is about exceeding those expectations, winning the customer's loyalty and making a profit, all at the same time. Excellent marketing might be about inventing a new currency for value, uniquely suited to your offer, so gaining yourself true market leadership. The multiplex cinema has redefined the experience of going to the pictures and raised a new standard of value expected from a good night out. Despite predictions of the death of the cinema at the hands of the video, the multiplex idea has seen cinema attendance reach levels not seen since the boom years before there was a television in every home.

Try another three scenarios, and this time put yourself in the supplier's shoes and ask yourself, 'What must I do to succeed?'.

1. You manufacture chocolate bars – not a major brand name, but a good product using top-quality ingredients. What do you have to be good at to succeed against the competition from the big guys, and why should a retailer, or anyone else, want to buy your product?
2. You sell pesticides to farmers who are growing increasingly concerned about whether they can sell their produce if it is treated with such chemicals. What could you do?
3. You provide an in-house business travel booking service to a multinational company that believes it can get a better deal on its own, through the Internet. How can you keep the business?

From the supplier's point of view, is the answer to these questions 'Marketing'? It is certainly about having clear propositions to put in front of potential customers, propositions that will give evidence of *your* value for *their* money:

1.   What value can you give to retailers who prefer the easy life of having big brand names sell themselves? Perhaps they want an own label? But are you cut out for that sort of business? The volumes may be more than you can cope with, and the economies of scale are less than the costs of expanding your capability and giving the sort of discounts the customer will expect. Perhaps there is a small demand, a niche market, for flavoured chocolate bars – liqueurs, orange oil, coconut? Perhaps there is a demand for organic chocolate, or chocolate made from ingredients grown in countries and on plantations that treat their employees with a level of respect you can live with? And maybe, just maybe, you can offer some of these things without breaking the bank, your business, or your word.

2.   Sell them less pesticide? Fine if you have some alternative solutions for them. Offer a service to manage the application of the pesticides to minimum levels? Or provide them with evidence that they can pass on to their customers that your products are not harmful in the food chain? (A recent report argues that organically grown food with its higher chance of harbouring bacteria is some eight times more likely to kill us than food sprayed with a cocktail of unpronounceable chemicals!)

3.   Sounds like they are determined. Perhaps you should find a new customer, one that values its own time more than the thrill of finding bargains through Internet searches?

Of course, the real answers to these marketing problems are to be found somewhere beneath a pile of 'it depends'. And that is also marketing – understanding the dynamics and interactions of all those overlapping and competing 'it depends'. What these examples start to suggest is that marketing is more than finding customers for your offer; perhaps it is also about adapting that offer to meet the needs you encounter?

WHAT THE MAN ON THE CLAPHAM OMNIBUS THINKS

Ask a sample of people in a pub or standing in a bus queue or even the proverbial man on the Clapham omnibus what they understand by 'marketing' and it is unlikely you will hear anything much like the points we have been discussing. You are more likely to hear something like the cynical 'Making people buy things they don't need', or the half-informed 'It's all about advertising', or even a passionate denouncement of the 'exploitative, consumerism-run-mad society we all live in'. It is a fair guess that the answers will bear little relation to the challenges confronting today's professional marketer.

Not so long ago a poll of opinions in the UK found marketing people rated at only one rung above politicians and tabloid journalists on the ladder of 'respectable careers'. Why the apparent contempt? (At least we don't need to ask the question for the careers on the bottom rung.) The cliché has it that familiarity breeds contempt. Well if that is so, then it is a familiarity with a gross caricature of the marketer as an overpaid yuppie indulging in an irresponsible kind of spivvish behaviour that preys on people's frailties and is at best 'economical with the actualité' (to quote the late Alan Clark, MP).

WHAT YOU THINK

Which of the following six statements do you feel give the best definitions of what marketing is all about? Perhaps none of them matches your own understanding, but which come closest? Try to identify the three that you feel are the best, or if none of them appeals very much, then identify the three least bad!

Marketing is:

1. selling everything that you make;
2. making our customers prosperous;
3. making the best-quality product;
4. making whatever quality the customer wants;
5. getting out of unprofitable lines;
6. looking for future needs.

I confess that none of these statements is meant to be an adequate definition; reducing marketing to a four- or five-word definition is a tall order (though in the next chapter I will make a stab with 15). The point of the exercise is to establish whether you have any current bias in your understanding – are you a 'left sider' or a 'right sider'?

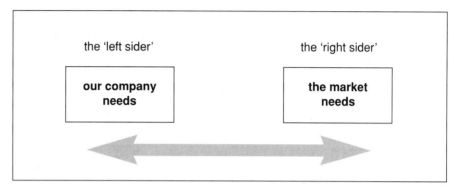

Figure 2.1 *The attitude spectrum*

Perhaps you can identify a commonality between statements 1, 3 and 5, and another between 2, 4 and 6? Definitions 1, 3 and 5 are the 'left sider' views: a concern with internal issues (achieving sales targets or efficient use of production capacity), an emphasis on the product and a focus on the present. Numbers 2, 4 and 6 are the 'right sider' views: their focus is external – the customer, and a concern for the future (see Figure 2.1).

Is one side any better than the other? Let's debate the 'left siders':

- *Marketing is selling everything that you make.* So what if the market doesn't want what you make? What if it prefers someone else's product or service? In such a situation your only option may be to drop the price and have a clearance sale. Is that good marketing?
- *Marketing is making the best-quality product.* So what if people feel they can do with something less than a Rolls-Royce? How do you force a cordon bleu meal on someone determined on eating a Big Mac? Indeed, why should you try? There are few restaurant chains more successful than McDonalds.
- *Marketing is getting out of unprofitable lines.* So what if you supply stationery items direct to local offices, and most of your lines are profitable, but not envelopes. Do you drop envelopes from the

range and make the customers go elsewhere? How would they feel about you, and what if they get to like where they go for their envelopes?

There are clearly some significant limitations to defining marketing solely in this 'left sider' way. So let's debate the 'right siders':

- _Marketing is making our customers prosperous._ Is this an act of faith? Does customer profit equal our own profit? The best way to make a customer prosperous might be to supply them top-quality product, with top-quality support and service, free of charge – not much of a plan you say, but isn't that just what is happening with suppliers of Internet access software?
- _Marketing is making whatever quality the customer wants._ But what if we can't, competitively? Let's say we make dyes for fabrics, top-quality dyes. Perhaps there is a demand for a low-quality, low-price dye for some applications, but we can't hope to compete with low-price imports. Do we supply at a loss, as an act of good-will?
- _Marketing is looking for future needs._ Of course, to argue with that would be dull, but how much of this 'future focus' is 'wild blue yondering' in reality? Might an overgrown fascination with the future blind us to the real needs of today?

These 'right sider' views might seem to be 'states of mind' as much as practical definitions. Making customers prosperous, giving them what they want, constantly thinking of their future needs – perhaps these are even acts of faith?

It is certainly true that marketing does represent a state of mind, a belief that getting it right for the customer will result in our own success – not a state of mind, it has to be said, that is necessarily shared by all in business. There are other states of mind. Our success will come from: cost reduction (the accountants' view?); increased volume (salespeople and factory managers?); developing better and better products (R & D?). Are they all right? Is business success a compromise between these potentially conflicting notions or does one or other of them have to win through? Is it possible that they could all be achieved simultaneously?

DO BANKS DO MARKETING?

Let's take an entirely fictitious bank and suppose that they have just had a study done on the cost to them of processing cheques. They were expecting a big number but are staggered by the huge scale of the cost when all its implications are considered. Clearly something must be done. Somebody suggests that they simply announce a long-term plan to remove cheques as a service in line with the natural increase in electronic payments in the market. Someone else suggests that they should levy a charge for using cheques, first to non-customers of the bank but eventually even to their own customers. The next person attempts to soften this by suggesting that they offer a discount to those people who use methods other than cheques. Is this marketing, or a fixation with their own issues?

The true marketer, the person who seeks to consider both sides of the attitude spectrum in Figure 2.1, would realize the benefit to the bank of not processing cheques and would then look out into the market-place and ask how the bank could help promote a faster move towards electronic payments. It would need to understand people's perceptions about using cheques versus electronic transfers and how questions of trust, confidence and security weighed against issues such as cost and convenience. And by people we don't just mean the bank's customers; we mean everyone out there who makes or receives payments – the market-place. If the bank were able truly to understand the needs of the market in this way it might then be in a position not only to influence the whole market-place, but also to gain competitive advantage, while securing all the internal benefits of reducing cheque processing. We might call this marketing.

Let's close this chapter (admittedly one that has posed questions rather than provided answers) with a definition from the UK's Chartered Institute of Marketing (CIM), and ask you to consider how far it goes to improving on the limits found in 'left sider' and 'right sider' views, and what issues it still leaves unresolved. According to this definition, marketing is:

> 'anticipating, identifying and satisfying customers' needs … profitably'.

3

The marketing model

The definition of marketing given at the close of Chapter 2 is fine, *as far as it goes*. It is good that it stresses the future. Marketing is a proactive task; it is about *anticipating*. It sees marketing as an inquisitive pursuit, not simply the result of what we know and do already; it is about *identifying*. It gives marketing a fundamental goal – *satisfying customers' needs*, and it provides a 'real world' test, that this should be done *profitably*.

So what is lacking? I would make three observations:

1. In the real world none of this happens in a vacuum. There are competitors struggling just like you to anticipate, identify and satisfy. This has an implication on *how* you will go about the task, finding ways to do it better, faster, more cheaply, or some other, preferably unique, advantage. At its core, marketing must be about seeking such *competitive advantage*.
2. As well as the *competitive environment*, there is also your own environment, your own business's capabilities. The real world again – resources, money, time, people and skills, factors that will impact on your ability to anticipate, identify and satisfy profitably.
3. Most written definitions of marketing suffer one or sometimes

both of two common problems. Either they say too much in their attempt to cover the nuances, or they use words that alienate all but the already converted. How about this definition? 'Marketing is the process of: 1) identifying customer needs; 2) conceptualizing these needs in terms of the organization's capacity to produce; 3) communicating that conceptualization to the appropriate focus of power in the organization; 4) conceptualizing the consequent output in terms of customer needs earlier identified; 5) communicating that conceptualization to the customer.' If you could be bothered to fathom its meaning there *is* actually something there, but frankly, who would be bothered? This brings us to a third problem – most definitions also lack what I might call 'the spur to action'. You read the definition at the close of Chapter 2 only a few seconds ago. Do you remember it? Does it *live* in your mind? Does it make you want to do anything new or different about your business?

I would like to propose another definition, a pictorial one, encompassing all that the CIM definition urges, and taking on board my three observations (see Figure 3.1).

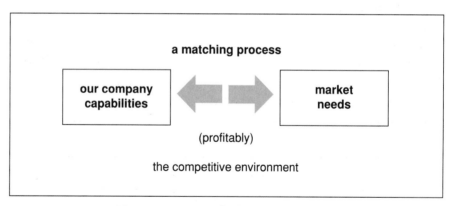

Figure 3.1 *Marketing – a definition*

I will also attempt the 15-word definition promised in Chapter 2. Marketing is: 'a matching process between our capabilities and the market needs, seeking a profitable competitive advantage'.

The model combines the 'left sider' views we discussed in Chapter 2 – our own company capabilities and requirements – with the 'right sider' view of the external world, and makes neither dominant over the other. Marketing is about finding the match between the left siders' realities and the right siders' enquiry and understanding.

The search for this match happens in a competitive environment. While everyone else is pursuing this same goal (assuming they know anything about marketing!), yours must be to seek some form of advantage over them, preferably through some element of uniqueness. And that edge, or source of _competitive advantage_, should be robust and sustainable. It is of little advantage or profit to find a match that your competitors can copy, and perhaps ultimately achieve at lower costs than you. (We will return to this particular challenge in Chapters 8 and 18.)

The model does perhaps lack one ingredient from the CIM definition – the notion of anticipation. Marketing is not static. Above all else it must concern itself with the future, seeking to anticipate needs, even to create them, and seeking to mould capabilities in order to meet those needs. The exact time frame will depend on the industry and the market. In the world of high fashion, clothes designers must always be looking a season ahead; for the manufacturer of military aircraft the future is a decade or more away; and in the world of IT, it could be only weeks.

This slightly more complex version of the model places the matching activity not only in the competitive environment, but also in the appropriate time frame (see Figure 3.2). Any company wishing a future must operate in the present while moulding its capabilities for an anticipated or planned future.

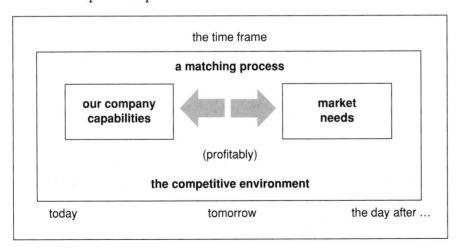

Figure 3.2 _Marketing – an anticipatory definition_

TESTING THE MODEL

The real test of any such model or definition has to be: does it make any difference to how decisions are made, strategies set, or resources applied? Would an understanding of this model have helped any of those businesses that have failed because of poor marketing?

The fall and rise of Triumph

The decline and fall of the British motor-cycle industry in the 1970s can be understood within the bounds of this model – in the omission rather than the commission of its strictures. Japanese manufacturers had better understood the needs of the market than the UK operators had, and they had a capability to provide the solutions. British manufacturers had failed to look ahead and anticipate, and when at last they saw the time had come for change they were not able to transform their capabilities at sufficient speed to keep up. Looking ahead means just that, looking for how things will be different, not planning the future based on the past. This is never easy for a business that glories in a successful past, as Triumph did.

Triumph had a great brand name with tremendous customer loyalty, but they let it slip away as they tried to move into the future by incremental steps based on the past. New features such as electronic starters and disc brakes were added to old designs, and all of this was done on old equipment that dated from the 1930s. Moreover, as they chased down the road of cost reduction and improved productivity they fell yet further short of the new standards set by market expectations, expectations that were being stimulated by the new entrants. The vicious circle of decline is not uncommon for companies that fail to understand what marketing is all about.

Could things have been different? Of course. There was no fundamental British inability to manufacture good motor cycles, only a deadening slowness to recognize that selling those bikes required marketing skills that had not yet been properly developed or in some cases even been seen as necessary. The 'marketing is for wimps' school of thought is not attractive in a boardroom.

The story has a happy ending with the rebirth of Triumph in the 1990s. The rebirth didn't just resurrect the brand name; it was realized that they also had to meet new needs, internally and externally. The new Triumphs were not retrospectives of the glory days; they were totally new designs made with totally different, computer-aided production techniques. Where reliability and quality had been sapped away in pursuit of reduced costs in the 70s, the new drive was for top quality and top reliability delivered by a workforce of passionate motor-cycle enthusiasts. Now the Japanese come to Britain to see how to build motor cycles and Triumph build more bikes than BMW, with their greatest success in Germany!

The death of a brilliant product – the slide rule

Let's take another example, this time of a long-dead business – slide rule manufacture.

Back in the 1950s and 60s we might imagine a manufacturer of slide rules, just south of Munich, making excellent profits because they made excellent slide rules. For those too young to remember, the slide rule was an instrument for calculating – multiplication and division, and for expert users a good deal more. It worked on the principle of logarithmic scales (don't worry, we don't need to know!) printed with great precision on something about the size of a ruler with a central slider that moved in and out to facilitate the calculations. All we need to know, perhaps, is that schoolchildren hated them.

The company had a match; they were good at making a tool that met a need – portable calculation. Unfortunately, the company didn't understand their activity in this way. They thought they made good slide rules, full stop. Their efforts and resources were devoted to making a better slide rule, a cheaper slide rule, a fancier slide rule – but in all cases, a slide rule. Of course, the moment someone launched the electronic pocket calculator, the slide rule's days were numbered. No level of price discounting would reverse the decline, nor any advertising campaign or up-market packaging – the idea was dead.

So how might the model have helped? Firstly, the company might have understood the basis of their success – a match of capabilities and needs, not simply a good product. Secondly, they might have spent some time defining just what needs they were meeting. It wasn't a need for a slide rule, but for portable calculation, a need that could be met in a number of different ways, including new technology. Thirdly, they might have identified more accurately the nature of their own capabilities – not making good slide rules, but the ability to make precision instruments.

Armed with such an understanding, the company would have had some choices, providing the basis for a long-term future: 1) to investigate new needs for their capability – manufacturing precision instruments; 2) to develop a capability to provide better means of portable calculation (a real need – remember how much schoolchildren hated them!).

In other words, they could have looked for a new kind of match, either by accepting their main capability and seeking new applications (a 'left sider' bias), or by seeking to change their capabilities in pursuit of a better solution to the market's needs (a 'right sider' bias).

At this point the time frame would be important. Once the first electronic calculator was on the market it would already be too late to start trying to change capabilities. A slide rule manufacturer cannot become an electronics manufacturer overnight. The 'right sider' focused on market needs would have needed to start work on its 'left sider' capabilities years in advance. To repeat an earlier comment: *marketing is not static; above all else it must concern itself with the future, seeking to anticipate needs, and seeking to mould capabilities in order to meet them.*

ISSUES RAISED BY THE MODEL

What the slide rule company really needed was an understanding of *what business they were in*. If we had asked them, doubtless the answer would have been, 'The slide rule business, of course!'. Such an answer would have betrayed their lack of understanding and application of marketing. For this company, we might guess, marketing meant designing the packaging and making sure the sales team had a good product brochure. The marketing department (if it existed at all) would have been about short-term tactical activities.

So what business *were* they in, if not the slide rule business? This is just one of several issues raised by the model, and perhaps we should list them first, and then deal with each in turn:

1. What business are you in? Are you product-led or market-led?
2. Should your activities be for the benefit of your own business, the customer, or the market? Is it market growth or market share you should strive for and promote?
3. Which side should you be working on – changing capabilities or influencing needs?
4. Does the model apply equally to consumer (fmcg), business-to-business and service industry marketing?
5. Is it market needs, or consumer needs (the concept of the market chain)?

6.   Is profitability the automatic consequence of a good match?
7.   How far ahead must you be looking?

What business are you in? Are you product-led or market-led?

The problem that our slide rule company had was a definition of their business by the product they made. This might sound an obvious enough thing to do, but it misses the point of the model. It is such a common mistake, made by businesses that are not marketing-orientated, that it deserves a lot of attention. It betrays a left sider's mindset, valuing tangible things (like products) above intangible concepts (like needs and customer perceptions). It is a typical state-ment of a *product-led* business. How about defining the company's business, not by what they make, but by what it does for their customer? Let's say they are in the portable calculation business. This is a *market-led* position.

This is one of those defining moments in our understanding of the marketer's mindset. If this definition of the company's business as 'portable calculation' seems only a matter of semantics to you, then you are not yet thinking like a marketer. The important test is: what might this market-led definition have done for them?

As a product-led business (defining themselves by the product they make – slide rules), they would spend money and energy on improving that product. Marketing would have been a function devoted to better packaging and sales drives, while R & D and production would have been the main forces in the business. Great, so long as the industry technology remained non-electronic, but terminal once that change occurred – like the paraffin salesman fighting against the advent of electric light.

As a market-led business (defining themselves by the solutions they bring to the market – portable calculation) they might spend more of their money and energy on developing alternative solutions – better means of portable calculation, attending to the hatred for their product from all those schoolchildren! This way might have led to a long-term position in the market.

So should they have invented the electronic pocket calculator? Unlikely, you say, unreasonable to expect it, even impossible? So what about seeking to work with a partner? Why not team up with

Texas Instruments or Commodore and offer to wed their technical capability with your experience in the market-place?

And if none of this was realistic or practical, at least they should then have been aware of their limitations in the portable calculation business, an awareness that would only have come from under-standing the business they were really in. Accepting their limitations, they might have started looking for alternative applications for their technology and its capabilities. This might find them defining their business, not by the product they make, nor by the solution it brings, but by the expertise they possess – the precision instrument business.

Is this second definition simply another kind of 'product-led' approach, replacing the product with a technology or an expertise? It could be, if the business isn't using the marketing model. By using the model they will understand that once they find a market for their expertise, it will be the needs of that new market that drive them, not the features of their current technology. Above all else they should remember the phrase drummed into salespeople at their basic training: *people buy solutions, not products*.

An interesting aspect of this product- or market-led debate is the way it highlights the competitive environment. Table 3.1 illustrates the comparison between product- and market-led approaches, indi-cating the likely 'business we are in' definition and the resultant understanding of where the competition might lie.

The product-led company will see itself largely fighting against fellow manufacturers – market share will be the goal. The market-led company has the luxury of a broader view, realizing that there are alternative solutions to its own. We have said enough about slide rules; let's consider lawnmowers. The product-led manufacturer of a hover mower might see the roller mower as a competitor. Hardly the case in reality; they exist in two different markets, performing two different roles – garden control and garden aesthetics. The true competition comes from alternative means of achieving those same ends – concrete or gravel!

Charles Revlon once said that other firms made cosmetics, but Revlon sold hope! The point was well made and cosmetic manufac-turers have always striven to convince their customers of their need – nature cannot be allowed to win; even the natural look needs make-up.

The manufacturer of exterior gloss paint knows that plastic window frames have been much bigger competition than any other

Table 3.1 _Product- or market-led? The competitive environment_

Product-Led	Competition	Market-Led	Competition
slide rule	other manufacturers	portable calculation	electronics
¼-inch drill	other manufacturers	¼-inch holes	lasers, adhesives
hover lawnmower	other manufacturers	garden control	chemicals, concrete
heavy roller lawnmower	other manufacturers	garden aesthetics	gravel or pebble gardens
make-up	other manufacturers	hope!	nature!
hats	other manufacturers	fashionable appearance	hairdressers
exterior gloss paint	other manufacturers	durability	plastic windows
three-piece suite suite of furniture	other manufacturers	lifestyle	holidays

paint manufacturer – not painting is an attractive option for the consumer.

The implication of this is clear to the marketer: there are competing sources for the money they hope to get from their customers. Some of those sources are competing manufacturers, but there are other sources apparently outside their market (as viewed by the product-led business!). A typical family might have the choice: new three-piece suite or summer holiday? The truly successful furniture manufacturer is the one that not only makes its offer better than that of the other makers of chairs and settees, but manages to make it more attractive than the prospect of lying in the sun for two weeks!

This leads us into the second issue arising from the marketing model.

Should your activities be for the benefit of your own business, the customer, or the market? Is it market growth or market share you should strive for and promote?

If the furniture manufacturing company is in reality in competition with the holiday firms, then they must devote much of their marketing activity to enhancing the value and attractiveness of furniture, anyone's, not just their own. Silentnight, a major bed manufacturer based in the UK, have long realized that the route to riches is more about getting people to change beds more often than it is about simply insisting they buy a Silentnight bed when the time comes. It seems that many of us keep our beds for over 20 years, with all the risks of bad backs. If only we would spend some of the money we spend on healthy living – food, exercise and relaxation – on a new bed a few years earlier, Silentnight would be very happy people, as would their fellow bed manufacturers, their competitors.

The decline in the hat industry from the dizzy heights of the 1920s and 30s was partly due to the war years, partly the more informal approach to dress, but also very significantly due to the increase in hairdressing and hair washing. There was a time when even the most meticulous would only wash their hair once or twice a week, and visits to the hairdresser were infrequent. As it became easier to wash hair at home more often and the number of hairdressing salons (not barber shops!) increased, so one of the uses of hats declined. Today's hat maker works in a different environment, where the hat is no longer a utilitarian item of clothing designed to hide a bad hair day but an additional adornment to an already pampered head. I heard a director of a hat firm complain recently that people don't wear hats properly. 'We make them to fit round the broadest part of the head and they want to wear them perched on the back, to show off their faces I suppose.' I couldn't help feeling that this missed not only the point but also an opportunity for a hat revival!

So which is right, looking after your own interests, or those of the market as a whole?

Fruit of the loom?

Consider the case of the UK carpet manufacturer. In the space of only 30 years the share of genuinely loom-woven carpets, as opposed to those made by cheaper manufacturing styles, has fallen from some 80 per cent to less than 5 per cent. This particular manufacturer is the UK market leader in loom-woven carpets, a big fish in a shrinking pond. The reason for the decline is money. Until recently, loom-weaving technology had not changed significantly in 100 years; it took as long to make a loom-woven carpet in 1990 as it did before the First World War. This made the loom-woven carpet very expensive and compared to the new 'tufted' carpets, positively exorbitant. But help is at hand in the form of a new loom that promises to increase the speed of manufacture fourfold. The result is that the yawning gap between the price of woven and non-woven carpets could close significantly.

The manufacturing company have a choice. Should they keep the new loom for their own use, so boosting their own market share, or license the technology to other woven carpet manufacturers, so raising the total share of woven carpets?

The answer to such a question lies in their definition of their business, and so their perception of the competition. If they see their competition as other uses for the consumer's money, then licensing the technology and making woven carpets more attractive in general would have much merit as a strategy. If they are certain however that their competition is only other woven carpet manufacturers, then selfishness is the best policy.

Ask any retailer whether they would rather be on a bustling high street in a thriving town where consumers are spending lots of money in all the other shops (including their competitors'), or the only shop on a quiet road in a run-down town, and you might guess the answer. Of course, the costs of being on the high street will be much higher, and the retailer's ability to compete will be more thoroughly tested. This brings us in part to the next issue raised by the model.

Which side should you be working on – changing capabilities or influencing needs?

Changing capabilities

Can a company change its capabilities? Can an independent food retailer used to trading from a corner shop hope to take on the big boys by moving to the shopping centre? Or should it stay where it is and concentrate on what it is good at doing, in its own way?

The answer has to be yes, of course capabilities can be changed, with the application of sufficient resource and skill, but an equally important question is for what purpose _should_ they change? An awareness that the market's needs are changing, or will change, is certainly one of the best incentives; this could be about survival. The problem is that a successful past can be a huge obstacle to change. How easy is it for the successful manufacturer of mainframe computers to see the implications of PCs, the busy corner shop to see the significance of the new mall, the thriving but traditional training firm to see the opportunities of training via the Internet? And even if they do, is it possible for them to change capabilities built up over years?

The greater the complexity of the technology, or the more

entrenched the business is in its mode of operation, the harder it will be to change. Recognizing that reality will be of value, not a reason for despair. If your existing capabilities really are the heart of your business then perhaps there is more sense in finding new applications for your expertise. The corner grocer could become a delicatessen rather than a supermarket; the training company could provide its materials and expertise to an expert Internet operator. But perhaps the mainframe manufacturer just has to make the change.

Being led by your capabilities – good or bad news?

Once a business gets to be good at something, that capability tends to affect its view of the world; it becomes the secret of its success. So long as the capability is relevant to customer needs then there is no problem (for the present, but see the IBM story below), but this raises one of the difficulties for conglomerates operating in a diverse range of market environments: can one capability be applied to all?

Gillette's problem with pens

Gillette has forged a unique match in the shaving market by applying 'hi-tech' capabilities to its global brand. It is an approach that it has found hard to replicate in some of its other businesses, like the three stationery brands – Parker Pens, Papermate and Waterman. With no significant technological breakthroughs in these businesses the alternative is a tough fight for market share in a very mature market – a situation that Gillette finds 'uncomfortable' when compared to its success in the shaving market. In early 2000 Gillette was looking for buyers for these three businesses.

We hear much talk about 'core capabilities', particularly when a business is considering outsourcing some activity *not* considered to be core. Great care should be taken that core capabilities are defined by reference to the needs of the market, and are not simply those things that you happen to be good at.

IBM... and a small outfit from Seattle...

IBM's core capabilities in the 1970s were in the manufacture of computer hardware. When they went into the PC business (coming from behind) they chose to outsource two 'non-core activities' – the microprocessor to Intel, and the operating system to a small software outfit based in Seattle... What business was IBM in – metal boxes, or solutions? If it was the former then they were right to do as they did, but if the latter, then the operating system was vital, a truly core capability and not something to be outsourced so lightly.

26

Buying new capabilities

One of the most common ways for a business to change its capabilities is to buy them through acquisition. This seems to be straightforward enough. If you are a pharmaceutical company with plenty of money but no pipeline of new drugs, then buy a competitor that has such a capability. Such has been one of the biggest motivations behind the bewildering number of acquisitions and mergers in this market over recent years. All is not so simple however and sometimes it can take years to bring together the different cultural and business values of two such one-time competitors. Perhaps retailers should buy Internet companies (and they do) as a means of jumping on the e-commerce boat? A good idea, so long as they understand the challenges involved – I am reminded of a front cover of Time magazine depicting the head of Sears (in appropriately serious suit) and the head of their burgeoning e-commerce business (in appropriately casual bags and sneakers). Nice picture, but wouldn't you love to be a fly on the wall of that particular boardroom?

Unilever and Myhome – set to clean up?

A new company offering home cleaning services to those cash-rich but time-poor households we hear so much about has recently been set up, Myhome. Nothing unusual in that, except that Myhome's parent is Unilever. Can a multinational manufacturer of soap powder, ice-cream, butter *et al* turn itself into a service provider? Unilever has approached this with care. First came a pilot, they bought an existing company, Mrs McMopp, and they have made Myhome an independent organization. But why the move? Margins are ever tighter in the manufacturing operations, and service offers promise better returns, but more importantly Myhome will provide Unilever with a vehicle for understanding the real needs that their product and service propositions must meet, particularly in the cash-rich, time-poor segment. What business are Unilever in – cleaning materials, or clean homes? If it is the latter, then capabilities must change and Myhome is a small but fascinating part of the process.

Influencing needs

Can a company create needs? How many of us knew we wanted a Mars Bar ice-cream, a Post-it note, alcoholic lemonade, or natural white paint before it was offered to us? Marketers thrive on what they call latent needs – the sort we all have, but just haven't yet realized that we do. The Mars Bar ice-cream created a whole new market sector out of nothing – the branded confectionery bar ice-cream. We hadn't been clamouring for it, but there was clearly an opportunity. Interestingly, in the light of the issue just discussed in point 2, it is arguably Nestlé (who purchased Lyons Maid in the mid-90s) that has gained most from the new sector, following on the Mars idea with a host of their own confectionery brand names. Mars had the idea, but perhaps Nestlé had the wider capability – their broad range of branded confectionery lines.

The lower the level of conservatism in the market, the more scope there is for such activity. It is harder to see a confectionery brand breaking into the wine or whisky market with a clever brand extension! In the 1980s the wine market looked set for a revolution with the advent of wine in a box, but the popularity of the idea was short-lived and now occupies a fairly small niche of the market. Wine drinking is still bound up with other factors more 'important' or of greater 'value' than convenience.

Sometimes however revolutions do occur, and in the most conservative markets. Health care before the Second World War was a complex but static mix of private provision, charity, self-help and 'just put up with it'. The National Health Service changed all that, and within a generation people were demanding treatments for ailments they had not even heard of only a few years before. A new capability in the market created new needs such that we now have a health service strained to the limits, fertile ground for new providers to offer alternative solutions, hence the rise of private health insurance and at the same time the growth in alternative medicines and treatments from acupuncture to faith healing.

Business, oddly enough, has always been one of the most conservative markets to influence. Note the continued reluctance of so many companies to move into the world of e-commerce – the 'dotcom' revolution is still more apparent in the financial markets than it is in the office. It seems that in this market, needs have to be as clear as day before there is an uptake of new ideas, and sellers to this market have their work cut out to *create* needs. Back in the 19th century Alexander Graham Bell had much this same problem with his telephone. A revolution for business communications, he said, and to one doubting businessman in particular: 'Just think, with one of these you can talk to a customer 300 miles away.' The doubting businessman's reply expressed precisely the inertia in the business market: 'But, Mr Bell, I don't have any customers 300 miles away.'

The Post-it note, developed by 3M by accident (as the story goes), is often raised as an example of a capability finding a use for itself. Of course the Post-it has been phenomenally successful, one of *the* products of the 20th century, but perhaps it should not be used as a role model. The path is too littered with failures, and expensive ones at that, to want to encourage anyone to develop products in the hope that *if* they are clever enough they will be able to create a need after the event.

Of course, *creating* needs is the most dramatic end of the spectrum for the right-hand side of the model. *Influencing* needs will be as important, and often a lot easier. We all need petrol for our cars, but the oil company that convince us that their petrol will be less damaging to the environment, or kinder to our car, or the most economical, will be the winner. This is the role of branding, helping customers make their minds up by influencing the way they think about their needs.

It is rare that any business will not need to work on both sides of the model. It may seem that business-to-business marketers will spend more of their time concerned with changing capabilities within their own organization while the fmcg marketer is busy influencing needs through promotion and branding. This might be the case in the grand scheme of things, but this thought leads us to the next issue arising from the marketing model.

Does the model apply equally to consumer (fmcg), business-to-business and service industry marketing?

The last issue left us with the thought: do fmcg marketers have a bias towards influencing needs, and business-to-business marketers a bias towards changing capabilities? If it is so in any given situation, that *is* not to say they should ignore the other side.

While Mars did a brilliant job on understanding and exploiting our latent desire for a Mars Bar ice-cream, they slipped up famously by asking retailers to put the new product in their existing refrigerators, owned by Walls or Lyons Maid! They lacked a capability and, though soon put right, it was an embarrassment and an expensive error.

Mars and the cold shoulder

Misreading the opportunity – ICI's alternative to CFCs

ICI did a brilliant job in the 1990s in creating an alternative for CFCs (chemicals used in refrigerants, air-conditioning and aerosols, said to contribute to the erosion of the ozone layer), soon to be banned by international agreement. Their capability as an inventive chemical company was seen at its best and there was much enthusiasm for the new product. Their reading of the market dynamics was less inspired. They failed to see how many aerosol-dependent manufacturers would prefer to change to roll-on or pump-spray applications rather than use the new CFC replacement. They also underestimated the speed with which competitors would have their own CFC alternatives on the market. This misreading of supply and demand caused a mismatch between their excellent capabilities and the true needs of the market: an expensive mistake. Confidence in their technical capability and an insufficient understanding of the dynamics of the market (a common syndrome in large and 'clever' companies) led to a significant over-investment in capacity. Now that CFCs have finally been banned the demand for such alternatives is increasing and there is a need to consider new capacity – as is so often the case in marketing, timing can be everything.

These two examples suggest a potential bear trap for the marketer. Whenever either side of the model starts to dominate the marketing process there is the risk that the other side will be ignored, either entirely or enough to cause damage. It is easy for a focus on either side to become the established culture of a business, with particular functions or departments growing to dominate and drive the business. A left-side focus sees, typically, production and R & D at the helm, while a right-side focus will often result in a sales-driven business. The task of marketing is to bring both sides together and to remember that brilliance on one side or the other is not enough; it is the quality of the match that matters.

The greatest challenge for many fmcg marketers is managing change within their own organization. Often they see this as an unnecessary burden, with other departments as obstacles to be knocked down, and consequently they go about it badly. Equally, the greatest challenge for many business-to-business marketers will be understanding the dynamics of a market in which they may be but small players, and this leads us to the next issue from the marketing model.

Is it market needs, or consumer needs (the concept of the market chain)?

When we look at the all-important subject of market segmentation in

Chapter 11 we will be reminded of a good piece of advice: _a market never bought anything; people do that._ When we speak of market needs then, we should always remember to identify clearly whom we mean, and it isn't always that easy.

For the fmcg company selling to the consumer through a retailer it is a relatively easy thing to determine what market they are in, who are their _customers_ and who the ultimate _consumers_. Customers – the retailers – buy directly from them while consumers – us – are the final users of the product. Defining what business they are in is that much easier as a result, and so is identifying where the attention is needed in the marketing model.

But what about the company that sells electrical wire to manufacturers of televisions, or sulphuric acid as a raw material in a product that is in turn a raw material for another, that may even end up in the electrical wire that goes into that television? What market are they in: acid, wire, television, electronics, or something else?

All businesses that sell to an intermediary before the final consumer are in a market chain. Those closest to the consumer tend to receive the greatest rewards as it is usually at that end of the chain that the most 'apparent' value is put in. I use the word 'apparent' as it is usually a matter of perception. Farmers have often complained that supermarkets make too much money selling their products and that farmers receive too small a share of the final consumer price. So why does it happen? For many consumers the final display of ripe apples cosseted in tissue paper in a spotlessly clean and air-conditioned superstore would convey more apparent value than the months the apples had spent hanging on trees in all weathers. Farmers may complain, but whatever the truth of the matter, when it comes to expressing what is of value, it is consumers' perceptions that matter.

Perhaps farmers have not done much of a job in marketing their produce to the final consumer? French supermarkets are now obliged to display how much they have paid for some fruit and vegetables in order to assure consumers that farmers are not being abused, and to allow consumers to make their own minds up about added value. This is a government-inspired attempt to regulate the flow of value and reward in the market chain, but sometimes those suppliers at the head of the chain will take matters into their own hands.

The growth of farmers' markets in recent years, where consumers can meet face to face with producers and select their own apples from reassuringly rural baskets (rather than tissue paper), or pick potatoes from the very soil in which they grew (rather than finding them ready-peeled and washed), demonstrates not only an attempt by farmers to capture the value from the chain but also the continuing truth that value is in the eye of the beholder.

The challenge for marketers, in aiming to meet the needs of the market, is to know how far down the chain they should be looking. Since most value tends to be added closest to the final consumer, the first question to ask is: does our product or service contribute to value as perceived by the consumer? In the case of the agrochemical company selling pesticides to farmers there is a very close relationship between their product and consumer value (see Figure 3.3), but a relationship not always seen in a positive light.

On the one hand, pesticides add value by helping to improve the quality of the final product, says one lobby. On the other hand, many people feel that pesticides are harmful in the food chain and that a

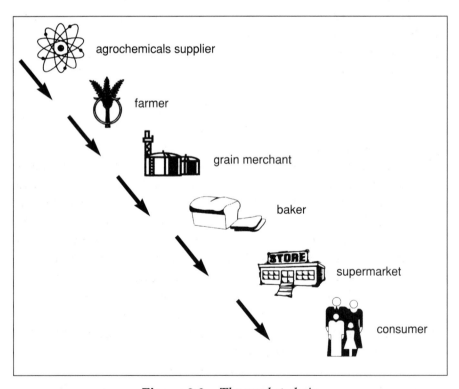

Figure 3.3 *The market chain*

proper definition of quality would be that the final product should be pesticide free. Whichever case is supported, there is little doubt that the agrochemical supplier needs to be very aware of the needs and perceptions at the consumer end of this market chain.

Understanding the farmer's needs goes beyond the interface between agrochemical supplier and farmer: it is necessary to understand the farmer's market chain. Not long ago, yield was the all-important measure of value. It determined the farmer's profits and the prices down the chain. In such an environment was born the focus on genetically modified (GM) crops. Many of the problems that have beset Monsanto in recent years could be said to have resulted from a poor understanding of how consumers in Europe feel about their GM products, exacerbated by their continued focus on yield as the measure of value. Times change.

Concern about food safety among consumers, spurred on by the press, pressure groups and supermarkets staking a claim to a point of competitive advantage, and fuelled by a run of food scares – benzene in Perrier, salmonella in eggs, E. coli, mad cows, dioxins in Coca-Cola and Belgian chickens – has entirely changed that measure of value in the chain. Safety is now the watchword. Supermarkets demand 'food passports' from their suppliers, demonstrating where and how the food was produced. The food manufacturers demand in their turn complete transparency from their suppliers – no more secret ingredients. The farmers' main concern now is whether they will be able to sell their product, not how much they can grow, and the challenge for agrochemical suppliers is a very different one.

The market environment is always changing and those businesses that focus only on their own part of the market chain are less likely to see the changes that will determine their future. In the early 1990s it was organic farmers who struggled to keep their heads above water, but they were looking forward, not planning their future on the successes of the past, and now they enjoy the rewards of that 'investment'. Farmers who find their livelihoods under threat through changing food fads or fashions make, like deserted mining villages, poignant stories for TV documentaries, and show just how hard it is for some businesses to work within the marketing model. They also show the dangers of working outside the model.

Working within the model and understanding the idea of the market chain is one thing; ensuring that a fair reward is gained for your efforts is another. The further from the end consumer, the harder it is to secure a large piece of the action, and remember, the goal of marketing is profit. Producers of raw materials might appear to be at the mercy of manufacturers who take their products and turn them into added-value, branded goods, but some raw material suppliers have found a way to secure their share of the reward.

Brands within brands – how Teflon ensures its reward

DuPont have successfully branded Teflon and Lycra, in each case a very small proportion of the finished product whether it be non-stick frying pan or sportswear, to represent the key ingredient in those products. A personal computer without an 'Intel inside' sticker would seem to be lacking something, and NutraSweet gives a badge of credibility to diet drinks.

These brands aim to secure ownership of the market chain, as viewed by the end consumer, for the supplier. The concept of ownership in this sense is an important one. Ownership brings power and security and, for wise marketers, the ability to change with the times. Teflon is no longer simply about non-stick frying pans, it is an important ingredient in paint, clothing and building materials, to name just three. Its success rests on its inherent qualities, but also on its ability to match up to consumers' needs and perceptions – not a bad definition for a successful brand.

Is profitability the automatic consequence of a good match?

Much stress has been laid in this chapter on the importance of finding a good match between capabilities and needs, but is that all that is required to make profits?

It is certainly the case that profitability, over the long term, is hard without a good match. Cases abound of businesses that touched a nerve in the market and shot to stardom but declined or even failed in the end through some lack of capability, very often a financial capability – Dicky Dirts, the trailblazing jeans retailer, Laker and Skytrain, Pineapple Studios, Sinclair, DeLorean, and the list goes on.

Philips, the Dutch conglomerate, has trailblazed more innovations in hi-fi and electronic gadgetry than seems credible from one company, an amazing fertility of ideas. Yet, when it comes to commercialized success the way is littered with tales of failure and losing out to a competitor from Asia Pacific. Their ability to identify with the market needs of the moment seems to lag behind their ability to invent and develop new products.

So matching is important, but is it all that is required?

The rise of the 'alcopop' is an interesting case in this regard. Manufacturers of beer and cider in the UK were concerned to see trends away from consumption of their products by the younger generation in the early 1990s. It seemed that youth had different (though no more creditable!) outlets for their money. The answer was a stream of alcoholic lemonades, fruit juices and other previously virtuous soft drinks. They hit a nerve and sales boomed. Here was a good match, manufacturers with spare capacity and all the right channels to market, and a latent consumer need that could be developed through advertising and, more importantly, the 'jungle drum' media of youth culture.

So far, so good, except that these new products needed huge marketing support and much bigger budgets than some of their more humble cider and beer predecessors demanded. Not only that, but the sales boom brought in competitors like moths to a candle, resulting in a price war at the retailers, the club and the public house. Profit and loss accounts actually dipped as a result of such success, but it was the sort of success that demanded more, sucking manufacturers in further. In such an environment even more promotion was required, starting to raise the concerns of parents that their children were being led down a worrying path – and this from the makers of good, wholesome, traditional cider! Marketers should never forget that their activities, however brilliant, take place in a competitive environment, and the demands of that environment can take a good idea and make it seem bad.

In the end (and the jury is still out) the re-branding of cider – Red Rock _et al_ – might appear to be a more successful strategy, and certainly one with lower risks.

What the environment does, in fact, is expose any shortcomings in the match. The low-cost, low-price airline has been a feature of the travel market ever since Laker, with more failures than successes, yet the idea seems such an obvious one. The premise is a good one, taking a leaf out of Henry Ford's book. He reckoned that if he could get the price of a car down below $500 he would be able to sell millions, a rather different premise from the idea that if he could sell enough cars the price would come down. The answer for Ford was mass production and any colour you liked so long as it was black. For the low-price airline the idea is that if it costs less than £30 to fly from the UK to Amsterdam then more people will fly, and the way to make this work is low costs. The theory is fine but it takes _genuinely_ low costs to make it work in practice. Airlines that pretend to low costs but actually support the same infrastructures as the 'full-price' airlines are doomed to failure. The mismatch is exposed and profits drain away or never materialize.

How far ahead must you be looking?

The ultimate 'how long is a piece of string' question. Each industry, each market, even each business has its own relevant horizons. There is the trading period, the mid-term, the long term, and the wild blue yonder. Each needs attention from the marketer. Any business that is ignoring the Internet at present because 'its real time is yet to come' is putting its future at risk. The marketer's job is more than hoping to predict the future; it is about managing the future.

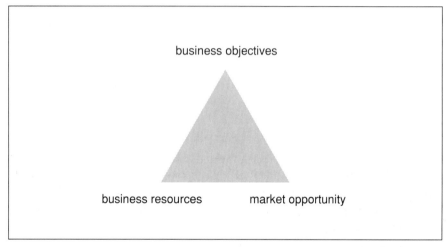

Figure 3.4 *Managing the future*

Managing the future requires a balance of three things: your objectives, your resources and the market opportunity (see Figure 3.4). Of these three, the market opportunity is the hardest to control, but the most important to understand, and this will be the subject of Chapters 5, 6 and 7.

For now, suffice it to say that a successful future depends on a match between capabilities and market needs, a match that establishes a basis for competitive advantage, if possible a unique basis protected by patent, or brand, or by fleet of foot, and a basis that will be sustainable over time and the onslaughts of envious competitors. In short, find a match, do it uniquely and sustain it. That's marketing, and in only nine words.

4

The marketing process

One of the joys of marketing is that there are always choices. This is also, potentially, one of its biggest burdens. The burden results if you have no appropriate means to make those choices, at least not the sort that allows you to sleep at nights.

Another joy is the way in which different choices can each lead towards success or failure – there are few absolute rights and wrongs in marketing. For one thing, the world changes, and in some fast-moving markets last month's good decision may already be looking suspect. As a colleague of mine once said, 'Marketing is a cerebral activity', not to be confined to simple rules of cause and effect, not to be reduced to crude black and white.

It may seem an odd way to start a chapter on the disciplines of the marketing process to portray the activity as some kind of intellectual free-for-all, for it clearly should not be seen that way. My purpose is to raise an apparent dilemma: on the one hand the complexities of the choices demand a high level of intellectual rigour, while on the other it remains hard, perhaps impossible, to apply the sort of scientific analysis that the implications of those choices would often seem to demand.

Marketing is a dangerous pursuit – big budgets are wielded, dramatic decisions are taken, products are born and raised, they mature, and they are put out to grass, all with huge impact on the health of the business. I have heard it said that marketing is a good place for new graduates to start in business because they can't do much harm there. OK, engineers can build factories that fall down, and R & D folk can design products that don't work, but marketers can do worse – they can wreck the future, without a disciplined approach.

The disciplines of professional marketing are not perhaps much exposed in its public persona. Media coverage prefers a flamboyant tycoon approach to a studied market analysis. It has been said of Rupert Murdoch, for instance, that he never does market research, and other high-profile captains of industry have shown similar allegiance to gut feel and personal flair. Don't think I'm putting down gut feel and flair – both hugely valuable things, but they cannot exist in a vacuum. (Of course, it's not true what they say about Rupert Murdoch. Of course he does market research; he just does it with his own eyes and ears, valuable tools of any marketer.)

In truth, most good marketing results less from inspiration or personal flair and more from good homework, rigorous analysis, detailed planning, regular review and tightly managed implementation – in short, a disciplined marketing process, as illustrated in Figure 4.1.

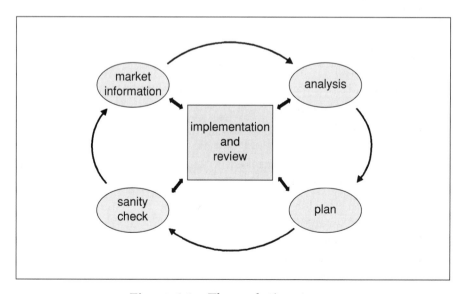

Figure 4.1 *The marketing process*

Except in the case of a new business set-up, most marketers inherit an existing business with all its strengths and weaknesses, opportunities and threats. In the real world the clock doesn't stop to give you a period of reflection or the opportunity for a clean new start – market planning happens in the midst of current activity. Implementation is continual, modified by the ever-changing market-place and so an equally continual planning process, fuelled by a constant research and analysis activity. The discipline of the marketing process is, as much as anything else, to help ensure that the pressures and demands of today don't get in the way of planning for tomorrow. It also banishes the excuse that as the market is changing we had best wait and see what happens before planning!

THE MARKET AUDIT

The first two stages – market information and analysis – represent what we might call the *market audit*: an attempt to understand what is going on out there and how well we are equipped to deal with it. The following stages – plan and sanity check – take this interpretation and put it into action.

Market information (market audit 1)

At the root of most good marketing is market information, the first step of the never-ending process and the first half of the *market audit* (see Chapter 5). In its raw form this information will be data – market size, market shares, profits, etc. It will include information on customers and competitors, current and potential. A broader kind of information will be the answers to questions such as:

- How do we define this market?
- How does it work and operate?
- What is our position in it?
- Who are the competitors?
- How do we define ourselves?
- What are our capabilities?
- What are the trends?
- What do customers think of us and our competitors?

As the information becomes more refined it starts to represent a fuller understanding of the dynamics of a market, its pressures, its demands. This refinement continues into the second stage of the process, and the second half of the market audit – *analysis.*

Analysis (market audit 2)

Analysis turns the data and information into knowledge. Knowledge in this sense is an understanding and awareness of the marketing model discussed in Chapter 3 – market needs, company capabilities, the competitive environment and the prospects for profitability. In short – what's going on out there and how well are we equipped to do what we want to do? A variety of tools and methods might be used and these will be explored in Chapter 7. They might include:

- the competitive environment;
- PESTLE analysis;
- Michael Porter's five forces or determinants of industry profitability;
- market needs – the opportunity;
- market mapping and options for segmentation;
- market chain analysis;
- value chain analysis;
- our capability;
- capability analysis;
- risk analysis – Ansoff matrix;
- the marketing mix.

As a result of this analysis we will be in a position to consider the options before us, and in pursuit of this to prepare two of the most useful of all marketing tools: 1) the SWOT analysis; and 2) the directional policy matrix.

These tools allow us to assess and interpret the market information gathered in the first part of the market audit within a disciplined structure. Structure is important for several reasons – the complexity of the data, the need to communicate the analysis to others in the business, but most importantly the need to use the analysis to develop options. Think about buying a car and the confusing profusion of makes and models. You will probably use a set of criteria (price, fuel consumption, 0–60 performance, air-conditioning, etc) to narrow the choice. Once your options are tabled it is hugely frustrating if in making your final decision you discover that the car of your dreams has a nine-month waiting list and you need a new car within four weeks.

In watching businesses prepare marketing strategies and plans it is surprisingly common to see this sort of backtracking because of omissions in the analysis stage. The moral of the tale is: first, get your criteria sorted out.

The analogy with buying a car is a good one as it points out a particular danger of poor analysis – doing what you had already decided to do and using the data to justify yourself. This is certainly how most of us choose our car – fall in love with it and then pick the evidence that shows we were right and none of the others will do! This may be fine for choosing a car if you end up happy with your purchase but it is no way to develop a marketing strategy (but so often the way it happens).

Plan

First, the options. Rarely are there no alternatives, and try to avoid the classic presentation of three choices: do nothing, do something, and do what I want to do. From these options a choice will be made and the marketing plan will emerge. This is not nearly as easy a process as that last sentence suggests. In many ways the more you know the harder the decisions are to take. In fact, the more obvious the choice appears to be, the more worried you might be that you were missing something in your market audit! In the end marketing is an activity that requires intelligence and judgement, and the better your information and analysis the better the decisions you will make.

The marketing plan determines what kind of business you aim to be, your scale, your style, and the detail of what to sell, how to sell it, where to sell it, and to whom to sell it (see Chapters 8 through 18). It will contain objectives – what is to be achieved, and strategy – how it will be achieved, and tactics – how it will be implemented. Chapter 10 looks at the actual preparation and writing of a marketing plan.

Sanity check

Remember that while all this is going on – market audits, options and planning – today's implementation is taking place (the result of a previous planning process). Remember also that the reality of today will have an impact on the way the future turns out. Your plan for the future will be affected by the reality of today, and of course some significant time will have elapsed since the collection of the data that forms the basis of your plan. Given all this we will see the value of the fourth stage of the marketing process – the sanity check.

This stage, perhaps the most important one when comparing success to failure, distinguishes professional, disciplined marketing from the 'seat of the pants' variety. The sanity check is a series of questions that recognizes that the real world involves change, the unexpected and the unknown, and attempts to take it all into account. It also aims to stop us falling foul of overexcited rushes of blood to the head.

This list is simply a starter to be applied to your plan before final implementation and should certainly include other questions of more specific relevance to your own circumstances:

- Are we being realistic?
- Can we trust the data?
- Are there things we don't know?
- Can we find out?
- Might the unknown have an impact?
- How will our competitors react?
- Should we have contingency plans?
- Are we headed in the direction we set out for?
- Are we being consistent?
- Has the plan won the support of those who will implement it?
- Will our customers support it?
- Is it worth the effort?

Implementation and review

The implementation stage is in reality less a stage and more a continuum. Despite that, it is necessary to distinguish it, in the eyes of those who need to do the work, as the result of the previous research, analysis and planning. At this point broad-scale marketing strategies must be translated into practical tasks and activities for a range of people across the business.

A vital and often neglected part of the implementation stage is the review of its effectiveness. This is not a one-off assessment at the end of the year or campaign period, but a continuous monitoring of progress measured against the objectives and performance standards established in the original plan. Disciplined monitoring and review is the oil that allows the marketing process to proceed as a continual flow rather than a series of lurches forward (the new plan) and staggers backward (the realization that another new plan is needed).

Part II

The Market Audit

5

Market audit 1 – market information

Rupert Murdoch doesn't believe in market research, or rather, he prefers to rely on his own instincts rather than Powerpoint presentations of numbers and statistics. He seems to do all right.

The Sony Walkman was launched in the face of some of the most adverse market research comments. Sony went ahead with the launch because its founder, Akio Morita, felt that market research couldn't ask the right questions in such new territory: 'I do not believe that any amount of market research could have told us that it would have been successful. The public does not know what is possible. We do.' It seems to have done all right.

So what is the big noise about doing market research – is it just research agencies justifying their existence (and their not insubstantial fees)?

I remember the day that the final degree results were announced at my university. I went with a friend to look at them posted on the wall, with some trepidation, as I feared the worst, not helped by my friend's absolute confidence in his having got a first. The place was crowded when we got there and we had to look over two rows of shoulders to find our results. They were posted in groups, by the class of degree – first, two-one, two-two and too bad to think about. I found mine pretty quickly – the advantage of an unusual name – and sighed with relief at my more-than-welcome two-one. My friend scanned the first-class list and twitched visibly as he failed to find his name, and then looked down the two-one list – nothing there – at which point he let out a whoop of delight and turned to me with a mile-wide grin, 'I knew it, a first'. It was two whole days later that he discovered to his horror that he had in fact got a two-two.

That's the problem with some very intelligent people: they know the answers already and strongly resist any evidence to the contrary. When my friend couldn't find his name in the two-one list the only possible explanation, to his overbearingly confident mind, was that he had in fact got a first but just hadn't been able to spot his name through the crowd.

This is also the problem with some very clever companies. The amount of brainpower and ability that goes into developing new products and services can often convince a company that what they are doing just must be right. At best this is wishful thinking but at worst it is sheer arrogance. Often, market research is commissioned with the intent of proving one's convictions to be right rather than as a serious test of trends or opinions. It is as David Ogilvy (guru and pioneer of the advertising industry) complained – market research is too often used as a drunk uses a lamppost, for support rather than illumination. Such an intention makes it very easy to ignore or reinterpret bad news.

Some companies don't feel the need to peer into the unknown, doubting the speculative nature of market research and finding ample support for their case in the facts of the past. But the evidence of the past is a poor guide in today's fast-changing business environment. Even the very recent past can mislead.

Star struck?

In May 1999 the new Star Wars movie, *Star Wars Episode One*, led to a boom in sales of Star Wars books for the publisher, Dorling Kindersley. 'On that basis, judgements were made about investing further in stock, believing that this could be a Star Wars Christmas,' said Peter Kindersley, executive chairman in January 2000, warning of an expected £25 million pre-tax loss for the second half of 1999.

It wasn't a Star Wars Christmas and Dorling Kindersley found themselves with 10 million books left in stock from 13 million printed in anticipation of the rush. Some hot things can go cold very quickly.

'Past performance should not be taken as a guarantee of future success,' warn the investment adverts; and it is useful advice for marketers. Marks & Spencer suffered a significant slip in its sales and profits in 1999, largely from a misjudgement of clothing fashions. 'Leggings and tunics lasted as the thing to wear for so long that we took our eye off the ball,' said Peter Salsbury, the M & S chief executive, his words serving perhaps as a microcosm of their wider problem.

Companies that use the past as a guide are perhaps less to be blamed than those that actually do the research into future needs, and then ignore the results. This is such a common scenario around new product launches that it deserves its very own name – I call it the 'Akio Morita syndrome'.

Dulux and a case of the blues

A company invests heavily in developing a new product; let's say a paint company develops a clever new system that allows consumers to mix their own colour in-store, by themselves, using a self-service machine. The market research says that people won't use the new system because of what the researchers call 'techno-fear' – they don't want the embarrassment of breaking the machine, or spilling paint, or any of a 100 other accidents waiting to happen. The launch team ignore techno-fear, quoting in their defence the words of Akio Morita, 'The public does not know what is possible. We do.' And the product fails. Not only does it fail, but it costs the company significantly in lost credibility. This is what happened to the Dulux brand in the late 80s with a system called Colour Options. For some time afterwards retailers were more wary of accepting 'good ideas' from a brand that had enjoyed success after success throughout the 80s.

The launch of the Sony Walkman was a great success, but it was not the norm. The fact that it is still quoted and discussed shows that it was not the norm, and while Akio Morita was clearly right in this case, we should take care in following his bold example.

And so the debate rages on – instinct versus statistics, the momentum of product launches versus the caution of researchers. Of course, research can get it wrong too.

Hoover's flights of fancy

Hoover UK ran a consumer promotion in the early 90s offering free airline flights to customers who spent £100 or more on their products. Research suggested a modest take-up, based on previous experience, but this promotion hit a nerve and Hoover were inundated. First off, they couldn't handle the demand and people waited weeks and weeks for tickets, and when the dust had settled they faced a bill for some £20 million and a reputation for naïvety.

Blind tests for a new formula Coca-Cola in 1984 suggested that they were on to a winner. Rarely had research been so compelling, yet the subsequent launch in 1985 brought howls of protest and after only three months the original Coke was back – Classic Coke was born. Cynics might say that this was a grand trick to effect a relaunch of an old product and give it a whole new life cycle – the redundant executives scattered around Atlanta, Georgia, might argue otherwise.

What all this suggests, I think, is that research has an important place, but must be used with care. It shouldn't command, but nor should it be ignored. The real skill of course is not in interpreting the answers, but in framing the questions in the first place. This is a genuine skill and, like advertising, should be left to the professionals. I have seen research surveys prepared by keen but innocent managers including gems ranging from the naïvely simple 'Is our product too expensive?' ('Gosh no, please put your price up!') to the impossible vastness of 'What do you want?'.

The value of facts and figures depends not just on the accuracy of the study, but very much on the choice of questions that created them. Suppose a car manufacturer had taken their clipboards on to the street 10 years ago to test the prospects for a new range of four-wheel-drive off-road vehicles. They might have asked, 'How often do you drive your car off-road?' or even more directly, 'How often would you like to drive your car off-road?'. The resultant statistics would have shown very small percentages in both cases. Had they used those facts and figures alone to determine their future strategy for off-road vehicles they would almost certainly have missed the growth phenomenon of the 1990s in the European car market. This was a task that called for more subtlety in questioning; attitudes and the realm of latent needs are rarely uncovered by such a direct approach – the very problem that Akio Morita observed.

Perhaps we should distinguish some types of research. The first distinction is between quantitative (facts and figures) and qualitative (ideas, attitudes and opinions).

QUANTITATIVE RESEARCH

Quantitative research includes such things as demographics (numbers of households, population aged 25–40, etc), market size, brand shares and price points. This is the realm of hard facts, though the famous dictum 'lies, damned lies and statistics' should be a warning to us all. The problems usually lie in the definitions and interpretations.

What is the size of the market for snack foods? Define a snack. What is the market share of brand A? Do we mean by volume or by value? How do we define the total market in which brand A has a share? (See the question above.) When companies ask, 'What is the size of the market?' they must take care not to limit their horizons. So many restrict their view by taking current customers as the basis for defining the market. Those with real growth aspirations take a different kind of view.

I once heard a senior executive from Coca-Cola ask an audience what Coke's global brand share was, with replies ranging from 20 to 50 per cent. He stunned us momentarily by telling us that it was a little less than 3 per cent, and then explained that he was measuring their share of all purchased liquids consumed, including tea, beer, wine, coffee... (The point was that they still had a long way to go – the important goal was an increasing 'share of stomach' or 'share of throat'.) This is an important notion when defining market sizes and measuring shares – are you looking at direct competitors (those with similar products) or at competing outlets for the customer's money? Coca-Cola's view that they were in competition with tea, beer, wine, coffee and the rest indicates a much greater ambition than simply looking at Pepsi – and their market information requirements are that much broader as a result.

A valuable quantitative data bank for fmcg marketers is what is sometimes known as the 'consumer diary'. A group of consumers is asked to keep a daily diary of purchases – everything from soap powder (with brands noted) to three-piece suites (with price and retailer). Over a period of time these diaries provide valuable trend information, as well as indicating short-term responses to factors such as seasonality, weather and promotional campaigns. Maintaining your own study is an onerous task but it is possible to buy into such diaries maintained by other non-competing companies.

As well as facts about the past (quantitative data by its very nature tends to be history), we might also use quantified studies to assess our current effectiveness. A typical example would be the use of *tracking studies* to measure the effectiveness of promotional campaigns. After all, if you are spending £5 million on an advertising campaign, perhaps it is worth £50,000 to test how well it worked? (See the section on tracking at the end of this chapter.)

Research and forecasting

As well as 'hard' facts there are also those studies that deal with such things as market forecasts or intentions to buy. It is important to remember that many such 'predictions' are extrapolated from past and current data and so are of course subject to the changing times. Benz are famed for having carried out one of the first predictive research studies into the UK car market as early as the birth of the 20th century. They predicted that the market would not exceed 1,000 cars, owing to the shortage of chauffeurs.

The forecasting of demand based on trend analysis is never straightforward, not least because of the way it is influenced by the current strategy of the company seeking the insight.

Airbus or Boeing – who's got the future sized up?

Airbus, the European aircraft manufacturer, plan to launch the A3XX in 2004 or 2005, a super-jumbo with 1,000 seats and the promise of on-board restaurants. They forecast demand for 1,500 such aircraft over the next 20 years, a forecast that is four times greater than that of their main rivals and existing jumbo supremo, Boeing. How much the Airbus forecast is based on their decision to build the A3XX, itself the result of having the technical capability, or the offer of government funding (and excellent job prospects), is open to debate, as indeed is Boeing's much smaller forecast based perhaps on their own strategy to stick to more conventional jumbos. Some people say forecasting is too difficult to attempt for the long term. Perhaps there is an equal peril in it being all too easy – whatever you happen to be looking for!

QUALITATIVE RESEARCH

Qualitative statements – preferences, opinions, latent wants and needs. Such comments are often prompted by the much-vaunted and oft-maligned focus group. A group of customers, carefully chosen to represent the target market, is encouraged to discuss the merits or otherwise of anything from chocolate bars to television programmes. How much reliance can be put on the remarks of half a dozen such guinea pigs is open to much debate – but what a great way to have your ideas challenged or tested. Many a successful consumer product has been aired, modified and launched on the back of such focus groups, with sample sizes as low as 12 or 18 people. The real requirement is not so much large numbers but expert facilitation – another job for the experts, not overenthusiastic sales or marketing managers who push the group to accept their product.

Qualitative studies are of great value to marketers seeking to understand and segment their market-place. Chapter 11, 'Segmentation', describes a market segment as a group of customers with similar needs, attitudes and perceptions. Quantifiable surveys might shed light on the size of such groups but the qualitative data from studies such as focus groups will be of vital importance to understanding the softer aspects of their attitudes and perceptions.

Expert opinion is often accepted as valid qualitative research, and can be hugely valuable where the experts are the intended customers. Customer surveys are most useful in this regard, but as ever the questioning requires expertise and subtlety. Sending the sales force out to canvas opinion is not the ideal way to conduct such research, especially if it is customers' opinions of the sales force! Trade shows provide excellent opportunities to gauge customer opinion, provided they are planned to include that purpose. The questioning must be disciplined and consistent, and the answers assessed with equal discipline and rigour, else the danger is a loose list of anecdotal stories that become folklore. Some businesses will attempt to set up 'advisory panels' of key opinion leaders in their market, particularly common in the pharmaceutical industry where specialists abound and interest and pressure groups prosper.

The expert pundit is another matter altogether, more fruitful ground for embarrassment than serious guidance. An 'expert' reporting on the unveiling of the TV at a 1930s New York Trades Fair foresaw a dim future for the invention as it involved the family sitting still in a darkened room and not talking to one another. Barry Norman, the BBC's top film critic, safely predicted the decline of the cinema as a result of the video, and was later honest enough to confess his mistake and his failure to foresee the rise of the luxury multiplex.

FOCUSING YOUR DATA NEEDS

One thing is clear: whatever your market, there is a lot of information out there. Even if your product, service or target market is so new as to be unrecognized by any published source or historical data, there is always qualitative opinion. Faced with the sometimes daunting task of starting from scratch the obvious question is: what to collect?

And the first riposte should be the equally obvious: what do you need to know? If you are a four-person company making widgets for sale in Devon and Cornwall, what use is it for you to know the world market size for widgets? Even if it's easily available information what does it matter to you? Our widget manufacturer will probably be much better served by a survey of local opinion and satisfaction that highlights a need for improved delivery times than by an inch-thick document of statistics on the global sale of widgets. Of course, the big picture might highlight trends that will affect the local picture, and in this respect trends and forecasts are probably of more value than the 'hard' facts.

The task is to identify your needs for information and focus your approach. There is so much data about that you must take care not to get bogged down in irrelevancies. If we remember the purpose of marketing as expressed in the marketing model, then we will see a good structure for our research activities: aiming to understand customer's needs so that we can develop the appropriate capabilities and secure competitive advantage.

That is a good overall guide, but we should be more specific about our need for information. Is it:

- to help us understand the market?
- to help us identify opportunities and threats?
- to help us develop a marketing plan?
- to help us develop a segment/product/activity plan?
- to present to customers as evidence of our capability?
- to help us forecast demand?
- to guide us in launching a product?
- to benchmark ourselves against a competitor?
- to help us understand our customers' perceptions?
  - customer satisfaction surveys
  - usage and attitude (U & A) studies
  - image and recognition studies

- to help us understand our customers' costs in use (see Chapter 13, 'Pricing strategies') and so assess the value and impact of our offer?
- to judge the success or impact of a particular campaign or activity?
  - pilot market testing
  - tracking effectiveness of promotional spend.

In other words, are we looking at a broad canvas or focusing on a particular issue? The nature of the information-gathering exercise will change as we move down this list. The more specific the need, the more individual the exercise will become, and expert advice will become more and more important.

The broad canvas

The following 10-point checklist is an attempt to guide your approach to the broader canvas of market information:

1. How do we define the market?
   - segments and product categories
   - size and value
   - market shares
2. Trends and forecasts.
3. Who are the customers?
   - current customers
   - potential customers
4. What share of their business do we have?
5. What are their needs, attitudes and aspirations?
6. How well do we perform, in the customers' eyes?
7. Who are the competitors?
8. How well do the competitors perform, in the customers' eyes?
9. What capabilities are required, now and future?
10. How well do we stack up against the competition?

Standard 'desk research' as it is called, gathering facts and figures, will only go so far in answering these sorts of questions. Not only are they almost by definition out of date but official statistics in particular are bedevilled by problems of definition. Commercially available reports, while useful, very often leave you wishing they had just broken it down by one level more: from the national to the regional, the market to the segment, the macro to the micro. This of course can give you the starting-point for commissioning your own research.

And one last reminder – beware of using your own sales statistics as a guide to the total market – there is no better way to limit your horizons!

COMMISSIONING YOUR OWN RESEARCH

You will soon be beyond the scope of 'desk research' and considering commissioning your own research. This is an area where a structured approach will be useful, to avoid the wrong turnings and blind alleys that await you. The following eight-step process will help you through the maze:

1. *Prepare the research brief, detailing*
   - Purpose of research (the outcome desired). Be sure you know why you are going to all this effort. What decisions are you hoping to be able to make? What sort of actions are you wanting to test? You might ask as a general 'test of value' at this point: 'If we are not going to do anything as a result of this research, why are we bothering?'
   - Scope of research (market/segment/customer).
   - Timetable for results.
   - Budget (and aim to stick to it!).
2. *Shortlist the agencies using the following criteria*
   - What experience do they have in this field (the market and the methodology)?
   - Are there any issues of confidentiality? A good agency will be able to work with your competitors, with all the benefits that brings of general awareness, and still maintain confidentiality, but you will need to be specific regarding your demands. (For really sensitive issues such as product launch testing, you should look for exclusivity.)
   - Are they able to respond to your timetable?
   - Will they work within your budget? A good agency should be able to suggest alternative approaches to help work within a tight budget.

3. *Brief the shortlisted agencies*
   - Ask for a presentation that demonstrates an understanding of the task, their capability, the proposed methodology, proposed sample size (where appropriate), timetable and logistics, and costs.
   - Be very clear if you require the agency to make recommendations or choices rather than simply gather information. This is very important to avoid any disputes post-research.
4. *Select the agency*
   - Issue a more detailed brief if necessary.
   - Be clear what involvement you want (if any) in the research – attending focus groups, etc.
   - Reconfirm timetables (particularly debriefings) and budgets (not because agencies are slack, but simply because such things suffer from the 'ooze syndrome').
5. *Field work*
   Where possible it is almost always advantageous to attend some sessions such as focus teams, provided that you let the agency get on with what they do best, without hindrance or undue direction from you. A good agency will welcome your presence, and the best agencies will manage you to perfection!
6. *Results debrief*
   - The research will have cost a lot in both time and money. Aim to maximize its value by involving as many people as appropriate. The debrief process itself can be as illuminating as the facts and figures presented.
   - Ensure that the aims of the research are restated at the outset. This will allow you to judge the effectiveness of the agency in their work.
   - Take care to listen to the agency's feedback before being tempted to put your own spin on the results.
   - Be clear on conclusions and recommendations.
   - Ask for a written report if required.
   - Commission new research as required.
7. *Action plans*
   Integrate results, conclusions and recommendations into your plans.
8. *Re-evaluate*
   Research data grows old. Have plans to stay up to date.

A final tip. Make sure that the research is kept available for use and that its aims and circumstances are carefully documented – corporate memories are notoriously short!

BUDGETS

The age-old question, and one more prone to short-termism than any other in marketing – how much to spend on market research? It is so easy *not* to spend money on research and nothing suffers, for the present. The professional marketer on the other hand might like to declare the research budget inviolate, a long-term investment and not something that is done only in good times when money is flush. Should you perhaps spend a percentage of sales turnover on market research, in the same way that some businesses aim to spend a percentage on R & D? Such an approach has one great advantage – there will *be* a budget! Unfortunately, market research is often a last-minute thought and there is no budget allocated. The result is either no research, or research of questionable value on a shoestring. The percentage of turnover approach also demonstrates a commitment to understanding the market environment – particularly important in a fast-changing market.

The percentage of turnover approach may even result in the maintenance of a full-time in-house market research department. The pros and cons of this are lengthy on both sides, including overhead cost and possibly restricted expertise on the downside, and the possibility of selling data to others on the up. The overwhelming plus is the development over time of some very deep knowledge that can be of benefit to you and your customers. This can represent significant competitive advantage. Perhaps the biggest concern is that horizons can be limited by the 'that's how we see things around here' school of thought.

In the end, perhaps the best approach is to spend by need and retain a good slice of common sense. Consider how much money is invested in the development and launch of a new product. If the figure is in the millions of pounds, then surely it is worth spending the tens of thousands on research to enhance the success of that launch? Let's consider here two particular circumstances to illustrate what I mean – *customer satisfaction surveys*, and *tracking of advertising effectiveness*.

CUSTOMER SATISFACTION

Perhaps you are losing customers at a rate and in a way that is beyond the normal trends. You might want to understand why and commission research into customer attitudes, perhaps a customer satisfaction survey. But is this the best time to do so, when something in the market (a competitor? your recent price rise?) is possibly prejudicing customers against you? Customer satisfaction surveys are not best used as one-off crisis management tools (nor are they intended to bring warm glows to the supplier!). They should be used to provide guidance to future activity. This is a case for long-term investment; indeed, jumping in and out of such activity can be more damaging to customer perceptions that not engaging in it at all.

Asking customers what they think of you is not as easy as it might seem. The question 'Are we expensive?' is unlikely to prompt a constructive response from a busy customer. A better approach might be to ask customers to consider first of all what is important to them in dealing with a supplier. By keeping this general you will help avoid sending them down an avenue prompted more by a recent failure on your part than by a genuine assessment of their own requirements. Of course, using an 'independent' research agency will help take some of the heat out of such a situation, but increasingly customers will not respond to such general approaches – they want to know who is behind the questions and why (and what they're going to do about it!).

If you establish a list of expectations from the customer, and ask them to rank them on a scale of 1 to 6 (1 being least important and 6 most important), you will be able to plot the horizontal access of the four-box matrix in Figure 5.1. (Incidentally, using a scale of 1 to 6 is much better than 1 to 5 for any of these sorts of ratings. The scale of 1 to 5 allows sitting on the fence – everything gets 3 for average – while 1 to 6 forces the respondent above or below the mid-point.)

Now ask the customer to evaluate how well you perform against each of these factors. This really does call for expert help. Questionnaires or interviews can be framed to get any answer you might want, but presumably you want the truth. This rating, 1 for poor through to 6 for excellent, will position the factors from the horizontal axis on to the vertical axis. The results of such a simple analysis are often most illuminating. Those factors that appear in the

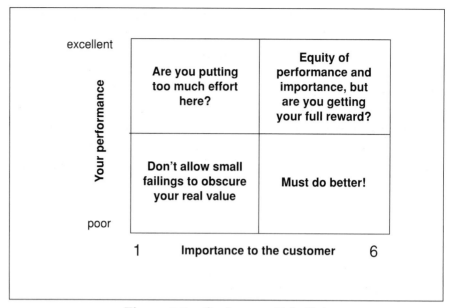

Figure 5.1 *Customer satisfaction*

top right-hand box are fine – they are important and you perform well, but you might like to ask – are we being properly rewarded for this excellent performance? But what of the top left-hand box? Excellent performance against things that don't matter all that much or at least not as much as some other factors. That in itself might not be too serious, some effort and resource misapplied, unless at the same time you have some factors in the bottom right box – very important to the customer but poor performance from yourselves. Such an outcome can help explain what might have been a frustration – you knew you did a lot of things brilliantly but the customer continually berated you for poor performance. The problem was in excelling at the wrong things!

Such an analysis can be used for many different purposes: improving performance on the bottom right factors, reducing effort and resource (perhaps) from top left factors, and getting a better reward for the value delivered through the top right factors.

Having plotted your own performance, another step might be to do the same for the competition. The value of this is more than the obvious benchmarking exercise. What it helps you to see is where you beat your competitors *when it matters*, not just where you beat them, and also where you underperform *when it matters*. Such an analysis is a good example of research that will illuminate your understanding and direct your efforts rather than support your current prejudices (remembering David Ogilvy's complaint).

This is a very simple description of a study that in the hands of a good research company can be taken much further. At its best such a study can be used directly with individual customers as a means of discussing and agreeing what actions need to be taken to enhance the future business relationship. Here market research, strategic planning and relationship marketing (see Chapter 20) walk hand in hand.

TRACKING

If you spend millions on TV advertising, surely you should spend tens of thousands to be sure of its efficacy? Henry Ford once said that half the money spent on advertising was wasted, but unfortunately you could never be sure which half. 'Tracking' is one way of being more certain.

Many big spenders in the area of fmcg advertising have started to look more carefully at the efficacy of that spend. In the old days they might have commissioned studies to measure 'top of mind' recollection (how many people polled would mention a brand unprompted) and slept happier when the results were 75 per cent plus. Then they started to wonder why a 75 per cent unprompted recollection turned into a 20 per cent brand share – clearly such a simple measure of advertising effectiveness was not enough.

A typical tracking study might ask three main sets of questions of its audience, and it would ask them before the campaign, during the campaign and after, in order to identify the impact and the 'stamina' of the campaign:

- _Cut through._ What awareness is generated by the campaign? Has it reached you and how well do you recall it?
- _Beliefs and perceptions._ What values and promises did the campaign raise, and what level of belief do you have in them? Has it enhanced your perception of the product/brand/company?
- _Disposition scale._ What action will you take as a result of this campaign? Will you buy the product now or in the future? Will you recommend it?

A typical study of this kind might cost about £80,000 using a sample size of 300 a month, tracking a campaign over three to six months. Expenditure of this kind would relate to an advertising spend of over £5 million.

ACT OF FAITH?

So is it all worth the effort? Much time and certainly much money will be required and a precise cost–benefit analysis is not always possible. For some it is an act of faith; for others it seems more like health insurance – so long as you're healthy it seems a dreadful waste but when your heart starts to flutter or your legs to wobble it seems the smartest move you ever made.

My company runs a marketing training event where delegates take part in a computer-based business simulation involving them in the investment of £500 million in plant and equipment for a new venture. It is frightening, but not uncommon, to see them balk at the idea of spending just a few million pounds on research in order to understand the market for which this huge investment is intended.

The toughest decision is waiting undoubtedly for the small enterprise with limited funds. And when is money tightest? Right at the outset, just when the most research is required. Of course, some research (and perhaps the most important if Rupert Murdoch is to be believed) can be done for little or no cost.

The White Company   Christian Rucker, founder of The White Company, a mail-order business specializing in household linens, towels, dressing gowns, bedspreads and the like, all of course in white, was spurred into action by hearing her sister-in-law remark that she couldn't find the right kind of white linen. 'I had to do it by mail order. I went away and couldn't sleep I was so excited.'

If money is an issue, perhaps the focus should be on enhancing your qualitative understanding of market and customer perceptions and needs. Listen to people, ask questions everywhere you go, involve everyone in the company in the thirst for knowledge and perhaps, even, conduct a few focus groups.

The next chapter, a short detour into the world of fiction, may help you galvanize your determination to know more.

6

Chakravarti's piano – or why you need market research

For those who might need further convincing of the need for market research, or identifying the right data, this chapter provides a brief respite from the author's assertions, and calls instead on the help of the maestro.

After a day of near-broiling heat in the big city, the cool of the evening wafts us across the greenery of Hyde Park and into the magnificent auditorium of the Albert Hall. London's traffic continues its roar just yards from the doors, but inside all is hushed. We have taken our seats, shared pleasantries with our neighbours, cleared our throats and now the house lights are going down. A single spot picks out the elderly man seated at the concert grand. He is alone on stage. He flexes his fingers, closes his eyes and hangs his hands over the keys.

V K Chakravarti, after 10 years in retirement, is back on the concert circuit and filling the halls as if he had never been away. We are part of a special audience this evening, here by special invitation for more than a piano recital – we are here to learn the mysteries of Chakravarti's piano.

Our senses flex as the great man's hands come down with a huge fortissimo to strike the opening chord of Chakravarti's Second Piano Concerto – only there is nothing, or rather just a single note, a lone tone of pathetic smallness, hardly enough for the grand emotion of his physical effort. His hands are moving quickly and there are more sporadic notes and the occasional remnant of a chord, but they are a surprisingly poor output for the frantic activity on stage. They form no recognizable melody or harmony, just isolated soundbites that confuse the audience into an uncomfortable shuffling of feet.

On stage Chakravarti seems oblivious to the confusion his performance is causing. Already there are beads of sweat on his forehead as he thunders on into his performance. Occasionally a recognizable snatch of music holds us for a moment, but then the mime show takes hold again and we frown and tilt our heads.

It is not long before we lean towards our neighbours. 'Is it just me or do you think his piano's not working?'

'Maybe it's the microphone?'

'Maybe it's the acoustics where we're sitting?'

'Maybe he's gone avant-garde in the last 10 years?'

We cough, we tut, somebody at the front is on his feet, and all of a sudden Chakravarti stops. He comes to the front of the stage and the single spot follows him down. 'And that, ladies and gentlemen, was the opening of my Second Piano Concerto, played with a very special arrangement – I call it my Business Variation.' And he smiles at us, just to confirm that he means the comment to sting. 'It takes just as much effort as the normal arrangement, only the final outcome is a little disappointing, I think you will agree? I have spent the last 10 years, what some people have called my retirement, watching people like you. You are all businesspeople here tonight, and I have the greatest pity for you.'

The audience is not taking this explanation well. First he performs three minutes of incoherent nonsense, and then he starts to insult us. At least we think he is insulting us; nothing is clear about Chakravarti.

He continues unabashed. 'I am a musician and as such the last few minutes have been terrible for me – far more terrible than for you. And why? Because I know what you should have been hearing. Most of you do not. You only know that you didn't hear very much at all. And why do I say I pity you? Perhaps you think me very rude?' The same smile, only this time a little more engaging. 'As I said, I have been watching you for the last 10 years, watching your struggles and your frustrations – and wincing at your blind ignorance.'

No smile could engage us after that, but he carries on, as oblivious to our mounting annoyance as before. 'You spend your business lives like poor Chakravarti's piano. My piano has 94 notes divided into eight octaves, each of 12 notes – yet just now you only heard 12, one octave.' He breaks off, seemingly concerned for the first time at something he has said. 'I must be confusing you – an octave with 12 notes. Perhaps you were expecting eight – octagons, octopuses, octogenarians, like me, and the rest of those octs. Well, there are seven white keys and five black, and eight tonal progressions, but perhaps I should say no more of that. It is unimportant, like sales statistics.'

A finger seems to come out from Chakravarti and poke a thousand eyes. 'Most of you, I suspect, think I was not doing my job up here just now, short-changing you, but I promise you I put every effort into every moment – I always do. I have practised this piece for weeks, for months, every day. Practice is important. If I miss a week my audiences notice. If I miss a day, I notice.'

He seems to relax at that thought and leans towards us a little more kindly. 'No, it was not I, Chakravarti, who let you down; it was my piano, poor Chakravarti's piano. You see, only the middle octave, only 12 notes, work. They are all you heard, and yet in only three minutes I had covered most of the keyboard. And that is how you spend your business lives, hearing only the same 12 notes, while you scatter your hands all over the keyboard.'

He walks back to the piano and sits as before, hands hung over the keys, only this time, as he brings them down, we leap from our seats, struck by the volume, the force and the complexity of the sound – every key is working now. Chakravarti turns on his seat and looks at us, it has to be said, with very evident pity. 'Do you remember how you heard that the first time?' He takes a finger and lazily hits a single key. 'That is how you heard it and how you hear in your business lives – I hope for your own sakes it is not a disability that clouds your private life. You have only your middle octave working and you miss so much. Perhaps you miss the whole point.'

We murmur, though more in complaint than any sense of self-realization.

'You are displeased with poor old Chakravarti. You think he goes too far, but you forget, I have been watching you. That single note, that is your sales statistics – isolated numbers and history, quickly gone and faster forgotten, almost pointless. You have already forgotten my one puny note.' He strikes it once more to remind us. 'But you will perhaps never forget that first mighty chord.' We leap a second time as he twists like a snake to strike that huge sound once again.

'You know what the rest of those notes are, in your business lives of course? Perhaps you don't – Chakravarti forgets himself. Blind ignorance cannot be overcome in a moment.'

The monumental cheek of the man bites into us, but at the same time perhaps we are beginning to see the point, slowly and reluctantly.

'If the middle octave is the past, sales history expressed in volumes and values, then go one octave down and we are already exploring much richer territory; this is where rhythm resides, the beat of your business – your customers. Here we find what your customers think of you, the spoken and the unspoken – the realm of their perceptions. Let me show you.'

He plays a simple melody in the middle octave, the sort that a child would pick out with two fingers; we guess that is what he thinks of sales history! Then comes the surprise, the same simple melody but with the addition of rich, complex harmonies and rhythm, just one octave below. The transformation is amazing, and the point is made. 'Go further down the scale and we find those foundation notes, the needs of the market, the real needs, and I mean real, not just the ones you chose to hear because they suit you. Further down again and we are in those profound bass notes of the unspoken needs, perhaps as yet unimagined.'

Chakravarti plays the same melody again, this time with a progression of deep bass notes, and we have to admit that the addition does indeed sound 'profound'. 'If we come back to the middle and start moving up the octaves we are in the realms of the potential future, a fascinating place that should interest us a great deal more than the plodding present. See how much more interesting a small addition can be.'

Again the same simple melody but with just a few unexpected leaps into the next octave, just a few notes, but a step change of sophistication. 'In these treble octaves we find excitement and melody. At first we hear the potential that lies already in your own capabilities, the genius of your people, the brilliance of your technology. Moving up the octaves we find new capabilities hungering to be used.'

We are treated to a rush of melody that makes us feel the future at our fingertips, and then Chakravarti stops abruptly and turns on us. 'So why don't you hear these things? Why the fascination with history, that dull middle octave, when the rest of the keyboard is the rhythm of your market, and the melody of your future?'

Put that way, we begin to wonder. At first it is quiet contemplation but soon the whispered asides turn to a chattering, and then a bubbling torrent that fills the hall. And just above this building hubbub, we can hear Chakravarti speaking slowly and quietly. 'And if you want to hear the sound of your market, the rhythm of your business and the melodies of your future, then you must expand your consciousness, octave by octave, up to the trillest treble and down to the deepest base. You cannot listen to notes; you must listen to the music, the whole thing. Let's start this very evening. Let's explore the music out there, and start by learning the secrets of Chakravarti's piano.'

We were well entertained that evening, with more from Chakravarti's Second Piano Concerto, slower and quieter passages, as well as more thunder and lightning. His piano was most remarkable, expanding and shrinking its playing range at his command. He was able to show how by the addition of each octave we were able to appreciate more and understand more of the music, but the most interesting demonstration was this. He played a melody, a new one, backed by the whole piano, and then subtracted a few of the lower octaves. The melody was still clear, but the end result was not nearly as satisfying. He asked our opinion on the matter, and we all agreed the full piano was better.

'Why?' he asked, and the best we could come up with, a thousand opinions, was that it just sounded right. 'In that case, I am satisfied. Your opinion is good enough for me, and the answer is – it just is. But your bosses might want a better explanation. How will they react if your explanation for launching product X is that it just felt right? Will they sanction that million-pound spend to make it happen? Perhaps you, a true musician with the instinct of a maestro, perhaps you can just tell, but others? They need the proof and the evidence. They want someone to say to them – we've tried this out on a lot of folk, they say it's good and they've even helped us improve it – we've researched it. And you know what? Even a maestro like me, even I need that too. Feedback, it sometimes hurts, but you're almost always the better for it.

'Let's say I want to know how well my comeback is going down. I could wait for the royalty cheques from the CD companies. Accurate, but a little late if I'm a flop. I could measure how fast I manage to play a piece and compare that to how fast I was 10 years ago to see if I'm likely to be more successful. You think I'm crazy? What about seeing if I could take some of the notes out – Bach without all those time-consuming semiquavers, so much more efficient.'

And Chakravarti entertained us with the fastest and undoubtedly the most efficient Bach's toccata and fugue ever played – a comic rendition of great application, but a musical monstrosity.

'Crazier still? You're right, who'd want it? Of course, I shouldn't count seconds or engineer out semiquavers just in the pursuit of efficiency. I should do research. Of course there is research and research. There is measuring and knowing stupid things, because you can – how many notes, how fast – and there is ignoring the really important stuff, because you don't know how to get to it – what people think.

'If I were brave, and I am not – most artists are scared silly of feedback – but if I were brave, I would go out and ask people. I might ask their opinion, their advice even. I would listen to the other music that was going on around me, my competition you might say, and I would try to understand what inspired it, what made it work. I would try to understand what people wanted, and who was giving it to them. I would do research.

'So how about you, do you do research, or do you just improve things by playing it faster or taking out the semiquavers? Let's say you want to improve your service to customers and you start with some easy stuff, like answering the phone. Someone suggests you should answer it within three rings, and you can measure that, so you're happy. Is that it?'

He waited, clearly expecting one of us to answer, but a thousand people around you is a daunting thing – we said nothing.

'Do you know the worst thing about such measurements? It is that they become the only important thing. They become the truth, the whole truth, and nothing else matters, so help you God. Consider: because you can measure something, this doesn't always make it important. You could measure how many watts of electrical energy go down the line during a call – does that matter? Does anyone care how many number eights are in the numbers you dial? But you could measure that if you wanted. Such data is not important.

'There is worse to come. Because you can't measure something, that doesn't mean it isn't important. Let's suppose you measure two aspects of all calls received – the number of rings before calls are answered, and the length of calls. Let's also suppose that both the number of rings and the length of calls have been reducing, and you conclude that customer service is both improving and growing more efficient. Does anybody want to hear my rendition of Bach again?'

We laughed, but only to relieve our discomfort at what we were being told.

'How would it be then if, at the same time, your staff were growing ever ruder to customers, to get them off the line so that they could answer the next call promptly, and the shortness of calls was because of them not knowing the answers to customers' questions or not caring enough to find out – what then? If we asked customers what they valued most in customer service, the speed with which calls are handled or the manner in which they are handled, we might get an answer that upset our peace of mind and the appropriateness of our data measurements.'

We were uneasy in our seats. This seemed like a trick, and someone, a brave soul given the domineering presence of the maestro on stage, stood up and asked in a clear, loud voice, 'But, sir, surely we could measure whether people liked Bach fast or Bach slow, and that would be worth knowing, and then we could start asking why. And surely we could ask our customers what they thought of our telephone service. We could even ask them to rank in order of importance things like availability versus helpfulness versus politeness?'

'My dear sir, you are quite right, and let me say, your question shows a profound understanding of the secret of Chakravarti's piano.'

There was a moment of silence, and then a ripple of applause around the hall – we all felt we were getting somewhere.

7

Market audit 2 – analysis

The analysis stage of the marketing process is intended to help us take our market information and transform it into knowledge. We need to understand how the information impacts on each part of the marketing model described in Chapter 3. The purpose is to see what options there are for serious consideration when we move on to the planning stage of the process.

We will look at a variety of possible tools (some already encountered) that will help us with our analysis. Each tool may be used in a variety of ways but for simplicity's sake I have attached each to one or other of the three main parts of the marketing model. This is not intended to limit their use, merely to make their description the easier. If a particular tool is described elsewhere in this book and it is more appropriate to discuss it in detail in that context, then this chapter will direct you there and make only a brief reference to it as a part of the analysis stage.

As noted in Chapter 4, tools and methods include:

- the competitive environment;
- PESTLE analysis;
- Michael Porter's five forces or determinants of industry profitability;
- market needs – the opportunity;

- market mapping and segmentation;
- market chain analysis;
- value chain analysis;
- our capability;
- capability analysis;
- risk analysis – Ansoff matrix;
- the marketing mix.

Considering the options

As a result of this analysis, not only will the options for future strategies become clearer, but we will also be in a position to consider those options within a disciplined structure. The tools discussed form, in this sense, a bridge between market data and the market plan. We will encounter many of them again at the planning stage, and their inclusion here is not intended in any way to restrict their use to the analysis stage.

Two tools in particular will help us bridge this gap between data and plan, and the analysis completed at this point will help us to prepare them: 1) the SWOT analysis; and 2) the directional policy matrix.

THE COMPETITIVE ENVIRONMENT

PESTLE analysis

A good starting-point is to understand the impact on our own markets of the large-scale external factors: the political, economic, social, technological, legal and environmental changes going on around us. The PESTLE acronym has grown out of PEST (before environmental issues were so important), adding legal to become SLEPT and now environmental to become PESTLE, and there will be many more variations. Use whatever you wish, so long as you are looking. (Incidentally, I am tempted to suggest a new acronym for the internal factors – money, organization, research, training, assets and resources – MORTAR, and watch as marketing departments grind themselves to dust…)

For much of the time these factors are simply things that we read about in the press, but from time to time they have a dramatic impact on the working dynamics of our own market-place.

Political change can bring large-scale revolutions, such as the opening up of Eastern Europe after the fall of the Berlin Wall, but they need not always be so dramatic. Changes in government can signal shifts in values and priorities in the country (even if they don't cause them). The more caring society heralded when New Labour replaced the Conservatives in 1997 was reflected in the messages and marketing strategies of many consumer products. Red-braced executives became stock jokes rather than role models, and cars became less clearly defined as symbols of power and status, with a consequent rise in values such as safety and environmental impact.

Government intervention is sometimes said (usually by economists and purists) to distort the market-place, but the political institutions are just as much a part of the fabric of commercial life as are suppliers and customers – they just attract more criticism! One of the debates during the 2000 US presidential election campaign was over whether Internet business should be taxed. Traditional businesses, especially retailers, called foul, while new start-up companies praised the foresight in wanting to nurture a new and vital sector. Whatever your view there is no doubting the impact on competitiveness of a decision either way.

Deregulation in the European airline industry and the rise of the new low-cost, low-price operators helped prime a 50 per cent increase in passenger traffic in 1999. It is noteworthy that the majority of the operators fly out of the UK, and that British travellers represent the main part of the leap in traffic, due in great part to the UK government's deregulation policies over some years. The same cannot be said of the transatlantic market. There are still limits on the number of airlines allowed to fly out of Heathrow to major US destinations, and the US government prevents foreign airlines from operating in its domestic markets, a combination of policies that puts a serious damper on the low-price offers that have swept Europe.

Moving back on to the larger canvas, moves towards (or away from) greater European unity, control over (or loosening of) trade, uniform currency, etc, will have impacts as yet unrealized on the future prospects of many businesses. Marketers should be interested in such things.

Economic change includes the 'big picture' cycles of growth and decline that impact so greatly on markets like chemicals or building, with a knock-on effect for other businesses such as engineering suppliers or estate agents, but also the more immediate impact of an extra 20 pence on wine at the budget. Many businesses put a lot of effort into understanding economic trends and forecasts as an important element in their own planning – when to build new assets, when to expand the workforce, when to batten down the hatches. A squeeze on consumer spending in the high street can impact on a host of businesses far removed from fmcgs, including catering, building, decorating and cleaning services.

Hard times don't always hurt everyone of course. In times of general economic depression, when people start to worry about the underfunding of the NHS, there is often a rise in subscribers to private health insurance. I also remember from my days in the paint industry how during the 1984–85 miners' strike there was a mini boom in sales in mining districts (for the first few months) as stay-at-home miners had brushes and rollers thrust into their hands.

Social change, such as the increasing number of 'double income' families, particularly the dinkies (double income, no kids), has led to a combination of more prosperous households, but with less time to enjoy their prosperity! Ready-cooked, microwavable meals have **'Ping Cuisine'** enjoyed great success in this environment, as have Internet shopping services. The 'double pension' household is fast on its way in large numbers, and with the addition of time to enjoy this continued prosperity we might expect an increase in leisure activities designed to *fill* time rather than save it – perhaps even a return to shopping trips?

Technological change has been the norm of the last 100 years and perhaps the expectation of change in this area (more so than any other PESTLE factor) is well integrated into the marketing process. Even so, many businesses are still well behind the pace in responding to the rise of e-commerce. Whether the Internet Luddites will be dead and gone in five years' time, as some predict, only time will tell. We can only observe that there is scarcely a business in existence today, from major corporation to corner shop, that doesn't have a computer sitting somewhere on a table. A whole army of consultants made a **Remember Y2K?** thriving trade out of Y2K worries (technological failings can have just as significant an impact as technological successes), and no one would deny that gene technology has opened up huge new vistas for the pharmaceutical and agrochemical industries. Technology used in the marketing process itself promises to shift the boundaries of so much marketing practice, speeding the development of new products, giving instant access to information and knowledge, and facilitating an entirely new way of working with customers (see Chapter 18).

Legal changes can have instant impact – the banning of beef on the bone being a dramatic example of the sudden removal of a market opportunity. They can also raise new opportunities – the deregulation of the transport industry from aeroplanes to buses being a prime example. Safety is an important issue in the public's mind and lawmakers are continually tightening the standards for businesses that supply the public. In Germany there is a serious debate over whether to make leather seats mandatory in cars and aircraft, as a fire prevention measure. Makers of fabrics beware; tanneries and cattle farmers rejoice?

There has been controversy recently over the success of a building company in installing seating into football stadiums following on from the Hillsborough disaster and the subsequent tightening of safety standards. The controversy surrounds the fact that the company gained advantage not only from a disaster but from a report that had criticized some of the people in the football industry who were now involved with the building company.

Environmental issues and concerns have demonstrated quite clearly their impact on business from the banning of lead in petrol to the Monsanto story. This factor, along with technological change, appears to be the most easily seized as a means of gaining competitive advantage, whether it be supermarkets declaring the absence of GM foods in their stores or hotels telling us that they won't be washing our towels, in order to avoid pouring more detergents down various drains.

It might seem, as so many of these issues are outside the control of the marketing process, that surely they cannot be worth worrying about until they happen? Who seriously planned for the fall of the Berlin Wall? Who honestly prepared for the rise in one-parent families? Who anticipated the Hillsborough disaster or mad cow disease? This is missing the point. Those marketers who keep their senses attuned to such broad canvas changes will be the ones who are fleetest of foot. Avoiding the pain of unexpected change and gaining from the opportunities presented is not a matter of accident. My own business opened an office in Kuala Lumpur almost on the day that the currencies and economies of the Asian 'tigers' collapsed. We didn't predict it, but we certainly responded (and stayed!) and have emerged from the other side with a lot of credibility and strength in the region.

Some folk just don't like success; they talk about businesses getting lucky. Virgin was 'lucky' to be around when the airline industry was deregulating and a whole new generation was looking for a new way to travel the globe. What this tends to ignore is the important truth that the most successful businesses have a way of making their own luck. Virgin's success lies substantially more in the hands of its market researchers and brand managers than it does in those of fortune. It is just as the famous golfer once said when told he was lucky to be so good at golf. 'You know, the more I practise,' he said smiling, 'the luckier I seem to get.'

Michael Porter's five forces, or determinants, of industry profitability

In analysing the competitive environment, we are seeking to understand where the opportunities lie and from where the threats might come. Michael E Porter, in his book *Competitive Strategy* (1980), has provided a model much used to assess the different competitive forces that bear in upon a business, and so formulate strategies that aim to raise barriers to those forces, or take advantage of them. Figure 7.1 shows how a business operates within the ferment and flux of five different competitive forces. As well as some general comments on each, we might look at the position of the UK food supermarkets in the early 21st century to illustrate the different forces at work.

The forces are:

1. *The current competitors* – each jockeying for position through price, quality, or service. There has been an ever more heated 'battle of the giants' between the big players in this market – Tesco, Sainsbury's, Asda, Safeway, the Co-op and Morrisons. The **Store Wars** fallout has manifested itself in everything from price wars (baked beans for 2p a can, bread for 5p a loaf) to the race to launch new services, from home shopping to ever more generous loyalty cards. This latter service has taken a particularly heavy toll on supermarket margins over recent years. These

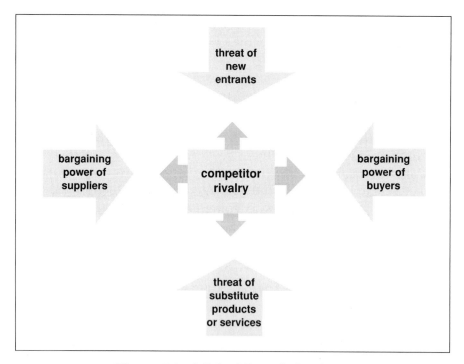

Figure 7.1 *Michael Porter's five forces*

are high-profile competitors and a slip in the rankings is public knowledge with consequent damage to consumer perceptions. It would seem that we like to buy from successful companies. A very significant feature of recent years in markets such as telecommunications, pharmaceuticals and financial services has been the tendency towards take-overs and mergers, changing at a stroke the competitive landscape. For those merging, the objective is improved security, enhanced capability and higher profits through scale and market presence. For those left independent, the rules have just changed.

2. *The threat of new entrants* – perhaps attracted by the profitability or growth of this market. New forces are continually hovering, spotting gaps in the market left by the ever repositioning major players. First there were Aldi and Netto, promising cut-price shopping, and recently the most dynamic grocery chain in the US, Wal-Mart, has threatened to bring its 'category busting' tactics to the UK through its acquisition of Asda. Not all of these new entrants are as successful as their aggressive launch plans

'Category busting'

76

promise, but their very presence reshapes the competitive dynamics of the market. New entrants come in many guises – Aldi opened new stores, Wal-Mart acquired existing ones. Sometimes they expand the market, and sometimes they just steal share.

3. _The threat of substitute products or services_ – replacing your offer, perhaps through new technology, or a lower-cost alternative, or a 'simpler' solution. Will the Internet and home shopping replace the supermarket as we know it? Certainly the supermarkets themselves are spending heavily on ensuring their own salvation through this medium, attempting to be their own substitutes before someone else does it to them. Xerox and 3M have formed an alliance to manufacture and market 'electronic paper', a technology that threatens to replace newsprint. A thin plastic sheet can be 'charged' with words and images, erased and recharged, allowing the owners to hang on to just one 'page' but have as many newspapers (for instance) as they wish. Newspaper publishers are interested, yet the American Forest and Paper Association hangs on to a prediction of 3 per cent per annum growth of paper usage through to 2010. Is it ignoring the threat of a substitute? Perhaps its prediction is just an example of the sort of broad but unhelpful statistic for the marketer – paper for what use: newsprint, books, packaging? For suppliers of newsprint, as well as printing machines, inks and a range of other associated products and services, putting their heads in the sand is not an option.

Xerox and 3M aim to save some trees

4. _The bargaining power of customers_ – often reducing in numbers through amalgamation, and consequently increasing their buying power. In the UK retail industry, consumers still have the ability to vote with their wallets as Marks & Spencer found to its cost in 1999. Food supermarkets working on relatively low margins need steadily growing volume in order to prosper. It is no surprise that there is so much noise about who sits on the number one position and why chief executives find their jobs under threat if they allow their store to slip down the rankings. The customer has genuine power in this regard. Consumers find other routes to apply their bargaining power, through pressure groups for more organic produce or campaigns to remove GM food from sale. Of course, the retailers aim to

turn such pressures to their own competitive advantage, with high-profile campaigns promising an end to battery-farmed eggs (Marks & Spencer) or a banning of genetically modified food products (Iceland). These are examples of retailers assessing a potential threat and acting to turn it to an opportunity.

5. *The bargaining power of suppliers* – sometimes through merger and consolidation, and often through the provision of increasingly specialist, high-value and unique services. At the other end of the supply chain, major suppliers can wield enormous power, either through brand names (who could envisage a major supermarket without Coca-Cola or Cadbury's?) or simply through the scale of their operation – genetically modified food products will be on the shelf simply because of the scale of supplier activities in such a wide range of food areas.

How these forces appear to you will depend on your starting-point. A company with a well-established position in the market is somewhere at the centre of the model, and will tend to see these forces as threats to its position. Its strategy might be to raise barriers to each one of them.

A company seeking to enter a market will be on the outside of the model – a new entrant – and will tend to see the various forces either as obstacles or opportunities. Its strategy will be to find means to overcome them, or take advantage of them.

In either case the object is to gain competitive advantage, and Porter's analysis is valuable in understanding the forces at work and your position relative to them, and as a spur to action. This last point is the most important – how does the analysis turn into action? Porter identifies two main options for gaining competitive advantage: a strategy of differentiation, and a strategy of becoming the lowest-cost supplier.

The PC is dead; long live the PC

Do Porter's definitions matter? Competitor, new entrant, substitute – aren't they all just competitors? They matter because the purpose of the Porter analysis is to prompt your reaction, to help you build an appropriate competitive advantage as a defence or offence. Let's suppose you are the manufacturer of a leading brand of PCs, the *traditional PC* that is, the personal computer. You are now faced with the rise of the mobile personal communicator, the 'new PC'. How you define the new PC will in turn help define your reaction.

Does it represent a new entrant or is it a substitute? If it is a potential substitute threatening to replace the traditional PC, then you might have to consider developing your own new-PC response. If it is a new entrant in the traditional PC's market, does it fight on the same ground, for the same customers, or does it redefine the market? If the former, then you will need to argue the superior benefits of your product's approach. If the latter, then perhaps the market will divide into two separate kinds of applications, with room for both new and old PCs.

MARKET NEEDS – THE OPPORTUNITY

Market mapping and options for segmentation

Chapter 11, 'Segmentation', goes into specific detail concerning market mapping. This is a process of drawing out the route your product takes to the final consumer, through the various channels of supply. There are many reasons for doing this at the analysis stage:

- to gain an understanding of your current routes to market;
- to assess potential new routes to market;
- to establish where your current strengths and weaknesses lie in comparison to the competition;
- to highlight opportunities for growth;
- to highlight areas where your position may be at risk;
- to establish the options for segmentation.

This last point, establishing options for segmentation, is of profound importance and will be dealt with in full in Chapter 11.

One of the most valuable aspects of market mapping is the way that it helps you look beyond your current customers. It is a fault of many successful businesses that they define their market and so their opportunity by their current and immediate customers.

Market chain analysis

In Chapter 3, 'The marketing model', we discussed the idea of the market chain, recognizing that unless we are the ultimate supplier to the end user there are steps in between us and that end user that will either add value or add costs. What market chain analysis allows us to see is the relative importance of each step in the chain towards the end consumer. Market chain analysis aims to understand the current picture, assess the opportunities for greater influence in, or 'ownership' of, that chain, and identify at which point of the chain contact must be established in order to secure the rewards for your efforts.

Let's suppose that we sell film material that is used in the consumer goods packaging industry. Our direct customer is the 'converter', the company that takes the film, prints it and manufactures the final packaging item whether it be a crisp packet or a 'glossy' box for an up-market perfume. A summary of the market chain is shown in Figure 7.2.

What this chain demonstrates is that the film supplier that only understands the needs and dynamics of the converter will be potentially disadvantaged when competing with one that understands

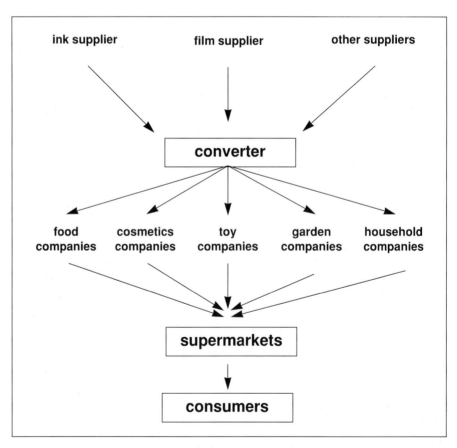

Figure 7.2 *The packaging market chain*

each user beyond the converter. The specific end uses of packaging material each have their own demands: food companies require high standards of hygiene and safety, cosmetic manufacturers are concerned principally with image, the toy producer will look for 'on-the-shelf impact', the garden chemicals company will want to ensure absolute clarity of instructions, and the household goods firm will perhaps be interested in costs above all else. If the film manufacturer is unaware of these differences, then the converter, its customer, will justifiably 'own' the market. The importance of this becomes clear if we consider the development of a new product. If the converter urges the film supplier to develop a new product to meet a specific need in the chain, then it will be the converter that owns the value of that development and receives the lion's share of the reward. If the film producer, through its knowledge of the end users, spots the opportunity and pushes the development, then it is far more likely to gain a proper share of the value added in the chain.

Of course, the supplier may choose to go one step further, to the retailer that sells the packaged goods, or beyond that to the final consumer. At each step the demands and measures of value will be different – the retailer may value display and space characteristics while the consumer may value convenience or environmental impact more highly. Each step in the chain must understand the next step to succeed, but to maximize the chances of success an understanding of the step beyond, and then beyond that, will often justify the effort.

It is not only down the chain towards the consumer that you must be looking. The other suppliers could have an impact on your business – a new type of ink that requires a different kind of film, for instance? The 'owners' of markets are those that understand the chain in all directions and seek to make their part of the chain the most significant. Using Porter's analysis of the five forces in a market they will seek to lock the other parts of the chain in to them (suppliers and customers) and build barriers to entry for new entrants or substitutes – brand names such as Intel, Teflon, NutraSweet, Gore-Tex and Lycra each has this dual effect.

Value chain analysis

Chapter 20 will give an extensive analysis of this important marketing tool. It goes one step further than market chain analysis, described above, and focuses on the steps taken by an individual customer in using our product or service. The objective of the analysis is to find steps in the customer's chain at which we can add value, and at which we can establish a point of competitive advantage. The analysis will help us to:

- highlight gaps in our knowledge of the customer's chain, so prompting research required;
- identify priority areas for action;
- compare the value provided to the customer from our offer to that provided by a competitor, so indicating areas for improvement and opportunities for gaining a competitive advantage;
- understand the capabilities required to succeed in the market.

OUR CAPABILITY

Capability analysis

This is more than asking 'What are we good at?'. The problem with such a question is that the answers are necessarily founded in the past. We are more interested here in what we *need* to be good at, and how well we match up. The tools for understanding the competitive environment and the market opportunity discussed above provide the starting-point. These will have highlighted the opportunities and the threats, the 'bottom half' of the well-known SWOT analysis (strengths, weaknesses, opportunities, threats) discussed towards the end of this chapter. We now must turn to the top half, our strengths and our weaknesses.

Risk analysis – the Ansoff matrix

Chapter 8, 'Business and marketing strategies', will deal in full with the Ansoff matrix (shown in Figure 8.5) as a means of considering the level of risk involved in your marketing activities and so indicating the sort of actions that you need to take to contain and minimize that risk. At this analysis stage it will be helpful to audit your current activities – are you trying to work outside your existing markets or existing product range, or are you focused on penetration? Look at how successful you have been and what obstacles you have encountered, and assess how well you have handled the risks involved, _but don't regard any success in the past as a passport to future prosperity._ When you look ahead to the options for your future, you will be able to compare the level of risk anticipated with the level of risk you currently undertake. This comparison will alert you to any need to reconsider your capabilities.

If your options include a significant increase in risk, moving into new markets, an increase in new product development or even diversification, you will want to increase your efforts at the market audit stage. You will need to gather more information, understand even better the dynamics of the markets, customers, competitors and products, and take even greater care to ensure your capabilities match the markets' needs. There are many ways to reduce risk, including buying in expertise, acquiring another company or finding suppliers to share the risk, but one of the most effective, lowest-cost ways is to do your homework properly at the market audit stage.

The marketing mix

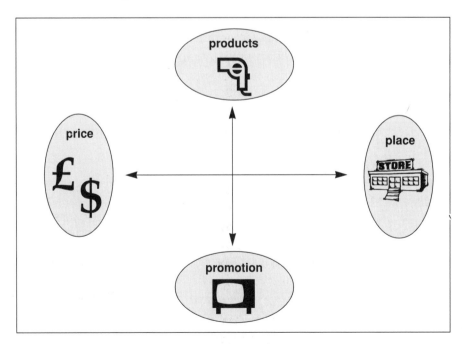

Figure 7.3   _The marketing mix_

As with the Ansoff matrix, you can use the marketing mix (the four Ps as discussed in Chapter 11, 'Segmentation') as a means of assessing your current strengths, weaknesses and capabilities based on your current activity, and comparing that analysis with what will be required for you to succeed in your future strategy. As already stated, but it deserves repetition – don't take current success as a guarantee of future prosperity. The purpose of this analysis is to highlight where you may need to change or enhance your capabilities.

How much will the mix change from your current experience and what will that imply for your ability to manage the mix? Will your new mix be in balance? Are you trying to raise prices with no supporting changes to product, place or promotion, or do you plan a massive promotional spend with no consideration of the implications on place?

The world is full, right now, of companies that think they can capture the market through the Internet simply by launching a Web site. What they are failing to consider is the effort, the expertise and the resource required to back up the promises made on that Web site. This is far more than a new twist on promotion, the P in the marketing mix concerned with getting your message to the customer. We are looking at a whole new capability requirement in the area of place, the P in the marketing mix concerned with getting your product or service to the customer. Companies offering Internet share trading services, and supermarkets offering Internet shopping and home delivery have had great success in promoting their offer, but have started to creak at the edges when it comes to delivering the promises.

Tesco say sorry for being a hit

In early 2000, Tesco were delighted to report that they led the market in providing a home shopping service, streets ahead of nearest rival Sainsbury's, but were having to apologize to newly signed-up customers that delivery dates might sometimes be as far as a week ahead of ordering because of the enormous popularity of the service. A nice problem to have, or a lesson in considering all aspects of the marketing mix?

CONSIDERING THE OPTIONS

As a result of the market information gathered in the first part of the market audit and the analysis done in the second we will be able to move on to a consideration of the main options before us. These can be complex and, quite frankly, beyond proper consideration without the sort of analytical tools being described here. Consider just the options available to improve profit as shown in Figure 7.4 – and these are far from the whole story.

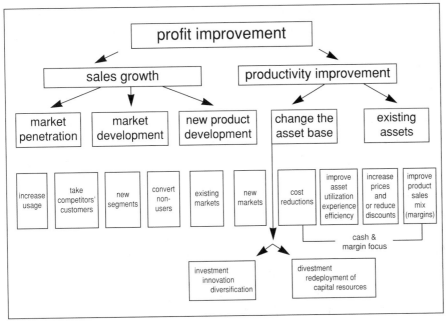

Figure 7.4 *Options, and more options ...*

(from: McDonald (1999) and after Professor John Saunders, Aston University)

The question – which to choose? – sparks a series of questions in reply. Which looks most attractive? Where do we have the most ability? Which is most likely to succeed?

Chapter 8, 'Business and marketing strategies', aims to provide some means to answer these kinds of questions, but before we leave the analysis stage we should look at two last tools that help bridge the gap between market audit and marketing planning, and so start to provide answers. The analysis done thus far will allow us to prepare two of the most useful of all marketing tools – the SWOT analysis and the directional policy matrix.

The SWOT analysis

Illustrated in Figure 7.5, this is one of the best-known of the marketing tools, one of the most used, one of the easiest to comprehend, but unfortunately one of the most poorly used in practice.

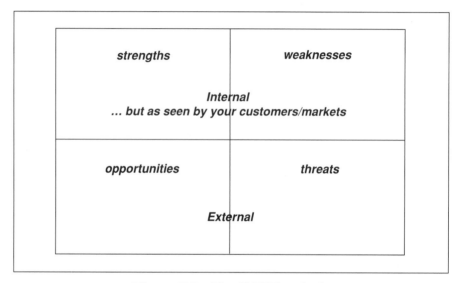

Figure 7.5 *The SWOT analysis*

Typical failings include a tendency to be too general and superficial. For a multinational manufacturing company, I could almost write the items that get put into the four boxes here and now:

- strengths – our people, our technology, our experience;
- weaknesses – our speed to respond, flexibility, internal constraints;
- opportunities – the Far East;
- threats – the Far East.

Such an analysis will get us nowhere. Stating the purpose of a SWOT analysis will make clear its importance and so the rigour with which it should be completed. The SWOT analysis provides a set of traffic lights for our options – go, stop, or more research required. It assesses our capability in seeing off the threats and seizing the opportunities, and it highlights the priorities for enhancing or changing that capability.

Another failing is to use the SWOT analysis at too high a level, typically as a means of assessing the position of the whole company. First of all, a SWOT isn't about the company, but the company's position in the market-place. Secondly, the value of a SWOT analysis tends to increase as we move from a SWOT of the market down to a SWOT of the segment, and even down to a SWOT of the product or service.

The third main failing is a tendency to see the world through the rose-tinted glasses of our own perception. The strengths and weaknesses highlighted in the SWOT should be based on the market's and the customer's judgement and perception of our capability. I once remember being involved in a top-level SWOT of the business in which at the time I was but a small cog, and seeing identified, somewhat to my surprise, that our global scale (we were the largest in the world) was a strength. What that scale meant to my customers in Norfolk and Suffolk I never did discover.

The opportunities and threats should be external factors, not issues within your own direct control. The fact that you have money available to expand your production capacity is not an opportunity – it is a possible strength (if such an expansion is relevant to the market's needs). The opportunity (if it exists) is that the market will stand more capacity, or even demands more capacity. This may sound like pedantry; what does it matter in what box we place something, provided we know what we are good at and what is out there to be grabbed? This is of course the point, going right back to the marketing model described in Chapter 3. The SWOT allows us to assess our capability (strengths and weaknesses) as a match for the market needs (opportunities) in the light of the competitive environment (threats). Precision in completing the SWOT will not only highlight imbalances in the match, but help us communicate these to all in our business concerned with securing that match.

The rigour of a SWOT should go beyond general phrases. We should attempt to measure the scale of strength and weakness, in comparison to our competitors, and the scale of the opportunities and threats in comparison with one another. This takes us to the last tool of the analysis stage, the directional policy matrix.

The directional policy matrix (the DPM)

Chapter 12, 'Product strategies', looks in some detail at this tool, and the associated tool of the Boston box. In that context it considers the management of a product portfolio – what products to give priority and resource to and where to remove resources and manage costs more tightly. It is an excellent tool for considering options where you have a finite resource to apply. At this stage of the marketing process you might use it first to consider the broad scale of options in front of you – what countries or territories to work in or chase, or what markets.

If you are already focused on a particular market then the DPM will help you focus on what segments, and if you are already focused on a segment then it will help you consider your product portfolio (as used in Chapter 12).

The principle is to take the elements of the SWOT analysis, and put them to a more rigorous test, quantifying your strengths and weaknesses as seen by the market, and ranking the attractiveness of the different options before you. The result is a four-box matrix (or nine-box if you want to indulge a penchant for 'greyness', for the world is rarely black and white) that will position your markets, territories, segments, customers, or products (the choice is yours and the DPM is a very versatile tool) in a way that helps you to allocate resources, effort and attention.

Figure 7.6 shows the matrix used to consider a choice of market segments (defined at a fairly high level) for a company providing training services. The 'advice' given in the boxes is only that – advice. It is not mandatory, simply a guide to your choice from the options available. The ranking and rating of the vertical axis, attractiveness, is of course in your own hands. There are other training companies, for instance, that would see NVQ training as very attractive based on their own capabilities and future ambitions. The horizontal axis is in the eyes of the market and should always be viewed from the perspective of the customers in those markets or segments.

Going back to the market information stage of the market audit (Chapter 5), we might now see our ability to complete such a DPM as a useful end objective for determining the sort of market information required. We will need a means to measure attractiveness and we will need information to understand our strength. This will come from

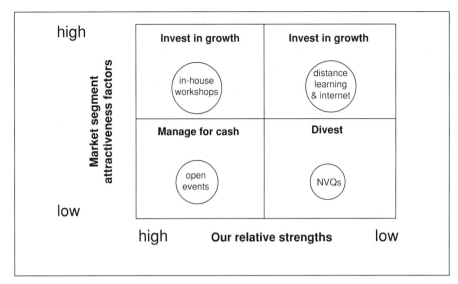

Figure 7.6 *The directional policy matrix*

research and it will also come from practical experience. We see in this model how the stages of the market process can, and must, be active together; both research and experience define our options and strategy.

If we are able to complete the DPM with confidence (not too many guesses and no wishful thinking) then we are also ready to move into the planning stage of the marketing process. We are already able to consider the options and move down to the next level of thinking – practical strategies. Chapter 8 deals with some of those strategies, followed by the CONNECT case study (Chapter 9) dealing with the task of the market audit and assessing strategic options. Chapter 10 will then outline the possible contents of a marketing plan, and the following chapters will deal with the specific contents of those plans, the segments and the marketing mixes.

The CD ROM that comes free with this book contains a simple and ready to use DPM software package.

Part III

Marketing Strategy And Planning

8

Business and marketing strategies

Throughout the analysis stage of the marketing process the clarity of the options before you begins to emerge. Marketing is about options and choices, but these never exist in a vacuum. The pace of change in the external environment imposes one set of limitations, or perhaps it would be better to see, rather than limitations, guidelines. Your own company's resources and capabilities impose another set of conditions on what can be done – the reality check. The task of the marketer is to seek the match between internal resources and external opportunities, sometimes seeking to influence the market, sometimes seeking to change company capabilities (see Chapter 3, 'The marketing model').

Taking one step back from this match we can see another set of guidelines for the marketer; as well as the external environment and the internal capabilities, there is what you and your colleagues want the business to be – its objectives. Things such as your intended size and scale of operation, target markets and segments, market share, geographical presence, style of operation and profitability provide an overall purpose for the marketer's matching process. What we are talking about here of course is business strategy.

Business strategy is about managing the future, and that is in essence a question of finding the right balance between the three things that we have been discussing, as shown in Figure 8.1.

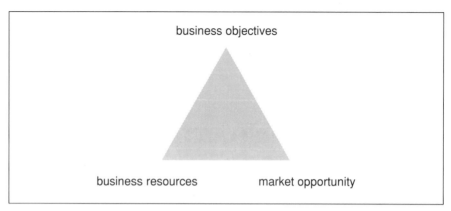

Figure 8.1 *Business strategy – managing the future*

The business objectives are what you want your business to achieve in the future. The market opportunity is the set of forces that will help you or hinder you – customers, competitors, Porter's five forces (see Chapter 7), etc. The business resources are those things that will support or constrain your progress: your own capabilities, production capacity, R & D, logistics, money and, not least, your people.

If business strategy is about managing this balance, we can see that it cannot be a once-and-for-all statement or document. Managing the future is a challenging exercise; as the future gets closer, so the opportunities change, not least because of your own impact on them, and so must your balance of resources and objectives. Managing the future must be a continual process of analysis, reassessment and change.

This is not to say that a business must be in continual turmoil with no direction. The trick is to retain as much flexibility as possible, while holding to some firm strategic goals as long as it is sensible and realistic to do so. At one time banks aimed to increase their market share by opening new branches. The winners were those who sat on the most property. The opportunity was there, and developments in IT provided the capability to manage large chains. The objective was realistic and the strategy was workable, until times changed. Market share is still the goal, but the specific targets have become more sophisticated and the means to reach them have changed. The new strategy looks at targeting particular groups of customers, and creating new banking brands such as Egg or b2 to exploit specific market segments. It aims increasingly to use home banking and call centres as the vehicle rather than a branch on every high street, and the cost structures of banks are changing out of all recognition as a result.

STRATEGIC INERTIA

In many businesses you will find evidence of an old strategy (right for its time) having been carried on for too long – the larger the company, the greater the inertia. Perhaps the banks we have been discussing were still opening new branches, only to see them closed again within a year, just as the new strategy took hold. Some super-market chains were still selling their smaller high street stores just at the moment they were deciding to re-establish themselves there with convenience store concepts.

The analogy of a large business with an ocean-going oil tanker is a good one; both take a lot of time and effort to change direction. Any consideration of a new source of power for the tanker is beset with the problems of keeping the existing one running. For large compa-nies, business strategy becomes ingrained to the point that often in the past a change of strategy has had to wait for a generation of managers to move on. The change process is made harder still when a charismatic company boss puts their guiding strategy into print and becomes a temporary best-seller on the bookshelves. Here is the dilemma: strategy must be able to change, but it must also have clarity while it is still in operation. Much of the movement towards smaller business units within a larger parent company has been in pursuit of this blend of clarity and flexibility.

Not that small businesses are without their problems. For them, looking into the future is often the difficult thing. In such a case it is not unusual for a business to run without a strategy at all! Day to day, this causes no problem, perhaps, but in the longer term it can have a serious effect on attempts to grow. Activities become disjointed, effort is wasted on wrong turnings, staff become confused about the company's direction, and fire fighting becomes the order of the day. Once in this trap, escape is difficult.

The 'resource escalator' and the perils of missing the bus

Working in an under-resourced business is no fun; everything is strained to the limit, including you. The reasons for under-resourcing are many. Here are three common ones:

1. lack of investment – either because of insufficient funds, or perhaps because of insufficient vision;
2. the inevitable time lag between a new opportunity appearing and the organization getting its act together;
3. the desire to use available resources as efficiently as possible – the 'lean and mean' school that takes things to the limit and sometimes beyond.

Whatever the reason, in a growth market the result is the same: a period of stress and then time for bold action and an injection of resource sometimes beyond the immediate need. This is particularly common in the service industries where the prime resource is people. You may only need half a new person but you have to take on a whole one!

We might call this situation the 'resource escalator' and it is illustrated in Figure 8.2. Its characteristic pattern is one of feast and famine with only the briefest period of perfect balance in between.

If the only problem with this situation were an imbalance of resource to opportunity then that would be one thing, but Figure 8.2 also shows what is perhaps the real problem with the resource escalator. The fixation on finding the right level of resource can easily turn into an internal focus driven by a desire to maximize efficiency. In a growth market this can be seriously bad news. Perhaps the resource escalator keeps reasonable pace with the *observed* opportunity, but is that the same thing as the real opportunity? When your business is growing, particularly if you feel smart (not to say smug) about how you manage your resource in line with that growth, it is easy to feel satisfied. Satisfaction and complacency are near neighbours and you can soon be missing the point that the *real* opportunity

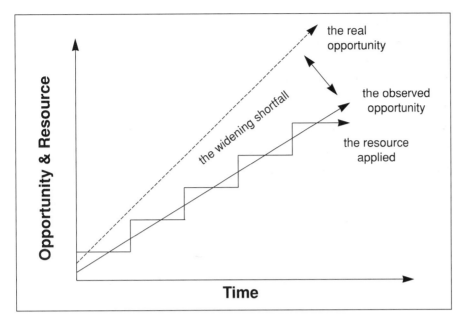

Figure 8.2 *The resource escalator*

is much larger and that, in fact, a gulf is appearing between your own performance and that real opportunity.

A common story, but what can we conclude? Perhaps the lesson is that, of the three elements in managing the future – objectives, resources and opportunity – it is the opportunity that is most important for the marketer to focus on and understand. This of course was the purpose of the market audit discussed in Chapters 5, 6 and 7, and it should remain uppermost in our mind when considering business and marketing strategy.

HOW FAR AHEAD?

The point raised here is about time lines. For how far ahead can a strategy be designed? This must depend on the pace of change and development in the particular industry and market. The time horizon for the banking industry has got a lot closer in recent years, it is still a long way off in the pharmaceutical industry, and in the food industry it shortens by the month. Understanding the trends that impact on the speed of change will be vital to success.

'In the long run, we're all dead.' John Maynard Keynes

For the pharmaceutical industry it is a combination of the research technology, regulatory controls on drug development, and patent protection laws that keep the time lines long. So long as it might take 15 years to bring a new drug to market, so business strategies will revolve around huge in-house research and development capabilities and large field sales forces. The pharmaceutical companies have identified that tomorrow's winners will be those that increase their 'speed to market', and business strategy is changing to bring this about. We have seen massive mergers of one-time rivals in pursuit of instant R & D expertise, investment in new fast-track testing procedures and techniques, and outsourcing of once-cherished activities from production to sales. Companies like Innovex have grown rapidly by providing flexible contract sales teams to the pharmaceutical industry, helping them with their new strategies of speed and focus.

Many businesses will have two or three strategy and planning horizons:

- the 10-year view;
- the 3-year plan;
- the 1-year plan.

The longer-term plan will encompass many of the 'ifs and buts' of predicting the future. The fact that these predictions don't come true does not negate the process. Businesses that think about the future are usually faster on their feet when changes happen in the shorter term. The short-term plan is very much more the tactical implementation, while the medium-term plan probably represents the realistic *hows* of running the business.

Where does the marketing strategy come in to all of this?

MARKETING STRATEGY

How does a marketing strategy or plan differ from a business strategy or plan? Is the latter simply longer term, or larger in scale, or broader in concept?

Looking at many business strategies or plans, there is often an inclination to criticize them for their overconcern with internal issues – assets, investment, HR issues, etc. Looking at many marketing strategies or plans, the inclination is to criticize *them* for being too limited, too short-term, too concerned with the tactical implementation of products, price, promotion and place.

Perhaps there is a need for each to become more like the other? The issue is really: how much is marketing in the bloodstream of your business, and what definition do you give to marketing as an activity? In a publishing company, for instance, marketing tends to mean promotion, and the business strategy is in the hands of the editorial team. Of course, what the editorial team are doing is marketing, and the marketing department is looking at just one of the four Ps in the marketing mix. In a multinational manufacturing company with big growth aspirations, the marketing and business plans might be almost indistinguishable. The marketing plan in such an environment must deal as much with assets and investment as does the business plan or else it runs the risk of being mere wishful thinking – all objectives and opportunity and no resources to make it happen.

In general, the thing that should most distinguish the marketing strategy, and indeed the practice of marketing itself, is the focus on the opportunity. Marketing strategy arises from an understanding of the dynamics and the requirements of the market, and the identification of opportunities for your own capabilities. Sometimes this may be to *create* whole new opportunities, such as the Mars ice-cream, sometimes simply to understand the true opportunities by looking into the market chain beyond the immediate customer.

THE STRATEGY ROAD MAP

Marketing is about the pursuit of sustainable competitive advantage, and with a variety of options to choose from (if you are lucky!) a key step in achieving this goal will be deciding what type of business you are, and wish to be. The strategy road map (Figure 8.3) will assist you in this part of the marketing process.

Starting with the mission statement and business objectives (see Chapter 10, 'Writing the marketing plan', for more on this), the marketing strategy is summarized in three broad slices (or sets of issues) – what products to sell and where, the source of your competitive advantage, and what values drive your business. Any change of strategy will almost certainly call for a reconsideration of each of these slices, as they do not work independently of one another.

Each set of issues raises its own specific questions, and an array of

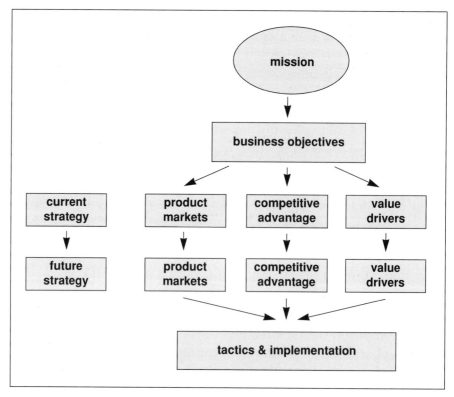

Figure 8.3 *The strategy road map*

options and choices to be made. Table 8.1 summarizes the key questions and suggests a model that will help in the analysis of each set of issues.

Gap analysis

Before we look more closely at these issues we should consider a helpful, and in this case pictorial, means of representing the challenge ahead. We probably have objectives for growth, whether in volume or value or share, and there will be many ways to get there. One thing is usually certain: doing nothing, or continuing as we have been doing, will rarely move us forward. It is a typical observation of people with 'long experience' in business, but a true one all the same, that the hardest thing of all is to stay just as you are. Attempts to do that almost always send you backwards.

Table 8.1 *The strategy road map – questions and issues*

Strategic Issue	Questions	Model
What Products, in What Markets?	Are these old or new? What risk is involved?	The Ansoff matrix
Source of Competitive Advantage	Is there an opportunity to be different? Is there an opportunity to be lower-cost?	Michael Porter and competitive advantage
Value Driver	Are you driven by functions, products, or customers?	Treacy and Weirsema's value drivers

We might represent this on a gap analysis, as shown in Figure 8.4, as the line of slow decline if we do nothing. The steepest line is of course out-target – some managers like to give targets and then what they call 'stretch' targets, as if to say that ordinary targets are too easy for the likes of us. Between 'do nothing' and our target is a choice of 'do somethings'. The choices for growth in attempting to close this gap are in fact outlined by the first tool to be considered in our strategy road map, the Ansoff matrix.

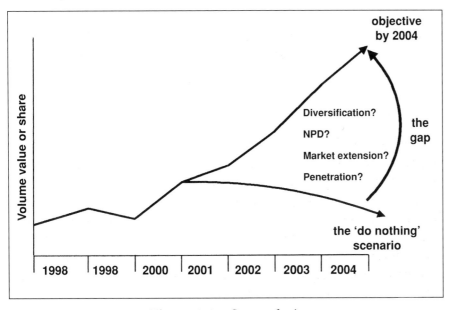

Figure 8.4 *Gap analysis*

Products and markets – the Ansoff matrix and risk

For any business wishing to grow, there are four choices based on what it sells and where it sells, expressed by the four boxes in the 'Ansoff matrix', named after its developer, Igor Ansoff of the Boston Consulting Group (see Figure 8.5):

1. Sell more of existing products into existing markets – *penetration*.
2. Sell existing products into new markets – *market extension*.
3. Sell new products into existing markets – *NPD*.
4. Sell new products into new markets – *diversification*.

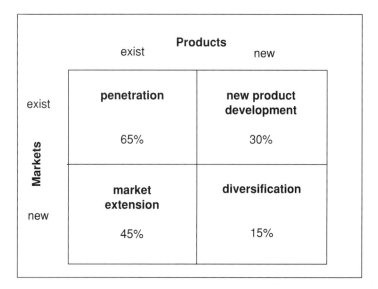

Figure 8.5 *The Ansoff matrix*

Penetration

Provided that there is more business to be had in your existing market (you do not already 'own' the lion's share), then penetration is usually the safest strategy. You already have a presence, you know the requirements and you can measure your activities with some confidence. The figure of 65 per cent shown in Figure 8.5 represents a typical 'success rate' for such a strategy, based on studies across a wide range of businesses. 'Typical' means very little, of course, when we turn to the particular. You may have only a 20 per cent chance of success in your market given your set of circumstances, but the number is useful as a marker in comparison to the figures in the other three boxes.

Each circumstance is unique, of course, but penetration becomes less attractive in a declining market, or where your share is so high that further growth is unrealistic. Shifting share from 5 to 10 per cent may sound a huge leap, but it is often a lot easier than moving from 80 to 85 per cent. For one thing, customers won't allow you this dominance, and for another, perhaps, the government will restrict you (remember PESTLE, Chapter 7), and there are always competitors who refuse to die whatever you do.

Risk

As your chosen growth strategy moves around the matrix from penetration to market extension, to new product development (NPD), or even to diversification, the risk of failure increases. With each step away from your existing market and your existing products you are moving further into the unknown, hence the smaller percentage success rate shown in each successive box. Again, these are typical numbers. Turning to specifics, an fmcg food manufacturer might be very pleased indeed with an NPD success rate of 30 per cent (the average is in single figures), while a training company like my own would be distraught!

Of course, some risk is necessary if you wish to grow, but any sensible business will always seek to manage or contain that risk, as far as they can. There are many things that can be done to manage risk:

- market research;
- market testing;
- alliances or joint ventures with experienced partners, including suppliers and customers;
- taking on experienced staff, or training;
- acquisition and merger;
- brand extension and the 'brand halo' (see Chapter 16).

The key to using the Ansoff matrix is in an honest assessment of which boxes you are operating in, so allowing you to take the necessary risk-reducing actions. So often a business will enter into a new activity, launching new products (NPD), entering new markets (market extension), or both (diversification), while underestimating the risk involved because it seemed just like the existing product/market (penetration). The peril of this underestimate is that you do insufficient homework and involve insufficient resources.

Diversification

The Mars ice-cream – a bumpy road to success	Mars scored a famous success with their launch of the ice-cream Mars Bar in the UK, creating a whole new market out of nowhere. The launch was diversification, a very new and novel product for Mars, and a new market, ice-cream buyers not confectionery buyers. Perhaps, however, one failing marred their success. Perhaps they saw this simply as NPD. Surely the markets were not that dissimilar? The result of this underestimate was a launch hiccup that could have wrecked the whole project, and certainly cost Mars time and money, not to mention some bad PR. It turned out that Mars were asking retailers of the new ice-cream to put it into their existing freezer cabinets. Unfortunately for Mars, these cabinets were rarely the retailer's own property. More often they were owned by one of the two big ice-cream brands, Walls or Lyons Maid. The response from these manufacturers was fast and litigious. Mars had to react in double-quick time by providing their own cabinets (I always think of that refrigerator supplier – it must have seemed like Christmas!).
	In the end of course the diversification was hugely successful, not least because of the heavy promotional spend behind the launch, but also very importantly because of the strength of the Mars name. Using an existing brand to enter new markets or launch new products can be a very effective way of reducing risk, provided that the values attached to the brand are transferable. In the case of Mars this was apparently so.
Virgin – breaking the rules?	In the case of Virgin, the success is even clearer. Some say that Virgin break all the rules of the Ansoff matrix, that moving from record label to airline to hotelier to cola producer to financial services to rail operator is diversification with a vengeance and that they should have failed more often. The point is that, far from breaking the rules, they have observed the most important rule: understand the challenge and the risk, and aim to minimize the risk when away from home territory. In Virgin's case, it is a combination of the brand halo, meticulous market research and their use of expert partners and suppliers that gives them their success.
Diversifying to escape decline – will it work for Marlboro?	Philip Morris, owners of the Marlboro brand, envisage a slow decline of that brand as a result of increasing restrictions on tobacco advertising. This is not a situation that they are about to take lying down, not least because the brand is one of their most important assets, valued at $23 billion. Plans under consideration include diversification into hotels and leisure, under the Marlboro brand. One way of reducing the risks of diversification is *brand extension*, taking an existing brand and using its 'halo' effect (see Chapter 16) to establish a presence in the new market. But some of the challenges are clear – can the Marlboro brand values be translated to, say, a hotel stay (presumably guests will still be warned about smoking in bed!), and will the

attempt be accepted by the market (the US government, for one, prevents such activities). Philip Morris must weigh the options, including diversification, to keep the brand alive, or perhaps conceding to its long-term decline and milking it for funds to invest in penetration strategies for growth brands in the portfolio, such as Kraft or Miller Brewing.

Market extension

Entering new markets with existing products, market extension, is perhaps the most fertile ground for horror stories. So many otherwise successful businesses assume that what works here will work there (when thinking of new markets as new countries). Very few companies are able to sustain a standard offer world-wide – even McDonalds has to call its quarter-pounder with cheese a 'royale' in France (as any watcher of *Pulp Fiction* will know!), and Kentucky Fried Chicken had to take the coleslaw out of the package when Colonel Sanders went to the land of the rising sun. Yet time after time corporate ego gets the better of a business and they come to grief.

Ben and Jerry's ice-cream was a phenomenal success in the USA with the company's quirky mix of showmanship, fun, local referencing, entrepreneurial spirit and social conscience, a formula that meant very little when the product was launched in the UK. Not only did British consumers care little for the plight of Vermont dairy farmers (the brand's support of this beleaguered group in the US won it a warm following), but few Brits got the jokes in ice-cream names such as Cherry Garcia (work it out for yourself).

Ben and Jerry – an ice-cream or a double act?

Even brand names can let you down – the Vauxhall Nova flopped in South America where Nova means the Vauxhall 'won't go', and Coca-Cola can sound like 'lice in the carpets' in some parts of China!

ICI Dulux, for many years predominantly a UK brand, acquired a number of non-UK paint companies in the 80s, including the largest operators in France (Valentine) and the USA (Glidden). It was some time before they stopped trying to force the famous 'Dulux dog' on to their new colleagues. In France, Valentine finally accepted an animal in their advertising, but a black panther matched their positioning and message better than the dog, and in the USA the use of animals to express brand values never did catch on. One of the ironies of this is that Dulux is a brand that conducts more market research than any other in its market, and is in the top league of research among fmcg companies, yet corporate ego held them back from asking

The dog that wouldn't travel

some simple questions when entering what to them, if not to Valentine and Glidden, were very new markets indeed.

Retailers often make the same mistake – Marks & Spencer struggled with their ventures into North America, Texas Homecare had an expensive flop in Spain, Aldi and Netto have never captured hearts and minds in the UK in the way they have on the continent, and Wickes Building Supplies, a leader in profitability in the UK market, ran a chain of poorly performing stores in Holland and Belgium throughout the 80s – the winning formula did not transfer as easily as they had hoped.

The challenge is bigger than usually envisaged. Products that have been carefully honed for their current market may need revision (and more than new labels) for an overseas market. They may need reworking to such an extent that they become new products and the business teeters close to diversification. Not that diversification is the problem: Virgin for one show how it can be done successfully. It is diversifying without ever realizing it that leads to tales of disaster.

New product development

This will be dealt with more fully in Chapter 12, 'Product strategies', but for here suffice it to say that in most businesses not only is the risk high, but the costs of development should not be underestimated when calculating the return on investment. As ever with the Ansoff matrix, this is not a signal to abandon all NPD; rather it is a caution to concentrate on the winners.

3M have long been heralded as an innovative company, with much talk about their policy of allowing employees to devote large chunks of their time, and 3M's money, on developing, well, almost whatever they like! They make the proud claim that the majority of their profits in only five years' time will come from products not yet launched, or even off the drawing board; and it works, *for them*. One of the problems of using such high-profile examples to illustrate winning strategies is that it is easy to forget the circumstances that make that strategy work. A company that plans a high level of NPD needs to ensure it has the capabilities. These might include a well-supported R & D resource, an ability to work collaboratively with partners and suppliers, an ability to get new products to market *fast*, a management structure that both allows and stimulates creativity, and an acceptance of failure and an ability to learn from it. It will also need a way to deal with the large numbers of ideas that inevitably get thrown up in such an environment, choosing which should be supported and which should be rejected. We might call it a *stage-gate* process, and we will look at this more closely in Chapter 12.

In global markets the cost of NPD can be almost prohibitive for any one player, and we see an increasing number of partnerings, alliances and joint ventures, to share the costs, reduce the risks and ensure that the capabilities are in place.

Hewlett-Packard dominate the market for small-sized inkjet printers for the business user. Xerox have a 2 per cent share but target 10 per cent by 2004. Arguably this is a penetration strategy for Xerox – they have products in the market already – but 2 per cent is barely a toehold. Such growth plans will require NPD, and the scale required calls for new capabilities and resources, so they are partnering with Fuji Xerox (their Japanese joint venture) and Sharp of Japan.

Partnering for NPD

Growth options in a mature market

If anything other than penetration is so risky, why do it? Growth is always the objective and, when a business is operating in a mature or declining market, penetration is not always the best route.

Few consumer markets are more mature than that for breakfast cereals in the USA; the big brands have slugged it out consistently for decades on the battleground of market share. General Mills recently scored a victory over Kellogg's by knocking its long-term rival off the number one spot for the first time, but the champagne is flowing less freely than might be expected with the realization that the battleground needs to change. General Mills are looking at genomic research to design foods for treating or preventing specific illnesses.

Escaping the breakfast battleground

Quaker, a smaller player in the cereals market, but of equal heritage, have recently partnered with Novartis, forming Altus Foods, in order to escape the price and share demands of this mature market. Altus Foods will pursue opportunities for food as a form of health treatment. 'We need to change food companies to nutrition companies,' says Robert Morrison, Quaker's chief executive. What might sound like NPD is really diversification, and the risks involved and the new capabilities demanded call for such partnerships and alliances. Novartis have launched the Aviva brand in the UK with a muesli that promises heart benefits, an orange juice drink with bone benefits and a crunchy wholewheat biscuit with digestive benefits. The promises are up-front and packaging carries a clinically proven badge with the tag line 'Enjoy the taste today – enjoy a healthy tomorrow'.

Almost nothing is inevitable in marketing, however. There are always choices, and Kellogg's are choosing to go a different route, aiming to reduce their dependence on cereals through the growth of successful convenience foods such as Pop-Tarts – penetration is still an option when a company operates in multiple segments.

Source of competitive advantage – Michael Porter

In Chapter 7, 'Market audit 2 – analysis', we discussed Michael E Porter's model of competitive forces that bear on a business. Porter goes on to argue that a business has two principal ways to respond to those forces in its pursuit of competitive advantage: 1) be the lowest-cost supplier; or 2) be a differentiated supplier.

The options may sound simple and rather stark, but the reality is that many businesses fail to make the choice and linger in a never-never land of compromises. What they often lack is the discipline to focus the whole business on whichever route is chosen. A typical outcome is, for instance, a production function devoted to becoming the lowest-cost supplier and a marketing function wishing to offer flexible product ranges.

In most markets there is usually the option to choose to be either lowest-cost or differentiated as a means to competitive advantage. The airline industry is an excellent example where both strategies are in evidence, even within the same parent company. British Airways chases the added-value, differentiated route, while launching Go as a low-cost operator to take on the likes of easyJet and RyanAir. What is important to note about the British Airways strategy is the need to operate Go as a stand-alone company. The sets of company capabilities required to succeed in each of the two options are so different as to make such a divide essential. We are looking at two different strategies, two different mindsets and two different cultures.

Lowest-cost supplier

This does not mean cheap or slipshod. It does not mean that the company will necessarily sell at the lowest price, though they will be able to do this should the need arise, or if, indeed, this becomes the key to their success. A successful practitioner of this strategy once said to me, 'The trick is to be the lowest-cost supplier, but not let the customer know that!'.

Where the strategy *is* to sell at the lowest price then the disciplines of such a business must be very tight indeed.

EasyJet is an example of such an operator and success depends on reducing the costs of its operation at every possible point in the supply chain. Starting from the top, the management team occupy a utilitarian open-plan office – part of the strategy, and very much a symbol to the rest of the organization. More importantly, costs are reduced by operating from smaller airports – Luton and Liverpool rather than Heathrow and Gatwick. Critically, the turn-around time on the ground is shaved to the shortest possible, allowing each plane to make more flights and carry more passengers. This requires close liaison with the airport operators and constant attention to detail. The sales operation must be honed to work efficiently, effectively and at lowest cost. Efficiency comes from use of the Internet – over half of easyJet bookings come that way. Effectiveness is about ensuring that where seats can be sold at higher prices, they are. This ability comes from understanding the demand patterns for each route, forecasting usage and developing pricing strategies that will fill planes at the optimum price. The sales effort is run at low cost by declining to work through intermediaries, the travel agents, so saving commission payments on every transaction. Promotion is a key ingredient, but rather than heavyweight high-cost TV campaigns, easyJet make excellent use of price offers through the national press.

EasyJet – investing in spending less

Over and above all of this, success depends on there being a demand for a low-price no-frills service, and easyJet have been able to capitalize on just such a demand as more people see air travel as an option to be compared with rail or bus.

None of this means a company that doesn't invest. Don't confuse low-cost operators with cheap-jacks. Where investment will reduce operating costs, such as investing in an Internet ticket-booking capability or in a call centre that allows the airline to cut out the travel agents' commission, that investment is made with alacrity.

Differentiation

Just as easyJet and Go aim to meet the needs of those travellers who simply want to get from A to B at the lowest price, so there are airline operators, indeed the majority, who aim to provide more than that, and provide it to a different segment of the market. Segmentation is what allows two such different strategies to succeed in the same market. There is no such thing as an air traveller; there are air travellers who want speed, those that want comfort, those that want fun, those that want to be excited, those that want to be calmed, those that want their egos stroked, those that want to make business deals, those that want a relaxing holiday, those that want to 'fly the flag', those that want to feel safe, and many more besides. The differentiated airline aims to offer a package that appeals to a particular mix of these needs, so hoping to stand out from the competing crowd.

Differentiation can be many things in such a market, but above all it must be seen by the customer to add value. A business-class ticket will have many facets of added value, perceived in a variety of ways depending on the customer and the circumstance. Business travellers needing an earlier flight will perceive huge value in a ticket that allows them to make that change, at no extra cost, with priority attention, even if they have to travel in an economy seat! On another occasion, waiting for a delayed flight on a busy Monday morning, the business-class lounge will seem more than enough value for the premium price paid.

To develop a successful differentiated strategy a business must be able to understand the complex interactions of price and value in their market, and must be able to present offers that meet real needs, while distinguishing themselves from the competition.

No longer just 'flying the flag' – British Airways goes global	For many years British Airways made great play of being the nation's airline, 'flying the flag', giving them a unique piece of differentiation. As deregulation in the industry loosened the ties between airlines' routes and airports, so competition grew and this patriotic positioning became of less value to passengers. Amidst a storm of protest from traditional supporters (including Margaret Thatcher and a handkerchief on one famous occasion), British Airways removed the Union Jack from their tailplanes and took on the mantle of a global airline. Adverts stress how many Americans travel by the airline, not how many British, with the implication that in business circles they must of course be doing the right thing. A new positioning, but still a very differentiated one.

Just as we should not mistake the lowest-cost strategy for stinginess, so we should not equate differentiation with massive promotional budgets or a spendthrift attitude. Differentiation can of course come from a high-profile advertising presence, but more significantly it comes from identifying and providing things that customers value and will pay a premium for. For such things, investment should flow, and for things of no value, the accountant's knife should be sharpened to the full.

Is it 'either or', or is it 'and'?

Porter advises marketers to make their choice, differentiation or lowest cost, and so avoid the perils of the 'inbetweeny'. But must it always be such a choice? Is it not possible to combine both? Certainly there are examples of companies that because of their scale will almost certainly have the lowest costs in the business but are nevertheless highly differentiated – Coca-Cola is one, Microsoft another. The real question is not whether they achieve this position, but how they use it and which of the two gains them their competitive advantage. When we look at pricing strategies in Chapter 13, we will see how the company that has an opportunity to both reduce costs *and* differentiate is likely to find itself in the role of 'price leader' in the market – an enviable position, but rarely achieved outside large-scale mass-market producers.

The 1980s was a decade when marketers made bold choices (it was definitely 'either or'), largely as a reaction to the blur and inertia of the 70s, but more recently businesses are asking for both differentiation *and* lowest cost (the era of 'and' is well and truly with us). Chapter 20 will look at the idea of the value chain and in particular at the example of Formule 1, a hotel chain in Europe, which through its understanding of customer value, combined with a drive to reduce costs (and a genius for segmentation), appears to be achieving the 'and' result.

Value drivers – Treacy and Weirsema

A value driver is a set of ideas or notions, a business culture, or a guide map that allows all members of the business to identify with what they should be doing to achieve success. It is what makes the business tick or, better, what makes it hum.

Treacy and Weirsema in their book, *The Discipline of Market Leaders* (1995), identify three value drivers. All may be present in any successful business, but for a *really* successful business, one or other of these drivers will stand out, distinguishing the business for its staff and its customers, and distinguishing it from its competitors (see Table 8.2).

Operational excellence is about doing what you do, well. It is about effective processes, smooth mechanics and the efficiency with which products or services are brought to market. Efficiencies of

Table 8.2 *Value drivers*

Value Driver	Examples
Operational excellence	McDonalds, IKEA, Dell, Wal-Mart
Product leadership	Microsoft, 3M, Merck, Intel, Nike
Customer intimacy	Kraft, Quest International, INSIGHT Marketing and People

production, economies of scale, uniformity and conformity, accurate forecasting, slick distribution, fast response – these are the sorts of things that might be important to a business seeking 'operational excellence'. Such 'excellence' can bring significant competitive advantage in a market where reliability is important or price is competitive. Businesses in the mass-market, no-frills, low-hassle, low-price arena will often be driven by this value.

IKEA and Wal-Mart – paragons of efficient virtue

IKEA achieve huge efficiencies through their logistics chain from manufacture to store, and in-store the 'self-selection, self-collection' formula completes the operational excellence of their supply chain, reflected in excellent value for customers. International uniformity (Swedish product names like 'Gutvik' and 'Sprallig' make it all the way to Australia), modular ranges and a carefully honed (limited, but it doesn't seem so) offer are some of the watchwords.

Wal-Mart achieve incredible cost savings through the logistical efficiency of their EPOS (electronic point of sale)-based ordering system. As each product goes through the check-out scanner it is reordered to be back on the shelf within 48 hours.

Product leadership is about producing the best, leading-edge, or market-dominant products. Businesses with high rates of innovation and patent application often have this value at their heart. It is hard to imagine a successful pharmaceuticals company that is not driven by this value. Investment in successful NPD is the key to success; the market for 'nearly there' or 'almost as good as the best one' drugs is rarely good. One of the biggest threats for a business driven by this value is that of falling behind, and it is necessary to push the boundaries of performance continually, and be seen to be doing so.

The pace of innovation achieved by Microsoft is amazing, the downside being that you can sometimes feel out of date as soon as you carry the new product out of the store. They walk a very difficult tightrope – innovate and risk upsetting customers who feel forced to replace what they saw as perfectly good products, or slow down and be seen as dull. They must also ensure reliability (just witness the publicity when there are doubts over the new version of Windows) and yet keep their foot on the accelerator. Occasional failure is almost inevitable for such a company, yet the costs of failure are huge, financially and perceptually – a difficult tightrope indeed.

Microsoft work at the edge

Customer intimacy is the ability to identify with specific customer needs, and match products and services accordingly. What distinguishes customer-intimate businesses is their stated determination to develop close customer relationships, and to act on the resultant knowledge at all levels of their operation. They will probably have a wide menu of products and services, and the ability to mix and match these to suit individual customer requirements – or perhaps they will go further than this and offer a totally bespoke service. There is a limit to how many customers this can be done for, and customer-intimate businesses will think carefully about segmentation and key account identification. Something else that often distinguishes businesses driven by customer intimacy is their willingness to share risks with their customers, and to expect a concomitant share of the rewards.

Quest International (a part of ICI) supply fragrances to the perfume industry. Each of their customers' products is unique, and the fragrance is equally unique – there are few off-the-shelf solutions. The perfumer's art is as much one of black magic as chemistry, and Quest must be able to identify with this. Customer intimacy is essential for success: absolute identification with the customer's needs, and the ability to focus the whole organization on meeting them. Many of Quest's customers are themselves driven by product leadership – branding is all – and Quest must be intimate with *that* value driver in order to be regarded as a key supplier. Their success is evidence of a broader observation: truly customer-intimate suppliers must be able to identify with value drivers in their customers that are quite different from their own.

'In this business, we get so close to our customers we can smell them – literally.'

Implications for the business

Clarity on these drivers is of huge importance to the resultant clarity of the business and marketing strategies. Those businesses that find it difficult to define their direction are often those that allow a random mixture of these value drivers throughout their operation. A business where distribution adheres to operational excellence, sales to customer intimacy and marketing to product leadership is a business heading for trouble, both internally and in its market.

The task of the marketing strategy is to make it clear which of these drivers must lead. Only then can the functions and operations within that business focus their activities accordingly. If customer intimacy is the goal, that doesn't mean the factory should throw operational excellence out of the window. What it *does* mean is that they should seek to identify *appropriate* operational excellence – perhaps measured by customer satisfaction as well as by the running efficiency of the plant.

Value drivers and strategic change

A particularly valuable aspect of this model is the way it can be used to handle the problem highlighted earlier in this chapter, that strategy needs to be flexible enough to change, yet clear enough to be operable.

While there will almost certainly be a lead driver, the other drivers will still be apparent in the business. No business can be 100 per cent customer-intimate with no ability to operate excellently or develop leading products. In reality, there will be a ranking order of the three. That ranking will be the result of the marketer's search for the match between company capability and market need – the marketing model.

Looking at the market, businesses should attempt to identify what balance of these three drivers is wanted by their target customers. By understanding their customers' needs, attitudes and perceptions, they may be able to identify minimum standards for each of the drivers, or what we might call 'givens'. A fast-food chain must be able to produce a product to a certain minimum standard, and must be able to offer a sufficient choice to allow for consumer preferences. Provided those standards are met, the chain might then choose to excel at the product aspect of the business – the best burger in town – or on the operational aspects of the business, with a slickly efficient supply chain from purchase through to delivery, and the fastest service in town. Table 8.3 represents the result of this analysis and the decision to chase the latter of these two strategic choices.

Table 8.3 _Value drivers and the strategic mix_

Value Driver	Customer Requirement	Strategic Mix
Operational Excellence	60	80
Product Leadership	30	30
Customer Intimacy	10	10

The minimum or 'threshold' customer requirement is shown in the first column. Matching those demands are the 'givens' to operate in this market. The business must now match those thresholds and then decide where it will exceed the requirement, so establishing its particular position in the market and defining its lead value driver. If customer demand is expressed as points out of 100, then expressing the strategic mix as points out of 120 allows marketers to express their chosen preference.

This suits today just fine, but will it suit tomorrow? Perhaps the business is identifying an increasing demand for wider menu choice. Perhaps it has established itself as a regular Sunday lunch call for families, and those customers would now like to think they could ring the changes a bit without going elsewhere. In such a case, the attention given to customer intimacy must grow. Table 8.4 shows how a business might represent this strategic shift using this model.

Table 8.4 _Value drivers and the future strategic mix_

Value Driver	Current Customer Requirement	Current Strategic Mix	Future Customer Requirement (5 years)	Future Strategic Mix (5 years)
Operational Excellence	60	80	30	30
Product Leadership	30	30	30	30
Customer Intimacy	10	10	40	60

Of course, the numbers are not precise: they are indicators, aids to analysis and strategic thinking. What Table 8.4 would help the marketer understand is the scope of the change required if this strategy is to be achieved, enabling a realistic conclusion as to the feasibility of such a strategy. The choice may be to remain as a business driven by operational excellence while meeting the threshold required for customer intimacy. This is not an unsupportable strategy. A business may choose to excel at a driver that is not in fact the most significant in the market, and succeed, provided that it meets the threshold standard for the other drivers. This choice may well mark that business out as special, and if it allows it to make a genuine, sustainable and unique match between company capabilities and market needs it will have every chance of success.

9

The CONNECT Inc case study

It is 1992. After two and a half years as Chief Executive, Simon Clark felt satisfied that he had at last begun to get to grips with his marketing problems at CONNECT Inc. He had started work on these problems two years before and had made a series of changes in an effort to secure the future growth of the business into the next millennium. His actions had been undertaken in the context of the business objectives of the parent group, a complex organization based in the USA.

THE COMPANY BACKGROUND

CONNECT is the Canadian subsidiary of an international organization that, while the parent company does not much like the word, is a conglomerate. The parent has some very clear operating principles. Over the last 10 years, and certainly until recently, it had grown its profit before tax by 15 per cent per annum. This was despite many difficult situations that had been encountered. As a result, 15 per cent annual growth of profit before tax has become a requirement placed on every operating division and subsidiary in the entire international operation.

The parent operates in many markets, grouping companies into 'sectors'. It is strong in the automotive components sector, timber and pulp, and has an interest in telecommunications. It is also very large in electronic components – CONNECT is a part of that sector. It is well represented in the service industries, owning a major car-hire company, an international hotel group and a number of life and fire insurance companies.

CONNECT itself is headquartered in Toronto. It has a manufacturing operation in Montreal, with smaller ones in the USA, UK and France, and marketing operations in Toronto, Los Angeles, London and Paris. There are small sales operations in Italy and Germany, while the rest of its world markets are covered by a variety of long-established agents and representatives.

The greatest strength of CONNECT, indeed its core capability throughout the 70s and 80s, has been its ability to manufacture high-specification electrical connectors sold to the aerospace industry. The connectors range in price from $500 to as high as $7,500. At the upper price bracket these connectors are made to very low tolerances for use in critical applications such as flameproof bulkheads and aircraft engines. Such connectors are of course critical to aircraft safety.

In common with other major suppliers to the aerospace industry, CONNECT has suffered from the major cutbacks in purchases that have taken place in recent years owing to defence programme reductions. After a decade of growth in the 70s, the more difficult trading environment of the 80s presented CONNECT with severe problems in achieving the parent's 15 per cent growth targets. Put quite simply, it couldn't do it any more. The collapse of the Berlin Wall seemed to signal the demise of its own business.

Most projections for the future of the aerospace and defence industries were gloomy, and the best that could be hoped for – and that was somewhat wishful thinking – was a static volume requirement for connectors. Clark believed that CONNECT could hold its own in the current market, but even an increasing market share would probably mean overall decline. Growth as demanded by HQ would require some big changes.

SALES ORGANIZATION

One of Simon Clark's first tasks had been a close look at the sales force and the part it played in CONNECT's marketing mix. The North American sales force, to take an example, had consisted of 20 field salespeople, with a back-up staff of nearly 75. This large HQ number was required because of the technical nature of the product. Technical service was a major department, with both pre-sale and after-sales service, a key part of the CONNECT approach. There was also a large inside sales operation, because of the number of enquiries to be answered by letter and telephone. Individual enquiries required individual quotations because CONNECT products were usually tailor-made and there were no standard price lists.

It was clear to Clark that he had a superbly well-qualified team from a technical standpoint. The North American field sales force was organized on a traditional basis with a VP sales and three area sales managers – Canada, eastern USA and western USA, each with a team of representatives. They were experts in their market, having developed close relationships with key customers over a number of years.

THE NEW MARKET

Very early in his time with CONNECT, Clark had decided that they should enter a new market for electrical connectors – commercial and industrial. He wanted to attack this market vigorously. This 'new' market was composed of companies in areas such as automation equipment, process control equipment and consumer durables – washing machines, refrigerators and televisions. CONNECT was also interested in entering the automobile market.

Clark was aware that this new market highlighted a big weakness in his sales team – their call rates. Call frequencies were less than one call per day. This had not been a problem in the old days, but the decision to go for a new market put this into a new context. The connectors required by the customers in this new market were very different from those that CONNECT had designed and manufactured for the aerospace industry. They were low-tech, standard items, made to what seemed to CONNECT's staff enormously broad tolerance specifications, and they were required in huge numbers.

CONNECT had to undergo a number of changes to manufacture these new connectors, starting with engineering. Clark engaged a new team of design engineers, knowledgeable in commercial connectors. After that he began the changes necessary in the manufacturing operation. The main impact was the construction of a new building on the Montreal site, housing the manufacturing plant for all CONNECT's commercial connectors.

THE NEW SALES TEAM

Now CONNECT had to find some sales, and this was where the call rate problem arose. It was clear to Clark that if one was trying to sell connectors at $2 a time rather than $500 or $5,000, then volume was vital, and the sales activity needed to get that volume was very different from that in the aerospace market. For a start, CONNECT's sales representatives would have to call on a much wider range of customers. When Clark looked at the market opportunity, he was impressed by the huge number of potential customers, compared to the small number in the aerospace market. If they could make an impression on only a small number they would still be achieving big sales volumes.

Clark's corporate targets prevented him from increasing the size of the sales force to any great degree, so the answer was to increase call rates to at least 5 per day. This brought him to a more knotty problem – psychology.

The CONNECT sales people knew their market and their customers well. They enjoyed high prestige with their customers, due to the significance of their products and their own technical knowledge, and they were used to dealing at senior levels. This was the root of the 'psychological' problem. Put quite simply, many of the representatives were neither willing nor able to change their style of working. As they said at team meeting after team meeting, it was a hard thing to do – selling to the VP of development at a major aircraft company before lunch, and then fitting in three calls to junior buyers in the household goods business in the afternoon.

More than this, many of CONNECT's employees were apathetic about this new market. They did not see why CONNECT needed it when after all it was still the industry leader in its traditional market and, while not buoyant, customers like McDonnell Douglas were not about to go away.

Clark's solution was to split the sales force into two, appointing a new VP sales and marketing for the commercial connectors market with a team of 24 sales representatives. VP sales and marketing was a new title in CONNECT, a company that had seen marketing as something done by soap powder manufacturers. The challenge for this side of the business was clear – it was an almost unknown market.

The VP sales and marketing for the aerospace market also had a new challenge (and the same new title, which made him smile a cynical kind of smile). His sales force was now only 6, to cover the same list of customers.

THE 'UNKNOWN' MARKET

One of the first jobs for the new VP sales and marketing commercial connectors was to commission some market research. The range of opportunities was huge, and Clark needed to target some key ones.

A not insignificant problem was that CONNECT had relatively few products to sell. The new design engineers had been slower than anticipated in getting new products off the drawing board and into production, and so CONNECT found itself contracting out a number of products to other manufacturers. The sales force referred to these products as their 'imports'. Though actually manufactured in Canada or the USA, they were regarded as inferior to their own manufacture. The label soon developed into a reality as CONNECT turned to the UK's manufacturing plant to help with production. The UK plant had specialized in the highest-spec products, but they had a lot of spare capacity as a result of the market's downturn, and working on the new connectors would help them to cover their costs.

There were now several reasons why the sales team began to lose their enthusiasm for the new task. They felt that some of the products were inferior to their own and to the competition's. There was a lack of in-house expertise about these products. There was an ever-present doubt about security of supply. And not least, there was the problem of transfer pricing – the UK people would regularly want to charge more than the local contract suppliers, as they had some very high costs to cover.

Against that background, the VP sales and marketing had the task of deciding whom to sell to, and how to sell to them. The inside sales team and the technical service people were available to Clark, but he didn't know what use he could make of them. Indeed, he didn't yet know what platform of customer service would give CONNECT competitive advantage.

TARGETS AND FORECASTS

The VP sales and marketing had been given very clear volume targets by Clark. These were based on some calculations of market size, and a goal of 20 per cent market share within three years. Clark had talked of a penetration strategy based on CONNECT's core strengths, and a dose of new blood. A small number of the new sales team came from outside CONNECT, from the commercial market, while the majority were from the original aerospace sales team.

High-volume targets brought a relatively new issue to CONNECT's attention – the need for accurate long-range forecasts. The new connectors were not 'custom-made'; they were made for stock. Many of the customer sectors in this market were cyclical, responding to changes in consumer spending and buying behaviour. Good forecasts were vital if CONNECT was to avoid major over-stocks or, worse, no stock at all in the middle of a consumer spending boom.

CONNECT had to develop a new system fast. It established a system based on historical usage, added inputs from the field sales team and overlaid this with the new market research data. Clark demanded six-month forecasts minimum, with trends two years out.

THE BUSINESS IN 1992

The sales forecasting system has become the operational core of the CONNECT business. The company is now manufacturing for stock, in a way it had never done in the aerospace market where nearly every order is unique. It now has a price list; that one change had been quite something, and the people in the quotations department had resisted it for months. As Clark explained to them, it was simply a question of customer needs.

In the aerospace business, customers normally know a year ahead of time what their requirements are, and CONNECT still builds more or less to order. A delivery time of eight weeks or more is quite acceptable, and price is something that is negotiated contract by contract.

In the commercial sector, customers demand delivery within 24 hours, with tough JIT and OTIF targets. Customers do not normally declare their requirements very far ahead of time and they require up-to-date price lists to allow them to shop around in a market that is very price-sensitive.

A similar transformation has also taken place in the field of promotional activity. The aerospace market remains one of personal contacts and long-standing reputation. In the commercial market there is a need for broader promotional activity. CONNECT's presence is still not that great (they have fallen well short of the 20 per cent market share target), and there is a need to amend, and indeed establish, its image. An agency has been approached to help with this work.

The agency's challenge is to take a company with a strong image as a manufacturer of specialized high-performance connectors and reposition it as a mass market supplier of low-cost connectors, and to do all of that without damaging its image in the aerospace market.

Because of that potential dilemma, and because of the high costs involved in promotion, Clark has retained control over the promotional budget for both markets. If all else should fail, this budget remains a useful 'escape hatch' in order to meet the parent company's profit targets.

CONNECT is at last able to manufacture most of its products for the North American market in Montreal. Using the UK operation was only ever a temporary solution. An unfortunate side-effect of that had been a number of problems on the UK site, now refocused on repairing its reputation in the aerospace market.

Distribution has become an important factor in the new business. High volumes have put a strain on the existing set-up, and Clark has considered the possibility of working through a network of independent distributors. He would like to feed the smaller customers through those channels, keeping the major customers direct. This, and the promotion issue, are his next main challenges.

THE MARKETING REVIEW

Progress has not been as good as hoped and there are big concerns that future targets will not be met. Clark has ordered a full marketing review of activities, with an emphasis on cost reduction and increased sales volumes. Clark himself has not yet begun to panic, although some of his lieutenants are getting worried.

CASE STUDY QUESTIONS

1. Assess CONNECT's original plan to enter the new market. How good was their assessment of the opportunities, and of their own capabilities?
2. If you had been employed as a marketing consultant, how would you have advised Clark when he first considered this new venture?
3. How do you rate their actions and progress to date?
4. How do you rate their chances of success in the future, as they are currently set up?
5. If you were now employed as a marketing consultant to help with the CONNECT marketing review, how would you advise them to proceed:
   − in the new market?
   − in the aerospace market?
   − in any other way?

If you would like to e-mail your answers or any other comments on this case study to INSIGHT at customer.service@insight-mp.com we will gladly critique your report and send you our own thoughts.

10

Writing the marketing plan

We have arrived at the planning stage of the marketing process, a stage more often 'skipped past' than you would credit. Why? So many textbooks make it seem such a daunting task that surely good common sense and skilful tactical application will do?

FAQS

Of all the questions asked by delegates on marketing courses I would bet that the most frequently asked is, 'How do I write a marketing plan?', and not always for the best reasons. Too often marketers are asked to write plans as if the very writing of them would conjure success out of thin air, and the thicker the document the greater the chance of success.

Perhaps more time is wasted on this exercise than any other in marketing, not because it is not a worthwhile activity – it is absolutely vital – but because it is approached for the wrong reasons and so handled in the wrong way.

The deadly sins of marketing plans

- Too many marketing plans are tomes the size of telephone directories that will never be read.
- Too many marketing plans have 'company secret' stamped on the front and are never seen by the very people who have to implement them.
- Too many marketing plans have so much energy poured into them that the thought of doing it all again is far too daunting and the plan gets set in stone, until it dies.
- Too many marketing plans get put off and put off because, with the market changing so fast, what's the point of starting?
- Too many marketing plans are written with an eye (even two eyes) on impressing the boss and showing off the writer's knowledge of all the latest four-box matrices.
- Too many marketing plans are full of so much data that their conclusions and actions required are lost in a mass of numbers.

SO WHY WRITE A PLAN?

The reasons are many, but perhaps the best is summed up by the matrix in Figure 10.1.

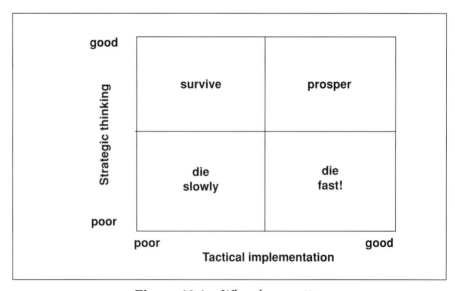

Figure 10.1 *Why plans matter*

A good plan should capture and communicate the driving marketing strategy of the business. Businesses with good clear strategies tend to prosper, and even if they are run inefficiently day to day they survive. Businesses without good clear strategies are doomed to die slowly though, ironically, those that are best at day-to-day tactical implementation of a poor or non-existent strategy will die the fastest! Making the wrong choices and then applying resource with energy and enthusiasm is a terrible way to die.

Reasons to write a marketing plan

Here then are 10 reasons to write a marketing plan – and there are plenty more that you might like to add to the list:

1. to ensure that everyone in the business knows where we are headed and how we will get there;
2. to ensure that our customers know where we are headed and how we will get there;
3. to be able to measure the success of our activities against clear objectives;
4. to remove the tendency for drift, a dangerous malaise that can afflict the best of businesses if they stop looking forward;
5. to ensure a disciplined approach to the selection of activities and the allocation of resources against them;
6. to secure the commitment of senior management, shareholders, staff and other stakeholders;
7. to focus the business's mind on change;
8. to focus the business's mind on the future;
9. to maximize our chances of success;
10. to evidence a professional approach to an activity that has too many cowboys playing tactical games.

General guidelines on writing a marketing plan

Above all else, the plan should be written to be read, and this leads me to some early recommendations:

1. Don't make it a company secret.
2. Keep confidential data, conclusions and actions in appendices that can be separated from the main document.

3. Keep data and analysis in appendices – let the plan focus on the conclusions and the actions.
4. Have an executive summary that condenses the plan into a one-page 'essence'. (The discipline of achieving this is most valuable in itself as it focuses the mind on to the essentials.)
5. Avoid jargon, and avoid using models and tools just for the sake of it.
6. Ensure that the plan is written at the smallest level possible as well as on the grand scale – the plan should have actions starting with the market and drilling down to segment, product and customer.
7. Involve the team in writing the plan.
8. Write the plan in a format that is easy to update (there are software packages available that reduce the task of rewriting and will even 'amend' your conclusions for you if important data changes).
9. Focus on the future, avoid too much history and don't use the past as a guarantor of future success.
10. Avoid unsubstantiated hype, especially the 'hockey stick' graph (see Figure 10.2) that shows years of decline changing to immediate success with no apparent effort other than the writing of the plan! If the future really is projected to look like this then the plan should make clear what changes there have been to the

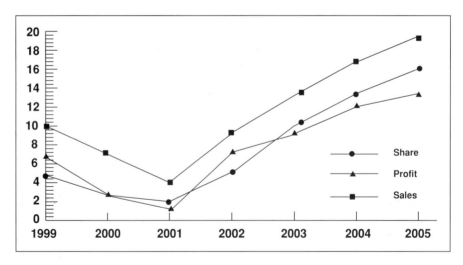

Figure 10.2 *'Hockey stick' graphs*

opportunity and what changes have been made to resources in order to seize that opportunity, otherwise why should it happen?

These guidelines will help you to avoid the most common pitfalls, but let's not pretend that this is an easy activity. There is so much to consider – not only the content but also the style and communication of the plan, and before any of that the context in which it is written. We should start by placing the plan in its context as a part of the wider business planning process (the planning cascade), in its time frame (the planning time horizon) and not least in the hustle and bustle of the ever-changing market environment.

THE PLANNING CASCADE

The marketing plan exists within the context of a business plan, and in a complex organization there may be a divisional plan and a corporate plan above that, as shown in Figure 10.3.

The cascade continues beyond the market plan into segment plans and individual plans for the elements of the market mix – a promotional plan, a product plan, etc. There will also be key account plans within each segment (see Chapter 19, 'Relationship marketing and key account management').

The implications of this are clear – there must be consistency between the plans, and so marketing planners must be both aware of and involved in the planning process that precedes their plan and that follows on from their plan. The marketing plan itself must make some reference to the business or corporate objectives that give it its context and its reason for being.

THE PLANNING TIME HORIZON

Every industry, market and business has its own 'natural' planning horizon. This might be considered the period in which it is safe to assume things will stay similar enough for plans to be developed and implemented. For some, like an aircraft manufacturer, this might be as long as 10 to 20 years. For an IT service provider we may be talking

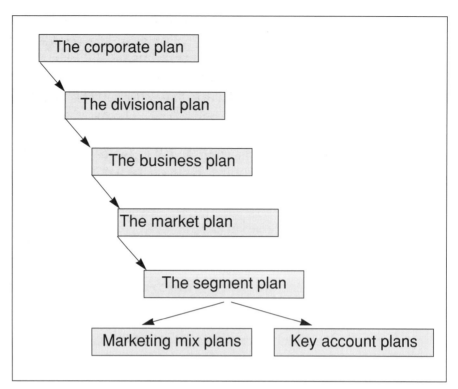

Figure 10.3 *The planning cascade*

of months. This is not to say that IT service providers should not plan for more than six months ahead, but rather that they will have a hierarchy of plans from long-term strategic to short-term tactical implementation. A typical manufacturing business might have a long-term plan of 10 years, a medium-term plan of two to three years (reflecting the 'natural' planning horizon) and an annual plan for tactical implementation. The certainty of the outcome should of course increase the shorter the time horizon considered, as should the detail of the contents. The annual plan will deal in the realm of prices, promotional spend and new product launch dates. The medium-term plan will focus more on the analysis of the market opportunity, the choice of market segments and the allocation of resources. The long-term plan will be considering the forces and trends that will shape the market in the future and the capabilities required for success in that future. The three plans in the hierarchy are not exclusive of one another and there will of course be overlaps.

A PLANNING PROCESS

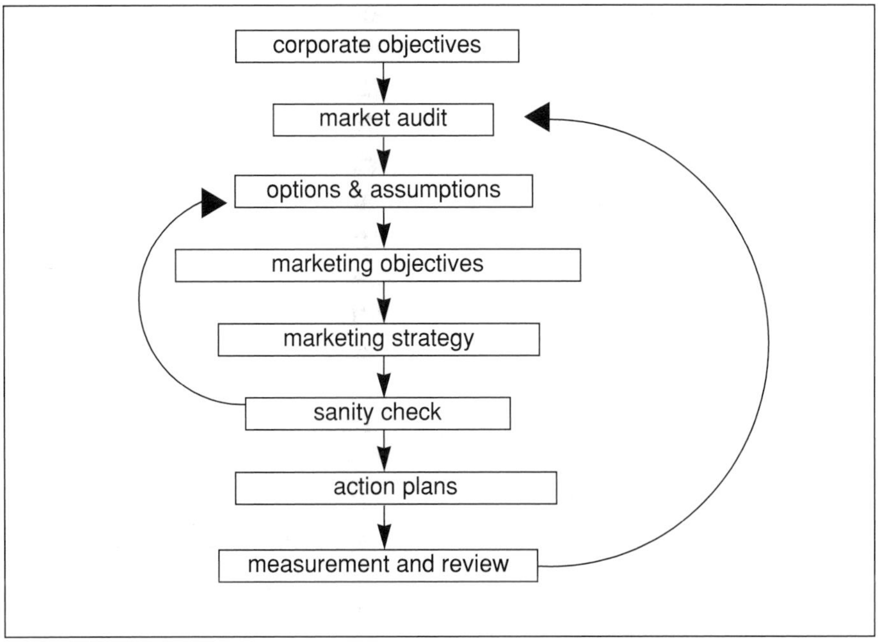

Figure 10.4   *The planning process*

As well as in a business context and a time frame, the plan also exists in the heat of the market environment. The planning process must allow for change to the plan itself as competitors enter and leave, customers prosper or die, and other factors make themselves felt. This is one key purpose of the sanity check (see Chapter 4): to make sure that all is still well with the many assumptions that will have gone into the plan. Use the sanity check to reconsider your options – the best choice may have changed – and to work through again the resultant objectives, strategy and implementation tactics. It is also important continually to measure and review the impact of the plan on the market. A sure sign of your success will be that your own activities will be having an impact on the shape and dynamics of the market. Use the measurement and review stage to revise your information in the market audit stage and to review your analysis and conclusions.

This last point is particularly important if you are a major player in the market – your activities and your own success can cause changes in the market that may bring problems. The National Health Service is a wonderful example. Its very success changed the whole shape of the health care market with the resultant (but completely unexpected) rise in demand. It was believed by the planners that the NHS would improve the nation's health and so reduce demand. It achieved the first part of the forecast but failed to see how the existence of a 'free at the point of delivery' service would encourage people to use it, and to bring new complaints and diseases for treatment. Throughout the 1950s, 60s and 70s, generations grew up expecting the NHS to treat every new disease or complaint that could be labelled and to use the very best drugs and equipment in those treatments. Today we see debates over whether Viagra should be available on prescription, and the shape of the health care market is still changed by the decisions of government and the NHS.

A MARKETING PLAN TEMPLATE

There is no perfect layout for a marketing plan – situations differ and the plan should accommodate and reflect any specific circumstances. There are however some broad guidelines. (You will find an expanded version of this template on the CD ROM attached to this book, to be used for preparing and presenting your own marketing plan.) First, there are some clear divisions in the plan:

- executive summary;
- the mission statement;
- the financial overview;
- the market overview;
- our position – SWOT and DPM;
- assumptions;
- marketing objectives;
- gap analysis;
- the strategy;
- the marketing mix;
- project plans;
- resources required;
- risks and contingency;
- appendices for confidential issues and data.

For each of these main divisions we will consider the content that might be included.

Executive summary

Keep this to one page if possible, with clarity of objectives, actions and resources required.

The mission statement

Is this a one-line slogan, with the merit of being remembered by staff and customers, like 'never knowingly undersold', or 'to double sales and profits by 2005', or even 'to win!', or _are_ they just slogans? The trouble with such statements is that in their attempt to be memorable they end up giving very little guidance, leaving just too much to the imagination! Is it 'to win!' at any price? How will we double sales and profits? Is never being 'knowingly undersold' (the slogan of JLP, The John Lewis Partnership) a mission for the business, or a slogan for the customer? Of course, a good mission statement will be one that _does_ mean something to customers, staff, suppliers and stakeholders. For JLP, the UK department store retailer, it is a policy, for the customer a promise, and for staff it guides them on how to behave – how to procure, how to sell, how to watch the competition.

In the end, a good mission statement will guide the organization through the choices that it will have to make, consistently. To do this without leaving too many holes for potential 'misunderstanding', there are perhaps five key ingredients to a mission statement:

1. What business are we in?
2. What future position do we aspire to? (This is often referred to as 'the vision'.)
3. What core competencies will get us there?
4. What segments and customers will help us get there?
5. What measure of success (including financial) will we use?

The clarity of 'What business are we in?' (see Chapter 3 and Table 3.1) is so important that it may even deserve its own short section before the mission statement. The definition should, wherever possible, be by the end use or benefit gained from your product or service. If this is not possible and your definition really is about your own product or technology, then perhaps you should be thinking hard about the market applications for what you do.

A publisher of business books is certainly not simply in the book market; it is in the market for improving business performance, or developing management capability, or improving personal performance, and there are many more definitions that would help that publisher carve a unique position. The publisher of this book, Kogan Page, is very much in what it calls the business practitioners' market, seeking to help develop the skills and knowledge of those working in the business environment. This gives its books a practical feel, with tips, techniques and real-world examples, easy to read, and hopefully even enjoyable! Its definition of the business it is in helps define the product itself. This needs to be in the context of market and segment, which leads to the next part of the market overview.

There is no need for justification of a mission statement, no need for statistics to back it up and no need to pin it down to specifics – a mission statement is a signpost, not the map.

It is tempting to list examples of various 'good' mission statements, but they will not be helpful. You cannot and should not 'steal' someone else's mission statement. This is not a matter of ethics, or even of competitive advantage. It is simply that a mission statement must suit your precise circumstances. It must fit like a tailored suit; off the peg is not good enough.

The financial overview

This provides a quick summary of your business performance, normally best displayed graphically, showing revenue and profit over the last three years (or whatever is the most relevant time-scale) and the projected outcome over the period of your plan. If your plan will require significant investment of any kind this is the best place to include details, with comments on the period of return.

The market overview

- The definition, shape and scale of the market.
- Financial analysis.
- Trends and future shape.
- Segmentation.

Defining the shape and scale of the market is important to getting all those involved with the plan looking at the same thing: size and value, the segments, levels of maturity, the competitor analysis including their market shares, customer analysis, and the significance of market chains. This might include any of the tools from the market audit – PESTLE, Porter, market map, market chains, Ansoff, etc.

A financial analysis showing levels of revenue and profitability of the major players – suppliers and customers – may be useful here.

After definitions come the main trends and future shape of the market, again using tools from the market audit (Chapter 7), customer needs, supplier capabilities, supplier consolidations, etc.

Segmentation is such an important part of marketing strategy and planning that it deserves a good deal of attention at this point: how the market is segmented, what your basis for segmentation is, how that is different from the competition's, whether that gives you any competitive advantage, whether it raises any additional challenges and what the priority segments are. (The DPM used in the next section may be a good vehicle for communicating the basis of segmentation and the priorities.)

Our position – SWOT and DPM

A comment on your own position and performance should come in here; the SWOT analysis and the directional policy matrix (DPM) provide excellent tools for summarizing a lot of commentary in a 'pictorial' form. (The DPM is discussed in Chapters 7 and 11 and in detail in Chapter 12.)

Assumptions

There are always assumptions made in preparing any marketing plan. These might include such things as: no new player will enter the market, exchange rates will not shift more than 10 per cent, or the US Food and Drugs Association will approve our new drug. Should these assumptions be proved wrong, then the implications on the plan could be very significant, hence the importance of listing the important ones here. This could become a very long list, so remember that we are not trying to say in our plan, 'This all applies if the world doesn't change an iota'; rather we are asking, 'What are the significant changes that might occur for which this plan does not take account?'.

Marketing objectives

The marketing objectives are quite different from the 'vision' element of the mission statement. Whereas the mission statement was a sign-post, the objectives are very specific destinations on that signpost. They should be written in strict accordance with the SMART acronym:

- **S** – specific;
- **M** – measurable;
- **A** – achievable;
- **R** – realistic;
- **T** – timed.

Those who have gone through a personal performance appraisal and objectives session with their company have probably come across something very like the SMART acronym – and the lessons apply just as much to marketing objectives as to personal ones.

Avoid objectives such as:

- We will successfully enter the market for high-price designer teddy bears.
- We will become the market leader.
- We will launch three new products.
- We will ensure full customer satisfaction.
- We will achieve a return on net assets of 25 per cent.

Define success. Define high price. By when will 'success' be achieved? What does market leader mean – highest volume, greatest value, best-known brand name? Again, by when? When will the three products be launched, and is launching them the only measure of success? What makes a customer satisfied? Does full satisfaction mean zero complaints? Is that realistic? At least the 25 per cent RONA is specific and measurable. We will have to assume it is achievable and realistic. We need to add a date, though, before it passes the SMART test.

Financial objectives are very important here (not least because they are often missing from a marketing plan, particularly in organizations where marketing is regarded as the 'creative' side of the business) – what are the implications of your plan for revenue, investment, cash flow and profit?

In a complex market where you operate in more than one segment, it may be best to post some market-wide objectives but then divide the plan at this point into a series of segment plans each with its own objectives. If that is so then all of the following steps will be repeated for each segment.

Your marketing objectives will drive your business for the next year, three years, maybe longer, so they deserve a lot of attention for both their content and their style of presentation. Use them to throw down gauntlets by all means, provided the rest of the plan shows how that challenge will be handled. Most people like to work in an organization that takes on challenges, provided they are not reckless or unrealistic. Your objectives will say a lot about the aspirations of the business, but also much about the level of professionalism involved in managing the business.

Stealing an idea from an earlier book of mine, _Key Account Management_ (1999), consider two different philosophies of 'making it happen', two extremes that might characterize different approaches to business and marketing objectives. We might label them the 'Viking' and the 'Gently does it'. The 'Viking' philosophy argues that you should row on to the enemy shore, disembark your troops and burn your boats. That way, making things work is your only option. Success in such circumstances is bold, daring and the stuff of legend. Failure is brutal and unsung. The 'Gently does it' philosophy argues that you should hold off-shore, viewing the enemy through long-range binoculars, looking for signs of weakness, hoping that they might fall into a hole of their own digging, and then creep ashore to take their place. Success is met by praise of your great wisdom and tactical genius. Failure brands you a coward.

Gap analysis

A gap analysis (Chapter 8) may be a good pictorial way of communicating the scale of change required, particularly if significant growth is the object, and indicating the kind of activities required to fill the gap – provided of course that this is not an unsubstantiated 'hockey stick' graph!

Large gaps and bold objectives are fine provided they are supported by plenty of 'how tos', and even burning your boats may be considered a suitable 'how to' in some circumstances, but whatever the case, the 'how tos' are vital, which brings us to the strategy.

The strategy

If the mission statement is the signpost and the objectives the specific destinations on that signpost, then the strategy is the route-map. Chapter 8 deals in great detail with the specific elements of marketing strategy; here we will simply list the tools or headlines you might use to write it into the plan:

● Ansoff matrix – growth and risk;
● source of competitive advantage – differentiation or lowest cost;
● value drivers – operational excellence, product leadership, customer intimacy;
● branding strategy (see Chapter 16).

The marketing mix

For each segment, this will include the specific plans for each of:

● product – portfolio management (DPM) and product management (product life cycles) (Chapter 12, 'Product strategies');
● price (Chapter 13, 'Pricing strategies');
● promotion (Chapter 15, 'Promotion strategies');
● place (Chapter 17, 'Place strategies').

This will include targets, budgets and detailed timetables for implementation.

Project plans

Your plans for the elements of the marketing mix may result in some specific projects – developing new point of sale materials, a new product launch, briefing a PR agency, passing a group of customers to distributors, etc – and the detail of those projects should be placed here:

- scope and objectives;
- project team – roles and responsibilities;
- timetable and critical path analysis.

Resources required

There will be a variety of resources required for you to achieve your plan, some existing and some that will need sanctioning. A budget outlined over the time-scale of the plan could be a helpful addition here. Indicate clearly the difference between existing resource and new requirements, and give some indication of the process for securing those new resources – don't expect the board to read your plan and send you down a blank cheque!

Resource elements might include:

- people – particularly their time;
- assets – equipment;
- financial investment;
- market research;
- agency support – advertising, PR, point of sale material, sales promotions, etc;
- training.

This comprises a list of the resources needed to achieve the desired outcomes. This is often summarized in a budget shown over the time-scale of the plan but could include other elements too.

Risks and contingency

There are risks involved with any plan. Detail these here and note the contingency plan in place should you experience the down- rather than the upside. In some cases it may be necessary to do the same for the significant upside if that would have implications on resources – production capacity, staff requirements, etc.

Your plan has been based on a number of assumptions. This does not mean that you have done your duty with regard to the outside world and can now use these assumptions as a means of protecting your behind! It is wise to identify those key things that could dramatically change the course of your plan and outline the contingency plans you would put in place to deal with such a turn of events. It is with such an issue as contingency planning that the truly professional marketer stands out from the 'also rans'.

Appendices for confidential issues and data

At the start of this chapter I stressed that the marketing plan should be available to a wide audience, not stamped 'company secret' and left in a cupboard to rot. In some cases you might even like to make your marketing plan available to customers, but in such a case there will be some things that are best not put under public gaze. These should be put in appendices, with careful control over who receives the plan within and who without.

Too many plans are unreadable because of the mass of data that clogs them. The data is important, it is evidence and it will change, so changing perhaps the direction of the plan. The right place for this is an appendix, for those who want or need to enquire further.

A well-written plan does not need a constant stream of justification and proof for its assertions; the discipline used in its preparation and the professionalism of its presentation should go a long way to winning the trust of those who must act on it and give it sanction.

THE WAPPIT MARKETING PLAN – A 'COULD DO BETTER' CASE STUDY

The following is an 'excellent' example of a marketing plan that on the surface may appear to be OK, but look more closely and you will see it is everything from lazy to dangerously incompetent. Unfortunately it is not so very far removed from the truth of some plans that we have seen over the years. Indeed it was modelled on some of the worst, and real, examples that have come before our attention.

I am indebted to my colleague John Andrews of INSIGHT for allowing me to use his brilliant pastiche, and encourage you to spot the howlers and promise yourself that you and your own plans will never fall victim in the same way.

Needless to say, Wappo is not a real company, has never existed, and if this were an example of their work, never could have existed! Similarities to any real company are purely shameful.

Top secret
Wappo Group Ltd
Wappit marketing plan
Period: 1996–1999

Mission

Wappo aims to be number one in Europe with Wappit.

Financial objectives

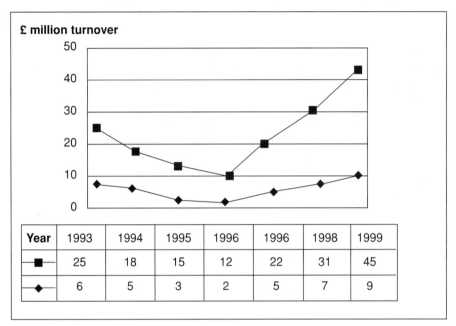

£ million turnover

Year	1993	1994	1995	1996	1996	1998	1999
■	25	18	15	12	22	31	45
◆	6	5	3	2	5	7	9

Figure 10.5 _Financial objectives for Wappit 1996–1999_

Market overview

The Wappit range of products is a family of sophisticated agrochemical products from Wappo Group for use with the cereal, coffee and fruit-growing markets:

- Wap 1 – fruit;
- Wap 2 – coffee;
- Wap 3 – cereals.

In all markets, competition is increasing, especially from companies like Zeneca, Ciba-Geigy, BASF and Sandoz.

The biggest market in Europe for cereals is the UK, and the UK has seen a tightening of regulations regarding the use of Wap 3. However, with our advanced technology and major research programmes we expect to see improvement in sales of Wap 3 through the planning period.

The combined efforts of the EEC Commission and the Common Agrochemical Policy are not thought to affect our market share over the next 10 years.

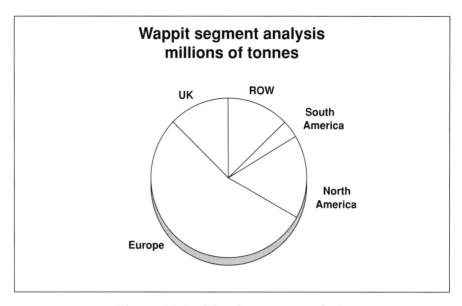

Figure 10.6 *Wappit segment analysis*

Portfolios

Boston box

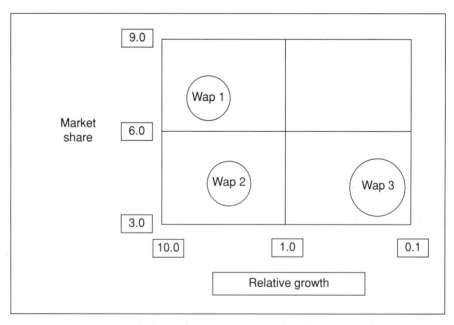

Figure 10.7 *Boston box*

As can be seen from the Boston matrix above, the Wappit portfolio is well balanced and the matrix shows a good flow of cash to develop the dog, Wap 3 (see also Figure 12.6, page 206).

Directional policy matrix

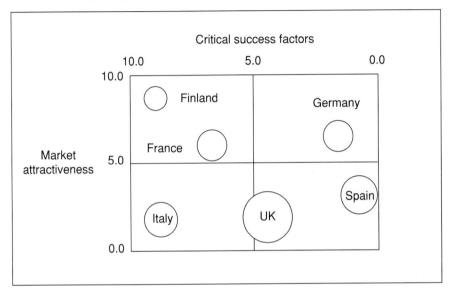

Figure 10.8 _Directional policy matrix_

SWOT analysis

Strengths

- Wappo has the biggest plant in Europe.
- The ageing population is stimulating the need for more garden products.
- Finland is expanding.
- Research shows novel ways to produce cereal herbicides.
- Wappit is a well-known and respected brand.

Weaknesses

- The market for agrochemicals is under attack from Brussels and environmentalists.
- Our plant is poorly located on the Isle of Skye.
- Wappo has limited access to good transport facilities.
- Local residents do not like the smells from our plant.
- Our proximity to the local airport prevents us from using high chimneys to vent off gas.
- We must purchase raw materials on the open market in competition with integrated companies like BASF.
- We are under increasing pressure to minimize our working capital.

Opportunity

- We have strong nuclear chemistry for microbiological analysis.
- There will be higher feedstock prices in 1998.
- BASF are under increasing pressure to reduce effluent from their German site.
- Our packaging is regarded as the best in the industry.
- We are registered to IS 9000 quality standard.

Threats

- There is a trend to use more environmentally friendly products in agriculture.
- Supplies of one of our key raw materials are purchased from a single Far East source.
- There is a reduction of sales effort as Wappo continues to cut costs.
- The reliability of our plant has been variable during the last 12 months.
- Our major UK distributor may be purchased by Ciba-Geigy.
- The Koreans have entered the Spanish market with a low-cost copy of Wap 2.
- Further testing of Wap 1 is needed for FDA approval.

Gap analysis

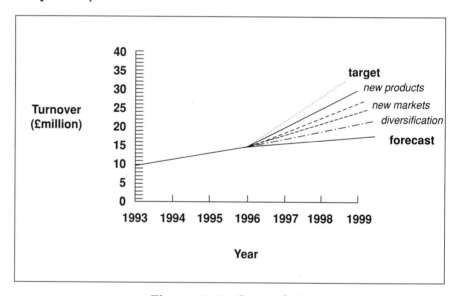

Figure 10.9   *Gap analysis*

As can be seen from the cautious gap analysis above, Wappo intends to grow sales to £45 million by 1999 mainly by cost reduction and acquisition. Some market share is forecast to be gained but this is likely to be minor. No new products are forecast to be launched in the planning period.

Marketing objectives

- Wappo will become number one in the supply of Wappit.
- We will maximize income from all products.
- We will ensure our portfolio meets market requirements.
- We will share our strategy with the sales force.
- We will grow our market share of the Spanish market by 7 per cent during the planning period.
- We will ensure the correct portfolio of products to meet environmental standards.
- We will identify and exploit new opportunities for Wap 1.
- We will maintain European Wappit prices at today's level against anticipated aggressive competition.
- We will grow sales in North and South America using sales agents.
- We will launch a blends business of multi-purpose domestic herbicides in 1998.

Marketing assumptions

- Raw material prices will increase with inflation over the next three years.
- There will be no increase in environmental regulation during the planning period.
- There will be a switch to more cereals and fruit grown at the expense of grass and animal growth.
- BASF will shut down in 1998.
- We will maintain our UK market share.
- EEC directives are likely to be relaxed over the next five years.
- The Koreans will not take a major stake in Europe.
- Finland will double production of fruit through their investment in heated greenhouses.
- There will be no new investment in Wappit-type manufacturing process plants in the planning period.
- Exchange rates of USD 1.6 – 1.7 to £ sterling will be constant through the next three years.

Marketing strategies

Product

- We will increase research on Wap 3 to improve its quality by a 3 per cent reduction of impurity salts.
- Cost cutting will take place on Wap 1, as little future is envisaged with this product.
- We will produce a globally accepted grade for all cereal crops.
- We will be competitive with Ciba-Geigy at all levels.
- We will modify the viscosity of Wap 1 for Finland to meet local cold weather conditions (reduce from 12 CP in 1997 to 5 CP by 1999).
- We will extend TV advertising on Wap 3 across the UK and Spain.

Price

- We will price aggressively but competitively to gain market share, but not at a price to lose money or invite BASF to increase its share.

- We will maintain vigilance for upward pricing opportunities.
- We will publish and deliver customer service standards.
- We will improve the lead times involved in the manufacture of special grades.
- We will increase Wap 1 prices by 5 per cent in line with expected inflation during 1998.

Promotion

- We will have active customer visits.
- We will invest £20,000 to promote the Wappit brand through trade press advertising in 1998.
- We will ensure that our sales force undergo at least five days' sales skill building development over the planning period.
- We will make extensive use of radio advertising in Spain and the USA.
- We will understand BASF's feedstock strategy in the USA.
- We will update all our literature to include the latest SHE requirements by end 1997.

Place

- We will maintain the use of distributors.
- We will establish more direct contact with retailers.
- We will evaluate cost-effective distribution options.
- We will ensure all our customer service personnel attend the two-day customer care programme and follow up with team meetings every six weeks to reduce complaints by 20 per cent in 1997.
- We will examine product swaps with BASF in the USA to gain logistic advantage.
- We will improve product labelling.

11

Segmentation

We have referred often enough in past chapters to market segmentation for it to be clear that this is a fundamental and vital part of modern marketing practice. So much flows from good segmentation – the marketing mix (the four Ps), positioning, branding strategies, key account management – that it deserves a good deal of attention. Of all the elements of the marketing process it is perhaps the one that requires the greatest commitment of effort and stamina – that is to say, segmentation doesn't always come easily! It is a game with endless possibilities, and almost as many right answers as wrong. It is a vital part of the bridge between company capabilities and market needs; indeed it is often the very thing that makes a genuine, sustainable and unique match possible.

When you are next standing in the soap powder aisle in the supermarket, or marvelling at the choice of restaurants in a busy city centre, just stop to consider why there are so many. Why not one soap powder for all? Why are the people evenly spread across the restaurants instead of all piled into one? The answer is segmentation. Each powder or restaurant is targeted at its own chosen clientele and, as a result of that targeting, is answering their needs, attitudes and behaviours with greater accuracy.

For a subject so important, and with such variety of outcome, it is important to observe some kind of disciplined process, and that is the main purpose of this chapter, but first some definitions.

What is a segment?

A market segment is a grouping of customers with similar buying needs, attitudes and behaviours. It is important to stress the words 'attitudes' and 'behaviours'. If we only looked at needs we would be limiting our options. We all need food, so on that basis there would only be one segment in the food market. Of course there are more because, although we all need food, we display an amazing array of attitudes to the stuff, and exhibit an equally large range of ways of going about buying and using it. Each of these facets of behaviour or attitude provides a potential market segment. Just consider a few of those in the food market:

- eating out – restaurants, cafés, fast food, food on the move, vending;
- eating in – breakfast, lunch, dinner, entertaining, barbecues;
- business – canteens, hotels, institutions, catering, airlines;
- retail – supermarkets, wholesalers, cash and carry, delicatessens;
- branding – brands, own brand, no brands;
- health – low sodium, diet, low fat, high fibre;
- diet – vegetarian, vegan, organic;
- ethnic – Indian, Chinese, Italian, Moroccan;
- family – 2.4 kids, single parent, retired, single;
- experience – cordon bleu, first-time cooks, professionals.

Add to this list the range of food fads, local tastes, traditions, income levels, time to cook, lifestyles and more, and you can see that the list is huge. Two things become clear at this point. First, segmenting a market into each of these individual pockets would leave it quite unmanageable, and second, such an exercise would result in a very unrealistic picture of the food market. In reality these facets of behaviour and attitude overlap one another in such a way that they can be consolidated into larger chunks or segments, for instance people who want to cook their own Chinese food to eat in but have little knowledge or experience, or hospitals that want to have pre-cooked meals prepared to strict dietary specifications for fast reheating on site.

In any market there will be many different options for grouping customers. Choosing the best way is the art and science of segmentation.

Some reality checks – the 'viable' segment

The hospital that wants pre-cooked meals to dietary specifications for reheating on site – that starts to sound like a segment for which an offer could be developed. What we might call a good or a 'viable' segment is one that meets that test and a few more. When identifying a market segment, it should stand up to these questions:

- Is it large enough to justify focused attention?
- Are the customers' needs, attitudes and behaviours similar enough to be aggregated together?
- Are the needs, attitudes and behaviours specific enough to be distinguishable from those of other segments?
- Is it possible to design an appropriate _marketing mix_ for the segment (see below)?
- Is the segment _reachable_? Can it be identified, measured, analysed, communicated to and sold to _discretely_ from other segments?

Positive answers to these questions will start to suggest that you are looking at a viable segment.

STRATEGIC OPTIONS

There is no rule that says you _must_ segment your market-place, nor, if you choose to, to what degree. There are some clear benefits of segmentation (discussed a little later in this chapter), but also some clear demands on your own business capabilities. Segmentation is one of the strategic options, and there are perhaps three main choices as shown in Figure 11.1.

Each strategy has its pros and cons:

- Strategy 1, by ignoring the segments, runs the risk of missing the precise needs of the market, at best forgoing some opportunities, at worst losing competitive advantage to a more tailored approach. On the plus side, if the market will accept a standard

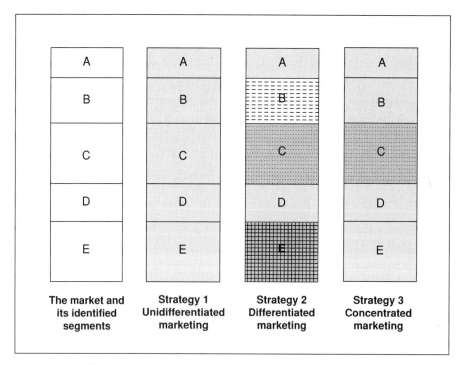

Figure 11.1 *Segmentation – the strategic options*

offer across all segments there is the potential for economies of scale and low costs. Many supermarket own labels might appear to follow this strategy but in fact the supermarket chain itself has targeted specific segments, Waitrose for instance chasing a rather different clientele to Aldi. Good examples are hard to find. Segmentation has become such a vital part of most marketing strategies that not even supposed commodities such as milk and sugar can be said to be totally untargeted.

● Strategy 2 recognizes the segments and spreads its risk by participating in all of them. If companies are able to manage this many separate offers then they may find themselves in a commanding position. If they overstretch their resources they may find themselves losing out to more focused competitors. Kellogg's follows this strategy in the breakfast cereal market (a market with a surprising number of segments identified by manufacturers), with a product offer in nearly every segment, from health to fun, children's to energy, traditional to novelty. Their promotional spend is consequently huge (£55 million per annum) but they occupy 8 out of the top 10 positions for breakfast cereals sold in the UK.

● Strategy 3 has the strength of focus – expertise, specialism, reputation, etc – but takes the risk of putting all its eggs in one basket. Weetabix is number two in the UK's top 10 selling breakfast cereals with a promotional spend of £15 million focused on a product once described as 'a dour, sugarless flaked wheat block that looks like it was designed by the Soviet cereal secretariat in 1951'. In fact, Weetabix is the SAS of the breakfast cereal market compared to the Kellogg's Red Army.

The right choice must depend on the circumstances, the market dynamics and the capabilities of the competing suppliers. If there is a strong demand for low-cost suppliers in the market then strategy 1 may be the preferred option. The greater the potential for differentiation, the more attractive strategy 2 or strategy 3 will become.

The 'wonder watch'

Suppose you had just invented the 'wonder watch', a wrist-watch that performed well against the whole range of requirements for it from different consumers:

● to tell the time;
● jewellery;
● an investment;
● a badge of status;
● fun;
● a fashion accessory;
● a stop-watch;
● a calendar;
● deep sea diving;
● a gift;
● a calculator;
● and many more...

What strategy would you follow? If it really does manage to do all these things (unlikely, I know, but just play along with me), then isn't strategy 1 the right choice with all its economies of scale?

The problem will be price. You might be able to sell this watch as an item of jewellery for £100, and as a badge of status for £500, but simply as a means of telling the time perhaps for only £30. (In other words, if that is what someone is looking for, that is what they would be prepared to pay.) In an open market with no segmentation strategy on your part, the lowest common denominator will win through – £30 for the most incredible watch ever invented.

Strategy 2 looks better, positioning the watch in different segments, but it would be necessary to do a lot of redesign for this to work – it can't be exactly the same watch – and before long you don't have one 'wonder watch' any more but six different products to suit six different sets of needs.

Strategy 3 will force you to focus, perhaps on the segment with the greatest potential for revenue, share, profit – it's up to you – but again it is no longer a 'wonder watch', just a great piece of jewellery, or a great sports watch, or…

The moral of the story? Perhaps the 'wonder watch' is not such a great idea. The one-size-fits-all approach will lead you down a path of missed opportunity unless the one most important driving force for you and the market is reducing costs through uniformity. Even here, this is segmentation by omission. You produce a low-cost uniform product but only certain groups of customers will buy it; the rest will look elsewhere. The real moral of the story is that you can't avoid segmentation, even if you want to!

SEGMENTATION AND THE MARKETING MIX

The *marketing mix* is the means of influencing demand and gaining competitive advantage. Marketers have four levers under their control: *product*, *place*, *promotion* and *price*, traditionally known as the 'four Ps', and shown in Figure 11.2.

Demand is influenced by the total mix, each of the four Ps working in relation to one another:

- product – the range, quality, packaging, after-sales service, etc;
- price – premium, discounted, terms, etc;
- promotion – communication of the offer to the customer, including advertising, PR, sales force, etc;
- place – the route to market and distribution channels, including direct, retail, wholesale, etc.

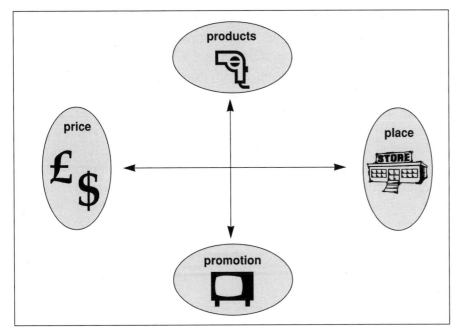

Figure 11.2 *The marketing mix*

Not only do the four Ps interact with one another, but they must balance with one another for a successful mix. New product launches are particularly prone to *misfits* in the mix.

From misfits to icons – Babycham and Range Rover

When Babycham was first launched, the product, promotion and place were well thought out, but the price was too low. This was a drink (fake champagne) that men bought for their girlfriends, to impress them (remember this was the 1960s!). But at such a low price, who was going to be impressed? The product was relaunched at a suitably ego-enhancing price and remains one of the icons of a different world.

When Land Rover launched the Range Rover, place was the misfit as customers had to go to traditional Land Rover dealers, with all the attendant imagery of agricultural machinery, for this new up-market premium-priced product. Smart new showrooms were opened in a hurry.

The 'proposition'

Each segment will require its own particular mix; indeed, if it didn't then the segment would probably not be a 'viable' one as defined by our test questions above. The sum total of this mix is what many would call the *proposition*, the reason a customer should buy your product or use your service. The proposition may well emphasize one element of the mix more than others: the lowest price, the most widely available, the best known, the most reliable. Where there is such a single-mindedness about the proposition, what marketers call a *unique selling proposition* or 'USP', it is helpful as a means of ensuring that the other elements of the mix support it. The most reliable product should be sold at a premium through channels that are also reliable (it doesn't support the credibility of such a product to be sold through 'Crazy Mikey's Discount Heaven'). The lowest-price offer may need heavy promotion to generate the volume required to keep cost down and the channels of supply will need to be mass-market.

By preparing a different and specific marketing mix for each segment, the business ensures that it will meet the needs of each grouping of customers in a more focused way. At the same time, it enhances its opportunity for maximizing profits through premium pricing, or differentiation, or the offer of a lowest-cost option – whatever the dynamics of the particular segment demand.

The airline industry provides an excellent example (Table 11.1 shows a much simplified summary) with the division of customers into classes – first, business, economy and standby – each with its own needs, similar enough *within* the class for aggregation, and different enough from the next for discrete treatment through four different marketing mixes. The result? On a flight from London to New York, passengers will be paying anything from £200 to £6,000 for the same seven-hour flight!

Table 11.1 *Segmentation in the airline industry*

	Product	Price	Promotion	Place
First	luxury/ego	£6,000	direct to 'club' members	direct
Business	priority/ flexibility	£2,800	business journals	company on-site travel agents
Economy	standard	£850	press, magazines	travel agents
Standby	'risk'	£250	Ceefax, Internet, 'small ads'	Internet, airport desk

Of course, it isn't the same *flight* at all, even though the passengers might take off and land together. The four classes paid different rates because they sought different things. Standby passengers have a different attitude to risk from business travellers, and are happy to purchase a degree of risk (they might not go!) for a discount. First-class travellers may behave differently in their purchase of the ticket from economy travellers: they may have a regular journey, which the airline 'manages' for them, while economy travellers prefer to shop around.

The seven Ps of service marketing

For some time marketers in service industries have seen the need for seven Ps, adding the following to the traditional four:

- people;
- processes;
- physical evidence.

Take training providers – the product may be marketing skills, the price attractive, the promotion effective and the place well targeted, but there are other critical determinants of competitive advantage. Who will deliver the training? The person is an extension of the product, or in some cases perhaps the product itself. Good training shouldn't happen in a vacuum, and successful suppliers will have processes that enable them to link training to delegates' work experience, before the event, during the event and after the event. When choosing training providers there is a great deal at risk – what if they waste our time, what if they don't understand our needs, or what if they send us down the wrong tracks? With a service that has many intangibles, there is a need to provide physical evidence of capability – references, an impressive client list, the opportunity to sample the wares, even perhaps a book on the subject that demonstrates a provider's credibility and status in the big wide world.

Problems with the mix?

The traditional marketing mix has four Ps, the service mix has seven, and perhaps this is sometimes just too simplistic. Where do we find branding – promotion or product? Is customer service part of place or product? Is packaging the product or the promotion? The sales team can find itself in all of them! An interesting debate, and all the better for engaging our thoughts, but the problem with where we put things in the mix is not the most important issue. There is a potential problem with the whole idea of the mix, if we do not take care. It is very easy for the mix to become a range of things that you will do *to* the market. Without care this can develop into an arrogance that says: 'What *we* do *to* the market must be right.' That way lies insensitivity and an inability to see change. The mix must be something you do *with* the market, sometimes influencing, sometimes reacting, but always in tune. Not an easy task, but one made much more manageable as a result of segmentation. This issue will be taken up again in Chapter 19, 'Relationship marketing and key account management', where a different approach is considered, focusing not on the marketing mix but on the customer.

BENEFITS OF SEGMENTATION FOR THE BUSINESS

There are many benefits to be had from good segmentation:

- an enhanced understanding of market dynamics, particularly the notion of the market chain running right through to the end consumer;
- an enhanced understanding of competitor strengths (the competition will differ by segment), and so the opportunities for competitive advantage;
- a greater understanding of the needs, attitudes and behaviours of customers;
- a better chance that you will see how to develop the capabilities of your business in order to match those needs;
- a basis for organizing and structuring your business, focusing the whole supply chain on the customer;
- improving your ability to manage the marketing mix in a customer-focused way;
- enhancing your opportunity to add value, gain competitive advantage and build barriers to entry for competitors or substitutes;
- enhancing your opportunity to create, maintain and defend price premiums.

Always remember, you are doing this in order to focus your limited resources on those areas of the market where you will have the best match between your capabilities and customers' needs – the best opportunities for competitive advantage. It doesn't mean that you will necessarily turn business away if it appears outside these areas, simply that you will be able to determine your priorities more clearly when faced with any choices.

Segmentation and the market chain

In a business-to-business market, if segmentation is done purely based on the supplier's immediate customers, there is a significant danger of losing the added value of what you provide. Take a supplier of film used by 'converters' in the manufacture of packaging materials. The converter supplies packaging to a range of different markets, as shown in Figure 11.3. This diagram also notes what we might call the _hot spot_ in each of these markets – the leading issue on which purchasing decisions are made.

Let's suppose that the film supplier has a good R & D department and is able to develop a range of novel products with different application features. Can this film supplier hope to add value and, more

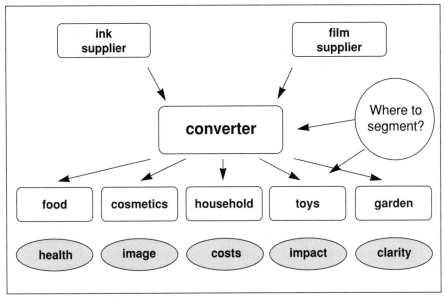

Figure 11.3 _Segmentation and the market chain_

importantly, retain its share of the value added, without understanding how those features might be of benefit to these different markets? If it waits for the converter to brief it on what is required, then it will be the converter that wins and retains the lion's share of the value. So it should segment not at the converter step in the chain, but perhaps by packaging end use? Maybe so, but such a decision will involve it in a whole new range of relationships and activities, calling on a whole new range of capabilities. Making the right segmentation choices takes us back to the demands of the marketing model (Chapter 3) and the need to match market needs with appropriate business capabilities.

Monsanto – picking the wrong link in the chain?	It hardly needs saying that Monsanto have had a rough ride over GM foods. In part we can see some reasons why in their choice of segments. Monsanto segmented at the farmers' level in the chain; the benefits of GM were largely for farmers, or at least that was how they were communicated. Of course the chain extended down to the consumer, and the consumer was far from convinced. Consumers buy products not technologies, and with large doses of hindsight we can see how Monsanto compounded their problem by promoting the technology as a means of communicating the benefits to farmers. Compare this scenario to the success enjoyed by Zeneca with a GM tomato (admittedly pre-BSE) used in the manufacture of tomato paste. The GM tomato had significant consumer benefits: a superior taste as it clung to the taste-buds, and a superior coating ability for things such as pasta. It is an increasingly recognized truth that most value in the chain is usually added closest to the consumer, and if GM suppliers are to break through the barrier of GM resistance they will need to develop and communicate genuine consumer benefits. Some are just on that line, seeking for instance to 'find a food that prevents osteoporosis' (a headline from a DuPont advertisement in their 'to do list for the planet' range).
'Wool is only wool if you let it.' Getting a price premium for Australian wool	The recent story of the Australian wool market is a nice example of how segmentation can be used in a mature and challenging market, in pursuit of a price premium. Synthetic materials have been slowly replacing wool for many years, and prices have been in what looked like terminal decline. The search began for segments that would offer price premiums, and the answer has been high fashion. The demands in this segment are for lighter-weight fabrics with close-to-the-skin comfort, perfect for fine and superfine grades of wool. Interestingly, before this segmentation began to be pursued in practice the prices of both 'broad' and 'fine' wool were falling together, dropping by 1998 to 35 per cent below the base of 1995. Since that time and the implementation of segmentation strategies, the two grades have seen prices diverge – broad wool prices have fallen still further while fine wool prices have recov-

ered and advanced beyond 1995 levels, resulting in a premium of well over 100 per cent against broad wool grades. The Australian wool industry is still in difficulty: supply outstrips demand and prices for broad wool are still in decline, but segmentation has at least allowed suppliers to find some prospect of better prices, and suppliers are starting to shift their emphasis towards more fine and superfine production.

Failure to segment will at best result in missed opportunities and at worst result in the inability of your business to gain competitive advantage and long-term security.

THE SEGMENTATION PROCESS

This is a complex issue, and an important one. Following a disciplined process will help you gain the most from the activity rather than ending up with an intellectually satisfying but sterile result, as often happens when a lot of top-class brainpower is applied to a subject.

There are three principal steps:

1. identification of the basis for segmentation
   - market mapping
   - opportunity analysis
   - leverage points, push or pull
   - who buys what, how, when and where;
2. targeting – the selection of segments
   - attractiveness
   - resources and capability;
3. positioning
   - the market mix
   - propositions
   - perceptual mapping.

IDENTIFICATION OF THE BASIS FOR SEGMENTATION

Market mapping

A good start will be to draw up a *market map*. This is a diagram illustrating all the routes to market for your product or service, what we might call the 'market channels'. The example in Figure 11.4 shows the main routes (much simplified) for a manufacturer of adhesives, industrial and consumer.

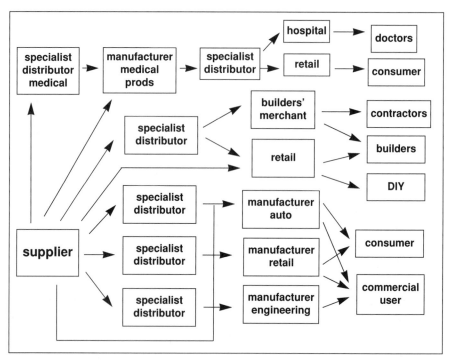

Figure 11.4 *The market map*

The map presents some options and choices for segmentation, some clearer than others. The next stage is to follow a process of focusing in on the best possible means of segmentation.

Opportunity analysis

● Note the size of the market, and the percentage of sales at each 'junction' along the different channels. This will normally be done as percentages of sales volume, although using sales value or profit may be more illuminating.

- Note the size of your own business, and the percentage share, at the same points.
- Note your ⋯⋯ ⋯the same points.

Doing this w⋯ ⋯ormance to the total opp⋯ ⋯inst in each area. Segmer⋯ ⋯t, not your historical sal⋯ ⋯tunities but you will ign⋯

Leverage

Where to s⋯ ⋯its pros and cons. At thi⋯ ⋯e must now engage our⋯ ⋯ve might call _leverage poi⋯_ ⋯l purchasing decisions a⋯ ⋯ut where are the big on⋯ ⋯ıy?

- Are de⋯
- Do di⋯ ⋯oducts to the marke⋯
- Is it t⋯ ⋯s, or the end user?
- Whe⋯ ⋯s, are you in comp⋯ ⋯ offer, or must you⋯ ⋯tention to you in p⋯ ⋯e more attrac- tive⋯

Push ⋯

If your⋯ ⋯a good brand name a⋯ ⋯ct to be in what we w⋯ ⋯e market-place create⋯ ⋯ınels of supply. Withoı⋯ ⋯u will be more used to⋯ ⋯⋯⋯f supply to use your products and services. Reality will combine both push and pull, but it is useful to understand the relative balance at different points of the chain.

Segmenting by end consumer might be easier and more effective for a pull strategy, while a push strategy might call for segmentation by the channel of distribution. The closer to the end user you can segment, often the more powerful the impact, but of course remembering the test questions from the start of this chapter – will it be a *viable* segment?

Getting a full understanding of these leverage points goes beyond market size and percentage shares. It requires a whole new set of questions, to understand the dynamics of how your market works.

In our example of a market map, based on a real map used by a manufacturer of specialist adhesives, the main leverage points might be found at:

- the manufacturers of medical products;
- builders and DIY consumers;
- specialist distributors to the automotive, electrical and engineering industries.

It is worth commenting on the choice of manufacturers of medical products as the leverage point in the medical chain. The adhesive is used in making syringes and neither the hospital nor the doctor will have much interest in whose glue is used. But, and I can hear you saying it, what if further enquiry led to us finding that different medical treatments required different kinds of syringe and that the design of those syringes was influenced in no small part by the choice of adhesive or other bonding technology? We are racing ahead in our level of sophistication at this point. We will return to this kind of analysis in Chapter 20.

Already we are finding that the leverage points in each of the three main areas are at different distances along the chain to the end user:

- medical – close to the supplier but beyond the distributor;
- building and DIY – the consumer;
- specialist industrial uses – the distributors.

We might then expect to find that the way the buying decisions are made and can be influenced will be different in each of the three cases. We are perhaps beginning to identify three 'segments' – medical, building, industrial – but there are more questions to be asked.

Who buys what, how, when and where?

In the excitement of all this analysis, it is good to remember a simple truth: markets don't buy anything – people do that! You need to understand the buying habits at each junction, and of each potential grouping of customers, particularly if you aim to segment by end user or consumer. There will be a lot of trial and error in your attempts to find the right basis for segmentation, and for each possible 'cut' you should be aiming to understand:

- attitudes and perceptions;
- motivations;
- needs;
- buying behaviours.

In our example, we might expect to find the following sorts of differences, at three different leverage points:

- _Medical manufacturers_ – have some very precise specifications for the product, and expect a good deal of help from suppliers in delivering bespoke solutions. They buy in large quantities, with long-term contracts. These are 'R & D buyers': price is of little significance; quality and security of supply are everything.
- _DIY consumers_ – have no expertise in the product, but are looking for something they can rely on, influenced by advertising and brand names. They buy in small quantities, irregularly, and want to find the product freely available in DIY superstores. These are no-hassle 'convenience buyers'.
- _Specialist distributors to the engineering industry_ – want to be able to present the best solutions to their customers. They want a range that meets the spectrum of demand, and buying terms that give them a large enough margin to justify the technical support they offer to customers. These are 'commercial buyers'.

What we are doing here is starting to look beyond segmenting simply by a point in a market chain to segmenting by a variety of additional bases, and the next sections will give more detail on how this might be done in a business-to-business environment and in a consumer/fmcg market.

Some bases for segmentation – business-to-business

Table 11.2 summarizes 10 typical bases for segmentation in a business-to-business environment, grouped into three main types of characteristic.

Table 11.2 *Bases for business-to-business segmentation*

Organizational Characteristics	Industry type
	Size of firm
	Geographic location
Product Characteristics	End use benefits
	Frequency and scale of purchase
	Specification
Buying Characteristics	Distribution channel
	Purchasing function and policy
	Buyer characteristics
	Lead influence on purchase

The paints example

Using brands to distinguish segments – Dulux and Glidden

ICI Dulux used a range of bases like these to assess the trade market for Dulux paint. They had identified, among others, two potential segments deserving of more attention, the small firm of decorators and the major contractor firm. They compared the two segments against the bases summarized in Table 11.3. They found the two segments to be so different that not only were two very separate marketing mixes applied, but a new brand was launched to target the major contractor segment, Glidden Paint, with Dulux Trade targeting the decorator firms. When they looked at buying behaviour in particular they found that the brand loyalty of self-employed professional decorators and the influence of their clients (brand-aware house owners) made the use of the Dulux brand a must. Buyers for major contractors demanded cost reductions that would have compromised the main brand had it attempted to work in both segments. A new brand was the perfect solution, and one already existed in the world group (Glidden is the main ICI paint brand in the USA).

Table 11.3 _Segmentation – trade paint_

Base	Major Contractor	Small Decorator Firm
Size of Firm	200+	1–5
Size of Purchase	industrial scale, larger pack size	domestic scale, smaller pack size
Specification	professional	from client, usually a homeowner
Distribution Channel	direct from supplier	builders' or decorators' merchant
Lead Influence on Purchase Decision	price and cost analysis	client specification and brand loyalty

Novel segmentation

There may be some fairly obvious ways to segment a market but the problem with these 'easy options' is that your competitors are probably seeing things just the same, and where's the competitive advantage in that? The pursuit of novel ways to segment (provided they pass the 'viability' test – see above) will often unearth new understanding of the dynamics of the market-place and gain you significant competitive advantage. Here are two such examples.

The fertilizer example

Back when ICI was still a manufacturer of fertilizer, it found its product to be in slow decline in a mature market. It decided to segment as a means to finding new offers, testing first the more obvious 'cuts': crop type, geography, seasonality, etc. Finally it hit on the simple truth noted earlier in this chapter – wheat didn't buy fertilizer, and nor did East Anglia: it was farmers every time! Farmers came from different backgrounds, with widely differing attitudes, aspirations and buying behaviours. Once the manufacturer started to explore these factors it began to understand (almost for the first time) what _really_ made people buy its product, or not. The final segmentation was done on the basis of attitudes and needs, the traditional family farmer for instance having a rather different outlook to the graduate of agricultural college managing a large estate. Division of the market into six segments allowed the business to prioritize its attentions on those that would respond best to its own strengths. The resultant marketing mixes helped the manufacturer target its product better, add more relevant value, structure its own operations to suit customers' needs and gain a significant increase in revenues and profits.

'When you finally realise that it's not East Anglia that buys your product, but farmers, then you're on to something.'

165

The pharmaceutical example

A supplier to the pharmaceutical industry had segmented for some time by therapeutic area; there was an asthma segment, a heart segment, a cancer segment, etc. This really did very little for it, as not only did every one of its competitors do the same but it found the behaviour and attitudes of separate customers to be quite different even in the same segment. What it found (with hard-won experience) was that it was not so much the therapeutic area that determined behaviour but the phase of development that the drug was at. A drug must pass through a series of checkpoints on its way from research to market, including efficacy tests, trials and regulatory approvals, and these fall into four distinct phases. A pharmaceutical company will have rather different concerns and needs moving from one phase to the next, but they are quite precise and uniform within a single phase, providing an excellent opportunity for segmentation for the observant supplier. At the earliest stage, the pharmaceutical companies want speed and flexibility from suppliers, with price and quality some way down the list. As the development proceeds this changes to a greater need for quality and reliability, and then an absolute ability to gain regulatory approval, and finally to issues of scale, capacity and the reduction of production costs. The molecule supplier was able to identify these stages, or phases, as quite discrete segments based on specification requirements, and develop offers that met the needs, attitudes and behaviours, almost regardless of drug type.

The nesting concept

Developed by Benson P Shapiro and Thomas V Bonoma, the nesting concept aims to help in working through the complexity of segmenting in the business-to-business environment. The number of options can be bewildering, so Shapiro and Bonoma suggest a hierarchy of bases on which to segment, as represented in Figure 11.5.

The idea is that demographics provide the most basic means to segment but that within that are four further levels of increasing specificity. Next come the operating variables such as the client's technology, capabilities and use of products and brands. The nest within that nest looks at purchasing approaches – the way that clients buy. Next come situational factors – the product application, the urgency, the scale. Finally comes the buyer personality – attitude to risk, motivation, etc. A general observation can be made that the closer to the central nest you get in your attempts to segment the market, the harder the task but the more likely you are to find a unique basis that will give you competitive advantage.

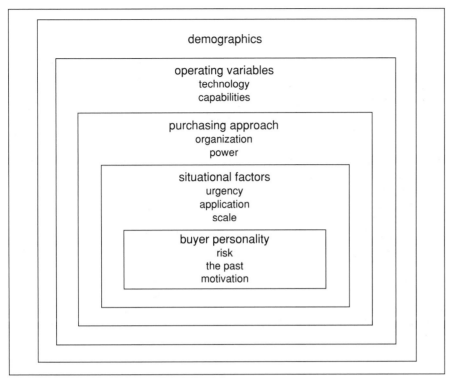

Figure 11.5   _The nesting concept_

(from: Shapiro and Bonoma, Harvard Business Review, May–June 1984)

Some bases for segmentation – consumer/fmcg

Table 11.4 summarizes 10 typical bases for segmentation in an fmcg environment, grouped into three main types of characteristic.

Some of these deserve a little more attention.

Table 11.4   _Bases for consumer segmentation_

Macro Characteristics	socio-economic
	demographics
	age and sex
	income
Circumstantial Characteristics	regionality
	family or household size
	house size/location
Lifestyle Characteristics	psychographics
	aspirations
	rate of adoption

Socio-economic classification

Probably the most common method of consumer segmentation in the UK, much used by the advertising industry, is the socio-economic classifications of A, B, C1, C2, etc. This is an attempt, increasingly crude but none the less popular, to classify people on the basis of their social class, status and occupation. It makes certain assumptions about disposable income (A has higher than B, etc) and about discretion and taste (A being more select than B, etc), which are valuable distinctions for marketers but probably not related to these social groupings in the way originally envisaged. As a shorthand for such distinctions it is still useful, provided you are happy that the established descriptions don't bear too much inspection. Table 11.5 lists the main classifications.

Table 11.5 *Socio-economic classifications*

	Class	Status
A	upper middle	higher managerial, professional
B	middle	middle management, administrative
C1	lower middle	supervisory, junior management
C2	skilled worker	skilled manual
D	working	semi- and unskilled manual
E	low subsistence	pensioners, casual, unemployed

A significant drawback of this method of segmentation is the look of sheer wonderment that greets you if you attempt its use outside the UK! Perhaps better suited to the targeting of communications, hence the advertising industry's continued use, the classifications are increasingly suspect as providing any coherent set of needs, attitudes and behaviours, vital for good segmentation.

Two observations perhaps cut a swath through this basis for segmentation. First, pensioners are far from a coherent group, as they include those on state pensions alongside those on two-thirds of final salary who have paid off their mortgage and whose kids have flown the nest. Second, one of the highest disposable income groups in the UK is the 18–22 age group, in work but still living at home, with few commitments beyond next Friday night.

Demographics

Simple demographics are fast losing their appeal as a basis for segmentation – people aged 25 to 35 are not exactly a coherent group with similar needs, attitudes or behaviours. Marks & Spencer long relied on the 'middle-class' and 'middle-aged' consumer as the yardstick for its positioning. A 54 per cent dip in profits in 1999 forced it into a rethink, including the launch of the Autograph range of clothes, targeted not at an age group but at an 'attitude' or 'lifestyle' group.

Lifestyle characteristics

The last 20 years have seen much attention given to lifestyles in preference to socio-economic classifications. A huge range of terms has arisen, including the yuppie–dinky terminology. One such classification, even giving percentages of the UK population, is summarized in Table 11.6.

It is easy to criticize any such listing, particularly out of context, although it does seem that any basis of segmentation that puts a 17-year-old unemployed seeker of 'fun' in the same segment as an elderly couple living on a meagre pension has something to explain. Is a possible explanation (though not an attractive one) that this 5 per cent of the population is what we have come to call an underclass, not to be considered as a prime target for the marketer?

Using generic lifestyle definitions is always going to lead to problems when faced with the specific circumstance. Much better, if the marketer has the time and the resource, is to construct your own distinctions that work in your own market. Such distinctions tend to evolve over time as experience and research hones the analysis. At this point, lifestyle segmentation merges with psychographics, an attempt to map out consumer attitudes defined by emotions and perceptions.

Psychographics

Having discussed ICI Paints in the business-to-business environment, we might look at how it deals with the consumer side of its market.

Table 11.6 *Lifestyle segmentations*

(from: Christopher, M and McDonald, M (1995) *Marketing*, Macmillan, London)

Lifestyle	Description	% of pop
Self-explorers	self expression and self-realization, reject doctrine in favour of individual awareness, 'spiritual'	15
Social Resisters	caring and altruistic, concerned for society and the environment, can be intolerant	14
Experimentalists	highly individual, fast-paced enjoyment, materialistic, pro-technology, anti-authority	11
Conspicuous Consumers	acquisitive and competitive, concerned with position and show, pro-authority and hierarchy	19
Belongers	conventional, traditional, seeking to fit in, family-orientated and resistant to change	18
Survivors	class-conscious and community-spirited, aiming to 'get by', hard-working and apparently happy with their lot	17
Aimless	a) young, unemployed, seeking 'kicks', anti-authority; b) old, focused on day-to-day existence in trying circumstances	5

Sixty years young and still changing – how Dulux keeps in touch

Dulux is an excellent example of a brand that has evolved through changing market circumstances, always keeping in touch with its consumers through a deep understanding of their needs, attitudes and behaviours, and updating its basis of segmentation accordingly.

In the 1960s the boom in DIY was based to a great extent on a raft of new products that were easy to use; Formica led the way, but there was also Fablon, hardboard and paints such as Dulux non-drip gloss. Segmentation based on product types and product usage was quite appropriate in such a climate, and so it stayed for many years.

Into the 1970s and attitudes were changing. DIY was an established norm and consumers were seeking more; they wanted to transform their homes. Dulux became an aspirational brand and new segmentation was required. Terms such as *planners* and *appliers* evolved, and soon became segments, each needing its own marketing mix, not least because planners had to be targeted early in the decision process, through magazines and TV, while appliers could be targeted in store, with advice and information.

The more demanding 1980s and 90s saw consumers seeking increasing personalization of their homes. The 'nesting' culture (an updated form of the Englishman's home being his castle, where a desire for personal and private spaces strongly influences attitudes and behaviours) called for another look at segmentation – planners were not just planners any more. Figure 11.6 gives a diagrammatic description of the new segmentation using psychographic terminology.

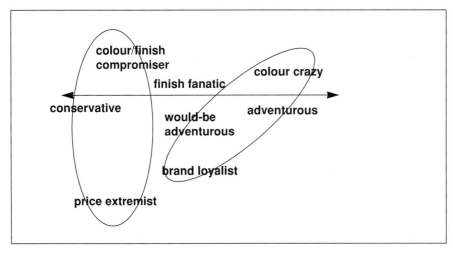

Figure 11.6 *Segmentation for paint consumers*

Consumers are identified as conservative, would-be adventurous or adventurous in their attitudes to decorating and their use of paint in particular. Around that spectrum of attitude there are other emotions going on. With regard to the end effect, there are those who want to use colour, those who focus on the finish and those who compromise between the two. Looking at their purchasing behaviour we can identify those who are brand-loyal (usually to Dulux as the brand leader) and those who buy on price (most often the own-label consumer).

Different slices of this spectrum can be seen to be more attractive than others, both in terms of premium pricing and as allowing a match with Dulux's main capabilities. The brand-loyal colour-crazy is a prime target, whereas the conservative price buyer is less attractive.

Rate of adoption – the 'adopters curve'

When a new product is launched there is usually a vanguard of ardent enthusiasts who jump on board, almost regardless of the product's merits. Sometimes it goes no further and the product dies, remembered only as a fad supported by a clique of fanatics; there were certainly a *few* enthusiasts for the Sinclair C5!

If a product is to succeed it has to go beyond that narrow following and find a wider audience. It has to progress beyond the *innovators* to find the *early adopters*. Everett Rogers captured this concept in his much-quoted 'adopters curve', shown in Figure 11.7. The curve shows how most new products or ideas go through stages of adoption, first by the innovators, a small but enthusiastic group, then by the early adopters who help make the product something of wider appeal. The early majority provide the volume sales that drive down costs and turn the product into a mass-market one, at which stage the late majority come sweeping in to buy. Laggards are those that resist till the very end, or perhaps never succumb.

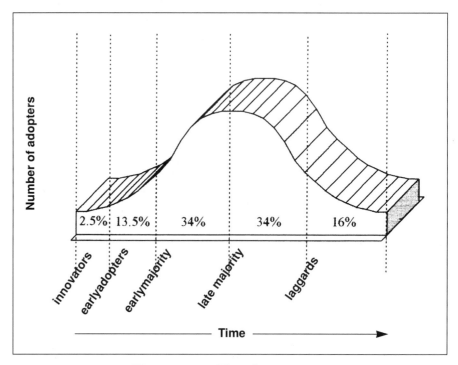

Figure 11.7   *The adopters curve*

(from Rogers, E (1962), Diffusion of Innovations, New York Free Press)

A classic example of such a development is the electronic pocket calculator. At its invention it was bought as an advanced scientific instrument, predominantly by businesses and institutions, doubtless requiring approval by the capital acquisitions committee. It was not long however before a new segment of the market opened up, spurred on by government legislation (PESTLE again – see Chapter

7). Once it was approved that calculators could be used in GCSE maths exams, every little Johnny and Jane rushed home to demand their parents bought them one, though they were cumbersome instruments with a mind-boggling array of functions. This new demand from the _early adopters_ brought prices tumbling down. Before long the pocket calculator was an established item for business people and this _early majority_ helped drive prices even lower until calculators were being given away free as promotional items; the _late majority_ was engaged.

An interesting feature of the model is the role of the innovator, sometimes a positive force, but not infrequently a drag on the market's uptake. The Internet is a case in point. Early users of the Internet were portrayed as 'nerds', sad characters with no social life who sat up late at night surfing the Net in search of other such lost souls. Whether true or not, this image of the early users served to hold back wider acceptance of the Internet, perhaps for as long as two years.

As a model for potential segmentation the adopters curve holds much promise. A marketer can plan the development of a product through these stages, changing the marketing mix as each new group is targeted. The proposition must be quite different for each group. For innovators, the talk might be of novelty, experimentation, leading edge and trial. Such a proposition would frighten the late majority, just as the innovators would be bored by talk of 'tried and tested' and lengthy evidence of success, such as would appeal to the late majority.

TARGETING – THE SELECTION OF SEGMENTS

It can be seen that the task of selecting the right basis of segmentation is not easy. The options are vast, and the complex interactions of different bases can be mind-boggling. There is no better advice than perseverance and stamina; the outcome will be worth the effort.

Having found the basis that suits your business, the next step in the process is to select those segments that merit targeting. At this point we must go back to the marketing model described in Chapter 3. The aim described in this model is to achieve a match between your company's capabilities and the needs of the market. This matching process will now help us in the selection of segments.

We might use a process already discussed in Chapter 10 and one that we will encounter again in more detail in Chapter 12 in the context of product portfolio management: the directional policy matrix. Figure 11.8 shows the matrix that we aim to complete, plotting segments against two sets of factors: 1) their attractiveness; and 2) our ability to match the needs, attitudes and behaviours.

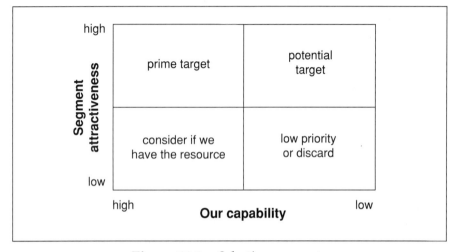

Figure 11.8 *Selecting segments*

Segment attractiveness

A range of factors should be identified that will determine the attractiveness of the segment to your business. These might include any of the following, or any additional factors that are relevant to your own circumstances:

- Size – volume, value, profit opportunity.
- Growth potential – volume, value, profit opportunity.
- Ease of access.
- Opportunity for a match.
- Are they 'early adopters'? Do they pick up on new ideas and products, or do they wait until the market has tested them?
- Will they value your offer?
- Level of competition, low being attractive.

Our capability

Again, a range of factors should be identified that will determine your level of capability. These might include any of the following, or any additional factors that are relevant to your own circumstances:

- resources – production capacity, etc;
- ability to differentiate;
- cost levels;
- budget for promotion;
- sales force;
- access to distribution channels;
- image and reputation;
- product quality;
- service levels;
- speed of response.

Chapter 12 outlines a process for scoring these factors so that you can plot them on the matrix. This tool is only an aid to decision making. It doesn't make the decisions for you, and the labels on the matrix are only suggestive of your outcome. In the end you must decide how many segments you can target, based on the strategic choice discussed at the start of this chapter (Figure 11.1): do you go for a spread or do you focus? Perhaps as many businesses overstretch themselves as restrict their growth by an overly pessimistic opinion of their own abilities. The 1960s and 70s saw the rise of conglomerates operating in a wide variety of businesses, markets and segments. The trend of the 1990s was for increased focus. Perhaps new technology will enable businesses to manage a wider range of segments in the 21st century?

POSITIONING

Earlier in this chapter we looked at the concepts of the _marketing mix_ and how the sum total of that mix represented the _proposition_ to the customers in your chosen segment. This proposition will _position_ your offer in the customers' eyes. The practice of _positioning_, then, is determining what you wish customers to think about your offer, and how you want them to react. Positioning must reflect the dynamics in the market, and so brands and offerings must reposition as those dynamics change.

Chemist, pamper parlour, or unofficial adjunct to the NHS? Boots marches on...

Boots the chemist has been more than just a chemist for some time, and after many years of moving towards a kind of variety store we can now see Boots repositioning into the service sector with in-store opticians, dentists and chiropodists. In part this is a continuation of the shift from chemist to 'pamper parlour', but it also sees Boots taking on (from the beleaguered NHS) a new role in auxiliary health care. This new positioning is one that its existing brand strengths based on responsibility, trust and confidence make particularly attractive.

We have stressed throughout this chapter how segmentation is based not only on the needs of customer groups, but also on their attitudes and behaviours. Dealing with the complexity raised by such factors is one of the key intellectual challenges of marketing, made all the harder by the fact that we are dealing here not so much with facts as with perceptions. Any salesperson of even moderate experience will affirm that when it comes to customers, it is perceptions that count, not facts. This is not an invitation to charlatans or those who wish to be 'economical with the actualité'; rather it is a warning to those who get too bound up with the intimate detail of their own product and fail to see how it is actually understood or regarded.

Clive Sinclair (now Sir Clive) had a clear view of his Sinclair C5 as an energy-efficient, environmentally friendly, low-cost means of transport. His potential customers saw it as a death trap. Predictor, the self-use pregnancy testing kit, has tried hard through its promotional messages to stress the positive, not to say joyous results of its use, but there are still large numbers of people who regard it as something that you use to discover the worst. Remember 'This is the age of the train'? The old British Rail may have had reams of statistics to back its claim, but few of us believed it for a minute.

Perceptual mapping

As with all communications, the message *received* is of more significance than the message *sent*, and this is a vital truth to remember when seeking to position your product or service in the chosen segment. The four Ps will help you to determine the elements of your proposition, but we need to turn to the idea of perceptual mapping to help ensure that we actually occupy the space in people's minds that we intend.

Figure 11.9 shows one of a variety of possible perceptual maps for the motor-car market. This particular one looks at two factors, price and performance, comparing a sample of makes and models based on consumer opinion in a particular segment. It is very important to remember that this map does not show _actual_ positions as based on any comparisons of list price and technical specifications; it represents the perceptions of a particular group of customers. Facts may argue another case entirely, but it is perceptions that make people buy. In this case it is a particular BMW model under consideration, and the map shows its positioning _vis-à-vis_ the competition on these two factors, price and performance. The question for BMW would be, is this where they want their model to be positioned, or should they be doing something to their marketing mix in order to alter customers' perceptions?

The perceptual map can be used in a number of ways. As here, it is

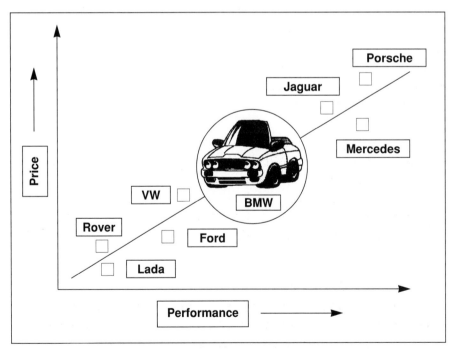

Figure 11.9 _Perceptual mapping_

used to assess where target customers place your proposition and to compare that with your intended proposition. Another use would be to plot the competition and to look for any 'gaps' in the map. Such gaps may be opportunities for you to offer a unique proposition. BMW were arguably the first manufacturer to position a middle-price, mid-sized, high-performance car (perceived), exploiting a gap that had stood open between the likes of Ford and Vauxhall on the one hand and Porsche and Ferrari on the other.

Another way to use perceptual mapping, and perhaps the most useful for the specific task of positioning in a segment, is to analyse positioning against a wide variety of factors. Few markets, and the car market least of all, operate on anything as simple as just two buying criteria. It is only for simplicity of explanation that I show this two-dimensional map; in reality we must consider as many dimensions as actually matter. We are seeking to understand what mix of factors really drives the customer's decision process, and at the same time to assess whether that mix of factors allows you the most competitive advantage.

MARKET RESEARCH

The last thing to say about segmentation is something that must by now be abundantly clear. The more you know about your market the more powerful will be your method of segmentation and the more effective your positioning. Market research is vital unless you are to rely on gut feel and inspiration. Quantitative data will be required for the market mapping exercise and, after that, qualitative data will be required as you delve further into customers' attitudes, behaviours and perceptions. The search for the right basis for segmentation will in fact help to highlight the sorts of questions that you should be asking. As the search progresses you will uncover more and more that you just don't know. Don't despair, this is good(!), provided that you have both the motivation and the budget to seek better understanding as a result. Time and money are issues here, and we are of course back to the basics of the marketing model – company capabilities. How many segments you can operate in will, in the final analysis, depend as much as anything else on your ability to understand them.

And heed the warning about market research given by David Ogilvy (already offered in Chapter 5), in the pursuit of viable segmentation strategies more than anywhere else. You will recall that he worried that marketers were turning to market research rather like a drunk to a lamppost, for support and not illumination. Use the research to open up the possibilities, not just to confirm your current practice.

Part IV

The Marketing Mix

12

Product strategies

Marketing as we know it today had its roots in the new manufacturing industries of the 19th century, so it is no surprise that the definition of a product was for many years an entirely tangible one – a product was something that was made. Sure, it could be anything from a pin to an ocean-going liner, but it was very much a 'real thing'.

In more recent years the application of the word 'product' has broadened considerably, not only in marketing circles but also in common usage. Now it is quite normal to hear a holiday, a pension plan, a theatrical performance or a premier league football match described as a product. Even a country can be seen as a product – the Seychelles tourist board recently employed an executive from Coca-Cola to help market their holiday islands.

The idea is much older than the application of the jargon. Doubtless David O Selznik spoke of Clark Gable and Vivien Leigh as marketable commodities (though as we will see, 'commodity' is a far from satisfactory term for what they represented to Selznik's film company), recognizing that people could be products. Now, even bishops in the Church of England call for new thinking in marketing their product, though whether they mean their church, their creed, or their Lord is not always clear.

This usage reveals more than the fact that marketing people have moved into the world of finance, art, entertainment and religion. It is a recognition that a product may be more than a tangible 'thing', indeed that most products are a complex of tangible and intangible elements. Much more than an item, the product is something experienced by the consumer.

Dinner at the Ritz is a product, and it is for more than the food alone that we go. We may find better food in a humbler restaurant, but dinner at the Ritz remains a unique experience. For that matter, a Big Mac is a product, and here too we are buying more than the food. The product in this case includes a whole range of associations and attendant benefits from familiarity to reliability, from convenience to mobility. In the end, what we pay for cannot be measured in itemized costings of bun, beef patty, or lettuce leaf; the experience itself has a value.

Product managers are responsible for more than an item. They are responsible for the image, the associations, the reputation and the ultimate value of their product. What people want from the product, how they use it or think of it, these are the concerns of product managers just as much as the product's physical form (if it has one) or its costs of manufacture. The ubiquitous can of Heinz baked beans (for so long a stock example on marketing courses) has more in common with a performance of Bizet's Carmen at the National Opera House than at first appears, and that is not to diminish either of these fine products.

THE COMMODITY

Economists speak of commodities as shorthand for things that are bought and sold, but the marketer has a more precise definition. For the marketer, a commodity is a failure. This is a product that really is just the 'thing', the item, the manufactured good. It has no value above the cost of its component parts. Any profit made by the seller of such commodities comes from the service of getting it to the customer, not from the product itself, and at such a point, of course, it ceases to be a commodity! If value has been added, then the product is not a commodity. By this definition it is hard to think of any real commodities. Water has long since ceased to be one, sugar is more subtle in its variations than ever before, even such 'known value items' (KVIs) as flour and tea have escaped the clutches of commoditization. The ease of self-raising and the healthiness of wholemeal, the convenience of the tea bags and the taste sensations of camomile, burdock and agrimony, such have been their salvation.

ADDED VALUE

We are talking here of added value, a concept that distinguishes the product from the commodity. Added value is not an artifice of marketers and advertisers. A product ceases to be a commodity and takes on some form of added value not when the marketer says so, but once a consumer perceives it to be so. Value is in the eye of the beholder. Of course, perceptions can be influenced but, even so, if a cardboard disc illustrating a cartoon character that comes free with a bag of potato crisps happens to be the one that completes your collection, then who is to deny its value? We will pay four times or more for a soft drink to drink it in a restaurant rather than at home. We will pay perhaps 20 times as much for the convenience of a diluted box of Ribena than for the equivalent amount made from the undiluted bottle requiring the addition of glass and tap water. The value of a lifebelt to someone drowning is beyond calculation...

The famous 'widget' beloved of marketing textbooks is a rare beast, the thing that has no value beyond its component parts, and that should be no surprise – it is the accumulation of value from manufacture to use that makes a product what it is. Value is added in countless ways. Let's take as an example a real-life widget, the thing at the bottom of those beer cans that makes the beer froth. Starting life as a bunch of component parts the value is not clear. Formed together and put in the bottom of a can they have added value by the fact that they have an effect on the beer when poured, but this is only part of the story. For the rest, and the lion's share of the value, we must turn to the consumer. The beer drinker has for long criticized canned beer as a poor substitute for the real thing from the tap. The 'widget' (as coined by Guinness) performs the miracle of translation, delivering draught taste with all the convenience of the can – true added value, if you're a beer drinker. In this example value was added by the beer manufacturer to the consumer's experience, so gaining it competitive advantage resulting in market share, premium price, or customer loyalty. Value was also added by the suppliers of the widget's component parts, by providing the means to such consumer value. Added value is a concept that traces back from end consumer all the way to the start of the supply chain, and products at all stages of that chain jostle for their share.

THE CORE AND THE SURROUND

The 'Pepsi Challenge' – when telling us we like it isn't enough

Back in the 1980s, Pepsi conducted a huge consumer research project in the UK asking people to blind-test Pepsi against the main competitors. The results delighted them: 55 per cent of people preferred their product. The tests led directly to a long advertising campaign showing the amazement on consumers' faces when they were asked to blind-test colas and found their favourite was indeed Pepsi. The campaign did not bring the hoped for ejection of Coke from the number one spot. The problem was that when people knew what they were drinking, not blind tests, 65 per cent preferred Coca-Cola! Pepsi changed their campaign to heavyweight endorsements from Tina Turner and Michael Jackson – simple factors like taste were clearly not enough.

Our preferences for products, whether colas, cars, or insurance policies, are affected by more than just the tangible issues such as taste, fuel consumption, or exclusion clauses. A host of less tangible associations combine to determine our final opinion and so our purchasing behaviour. A useful explanation of this phenomenon is the idea of the product as a core and a surround, shown in Figure 12.1.

At their core, both Pepsi and Coke are 'black sweetened drinks'. How much would you pay for a 'bsd'? Not much value added so far. The value is added in layers. First are the tangible elements – the ingredients, the taste, the design of the packaging and the availability of the product. These tangible things add value, but very often it is in the outer circles that the most added value is perceived, in the realm of the intangibles. Here, an array of images, associations and perceptions are conjured by the brand. With fmcgs in particular we find that the most value is often added at these outer layers. The preference for Coke is largely determined in these outer layers through a complex of associations with everything from youth to tradition, energy to relaxation, heritage to 'cool', and the American dream to the global family.

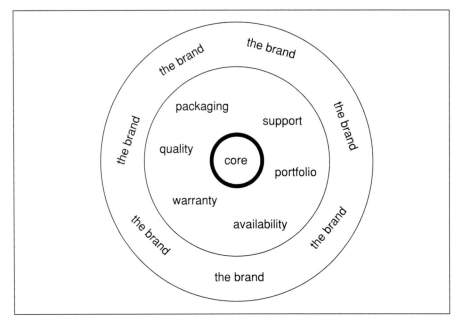

Figure 12.1 *The core and the surround*

Malt whisky drinkers will tell you that they can distinguish the taste of one malt from another with some precision – hence their preference. We will hear the same from the wine connoisseur. For many this may be so, but none the less the producers of wines and whiskies go to much trouble to build broader associations around the core of their product, its taste. For wine, it is any mix of the label, the shape of the bottle, the vineyard, the château, the pedigree, the grape type or blend, the skill of the producing family, the modernity of the technology or the antiquity of the method, and more. Whisky distilleries will weave even more magic around their product with images of ancient retainers practising time-honoured traditions with equipment that might just raise the eyebrow of a local food inspector. Would we value an identical taste so much if we knew it to come from a stainless steel vat in a chemical plant?

The battle of the petrol pump exhibits another version of this concept – how a product takes on a range of associations, tangible and intangible, well beyond its original essence. At its core, petro is petrol. It is not an unknown thing to see one company's tanker filling the underground tanks of a competitor's station. Even when a company develops a unique formulation, a genuine tangible difference, how much is this a factor in determining our purchasing behaviour? Each of us has his or her own reasons for choosing a make of petrol, some tangible, some less so. Here is a list, in no particular order of preference, culled from a consumer research study:

1. The station is on my way to work.
2. The station is on my side of the road, so avoiding turning across busy traffic.
3. The station has a shop.
4. The station has clean toilets.
5. There is good protection against the rain and the wind.
6. They've got a car wash.
7. I collect the loyalty points.
8. I'm collecting the free gifts.
9. They stock my favourite brand of cigarettes.
10. The pumps are fast.
11. The pumps don't dribble.
12. They always have a copy of my morning paper.
13. It's a great place to buy a quick breakfast.
14. I believe that their petrol is best for my engine.
15. I don't like the environmental record of the company across the road.
16. I broke down once and they helped me out.
17. The queues are short.
18. I like the people behind the counter.
19. I trust them not to put funny stuff in the petrol.
20. It always seems to be the cheapest.
21. It seems to give me the most miles per gallon.
22. I trust the name.

Many of these are tangible reasons, but less than half have anything to do with the petrol itself. The purchase seems to be more down to the mix of services and related products than the core product. And when we have reasons relating to the petrol itself they are about beliefs and perceptions as much as about known facts. Each of us would rate those reasons differently, each of us fitting into some segment of the petrol market – the business traveller, the convenience shopper, the tight budgeter, or the points collector, to name a few possibilities. Value is added in different ways depending on the segment, and the product is perceived differently depending on the segment. As a business traveller, I resent standing in queues behind people doing their grocery shopping, yet at the weekend I am the first to give thanks for late-night milk and bread!

Even for an unbranded raw material supplied in a business-to-business context there is a surround beyond the product's specification. Moving out from the product's core we might travel through the breadth of range, the mode of supply, the service package, and on to questions of flexibility in providing variants, and then out further to the increasingly intangible areas of confidence and trustworthiness. Many a buyer in such an environment will seek to measure the 'facts' of reliability and performance, but in the end will make a decision on the less measurable but more compelling grounds of trust and confidence.

Givens and differentiators

While it is very often in the outer circles of the 'surround' that the most value is added, this shouldn't lead us to suppose that the core is not important. Products that promise the moon in their surround but are rotten at their core are products that fail in the long run. Products have to work – drinks must refresh, and they must be good for us if that is what they claim. The higher the profile established by the surround, the greater the crash when something at the core fails. The withdrawal of Perrier water after it was found to have traces of benzene in it made front-page news.

There were more headlines in 1999 when Coca-Cola had to withdraw millions of litres of product in the Benelux countries after traces of dioxins were found. Food safety issues have become headline news, not just because we care about health but because food manufacturers make such public claims for the purity and freshness of their products and the general well-being to be had from them. Coca-Cola was criticized by many, not only for the product problem but for the way that they handled the problem. The management in Atlanta were slow to comment, and when they did it was to say very little. When that caused a problem they snapped to high-profile response mode with a dramatic product call-back. The watchers were not impressed – 'givens' are *very* sensitive things if they go astray.

Being high profile means never making mistakes

We might regard the core and those things closest to the core as 'givens', things that just *have* to be right or you are not in business.

189

Away from the core we are looking at what we might call 'differen-tiators', and the source of competitive advantage. We assume that all petrol will work, whatever the brand – that is a given. It is some mix of the factors listed above that determines our preference and so defines that chosen product's competitive advantage.

Packaging

For a fast-moving consumer good, the package might at any one time be a practical means of supply, the product's persona, its advertise-ment and sometimes its source of competitive advantage. Packaging can provide one of the best examples of a product's surround. Kodak film comes in yellow boxes, but not just any yellow. The colour consistency of that packaging is vital to a product that is claiming perfect colour representation. The package is a part of the product's credibility. The package can convey important messages about the product, through its style and appearance.

'To the marketer, packaging should never be just a wrapper.'

Limmits, the range of slimming biscuits, come in slim shapes with silky black wrap-pers, 'just as I would like to be' say many of its consumers, slim and sexy. The tradi-tional Coca-Cola bottle shouts heritage, the Angostura Bitters bottle positively screams its unique individuality (the label is way too large, the text on it far too small, but it is instantly recognizable and it works). Packaging can even communicate complex messages such as trustworthiness, provided it is given time. For many years ICI delivered its fertilizer products in distinctive blue bags and farmers would order 'blue bag' from their local wholesalers and heave sighs of relief when they saw it stacked in their own warehouse – a sign of a safe decision taken.

Novel packaging can allow new uses for existing products. The Tetra Pak has allowed a variety of drinks from milk to orange juice to be offered in ready-to-drink, long-life, or other convenience modes. In the convenience drinks sector it is arguable that the package is in fact the core of the product, not the contents. For many a food shopper with a busy lifestyle, the sight of a microwavable container is almost more important than what comes inside. I have often put back on the shelf the doubtless tastier but oven-cooked option and chosen instead the convenience version – conve-nient and value added, thanks to the packaging.

New materials have allowed suppliers of bulk materials to industrial users to supply in quantities that suit the customers' production schedules, not the limitations of the suppliers' packaging. The value of this is clear – deliveries of product direct to the point of use reduce lead times, remove the need for storage and allow the customer to concentrate on manufacturing rather than the management of inventory.

One of the dilemmas for the marketer is that novel packaging can often take longer to develop than the product itself. With an ever increasing emphasis on speed to market as a means of commercial success this must inevitably leave some good packaging ideas on the drawing board. The solution lies in seeing packaging not as a last-minute add-on, but as an integral part of the product, whether core or surround.

One of my favourite examples of this attitude is that of Dulux Paints, which developed a square can for a new product, Once Gloss. The novelty of the design suggested the novelty of the product, but this is not the story I wish to tell. The marketing manager knew that this novel design would be perfect to emphasize the originality of another product, only he didn't yet know what that product was – it lay in the future. He ordered a large production run in the confident assurance that it would suit 'some' future new product launch, and that waiting for the product would mean missing the boat on the packaging. A year later Dulux launched Kids Zone, complete with novel square can, which was a great success – brave, open to criticism of poor focus, but eminently practical and ultimately wise.

Kids Zone – it's square

Customer service

Still looking at the surround, another great source of competitive advantage for a product is customer service. This is not the place to go into detail on the elements of good customer service (Chapter 17 will explore this further), but rather just to say that it is an ingredient in the surround that will often reap rewards much beyond its apparent 'cost'. The key to success is finding the appropriate kind of customer service, and that means appropriate to the product itself.

The supplier of a unique and complex hi-tech product (perhaps a piece of software for use by engineers) may worry less about answering its telephones before the fourth ring and more about ensuring a fast-response after-sales back-up for users, on site. A hotel with its number on the board at a busy airport that answers its telephones on the fifth ring or beyond is a hotel going out of business. In the first example, customer service is about the product in use; in the second, it is about ease of doing business.

PRODUCT LIFE CYCLES

Products must be managed (hence product managers) not least because they are like living things. They are born, nurtured, encouraged to learn and grow, mature, grow old and perhaps at some future date die. The idea of a product life cycle is hugely valuable to anyone wishing to manage this process as it provides them with the same guidelines that a good parent would want for bringing up baby and sending it out into the big wide world.

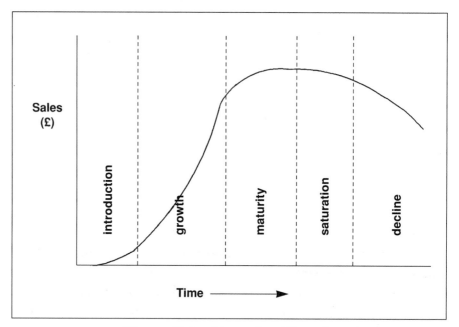

Figure 12.2 *The product life cycle*

A product can move through each of five stages of life, shown in Figure 12.2:

1. Introduction – this is typically a time of high investment and slow uptake.
2. Growth – if it takes on, it can take off, with resultant volumes bringing costs down, so fuelling more growth.
3. Maturity – the product's success brings in competitors to share the spoils and life starts to get a little harder.

4. Saturation – too many players are crowding around the honey pot, spoiling the game for everyone.
5. Decline – with the fun gone out of the game, the suppliers lose interest and the product declines towards death.

The development isn't inevitable. Many products die at their introduction. Many products get a new lease of life at maturity. People are born, they grow, they mature and they die, but products don't have to (they are after all only _like_ people): that is up to the market and the product manager. Nor is the time-scale uniform across all products. The life of a successful pharmaceutical may be measured in decades, a successful confectionery bar may come and go within two years, while a personal computer seems to have a life cycle that extinguishes on purchase!

The PLC analysis allows for three distinct uses by the marketer:

1. the comparative use;
2. the advisory use;
3. the dynamic use.

The comparative use

This is like taking your baby to the clinic to make sure that it's putting on the right weight for its age. Parents who are proud of their children might get strange ideas about their progress if they didn't stop occasionally to compare notes with others. Baby might be growing fast (babies do) but what if everyone else's is growing twice as fast? Your mother might tell you that little Sally is quite tall enough and that's how big you were at her age, but what if today's environment promotes much faster growth? The PLC can be used to plot your product against a range of benchmarks – other products in your own range, the competition and the market cycle. This last is particularly valuable as it encourages an understanding of that cycle and shows your performance in the only arena that matters. Knowing that you are down when the market is up allows you the choice of taking action. Without that kind of knowledge most of us would blunder on regardless.

The advisory use

The PLC can be used like one of those manuals on childcare, and with the same warnings – each child and each product is unique, and the environment is infinitely variable – but guidelines are none the less helpful and some are given in Figure 12.3.

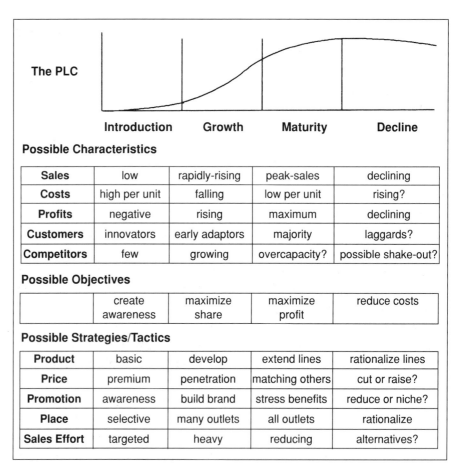

The PLC	Introduction	Growth	Maturity	Decline
Possible Characteristics				
Sales	low	rapidly-rising	peak-sales	declining
Costs	high per unit	falling	low per unit	rising?
Profits	negative	rising	maximum	declining
Customers	innovators	early adaptors	majority	laggards?
Competitors	few	growing	overcapacity?	possible shake-out?
Possible Objectives				
	create awareness	maximize share	maximize profit	reduce costs
Possible Strategies/Tactics				
Product	basic	develop	extend lines	rationalize lines
Price	premium	penetration	matching others	cut or raise?
Promotion	awareness	build brand	stress benefits	reduce or niche?
Place	selective	many outlets	all outlets	rationalize
Sales Effort	targeted	heavy	reducing	alternatives?

Figure 12.3   *The PLC – advisory use*

Take great care to note the use of the words 'possible strategies' in Figure 12.3. These are not prescriptions for success but generic advice. One of the loudest debates is whether prices should be cut or raised when a product enters the decline phase. The argument for raising price is the one of milking a product that will die anyway; the argument for cutting is that fewer and fewer people want to buy it and you have a factory to fill. The real answer must depend on three things:

1. What are your competitors doing?
2. What will the market stand?
3. What do you plan to do about this decline?

This third point takes us to the third and most important of the uses for the PLC analysis, the dynamic use.

The dynamic use

This is the use that least suits the analogy with a human life. Marketers have an advantage over parents: they can postpone nature, or bring it on. They can behave as no good parent would, yet still be doing the right thing. They can force their child to change its character, they can favour another child in preference to this one, they can raise new children that will chase this one to a premature grave, and they can even choose to kill their offspring outright.

Marketing is about choices and nowhere more so than in the choices facing the product manager with regard to the PLC. The tragedy is that so few product managers see the choices in time. In theory at least no product need ever decline, and maturity can be put off indefinitely. Continual growth is possible, provided that the marketer is on hand to do the right things. Even if maturity and decline become inevitable, there is always the option of a new product to replace the old, but the big question is usually when?

Consider a car manufacturer whose leading model has seen a few years of spectacular growth but is now showing signs of reaching maturity. Other manufacturers have caught up with what was once a revolutionary new design and market share is beginning to slip. There are choices:

1. Do nothing.
2. Take action to revive the existing model – augmentation, range extension, relaunch.
3. Launch a new model to replace the one in trouble – NPD.
4. Reposition the product.

The first is only acceptable if analysis of the market suggests that this is a temporary blip or that the market is no longer attractive. Incidentally, such an analysis is only too tempting for a company that resists change, and is so often a fool's paradise or a sanctuary for post rationalization. The second choice seems immediately the most attractive, appearing to call for a level of effort within the current capabilities and comfort zone, but is it enough, or is it even warranted? The third is a dramatic step but one that may already be too late. The fourth is less dramatic, but perhaps more challenging.

Augmentation

As products move through the growth stage, wise product managers will be on the look-out for opportunities to 'augment' their product. This may mean a range of activities including additional features and benefits, new design or styling, new packaging, or range extension. These are actions intended to give the product a 'kick', to set it on a new growth path away from the threat of maturity. The classic scenario is the 'new improved', whether it be soap powder or a motor car.

Cars are managed through this process to an increasingly pre-ordained plan. The launch model is quite basic, its novelty being enough to ensure success. As time goes by a stream of extras are applied, and things once optional become standard. A sure sign of a car approaching the end of its life cycle is when it carries every conceivable extra as the standard offer.

If we remember the adopters curve from Chapter 11, we will see the sense in such a strategy. The innovator's requirements are different from those of the early adopters, which are different again from those of the early majority. If product managers can identify the needs of these groups of customers, then they can plan the development of their product to meet them. The Japanese have long been regarded as experts in this practice of forward planning, a concept that has often been resisted by Western firms driven by a spirit of invention and technological expertise. Philips has been the source of more innovations in the electronics and hi-fi market than perhaps even they choose to recall – the reluctance being because of their failure to market so many of these new ideas well enough. If we look for a cause of their relatively poor track record we can see it in their apparent reluctance to manage the product life cycle. Too often they have launched a new product with a range of features and benefits more suited to an early majority audience, not the innovator, and too often an Asia Pacific competitor has captured the market with a more appropriate PLC strategy.

The concept of the core and the surround gives another insight into the strategy of augmentation. The first activities outside the core will be seen as differentiators by the market, but over time they become givens. The successful supplier must continually seek new differentiators, often searching further and further from the core, and in time these activities too will become givens. Doubtless the first petrol company to offer free plastic daffodils with its petrol stole a march on the competition, but soon it was the norm to pick up free gifts at the petrol station. Already the attachment of a grocery shop is almost a given. Now the search is on for yet more differentiators – cash machines, take-away meals, free newspapers and who yet knows what.

In the grand scheme of things, product augmentation is a relatively low-cost activity with attractive returns if done at the right time, and getting the timing right calls for a high degree of forward planning.

The product relaunch

Coca-Cola inadvertently relaunched their main product as Classic Coke back in 1985 after the failure of a new formulation Coke. The New Coke was a mistake, and a costly one, and the subsequent relaunch of the old product was a rearguard action, but nobody can doubt the new life they were able to breathe into an old product. Nothing had changed but for a logo and the word Classic, but after the outrage at New Coke the relaunch was greeted as a triumph and with much hindsight an act of genius!

When 'new' = bad and 'classic' = good

In January 2000 Subbuteo announced that their world-famous football game was to be withdrawn from the market. There was much talk of the attractions of video games and the like, and a good deal of news coverage of the announcement, and then a cry of protest from fans. By February 2000 the product was 'reprieved' amidst even more publicity. Famous footballers were called on to endorse the product – a vital ingredient for the predominantly young male audience – and sales of an old and mature product are set to see a revitalization.

An exaggerated death – Subbuteo

197

<table>
<tr>
<td>

How Kellogg's made an old story brand new

</td>
<td>

Kellogg's spent heavily in the 1990s on 'relaunching' Corn Flakes with a series of adverts that showed grown-ups 're-experiencing' the taste of the cereal as they took breakfast with their children. The messages were a clever combination of nostalgia and retro styling with simplicity and wholesomeness, all in a world of complexity and sophistication (which if we limit ourselves to breakfast cereals is, of course, largely the doing of Kellogg's!). An old and mature product was given a well-deserved boost based on values and qualities that were there all the time – they just needed restating.

</td>
</tr>
</table>

Range extension

Once there was white paint, but white paint was approaching maturity, so over the last 20 years it branched out. First there was brilliant white, then natural whites with just a hint of colour, ultra-white was fast on their tails, followed by one-coat white, classic white, romantic white and ever onward. Where once there was a single product, now there are a dozen. Such range extension is a common strategy in the fight against product maturity. Our beleaguered motor car might choose to revive its fortunes through the launch of new variations on the theme – an open top, a sports model, a diesel option.

The strategy can be played too far of course and the plethora of white paints led to confusion not only for the consumer but also the retailer taxed with ordering and displaying the many variants. Shelf space issues, a real-world factor, called a halt (or at least a slowdown) to some of the more rabid calls to 'Extend! Extend! Extend!'.

Sometimes the strategy can take the company far away from their original product. Virgin has come a long way from the original record label. Cosmopolitan has launched ranges of yoghurts and mineral water drinks. Dunhill is probably more noted for its up-market luggage and perfumes than it ever was for cigarettes. These are really examples of new product development, but at their outset perhaps they seemed more like simple range or brand extensions. The dividing line is important to note, however, as the statistics show without doubt the greater level of risk involved in genuine NPD.

New product development

Many of the examples cited in the sections on augmentation and extension might sound like new product development, and indeed they often are. One distinction that we might make to give clarity to the divide is to look at the NPD strategy designed to replace the original product. Why should companies want to cannibalize their own products deliberately? Perhaps the best answer is in order to get in first, before the competition, but this is not an easy concept for a business to accept, especially if its products are currently successful.

We need to revisit the PLC and redraw it, with the vertical axis measuring profit rather than sales volume or revenue. This is shown in Figure 12.4.

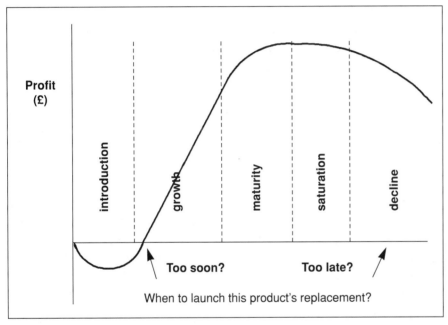

Figure 12.4 _The PLC and profit_

The question now is when to launch a new product. Many would vote for the maturity stage – the competition has entered the fray, perhaps the existing product is beginning to weaken, if cannibalization occurs then the loss is not so great. The problem with this timing becomes clear when we think of the PLC in profit terms.

A new product will require investment, a potential net loss, just at the time that profits are levelling out or even declining for the existing product. More than this, new product development will require sanction from senior management or the board. Will they sanction such expenditure when they look at your current business performance – maturity to saturation? We might add a third problem – NPD requires a great deal of corporate energy to succeed, energy that might just be starting to ebb away as the existing product enters maturity or saturation. And a final problem – NPD takes time, time to develop, time to launch, time to get established, and time is something you are fast running out of at the maturity stage. By waiting this late you are effectively raising the stakes on the success of your new product – if it fails, all is lost.

Very often the right time to launch a new product is while the existing one is still growing. Even though the launch will hasten the decline of a perfectly healthy product, consider the advantages. Profits are good, so investment can be accommodated. The business is still attractive, so the board will be happy to sanction your investment. Energy levels are still high, so the prospect for success is good. The only problem lies in that awful cliché, which should be banished from any business looking at its future: 'If it ain't broke, why fix it?' This cannot be the thinking of the product manager. Sure, your NPD may shorten the life of your current product, but isn't it better that you should be in control of that, rather than that your competitors should be? The challenge for marketers is taking the rest of the organization with them. This is really a question of inertia. If a business has been in the habit of NPD as prescribed here then the challenge will not be so great. If NPD is a rare thing, then watch out for the cries of 'If it ain't broke…'

NPD and 'stage-gate'

Watching out for the cries is of course not enough; it is much better to have a means of handling them in advance. The stage-gate process is often used by companies experienced in NPD as a means of assessing ideas and easing their development through the business. The exact process will be designed to be appropriate to the individual business, but there is a generic path described below.

Stage-gate is a process for managing the array of new ideas that come out of a market-orientated business. The closer to the market the business, the greater the pace of new ideas. How to prioritize, to ensure that only the best ideas get the inevitably limited resources available?

Stage-gate is also a process for ensuring the support of those functions that must contribute to NPD. If they are crying 'If it ain't broke...' then they won't be contributing as they should. Stage-gate ensures all are on board.

One warning, and an important one – design your process so that it speeds your best ideas to market and sends the poor ones back to the drawing board or into oblivion. Stage-gate is intended to quicken the pace of NPD, not hinder it, and if ever it starts to slow things down through committees and bureaucracy then it is time to change the process.

The generic path

Starting with an idea, a series of checks must be worked through, gates that say pass, stop, or think again. Perhaps it might look something like this:

- an idea;
- market research;
- analysis of the current and future position – PLC analysis;
- the customer proposition;
- issues such as cannibalisation and time to market;
- a detailed profit and loss case;
- performance criteria;
- technical feasibility;
- marketing sign-off;
- presentation of the technical and operational requirements;
- business sign-off;
- development;
- pre-launch checks, pilots, research, etc;
- launch;
- post-launch testing and review.

At any point the project can be sent back on a loop to an earlier stage, but heed the warning about slowing things down. Of course you need a process to weed out ideas that would be failures or would drain resources for poor return, and to ensure the successful launch of the good ideas, but above all else the process should be designed to speed your product to market. It is quite possible that over the next decade it will be 'speed to market' of new products that becomes the main beacon of competitive advantage – make sure stage-gate helps you to this goal rather than hindering you.

The rate of NPD

How fast the rate of NPD should be depends of course on the elements of the marketing model from Chapter 3 – what does the market demand, what is the competition up to and what can you cope with? Some businesses might see a decade go by between new product launches and be none the worse for it; it all depends. Rather than considering absolute timetables it is more helpful to consider the 'staging' of NPD. Figure 12.5 shows a 'perfect' scenario (though in only the most generic sense).

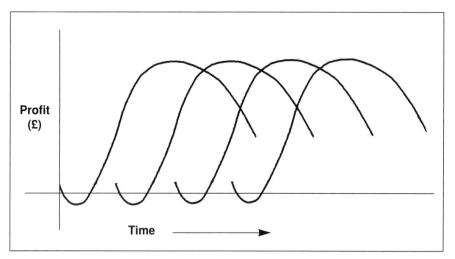

Figure 12.5   *PLC staging*

It is 'perfect' because the cost of investment of each new product launch is balanced by the profits of an existing product or range, and 'perfect' because the company has a balanced portfolio at any one time of launch products, those in growth, and those in maturity – a marketer's holy grail to be discussed further in the section on product portfolio management below.

Repositioning

Perhaps it is not a question of augmentation or NPD, but that your current product exists in the wrong market or segment. If analysis tells you that your own product's slow-down is the result of a similar slow-down in the total market, then the costs of augmentation or NPD will be hard to justify. Time to look for pastures new.

Lucozade is an excellent example. Time was when Lucozade was what your mother bought you when you were ill. Generations have grown up identifying the product with illness and recuperation. The brand had an excellent position in this segment, but the future was rather limited. SmithKline Beecham, the brand's owner, conducted a brilliant campaign over a number of years to reposition the product as a high-energy 'sports drink'. SB had identified the potential in this segment and they had a product with many of the necessary attributes. High-profile product endorsements from the likes of Daley Thompson were used to great effect alongside new packaging designs and new target retail outlets. Lucozade is still a favourite choice for those overcoming illness, but it now also occupies a position well away from the invalid's bedside table.

From sickness to health – the Lucozade story

The Lucozade success story is about more than a company with a substantial advertising budget. There were several requirements. First was an understanding of what the product and brand currently meant in the market, how it was positioned and how it was perceived. An understanding of the concept of perceptual mapping as described in Chapter 11 would have been important at this stage. Second was an understanding of where the product (and the market segment) sat on the PLC. Was there an attractive future? Would augmentation or range extension be enough? Was NPD an option? Third was a consideration of what opportunities existed in other market segments. At this point in the analysis the marketer had to think broadly, of existing segments *and* of potential segments. The high-energy sports drink was a relatively new concept, but one very suited to the circumstances of the time. Finally was the issue of budgets – yes, money matters – it is a matter of company capability.

PRODUCT DEVELOPMENT AND THE *CUSTOMER'S* PRODUCT LIFE CYCLE

Product improvement means different things at different moments in the life cycle. At the growth stage, improvement might mean quality; by maturity we might be looking more towards cost reduction and value through economy. This shift in the target for product developers can be a serious problem if R & D departments operate remotely from marketing departments, particularly as the lead times for some product improvement projects leave suppliers working on changes that were required years before and are now of little relevance. Translate this problem into a business-to-business environment where it is the customer's life cycle that needs understanding as much as your own, and the challenges become clear.

Intel – will the success continue?

For many years Intel have improved their chips by making them faster, as have competitors such as Advanced Micro Devices (AMD). Companies will develop a culture based on such experience – continuous improvement, with improvement defined as speed. While this is of huge benefit in the present, they must take great care not to allow this culture to blind them to the shifting targets brought by the customer's advancing product life cycle. As the PC market heads into maturity, will it still be speed, or might cost or service become more significant? Considering such questions is one of the many tasks of the marketer.

Watching the customer's market chain

How Intel aim to prosper by looking down the chain

Let's take this Intel example a little further and relate it to a notion discussed back in Chapters 3 and 7, the market chain. As the market matures Intel have to develop expertise well beyond their own manufacturing ability if they are to win the 'speed is best' battle. In order to persuade the PC manufacturer that speed matters, they must now influence the end user applications. Intel invests in companies that are developing applications where speed is of paramount importance – an example of influencing the chain beyond the immediate customer in order to support your own product development. So far so good, but a logjam has been reached. The Internet is now one of the key drivers of any PC manufacturer's strategy and here speed becomes an issue – the Internet is slow. It is the bandwidth available rather than the microprocessor that determines the kind of applications that can be used. Now Intel must look even further afield, for they depend on the development of more broadband access for the success of their 'speed is best' strategy.

The launch of the Pentium III Xeon microprocessor, Intel's most sophisticated to date, marks their attention to the customer's needs and PLC; the Pentium III Xeon is specifically designed to improve the performance of large Web sites and e-business applications. The benefit of such attention is clear: this is a high-margin area for Intel as compared with their lower-margin high-volume Celeron microprocessor line.

Product development cannot be carried out in a vacuum. The supplier must look well beyond its own R & D lab to understand the forces and dynamics in the market that will shape the nature and appropriateness of its product. Success for Intel is dependent on more than a slugging match over who has the fastest chip – first the debate must be made a relevant one.

PRODUCT PORTFOLIO MANAGEMENT

The CONNECT case study (Chapter 9) looked at a company with a tight range of products, which was attempting to launch a rather different range in a rather different market. Undoubtedly the existing market was at a late stage of maturity, with a number of external circumstances accelerating it towards decline. The new products had plenty of potential but also plenty of challenges. Which range deserved the lion's share of the company's attention?

Most businesses manage a range of products and the questions of priorities and resource allocation are continually pressing ones. Very often the answers boil down to the powers of persuasion of individual product managers or the personal preferences of the boss. Sometimes this gets the right result, but who would want to depend on it?

Managing a portfolio of products is undoubtedly harder than managing a single-product company, but if done well can lead to a far more secure and successful future. An excellent tool is at hand – the Boston box, complete with its exotic language of stars, cows, dogs and problem children. You may have heard these labels before, and if so don't allow familiarity to blind you to the significant value of this tool and its analysis. This is really one of those cases where familiarity has sometimes bred contempt, to the loss of all concerned.

The Boston box shown in Figure 12.6, developed by the Boston Consulting Group, seeks to guide the marketer in allocating resources to a portfolio of products. The tool can also be used to compare segments, markets, territories, businesses, even customers. Here we will use it in the context of a product portfolio. It is perhaps the classic four-box matrix of marketing, and none the less powerful for that.

The vertical axis measures the future growth rate of products in the portfolio, a judgement of their position on their PLCs. If you are comparing a portfolio of products all in the same market segment, then it will be the relative growth prospects of each PLC that principally concerns you. For a portfolio of products across a range of segments then the relative growth rates of those segments will also come into play. The horizontal axis measures the products' market share with high share to the left and low share to the right.

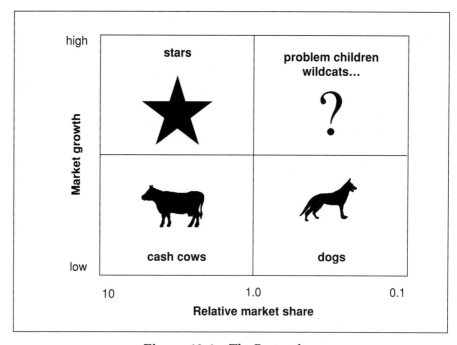

Figure 12.6 *The Boston box*

Why these two measures? We will argue their limitations a little later, but for now, growth is used as an indicator of attractiveness and share is used as an indicator of strength in the market.

A product in the top left box, a *star*, is clearly a good thing – there is future growth potential and you have a commanding position in the market with this product.

A product in the top right has a question mark against it – can this *problem child* be nurtured into a star? Can this *wildcat* be tamed? It occupies an attractive market or segment but perhaps you are a relative newcomer, or there is very strong competition. Will effort here be worth it and, with limited resources, which of the products in this box should get the investment?

A product in the bottom left, a *cash cow*, is there to be milked. Your high share indicates a strong position but the growth has gone – a place to be looking to reduce high-cost resources and effort.

The bottom right box contains the *dogs*, products to be divested or strictly managed at low cost of effort or resource.

It might appear from this rather simplistic summary that you should want all your products to be stars. But stop to consider what sort of business this would give you. Indeed, what sort of business would you have if all your products occupied just one box?

- All stars – apart from requiring huge investment to keep pace with success, this is perhaps a business with a cloud over its future. Products reach maturity. What then?
- All problem children – a business with a promising future, if only it had income to invest today!
- All cash cows – a business with plenty of cash, but to what long-term purpose?
- All dogs – a business soon to be out of business.

The ideal business will have products in at least the star, problem child and cash cow boxes – a balanced portfolio, just like a balanced investment portfolio. The sense of this becomes clearer if we consider the cash flow implications of products in each box as shown in Figure 12.7.

This analysis tells the same story, in a different way, to that in Figure 12.5, with the balance of PLCs staged over time. The positions are of course rather stereotyped. Some stars will have large positive

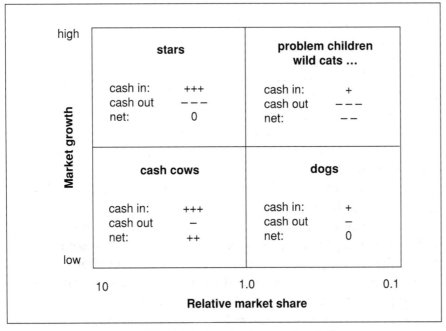

Figure 12.7 _The Boston box and cash flow_

cash flows, but it is not uncommon for stars to cost almost as much as they reap. Similarly some dogs will be positive or negative, but the point to consider is the need for a balanced portfolio. A business without cash cows will need to borrow heavily from outside. Cash cows provide the means to invest in the problem children, to turn them into stars, and as sure as eggs are eggs, today's stars will become tomorrow's cash cows.

This analysis is valuable in so many ways – allocation of resources, emphasis in the marketing mix (problem children are heavy on promotional effort, cash cows need careful price management), even determining the ideal product manager for each product. A cash cow might need an accountant's approach to cost control, an approach that might stifle a problem child to death, while a star calls for more careful management than might seem necessary – big products can steal resource and profits like nothing else in a business (except perhaps big customers). Table 12.1 indicates some generic strategies and activities for products in each of the four boxes.

Limitations of the Boston box

The simplicity of the Boston box is both its main attraction and its main failing. On the plus side, most businesses can make the measurements and comparisons required – growth and share, but on the minus side, is growth the only determinant of an attractive product or market? Must you have a big market share to have a strong position? Of course not, but here we see one of the strengths of the analysis rather than a weakness, the way in which it raises these very questions and encourages us towards a more sophisticated model – the DPM.

THE DIRECTIONAL POLICY MATRIX

A development of the Boston box is the directional policy matrix (DPM), already discussed in Chapters 7, 10 and 11. The DPM is a key marketing tool. It can be used, like the Boston box, to analyse and manage a portfolio of markets, segments, products, or customers. The essential difference from the Boston box is the way the DPM (shown in Figure 12.8) allows for a number of factors to be represented on the two axes, under two general headings. The vertical axis

Table 12.1 *The Boston box – generic strategies and activities*

Activity	Star	Problem Child	Cash Cow	Dog
Strategy	maintain growth	select priorities for invest	maximize earnings	divest or manage for cash
Share	maintain or grow	invest to increase	maintain	focus on profit rather than share
Product	augmentation and extension	NPD	rationalize	rationalize
Price	price leader	penetration	stabilize or raise	raise
Promotion	high level	aggressive, for share	reduce, for maintenance	minimize
Place	broaden	focused	maintain	rationalize
Costs	focus on economies of scale	controlled budgets	focus on supply chain costs	aggressive reduction
Working Capital	tighten controls	increase	reduce debtors	aggressively reduce
Production	expand	expand and invest	maximize 'occupacity' and efficiency	free up utilization
R & D	broaden application	expand, trials and pilots	managed projects	none?
Personnel	upgrade in key areas	increase, training and development	maintain and reward for efficiency	reduce
Investment	fund maintained growth	fund growth	limit fixed investment	none?

is a combination of factors that measure attractiveness. The horizontal combines factors to measure your relative strength in the market.

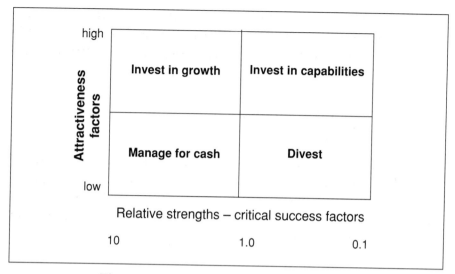

Figure 12.8   *The directional policy matrix*

'Market attractiveness' factors

We are asking here, if considering products, does our product occupy an attractive market segment? Is it a good place to be, and that must of course relate to your long-term goals as a business. We are considering here what kind of opportunities and market needs will be attractive to us – the right-hand side of the marketing model described in Chapter 2.

Some examples might include:

- Size – volume, value, profit opportunity.
- Growth potential – volume, value, profit opportunity.
- Financial stability.
- Ease of access – geography, openness.
- Portfolio fit – does the product fit with others in a range?
- Is your product 'valued'?
- Is there an opportunity for competitive advantage?
- What is the level of competition – low being attractive.
- Investment required.
- Specific customer demand.

Your own business circumstances must determine your selection, and the weighting you might give to individual factors. Whatever your final choice, you must be able to apply these factors to each of the products in the portfolio, measuring them against one another. In identifying these factors you will go a long way to identifying the sort of business you want to be, a useful exercise in itself.

'Relative strength' factors

These factors will measure how the market or segment perceives your capability, product by product. They are the determinants of your success or failure and will be unique by market and segment. Although we are dealing here with factors on the left-hand side of the marketing model (Chapter 2), internal capabilities, we must take great care to view them through the eyes of the market. The market's perceptions are more important than your assertions, whether grounded in fact or not.

Identifying these factors may well be harder than identifying the market attractiveness factors, and not surprisingly. Proper identification may call for market research, analysis of customer perceptions and satisfaction ratings, and if it does, then the exercise will have been useful even if taken no further.

While for market attractiveness factors the purpose is to compare your products against a common list, here you will need to measure each product against its competitors. Each product may be measured on a different mix of criteria, so each will require its own list.

Some examples might include:

- market share;
- brand awareness;
- innovation;
- price;
- costs;
- service requirements;
- quality requirements;
- investment in the market;
- value in use – value in the supply chain, total acquisition cost, etc;
- long-term sustainability;
- experience.

Compiling the analysis

The following tables are designed to help you compile your analysis. The attached CD ROM has a software package to help with the process, but it is no bad idea to commence with a paper exercise, however rough, for several reasons: it quickly identifies the black holes in your knowledge of the market, it makes a team-wide analysis easier to facilitate and most importantly it engages the brain rather than your typing fingers.

Attractiveness

Table 12.2   *Attractiveness factors*

	Products									
Attractiveness Factor										
1										
2										
3										
4										
5										
6										
Total										

Average score:
(total of all scores divided by number of products rated)

- Enter your products across the top of the grid shown in Table 12.2.
- It is advisable to select a list of about six factors – of course more may exist, but this will help to focus the analysis.
- Enter a score from 1 to 10 for each product, against each attractiveness factor. The higher the score, the better the fit of the product.
- Calculate the average score. This will be used to place each product on the matrix, higher or lower than the average.

Table 12.3 *Relative strength against the competition*

Product:	Competitors				
Critical Success Factor	You				
1					
2					
3					
4					
5					
6					
Total					

Relative strength

- For each product under consideration, identify six 'critical success factors' (CSFs) that represent the market's criteria for choosing a product. These are the factors that determine your success or failure against the competition.
- Complete one table (Table 12.3) for each product rated in Table 12.2.
- Insert your name and the names of your competitors across the top of the table, and enter a score from 1 to 10 for each, against each factor. Remember to ensure that this scoring reflects the market's perception, not your opinion!

Completing the matrix

Using the information from these two tables you can place each customer on the matrix shown in Figure 12.8.

From Table 12.2, if a product scores higher than the average score, then it will be in one of the two upper boxes, and if lower than the average, it will be in one of the two lower boxes. To identify which of the two, use the results from Table 12.3. Where your product scores better than your best competitor you will occupy the left-hand box, and the right-hand if you score worse.

And the outcome – perhaps not a revelation, or maybe so?

Whatever, the true value of such analysis is in the understanding that it generates, and that comes from the research required to complete the analysis. Once again we see the stages of the marketing process from Chapter 3 operating in sync with each other.

Figure 12.9 gives an example of a completed DPM for a selection of the training and consultancy products and services from my own company, INSIGHT Marketing and People, as seen about three years ago.

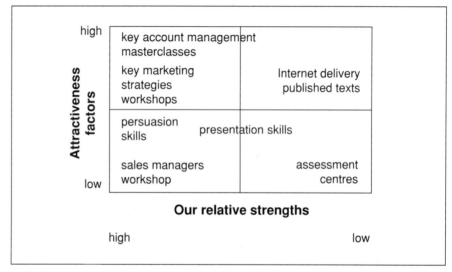

Figure 12.9 *INSIGHT product DPM*

An interesting debate develops at this point; is the wildcat product, training via the Internet, a new product development or an augmentation to existing products? There was certainly a need to invest in new capability, but in fact the development of this capability doesn't lead to a replacement of existing products, but is rather an enhancement of them. Traditional face-to-face training will continue, but the Internet will allow huge improvements to its efficiency and effectiveness through pre-event preparation and continuing post-event involvement and implementation. Sounds like an augmentation?

13

Pricing strategies

Price is probably the issue that most frightens marketers – get it wrong and you're stuck with it. How can you put a price up if you start too low and find that you're giving it away? Aim too high and you're dead before you start. That's what it can feel like when trying to fix a price on a new product; of course it is an important decision, but there are plenty of tools to help you get it right.

PROFITABILITY – PRICE, VOLUME, OR COSTS?

Before looking at them, let's just raise the stakes a little bit more and see why pricing decisions are so important to your profitability.

You are the marketing manager for a large company and your board has just given you your profit target for next year, a 15 per cent improvement without any damage to the long-term business. Unfortunately you have no new products in the pipeline so your choices are slim – sell more of your existing products, reduce costs, or raise prices.

Of course, these choices are not independent of one another. Sell more? Sure, perhaps by dropping the price. Reduce costs? But might that damage quality and so the price you can get or the volume you can sell? Raise prices? With what impact on volume?

A good place to start is with an understanding of the relative effects of changes to prices, volumes, or costs – there are perhaps some surprises. Let's get back to your problem, the 15 per cent increase in profit. Your business sells that world-famous 'widget', 200,000 of them last year at a profit of £50,000 (see Table 13.1). You have to improve profit to £57,500 and have the three options of volume, price, or costs (and for the sake of this case they will be thought of as working in isolation of one another). Option 1 is a volume increase, option 2 is the price rise and option 3 is the reduction in costs, each assuming all other things remain the same.

Table 13.1 *Comparing changes to volume, price and cost*

	Current Business	Option 1 More Volume	Option 2 Raise Price	Option 3 Reduce Cost
Units Sold	200,000	230,000	200,000	200,000
Cost per Unit	£0.75	£0.75	£0.75	£0.7125
Price per Unit	£1.00	£1.00	£1.0375	£1.00
Turnover	£200,000	£230,000	£207,500	£200,000
Profit per Unit	£0.25	£0.25	£0.2875	£0.2875
Gross Profit	£50,000	£57,500	£57,500	£57,500
Change needed		+15%	+3.75%	–5%

Of course, in the real world we cannot assume that all other things will stay the same, but the example shows something that surprises many people – the price rise required is much lower in relation to the volume required.

There is a simple equation that will help you make this comparison. If you ask the question, what price increase will bring the same profit improvement (all else being equal) as a given volume increase, the answer is:

$$\frac{\% \text{ gross margin} \times \% \text{ volume increase}}{100} = \% \text{ price increase required}$$

(Gross margin in this case means the sales price minus raw material costs.)

Ask the question the other way: what volume increase will bring the same profit improvement (all else being equal) as a given price increase? And the equation is:

$$\frac{\% \text{ price increase} \times 100}{\% \text{ gross margin}} = \% \text{ volume increase required}$$

A good ready reckoner, but let's not forget the real question: which of these three options is most likely to succeed, or what combination? This will get us thinking about the dynamics between these three factors in our own market-place. Lowering your costs, perhaps by bullying a supplier or two, will often be the easiest option. 'Suppliers are the soft underbelly of the market', a customer of mine used to tell me, usually just before demanding a price reduction to help _him_ meet his profit targets. Easiest, but perhaps not always the best in the long run. What happens when the supplier fights back, and the next rise is bigger to compensate for its short-term loss? What if word gets round about your success and every one of your competitors follows suit, and some of them reduce their prices based on these lower costs?

If we compare price to volume as our route to profit, we can start to ask: what extra effort might be required for more volume, and at what cost? We can also ask: what extra value will customers need to perceive in our product for them to pay a higher price? We are now in a more intelligent debate – no stock answers, but at least we are asking the right questions.

Trading price for volume

Let's now link price and volume together in a different scenario, cutting price to drive extra volume. Suppose you choose to drop your price by 5 per cent. What extra volume do you need to sell in order to make the same level of profit? An impossible question? Of course there are variables to consider – what if the extra volume drives your costs down? Most importantly, the answer depends on what level of profit margin you are working on before the price cut.

Table 13.2 shows the volume increase required (in the centre boxes) for any given price cut, across a range of percentage gross margins (assuming there to be no economies of scale from the higher volumes gained).

Table 13.2 *Volume increase required to match a given price cut*

% Discount Given	Current % Profit Margin							
	10	15	20	25	30	35	40	50
2%	25	15	11	9	7	6	5	4
3%	43	25	18	14	11	9	8	6
4%	67	36	25	19	15	13	11	9
5%	100	50	33	25	20	17	14	11
7.5%	300	100	60	43	33	27	23	18
10%		200	100	67	50	40	33	25
15%			300	150	100	60	43	33
20%				400	300	133	100	66

There is also an equation that will help you calculate the increase in volume required for a given price cut (assuming no economies of scale result):

$$\frac{\% \text{ price cut} \times 100}{\% \text{ gross margin} - \% \text{ price cut}} = \% \text{ volume increase required}$$

Perhaps the significant thing here is the surprisingly large volume growth required for relatively small price cuts, and at low profit margins the growth required is huge. The question raised must be – can you achieve such growth? If the answer is no, then don't chase prices down in pursuit of a volume-driven profit. We have a saying in my business: 'The pursuit of volume is vanity; the pursuit of profit is sanity.' If the answer is yes and in addition that greater volume will bring economies of scale and so lower costs, then a price for volume strategy may just work – provided that the competition doesn't follow suit, which of course it almost invariably does!

The table raises two other important points: the significance of high margins, and the importance of *knowing* those margins.

Low-margin businesses are very vulnerable to erosions of price, unless there are major opportunities for volume growth and significant economies of scale in that higher volume. Price wars can be fatal for such businesses; indeed, price will sometimes be used as a weapon for putting a low-margin competitor out of business. Most markets see price wars at some time, but they hurt most in low-margin environments such as at the petrol pump or on the shelves of the CTN (confectionery, tobacco and news) retailer. So why do they get started there? Often because the forecasts of volume growth are inflated or quite simply the sums are not properly understood.

Discounting is a dangerous game at the best of times, but a business that does this and yet doesn't know its own margins is flying blind. Most businesses will know their overall gross margin – the annual accounts will tell them that, but what about measuring margins by product, or segment, or customer? If you don't know your margins to this level, and you are involved in discounting or rebates, then this should become a priority action for you to find out.

Knowing your gross margins is one thing, but what about knowing the additional effect of your fixed costs on the profit of particular products? Without such knowledge some very strange decisions may be taken in pursuit of profit.

The business that went bust in pursuit of profit

Unfortunately most businesses 'marmalade' their fixed costs across products. Table 13.3 shows a typical allocation of costs to a four-product business, with the apparent outcome for net profit by product.

Table 13.3 *'Marmalading' of fixed costs (1)*

	Product A	Product B	Product C	Product D	Total
Gross Profit	100	80	60	50	290
Overheads	60	60	60	60	240
Net Profit	40	20	0	–10	50

The results suggest that product D is a loss-maker and so in the pursuit of overall profit the product is deleted. Unfortunately, overheads do not reduce immediately by the 60 that had been allocated to product D, but they do go down by 30, and people give themselves a slap on the back for a smart decision, the results of which are shown in Table 13.4.

Table 13.4 *'Marmalading' of fixed costs (2)*

	Product A	Product B	Product C	Product D	Total
Gross Profit	100	80	60	xxxx	290
Overheads	70	70	70	xxxx	210
Net Profit	30	10	–10	xxxx	30

The company is still in profit, but now product C is apparently a loss-maker. The same lack of knowledge of the true allocation of fixed costs is apparent and so unfortunately the same error is repeated and product C is deleted, though 'of course' the fixed costs do not reduce in line...

Table 13.5 *'Marmalading' of fixed costs (3)*

	Product A	Product B	Product C	Product D	Total
Gross Profit	100	80	xxxx	xxxx	180
Overheads	90	90	xxxx	xxxx	180
Net Profit	10	–10	xxxx	xxxx	0

I think you can guess what happens next.

FINDING THE RIGHT PRICE

As already noted, this mathematical analysis provides few answers, but it does prompt us to start asking the right questions. Some businesses don't worry too much about such questions, finding pricing a simple task to be handled by the accountants. Very often these are the sorts of businesses that are wedded to *cost-plus* pricing, and while that is very simple and straightforward as a methodology, such businesses will often find themselves in severe trouble when the environment changes around them. The classic case is of course British manufacturing industry in the 1970s.

For many of the long-dead businesses that failed to weather the storm of the 70s, price was directly related to their costs of manufacture. This made price calculations relatively easy, but when low-price Japanese imports started to arrive, when oil prices took off through the roof and wage demands chased inflation into double figures, sometimes the wheels of business just fell off. Manufacturers had to reduce prices to stay competitive (for most saw no salvation in 'added value' or 'differentiation', other than through _being British_ of course) and following the mechanic of linking price to costs, they had to reduce their costs in line. But here was the problem: compared to the Japanese the costs of production were huge and however much they might chase productivity they always lagged behind. Oil prices and wage demands added to the problem and so one after another the manufacturers started to strip not just costs out of their operations but also quality, service, reliability and, in the end, trustworthiness. The downward spiral was often fast and terminal. The dying British manufacturers' products were just not valued as much as the thriving Japanese's.

Yet cost-plus pricing is still widely used today, so we had best understand its principle, advantages and disadvantages, and compare it to three other methodologies – _marginal_ pricing, _market-based_ pricing and _value_ pricing.

COST-PLUS PRICING

Provided that you know the costs involved in providing your product or service, this is a fairly straightforward method of pricing. Take those costs and add the margin you require – instant pricing. The method has three things to recommend it:

1. It forces you to examine your costs.
2. It is relatively easy (even accountants can do it).
3. It ensures that you make the intended profit – _provided you can sell at this price._

After that, the negatives tend to outweigh the positives.

First, who is to say that you can achieve the margin you aim for? If the customer will not pay, do you sacrifice your margin by reducing price, or by improving the offer and so increasing your costs? If so, then why use this method in the first place?

Second, who is to say that you couldn't achieve a higher price and margin? The cost-plus method tends to make the supplier lazy; satisfied with meeting its target, it celebrates and looks no further.

Third, cost-plus encourages the supplier to focus on its own costs (the benefit noted above) but sometimes to the exclusion of looking at the market. For a business determined to drive costs down and use price to penetrate the market (see the section on competitive pricing strategies below) this may be less of a problem, but for any business seeking to differentiate its offer this could be a very serious failing.

Fourth, what happens when the customers discover your method? Professional buyers are trained to ask for cost breakdowns; they want to know your costs, and so your margin. Armed with that they are in control. They can use the discount table (Table 13.2) to tell you what price cut you can give in return for what volume increase. They can tell you that one of your costs, let's say technical service, is of no relevance to them, so please remove it from the price calculation and reduce the price accordingly. Quite simply, the customers are in control of the price debate and slowly but surely determine *your* pricing strategy. They may even seek to argue that your percentage margin is much greater than theirs and is that fair?

This last point is almost always bogus – comparing apples with pears – as businesses at different points of the market chain will work on very different percentage profit margins, because of their different circumstances and dynamics. The supermarket may make only a few percentage points on a product on which the manufacturer makes 30 per cent and a raw material supplier might make 50 per cent on their part of the product, but the dynamics of these three businesses are such that all remain happy with their lot. In the end it should be remembered that you don't bank percentages, you bank money.

This is not an issue solely for business-to-business or service marketers. Consumers, spurred on by consumer 'champions', are not particularly sympathetic to the suppliers' need for profit. They find it very easy to see a mark-up of 100 per cent (a margin of 50 per cent) as profiteering. Note the outrage sometimes occasioned by press stories that a restaurant chain, for instance, buys its wine direct from the vineyard and sells it for three or four times the price. Consumers often don't like what they hear from such cost breakdowns, but nor do they appreciate the dynamics of running a restaurant. If they knew the net margins, the other costs, the problems of peaks and troughs in business and all the rest, they might appreciate more the restaurateur's needs – but they don't. A little knowledge can be dangerous, and perceptions of a supplier can be damaged, unfairly perhaps, but damaged all the same.

The nightmare scenario...

A supplier of a prestige range of cosmetics and toiletries to a retail chain is having a hard time with the customer on its price. 'You never do anything for us,' the buyer asserts, 'and you charge a fortune.' Up against the wall, the supplier may be tempted to argue back, 'That's not fair. Don't forget our sales and merchandising force. They call on all your stores, take orders, build displays, offer advice and training, handle problems. Perhaps you don't realize that just that sales force alone costs us over £100,000 a year.'

The customer says nothing until three months later when it sits down to negotiate the next year's terms. 'We understand that your sales team costs you £100,000. Starting next month we no longer need it to call – we will do our own ordering. Instead, we would like the £100,000 as a discount or rebate.'

The nightmare gets worse. The supplier removes its sales force (it has no choice as they are banned from the store) and increases the customer's 'advertising support'. Three months later it finds that its sales have slumped. Its products are in less attractive parts of the store, there are gaps on the shelves, and complaints and problems are not being resolved, except expensively. It goes back to the customer and asks to be allowed to put its sales force back in. 'Sure,' says the customer, 'but you can't have your advertising support money back.'

The customer 'unbundled' the supplier's package, and worse, knew the costs involved in that unbundling. In truth it valued the sales force highly, but in pursuit of a significant financial gain for a short-term loss in service and sales it was prepared to 'forget' that value, at least in conversation with the supplier.

MARGINAL PRICING

For some businesses marginal pricing is just an occasional tactic rather than a long-term pricing methodology, but for others it is part of their everyday life. Let's return to the business described in Table 13.1, the world-famous widget manufacturer. They buy items for £0.75 and sell them for £1.00. They have a gross profit of £0.25 per widget or 25 per cent, the gross profit being what is left after subtracting the *variable costs*. We didn't discuss the other costs of this business, the *fixed costs* that carry on regardless of whether they sell their widgets or not. Let's say that this business has fixed costs of £30,000, or a further £0.15 per widget. This means that their net profit is £0.10 per widget or 10 per cent.

Now let's suppose that they have difficulty with a particular customer in getting their full price of £1. The customer offers to pay £0.90 and the supplier accepts, happy with the deal. How can they be happy when we have just seen that after variable and fixed costs are taken into account they only make £0.10 profit per item? This deal sees them making no profit at all!

The answer is marginal pricing. The £0.15 per widget fixed costs will exist whether they sell widgets or not. In fact, if they don't sell 200,000 widgets then the fixed costs per unit will go up, as £30,000 has to be divided across fewer items sold. By accepting a price of £0.90 the supplier is making no profit, but they are *contributing* money towards their costs.

There are occasions when such a policy will be very wise indeed. If they are to be left with surplus capacity they may as well use it and get some revenue in as a contribution towards fixed costs. Airlines and hotels practise this form of pricing with standby tickets or late arrival offers at reception. If the seat will be empty, then why not fill it with someone whose ticket price will at least contribute towards some of the airline's fixed costs? If the bedroom will be empty, then why not fill it with someone who may spend money in the bar or the restaurant? Of course, that person will cause the variable costs of selling the product or service to be incurred – the in-flight meal, the laundry bill – but provided that the price exceeds these items then the supplier will be making a contribution towards fixed costs.

Equally, there are circumstances when such a policy can run out of control. Salespeople armed with the contribution theory of marginal pricing can justify discounts that leave you selling everything on this basis! Hotels cope with this problem by having an allocated number of rooms available at marginal prices, to be sold only at the end of the day. Sometimes however they will calculate in advance how many such rooms to sell and promote them as special offers. This can work provided that their forecasting systems are good and they do not find themselves discounting rooms that could otherwise have been sold at full price. Airlines do something similar when they sell tickets in bulk at much reduced prices to travel agents. The critical issue is calculating correctly how many seats will be sold at full price and so how many can be discounted without loss.

Perhaps the worst scenario for marginal pricing is when it is managed so loosely that customers realize that they need never pay the full price again, whatever the circumstances of the purchase. The key to marginal pricing is in its control, and this is a real issue for the marketer.

MARKET-BASED PRICING

Market-based pricing in its purest form is selling at whatever price the market will accept. Economists will talk of supply and demand and the magic point at which they are in equity so that the perfect price emerges. Rarely are real markets so predictable as the graphs used to depict supply and demand, but the principle is a good place to start the discussion of market-based pricing. Figure 13.1 shows a typical supply and demand situation with supply curve A and the resultant price A.

If supply is increased with no increase in demand, as shown by the intersection of supply curve B with the demand curve, the price goes down to B. The amount the price goes down depends on what the economists call the elasticity of demand. If the demand curve is very

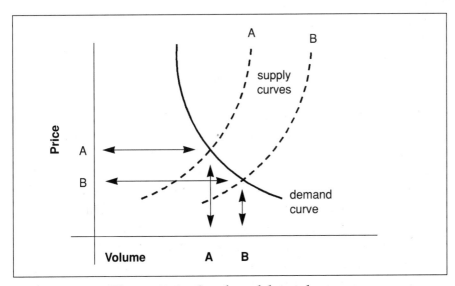

Figure 13.1 *Supply and demand curves*

steep, this means that price changes very little as demand changes; if it is shallow then prices shift a lot as demand goes up or down. What makes a demand curve steep or shallow? Some products are very price-sensitive – 10 per cent off house prices might drive demand sky high (represented by a shallow curve), while other decreases have less effect – 10 per cent off bread will not see us rushing to the stores (represented by a steep curve).

Supply and demand curves are only a start; they represent 'perfect' situations with no external complications. In the real world things are more complex, as neither suppliers nor customers can be relied on to behave as the textbooks say they should!

If there is a market for 100 units of a product and only one supplier, and that supplier has a capacity to make 80 units, the outcome will be in effect an auction to the highest bidder and price will move upwards. This is what happens when supply lags behind demand. In such a situation a competitor will doubtless see that there is profit to be had and will enter the fray with its capacity of, say, 40 units. All at once, supply is greater than demand and prices will fall as the two competitors start to slug it out for the customers' business. The first supplier might try to hold out for a higher price on at least 60 units (the volume demanded that cannot be supplied by the competitor) and may even choose to sell only 60, but if it seeks to sell its full capacity then prices will have to come down.

In the sole-supplier scenario above there are of course factors that will limit the supplier's ability to charge whatever price it wants. First of all it will test the 'elasticity' of the demand for its product – just how far it can stretch the price before the demand disappears either in pursuit of a lower-priced alternative solution or just to do nothing at all.

Secondly, it will have to consider the effect its price will have on the customers' perceptions – accusations of profiteering come to mind. An intriguing example of market pricing (or at least one said to be under consideration) involves a trial by Coca-Cola of a new vending machine in Japan. The machine is sensitive to the outside temperature, and as the mercury climbs so does the price of the drink inside the machine! A spokesperson for Coca-Cola has said that they have 'no plan to put them in the market-place.' If they did then this would be the principle of supply and demand applied with ruthless rigour, but at the possible cost of consumer trust. Market pricing is always working at this edge, and 'getting what you can get' can sometimes tip over into 'taking advantage'.

Some years back on the BBC _Troubleshooters_ programme, Sir John Harvey Jones was famously agitated by Morgan Cars' insistence on making only six cars per week leading to a waiting list as long as six years. Just as famously he was asked (politely) to leave on the grounds that such demand versus supply did wonders for prices. Morgan has chosen to increase production in recent times, though rather ironically this is now against a picture of declining demand. The market has changed, perceptions have altered and the old Morgan is not the catch it used to be – the economies of supply and demand have shifted and Morgan must grow its appeal with the launch of a new model, the Aero 8 – only time will tell.

The rationale of rationing

The protective price umbrella

A third factor that limits the extent to which your price can be anything you choose is the incentive your price gives the competitors to enter the market.

Stretching the market price to its highest level, especially when done by a dominant supplier, will sometimes provide a protective price _umbrella_ beneath which smaller suppliers can enter the market. This is a scenario experienced by IBM in the 1970s and 80s when their high market price (they were of course pretty much the only supplier of any standing at one time) allowed new entrants to gain a foothold by pricing below that level for a product and service that, if at first might have been inferior, would soon be comparable if not better.

The IBM umbrella

The attraction of having a greater demand than the supply available is such that suppliers will seek to limit supply by various means. A notorious example was of course the cartel of oil-supplying countries that rationed supply in the 1970s and managed prices upwards by massive leaps and bounds. A less dramatic scenario would be where a supplier simply chooses to remove some of its production capacity from the market. Such supply side initiatives are less common however than the demand side initiatives, which are after all the very stuff of marketing. Segmentation is practised in order to define groups of customers for whom a unique (and therefore limited) offer will be presented. If all suppliers segment the market in the same way then the effect is much reduced, but a novel method of segmentation (see Chapter 11 for examples) will serve to manage supply and demand in the supplier's favour.

Market pricing and the product life cycle

Chapter 12 introduces the idea of the product life cycle and the challenge to the marketer of revitalizing or replacing mature products. One reason for doing this is of course the question of price. If we think on the broader scale not just of products but of markets, we will see that a mature market is by definition one that is supplied by a number of competing suppliers with increasingly similar offers. The effect on price is to push it downward, and this process speeds dramatically if maturity moves into saturation. The market price for a product is determined by its life cycle – high at launch and reducing through maturity, but it does not have to be a slave to that cycle. The millions spent on 'whiter than white', 'new blue white' and 'revolutionary new white technology' soap powders are spent in pursuit of revitalizing a mature product life cycle. If the result is the ability to charge a premium (or gain significant market share by not charging a premium) then the augmentation strategy is a success – provided it all outweighs the cost of the activity.

Another escape is to launch an entirely new product. This will of course have an impact on the existing product (cannibalization) so it is important to consider the pricing strategy of such a move. Should the new product have a premium? Might it be possible to raise the price of the old product as it declines, simply because it might be possible to limit supply against a residual demand?

VALUE PRICING

One way to avoid the accusation of 'taking advantage' is to base your price not simply on what you *can* get, but on what you *should* get. This is the fourth pricing methodology we will discuss – value pricing.

Price, costs, or value?

What is a price, and how does it differ from costs, or from value?

A price is simply a marker, a point at which you are happy to trade. This is something quite different from costs. Customers' costs in buying your product might go well beyond the price itself. It will cost them money to find you, to deal with you, to put through the paperwork required to buy from you and to pay your bill. After that there are plenty more costs – storing your product, making use of it, repairing it, replacing it, disposing of it. What a purchaser would call 'costs in use' can make the original price look quite insignificant. And herein lies a clue for the supplier pitching for a price. Customers (at least ones who care about costs) will gladly pay a higher price for a product that will reduce their costs in use, providing that the savings outweigh the premium.

Consider your pricing strategy in the following scenario. You sell heavy-duty electric pumps used by a variety of manufacturing companies in a variety of plants. Your price is £40,000 and has been for some time. One of your customers has just informed you that there is a new kid on the block with a similar pump, selling at £36,000. What do you do? First you ask some questions.

- Is it the same specification as yours? More or less it seems.
- Is the supplier reputable? Very.
- Does its pump use the same amount of electricity? I'm afraid it does – no cost in use savings there.

So where does that leave you – cutting your price or losing the sale? A little more homework might find you a solution. As a good market-focused supplier you have of course good relationships with your customers and a few more questions furnish you with some interesting data. Over a five-year period, the average life of a pump, the costs in use look something like those shown in Table 13.6.

Armed with this data what would you do? Provided you had the capability, wouldn't redesigning your pump to save energy used be of potentially greater value to the customer than a simple price reduction? Sure, it might cost you to do this, and might mean a more expensive pump, but wouldn't a pump selling at £44,000 that reduced energy costs by 10 per cent be a good trade?

Here we come to two important points. First, price is simply one of the four Ps in the marketing mix, and by varying the mix it is possible to change the price. Many marketers maintain that the four Ps are

Table 13.6 *Costs in use – the pump*

Item	Total Cost over 5 years
Purchase Price	£40,000
Spares	£5,000
Installation Costs	£40,000
Energy Consumption	£230,000
Maintenance	£35,000
Disposal	£4,000
Total Costs in Use	£354,000

simply three Ps – product, promotion and place – that you juggle in order to justify the one P – price.

The second point introduces the third item from the trio that headed this section, and not before time – value. If price is simply a marker, and if costs are a combination of all the various prices of all the different services and activities encountered along the way, then value is what customers perceive they get from the whole exercise, and as such is by far the most important of the three terms. It is a justifiable criticism to make of the four Ps model that, in seeking the symmetry of a P for price, the marketer has often been focusing on the wrong thing. Shouldn't we be focusing on the C for costs to customers, or even on the V for value they receive? This section should perhaps be renamed 'Value strategies' instead of 'Pricing strategies', because only through getting your customers to perceive the value of your offer can you hope to charge any price at all.

We can take this notion further. If customers buy on value, not on price (and only the most ardent price hound does otherwise – you know the sort, 'I bought this *thing* in the sale, not sure what it is, but it was a bargain'), then if you can influence how they make their value judgements in your favour, perhaps you can command a significant price premium.

Figure 13.2 shows the different prices of a range of office printers. Based on price alone the Panasonic will win every time, but Kyocera aim to play a different game. It is not the price of the printer that matters, they say, but the total costs in use of cartridges, toner, etc. If that is taken into account, then the Kyocera wins through. Further than that, if they can persuade customers to use the cost per page printed as their measure of value, then the price of their printer is of

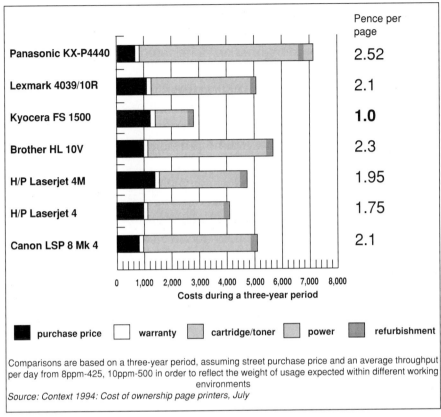

Figure 13.2   *The cost of printing*

much less importance and charging a premium over the competition is made all the easier. We might call this value pricing.

The secret of value pricing, as they say about chess, is simple in concept but hard to master in practice. Segment the market based on the value you can bring to each segment, seeking those segments where you can be seen to present the greatest *intensity of value*. Identify what we might call the *value hotspots* in each segment – where there is an opportunity to deliver that intensity of value. Target your proposition to those where this value will be perceived most clearly, and ensure that everyone in your business aims to do this in concert.

The Kyocera strategy, and that discussed for the pump manufacturer, is based on a complete grasp of the marketing model – understanding customers' needs and matching them with a unique proposition. It also calls on an additional capability – being able to communicate the proposition to the right person. Perhaps the buyer of the pump is not responsible for the electricity bill; perhaps the toner for the printer is bought by somebody other than the buyer of the printer. The supplier has to make contact with those people and argue its case. This aspect of the marketer's task will be discussed in full in Chapter 19, 'Relationship marketing and key account management'.

We might consider some examples of value pricing using some of the tools encountered elsewhere in this book. What they will illustrate is not only the variety of approaches and solutions but also the way that the tools of marketing combine towards a common end – the pursuit of a reward for the application of solutions to customers' needs.

Value pricing and segmentation – MCI WorldCom

Chapter 11, 'Segmentation', demonstrated how segmentation allows suppliers to maximize their pricing opportunities. This example shows how a service provider can use the technique even where the price for its principal service is set by the market. MCI WorldCom sell telephone and data communication services world-wide in a highly competitive market where the unit price of a call is both well known and well monitored. WorldCom segment their market by business type because they can observe hugely different needs for telecommunications between, say, an international bank and a manufacturing company.

My own experience brought this home to me most graphically when I was working with a client at one of their production plants in Scotland. I needed to send an e-mail and asked if I could plug my modem line into a telephone wall socket. 'Sure...', they said, and without waiting to hear the rest I pulled the existing cord from the socket to replace it with my own. Too late I heard them say 'but not that one!'. It turned out that I had blacked out most of the site's telephones for half a day. I thought that I would probably be dead by lunchtime. As it was, at lunch in the canteen I was approached by people wanting to shake my hand because they had got so much done that morning in the absence of all those disruptions from the telephone! The point that occurred to me was what would have happened had I done the same thing in the head office of the Chase Manhattan Bank?

Clearly it was not good to lose telephone communications for half a day, but the production plant coped. For the bank, five minutes' loss would perhaps cost millions of dollars. If that was so, how does a supplier like WorldCom use value pricing when the unit price of calls is so standardized? The answer is in the range of additional services offered. The production plant simply wants voice communications and a good rate for calls. The bank wants data transfer lines, belt-and-braces security (WorldCom call this installing a 'redundant line' – in other words a back-up) and a variety of other added-value services, all of which can be priced based on their huge importance to the working of the bank.

Value pricing and supplier positioning – Unilever

A customer views its suppliers in different ways. Just as a supplier will distinguish some of its clients as key accounts, so the client will look for key suppliers. The matrix in Figure 13.3 shows how some might go about this, positioning suppliers against two axes – the spend with them relative to other suppliers, and the relative significance of the supplier.

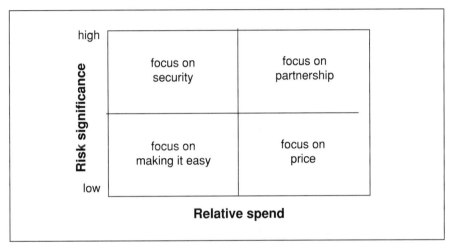

Figure 13.3 *Supplier positioning*

Significance will involve many and varied factors from technology, geography and the ease of changing supplier, to the use of brands or the financial security of the supplier. DuPont increase their significance to the client through the use of brand names that appear on the customer's product – Teflon and Lycra being two high-profile examples.

So what is the impact on price? If a supplier is positioned in the bottom-right box then the focus is very much on price, discounts for volume will head the agenda and the ability of a supplier to practise value pricing is greatly restricted. In the other boxes however the attitude to price may be somewhat different. In each of the other boxes there are factors that might come before price in determining the relationship with a supplier. In the bottom left the ability of a supplier to take on the burden of procurement for the customer – policing itself, managing inventory, managing forecasts, etc – might rank higher in importance than lowest price. Providing such services will allow a value pricing strategy. In the top-right box the supplier is of great significance to the customer's future, both financially and operationally – larger concerns than discounting will colour this relationship.

For a supplier positioned in the top-left box, let's consider as an example the supplier to Unilever of their main butter flavour. The flavour is a vital ingredient in the final product, placing the supplier well north on the significance axis. Of all the materials purchased by Unilever to make their butter products, this flavour accounts for

233

less than 1 per cent of the total cost, about as far left on the relative spend axis as it is possible to be. A supplier placed in this box is expected to provide absolute security of supply, without fault, and so long as the flavour supplier continues to deliver a completely consistent, fault-free product, then Unilever will continue to value it, and reward it accordingly. Both supplier and Unilever refer to the Unilever 'fat man' (Figure 13.4) in recognition of this fact.

Figure 13.4   *The Unilever 'fat man'*

The fat man represents the total costs of all materials purchased by the Unilever butter business. The small dot represents the flavour component, but note where it is placed – right on the heart. Nobody, both sides recognize, is going to have a heart transplant for the sake of a price discount!

Value pricing and the customer's product life cycle – Merck

The product life cycle, we will recall from Chapter 12, shows how at different stages of a product's life, from birth through growth and on to maturity and decline, the marketing mix must change if performance is to be optimized. The textbook theory has it that price can be high at the outset, will tend to fall as maturity approaches and may well rise again beyond maturity as the supplier tries to milk the last few drops of its life. I want to consider here, however, not the supplier's PLC but the customer's.

Consider the case of Merck, the huge US pharmaceutical company. What considerations do they have with regard to suppliers and suppliers' prices, as they move through the product life cycle of one of their drugs?

Before the introduction of the drug, their focus is very firmly on ensuring that it passes the various stages of regulatory approval. At this point they will certainly not jeopardize the success of a billion-dollar investment for the sake of a sharp discount on a supplier's product. Suppliers are key to their success at this point, bringing the expertise, services and products to get the drug through the stages pre-launch, and to ensure its maximum efficacy. The value placed on a supplier that genuinely helps in this way is sometimes beyond calculation.

Once the drug is launched the pharmaceutical company's attention shifts from efficacy and regulatory approval towards the supplier's ability to keep pace with volume growth. The supplier that can match the pace without any risk to security and quality will be valued indeed.

It is only as the drug enters the maturity stage that the company will start to turn its attention towards price, but even here it is not looking for discounts just for the sake of discounts, and most unlikely that it will be seeking to reduce its supplier's margins – if the supplier is a good one. The pharmaceutical company wishes to grow its profits at this stage by increasing the efficiency of the activity and the valued supplier is the one that can use its own experience at this point (the idea of the experience curve discussed below) to reduce its costs of production and so deliver lower prices to the customer. This is not price reduction through lack of value, simply a different price to reflect a different kind of value received – efficiency has replaced growth capacity, which in its turn had replaced efficacy.

Value pricing and risk – INSIGHT Marketing and People

As a provider of training and consultancy, my company, INSIGHT Marketing and People, gets called into some fairly hairy situations. Sad to say, many clients wait until they have a problem before looking for help and as any doctor will tell you, prevention is always cheaper than cure. A typical situation will be a client planning to launch a new product and realizing as the date approaches that it is far from certain how to go about the whole thing. If we think back to the Ansoff matrix from Chapter 8, we will recall that new product development is a high-risk activity, only one down from diversification. Businesses taking high risk need help from good suppliers, and the sort of help they get can be worth the difference between success and failure. Putting a price on a training course on new product development in such a situation has little to do with cost breakdowns. Even where the client prepares well in advance and the training is 'preventative' rather than 'cure', the value of such an intervention is well beyond the question of days spent. A supplier that helps its client reduce risk is a supplier to be valued, and that is at the root of value pricing.

I should hasten to add of course that such pricing is not in any sense a case of 'taking advantage of a man when he's down'. A value price allows a supplier to provide a value solution. It allows a service supplier to develop and apply the right expertise and capability, a win–win for both supplier and client.

Value pricing and the adopters curve – Jaguar

Chapter 11, 'Segmentation', introduced the idea of the adopters curve, representing the number of people who bought into a new product or idea over time. Consumer products in particular have long made use of this model in their pricing strategies. A product at its introduction is obviously new, novel, interesting and desirable to a particular segment of the market – the innovators. Innovators will see value in a product sometimes simply because of its novelty. A good example is the launch of a new car, especially if it is heralded by a blast of publicity and media coverage. Such publicity surrounded the launch of the Jaguar S type in 1999, a car that harked back to the glory days of the 1960s. There was without doubt a group of customers for the S type that would place great value on being seen to drive this car – early. Ego and prestige alongside exclusivity are powerful drivers for value pricing, and the new Jaguar responded to the opportunity.

Interestingly, this example can be seen to combine value pricing with market pricing. Jaguar took great care to promote demand, ration supply and charge a premium for the scarcity value.

Value pricing and the adopters curve – hi-tech

Another example much encountered is in the world of hi-fi, telecommunications and computing. The rate of technological change in these markets makes for a never-ending stream of new products, eagerly awaited by innovators and early adopters. At the other end of the adopters curve, the late majority are often buying products that are already well past maturity and about to disappear. This provides fertile ground for pricing policies that distinguish the different segments of the market indicated by the adopters curve. Buying a mobile phone almost implies that it is already out of date and we certainly don't expect to pay a lot for a model that has been around six months or more, but we will pay a significant premium to be the first to have the absolute leading-edge model, as the glass cabinet displays at airport duty-free shops make clear. Value in these markets is definitely denoted by newness, but then the markets themselves are new and technology drives them forward at a tremendous pace. A sign of maturity in a market is when the technology alone will no longer make the product or service saleable.

COMPETITIVE PRICING STRATEGIES

We have been discussing in the last section our ability to recognize or influence the customer's value judgements, and so follow a particular pricing strategy – value pricing. The examples cited all involve raising prices, or maintaining prices against market pressures to reduce them, but this is not the only outcome of value pricing. Perhaps your analysis leads you to realize that you are overpriced for the value perceived and that there is no opportunity to change that perception. Reducing prices in this circumstance is still value pricing – basing your price on value perceived. But value pricing is not the only choice open to you. Perhaps you choose to cut your price, not because of poor perceived value, but because you want to drive volume up and your costs down through economies of scale, and then cut prices again, and so on until the competitors drop dead of starvation. We are in the realm of competitive pricing strategy, a dangerous and complex place of action, reaction and counteraction, and we need a means to the right choice.

We will look at a two-step process: 1) the price/performance audit; and 2) the competitive pricing strategy matrix.

The price/performance audit

Consider your own current performance and place your product(s) or service(s) on the matrix in Figure 13.5. The matrix asks you to consider whether your price is higher or lower than the competition (the vertical axis) and then whether your business growth is faster or slower than the competition (the horizontal axis). We might then make the following general conclusions about your position in one of the four boxes:

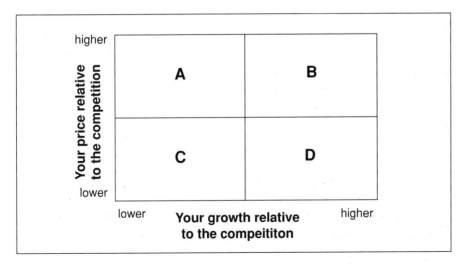

Figure 13.5 _The price/performance audit_

- Box A – Whatever value you are claiming for your product or service it is either not sufficient for the price you are asking, or is not wanted by the customer. Your competitors are offering a better price–value fit.
- Box B – You appear to be getting it right, but take care that you are not missing an opportunity for more, or perhaps you are offering *too much* value?
- Box C – There is obviously more to this market than price.
- Box D – Low prices seem to work, but are they necessary? Could you charge more?

The analysis is general, and raises more questions than it answers. The second step of this competitive pricing strategy process raises two of them.

The competitive pricing strategy matrix

The matrix in Figure 13.6 shows four possible pricing strategies that result from the consideration of two questions.

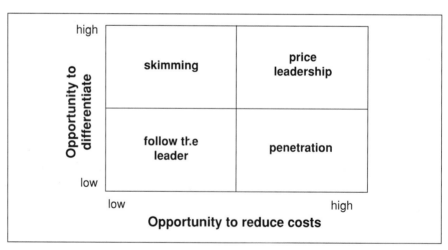

Figure 13.6 *Competitive pricing strategies*

The questions come from Michael Porter's choices for pursuing competitive advantage as discussed in Chapter 8: what opportunity do you have to reduce costs, and what opportunity do you have to differentiate your offer?

The opportunity to reduce costs may come from a number of factors, including:

- You have spare capacity and filling it with volume would bring unit costs down.
- Your product or service enjoys significant economies of scale from higher volume.
- You are able to invest in improved efficiency.
- A lower price for your product will allow you to reduce quality or service.
- _The experience curve_ – the notion that the longer you are involved in an activity, the better you get at it, so that a manufacturer should be able to produce at a lower and lower cost, the greater its experience (see below).

Remember that this matrix is about competitive pricing, so the question is not just whether you can reduce costs, but whether you can reduce them faster and further than competitors.

The opportunity to differentiate your product or service may come from a variety of factors, including:

- the use of brand names;
- promotional expenditure;
- PR activities;
- service packages;
- product quality;
- the impact of relationships.

Remember again that this matrix is about competitive pricing. It isn't just a question of whether you have good ideas, products or service packages, but whether they will outpace the competition and customers will regard them as being worth a premium.

Four generic competitive pricing strategies emerge from this analysis:

1. skimming – pricing above the competition and selecting the 'cream' from the market;
2. penetration – pricing below the competition to gain share;
3. price leader – being able to 'direct' the market price in either direction;
4. price follower – having to follow the price leader.

Skimming is the attractive option when chasing volume will not drive costs down, or there is no volume to chase – your capacity is full, you have such a large share of the market that further volume growth would be difficult, or economies of scale do not apply to you.

Penetration is an attractive option if cost reduction is relatively easy compared to differentiation, particularly if the market demands a low-price, mass-produced, uniform product or service. It is however fraught with problems.

Price cutting in the real world

A manufacturer of chemicals for the leather industry in the USA decided upon a penetration strategy, not because it believed it could reduce its own costs but because it believed it could stand the heat of lower margins longer than its competitors. The competitors would be 'shaken out' of the market. The low prices offered succeeded in winning volume, market share grew and competitors had to follow prices down, but then a problem was encountered. They reached capacity in their factory and competitors were able to edge prices up again because demand was still ahead of supply. A competitive pricing strategy came up against the twin realities of production capacity and supply and demand. Few pricing strategies can operate in complete independence of these factors.

The success of a penetration pricing strategy as described here depends on a *genuine* opportunity to reduce costs, through volume, through economies of scale, or through the *experience curve* (described below). Very often, of course, companies will use what looks like a penetration strategy to gain trial for their product – a common phenomenon in fmcg markets – but it is not a true penetration strategy in the sense described here; rather it is a short-term pricing tactic. Where such approaches often come unstuck is that they encourage a response from the competition that can scupper not only the tactic but also the profitability of the whole market.

Are we about to witness the UK supermarket 'shake-out'?

The opening months of 2000 saw Asda (newly bought by Wal-Mart) and Tesco slugging it out for the lowest-priced shopping basket. Industry experts are now predicting that perhaps two of the current top six UK food stores will fail to keep pace with these discounting moves and will be gone from the market within five years. What we appear to be witnessing is the classic 'shake-out' in a mature and oversupplied market where price is used to remove the weaker players. Of course, the definitions of 'oversupplied' differ depending on your perspective, and a reduction in suppliers is not always in the customers' best interest. Where that is so, and where markets are genuinely free and open, other options tend to appear to redress the balance.

The longer the downward spiral of price continues, the more debased the 'value' of the product becomes. As competitors' prices chase one another downwards, so the relative volumes remain the same with no real opportunities for cost reduction. More creative options for winning trial are required where this general debasement is the likely result of a (so-called) penetration pricing strategy, a good example being the way that Nestlé use sample packs of new breakfast cereals attached to existing products, whether cereals, coffee or confectionery. This doesn't impact on prices yet achieves its aim – intelligent marketing.

Price leadership comes from having a greater opportunity than the competition to both differentiate *and* reduce costs, and the discomfort of being a *price follower* comes from having neither opportunity. The price leader can choose to skim or to penetrate in pursuit of its own profit goals, or it can use price as a competitive weapon to encourage a 'shake-out' of competitors – this last being a strategy most often seen in mature markets where there are too many suppliers for the demand.

The experience curve – the Lopez factor

For most business activities it is true that the longer you are involved in the activity the better you become at it. Costs should reduce for a manufacturer as it learns how to make the product, improves its process, grows its volume, gets smarter with suppliers, etc. Customers have been known to use this theory as a means of persuading suppliers to lower prices.

Any supplier to the automotive industry will recognize the scenario, often referred to as the 'Lopez factor'. Lopez was a senior manager at General Motors, remembered for demanding price cuts from suppliers on a long-term basis. A supplier that could commit to price reductions this year, the next and the next would stand a chance of staying listed. The argument put forward was twofold – more volume would come your way as the number of suppliers able to oblige reduced, and the benefits of the experience curve would take effect. The theory was quite workable for some suppliers, but didn't work so well for those who had fewer opportunities for economies of scale.

The 'Lopez factor'

It is an important notion whether it applies to your own business or not, because it may just apply to your competitors.

Kodak vs Fuji – differentiation vs lowest cost

Back in the 1970s, Kodak had the lion's share of the European film market and enjoyed healthy prices and margins as a result. Then Fuji entered the market. Fuji came in with a price well below Kodak's, even below Kodak's costs to manufacture, and Kodak regarded this as a very short-term phenomenon – how could Fuji survive at such a price? Fuji were not making a profit at these prices and their own costs of supply were significantly higher than Kodak's at this point, but they were following a penetration strategy closely allied to the theory of the experience curve. As their price gained them volume, and as they became more experienced at operating in the European markets, so their costs came down. The Japanese are known for 'playing the long game', and Fuji were prepared to wait a long time before their cost curve dipped below their price line, but at last it did and it was clear to Kodak that Fuji was no temporary phenomenon.

At this point Kodak had a choice to make – to chase Fuji down the price route hoping to gain some of the cost savings for themselves as volume came back, or to differentiate their offer. The opportunity to differentiate (in comparison to Fuji's offer) was far greater than the opportunity to reduce costs (in comparison to Fuji's costs), and so they chose the product innovation route, and both, as they say, have lived relatively happily ever after.

The generic strategies discussed here are of course only a guide to what is possible and 'wise'. In the end, your final choice of price in a competitive environment will be determined by what you intend to achieve in that market – profit growth, market share, high perceived value, trial, etc. This brings us to one final pricing strategy – the zero price or zero margin strategy.

Zero price or zero margin strategy

This may seem a rather crazy strategy, selling for nothing, or selling for no profit, but it demonstrates just how price is but one part of the marketing mix, and just one means to profitability. Suppliers will often offer their products for free trial – sachets of shampoo taped to magazines, time-share operators giving trial weekends, agrochemical suppliers providing 'aid' to the Third World – each has its motive, ranging from encouraging trial to building desire to establishing dependency.

Retailers use the 'loss leader' tactic, offering well-known brands at cost (or less) in order to entice us into their store where we will doubtless spend our money on other 'full margin' items. Studies have shown, in fact, that shoppers who go out in response to these promoted bargains will very often end up spending more than they would on a normal shopping trip. Having said that, I recall the owner of an independent grocery store in East Anglia who took great delight in shopping at his competitors' whenever they made these offers, buying huge quantities of the 'loss leader' items, and only those, to sell in his own store at the normal rate (the supermarkets' sale price was often below the price he could get from the wholesaler). He saw this as a means of striking a blow against the unfair tactics of the big boys, and is doubtless still doing it to this day!

Service providers such as mobile phone network companies use the price of the mobile phone itself (much below its actual cost or even free) as a means to tie us into their service, at which point the real pricing strategies begin. Never was it more truly said that 'You don't get owt for nowt'!

New profit models in the 'new economy'

Commercial television offers a free service to viewers as a means of winning the advertiser's money. The offer of free Internet access is but a variation on the same theme. As I write there is a price war with a difference going on out there in cyber space. First AltaVista offer to provide their service with no phone charges (but not free access), only for NTL to follow with a completely free service if you subscribe to their telephone services. Profits are made in cyber space not by pricing the service to the end consumer, but by (for instance) the transfer of pennies and fractions of pennies for referrals in the 'clickstream'.

There are some wholesale cash and carry operators that take the zero margin idea to its extreme, making no profit on the sale of items to their customers. The secret is in the cash flow. The cash and carry, as its name implies, offers no credit, but takes cash payments only. If they are able to negotiate long credit terms with their suppliers, and if they concentrate on lines with high stock-turns, then they will generate enough free cash to invest for a return elsewhere. This kind of cash and carry operation is merely a means to an end – cash, and to be in competition with such a business and not understand their use of price would be a frustrating experience indeed!

'DISCUSSING' PRICE – OPEN BOOK TRADING

Many purchasing organizations have learnt that the supplier's choice of price, despite the theory of cost-plus, market-based or value-based, is often arbitrary and mysterious. An increasingly common policy in the light of this is to ask for *open book trading*. Suppliers are asked to disclose the make-up of their price, justifying the elements and its principle. This may seem just like asking for cost breakdowns (as discussed above under cost-plus pricing) with all the attendant risks of losing control of the package, which in some cases it is, but in others it is a genuine attempt to improve the effectiveness of the customer/supplier relationship. So how should the supplier respond?

One option is to refuse to comply, which generally works until the competition starts to comply and then the fun starts. Another option is to comply but with such complexity as to defeat the purpose – in the short term this is effective, in the long term very unpopular. Perhaps the only real answer to such requests is to ensure that your price is a value-based price. Examine your own activities and determine which of them *genuinely* add value to the customer. Make every effort to eliminate those activities that don't. And go further than this; ask the customer to respond with detail on its own costs in use, and use this information to tailor your offer to ensure that it provides the maximum value possible. (See the exercise at the end of this chapter.)

In the end, the only suppliers with anything to fear from this debate are the guilty ones: the cost-plus brigade, those with no true value to offer and, most importantly, those that don't understand the value they provide.

AND IN YOUR BUSINESS...?

Having read this chapter, and before reading the case study in Chapter 14, you might like to take 15 to 20 minutes to consider the following questions. It will be helpful to identify a specific product or service, and a specific customer, when considering your answers.

Viewed from your perspective:

1. Where and how do you add value to your customer's business? Is it through:
   - the product?
   - the service?

    –   the relationship?

    –   other?

2.   Where and how do you achieve value-based pricing?

3.   Where do you incur costs, without adding value?

4.   Under what circumstances do you fail to achieve value-based pricing?

Viewed from the customer's perspective:

1.   Identify for one of your products or services, and for one of your customers:
   - its features (tangible characteristics);
   - its benefits (what those features do for the customer);
   - its value (what value the customer derives from those benefits).

2.   Identify the customer's definition of value received.

3.   Try to quantify that value received. What would be the cost to the customer's business of not receiving the product or service?

4.   Is your price for this product or service based on its features, its benefits, or its value?

5.   What are the customer's alternatives to buying your product or service:
   - a competitor's products or services?
   - alternative solutions?
   - do nothing?

6.   What does your answer to question 5 indicate to you about 'price elasticity'? How far could your price go up before the customer chose one of those alternatives?

14

The Ambient Ltd case study

Ambient started life in the 1970s on the back of the North Sea oil and gas business supplying pipework sealants to the rigs. Still based in the UK but now supplying exploration companies around the world, Ambient has built a reputation for quality, largely through the success of a product introduced in 1993 – Ambo 5.

Ambo 5

When Ambo 5 was introduced, its unique properties established it as the clear market leader, and it was soon replacing most of Ambient's own existing products. The 'secret' was in the hardener, which allowed for a wide variation in setting times (depending on the dose) and in final rigidity. This made Ambo 5 particularly beneficial for use in difficult environments – ideal for the oil and gas exploration market.

The future?

Ambient's forecasts for the 2000s show a downturn in oil and gas exploration, at least in their main territorial markets, and their MD,

Martin Doyle, has been keen to look for new markets, with new applications. A lot of time has been spent looking at the European building market, in decline through most of the 1990s, but now showing signs of recovery. Since 1999 a small pack size of Ambo 5 has been on sale through UK builders' merchants, but early reports suggest that the product is seen as difficult to use – the instruction leaflet runs to four pages!

The competition

The success of Ambo 5 hit the competition hard, and before long two of Ambient's competitors were launching similar products. Lotus 'C' was launched in 1995 and, although the quality of early production was variable, it sold well because demand was greater than Ambient's then limited production capacity. The following year, X-Tec was launched by another competitor.

The market in the 1990s

Sales grew quickly throughout most of the 1990s as the three new products superseded most others in the market. By 1996 prices were very similar for all three suppliers and market shares were stable, with Ambo taking half of the market and Lotus and X-Tec sharing the rest.

Sales growth started to slow from 1997. It became clear that the market had not been growing for some time and that the sales growth of previous years was largely from replacing older technologies. The new smaller pack size for the building market was a tiny proportion of sales, but at least it was showing growth, unlike Ambo's total sales in 2000.

In January 2000, Ambient increased its price to £10.00 per kilogram from £9.50. Both competitors held their prices at £9.50. In Q1, Q2 and Q3, Ambo 5 sales volume was down by 10 per cent and both Lotus and X-Tec increased their market shares.

Pricing for 2001

By October 2000, it was clear that neither competitor was going to move its price up (there had been hopes they would do so in July or, failing that, in September) and Ambient were faced with a difficult pricing decision for 2001. Martin Doyle called a special board meeting to discuss the matter.

The Ambient board

- Martin Doyle – Managing Director;
- Barry Sellers – Sales Director;
- Walter Plant – Works Manager;
- Marion Marks – Marketing Director;
- Faith Mooney – Finance Director.

Martin (MD) made it clear that it would be a short meeting – he had a 12.30 lunch appointment – and that all board members should come prepared to argue their case. (Martin's 12.30 appointment was with an old friend, the boss of the company that supplied Ambient with their main production equipment.) Martin asked Marion Marks (Marketing) to circulate details of estimated market size and shares (Table 14.1), and also the quoted prices from 1994 to date (Table 14.2). Faith Mooney (Finance) was asked to circulate the confidential data on Ambo 5's production costs at different volumes (Table 14.3).

Table 14.1 *Estimated market size and sales volumes in kg*

Year	Total (est)	Ambo 5 (act)	X-Tec (est)	Lotus 'C' (est)
1993	60,000	60,000	–	–
1994	140,000	140,000	–	–
1995	350,000	210,000	–	140,000
1996	610,000	335,000	155,000	120,000
1997	830,000	410,000	210,000	210,000
1998	990,000	515,000	250,000	225,555
1999	1,140,000	630,000	260,000	250,000
2000	1,255,000	565,000	350,000	340,000
2001	1,330,000			

Table 14.2 *Quoted prices in £*

Year	Ambo 5	X-Tec	Lotus 'C'
1994	5.60	–	–
1995	6.00	–	–
1996	7.00	7.00	6.80
1997	8.00	8.00	8.00
1998	9.00	9.00	9.00
1999	9.50	9.50	9.50
2000	10.00	9.50	9.50

Table 14.3 *Confidential production costs*

Volume (kg)	530,000	560,000	590,000	620,000	650,000	680,000	710,000
Direct Costs	£/kg	£/kg	£/kg	£/kg	£/kg	£/kg	£/kg
Materials	2.10	2.10	2.10	2.10	2.10	2.10	2.10
Labour	1.12	1.05	1.00	0.98	1.00	1.06	1.10
Other Costs	£/kg	£/kg	£/kg	£/kg	£/kg	£/kg	£/kg
Manufacture	0.06	0.04	0.04	0.03	0.04	0.05	0.06
Selling	0.06	0.05	0.04	0.03	0.03	0.04	0.05
Admin	0.02	0.01	0.01	0.01	0.02	0.03	0.04
Fixed Costs	£/kg	£/kg	£/kg	£/kg	£/kg	£/kg	£/kg
Manufacture	3.75	3.54	3.36	3.2	2.93	2.80	2.68
Selling	1.58	1.50	1.42	1.35	1.29	1.24	1.18
Admin	1.06	1.00	0.95	0.90	0.86	0.82	0.79
	£/kg	£/kg	£/kg	£/kg	£/kg	£/kg	£/kg
Total Costs	9.75	9.29	8.92	8.60	8.27	8.14	8.00

THE MEETING

The meeting opened at 11 am prompt. Barry Sellers (Sales) and Faith
Mooney (Finance) had agreed to argue that Ambient should hold its
price at £10.00 per kilogram. Faith gave their reasons, turning to look
at Walter Plant (Works Manager). 'You have said it often enough this
summer, Walter. They must be mad to sell at £9.50. They surely must
be losing money at that price.'

Faith went on to forecast that prices for 2001 would converge at
£10.00; it seemed unlikely that the competition could hold prices for
three years running, even with low inflation. 'If that is the case, as I'm
sure it will be,' she continued, 'we will probably regain a market
share of 50 to 52 per cent.' She turned to Barry (Sales). 'I would
suggest a sales target of 680,000 kilograms, with a projected profit of
over £1.25 million.'

Marion Marks (Marketing) waved a dismissive hand towards the
Finance Director, and expressed her own view. 'Personally, I would
have thought that with our competitors' sales up by around 40 per

cent, they are more likely to be earning good profits than losing money.'

Walter nodded awkwardly. He was annoyed that Faith had referred to his rather rash remarks from earlier in the summer. Once he had seen the autumn sales projections for Lotus 'C' and X-Tec, he had recognized the improved plant utilization they were getting – both had three production units, each with a 120,000-kilogram annual capacity.

Barry passed a sheet of paper to the MD and went into presentation mode. 'As you can see, we have looked at the possibility of them holding on to £9.50. If they do that, we still think that a sustained sales push will recapture some lost volume. My estimate would be that a 46–47 per cent market share is quite possible.'

Faith nodded and added that at 620,000 kilograms the contribution to overheads was still over £4 million. Barry and Faith smiled at each other – they were pleased with their morning's collaboration.

The MD remembered that he had agreed only a year back to put the sales team on a volume-related bonus scheme, and now he always felt nervous whenever he heard Barry talking about a 'sales push'. He asked for views on putting the price up to £10.50 per kilogram.

'Everything I said,' Barry jumped in quickly, pushing a second sheet of paper towards his boss, 'everything depends on our holding our price,' he paused, and then continued, expecting a howl of disapproval from Marion, 'or dropping it.' The second sheet of paper showed Barry's calculations based on an Ambo 5 price increase – volume down to 530,000 kilograms, plunging market share and a slump in profits to £400,000.

As the MD read out the dire predictions, Barry nodded his head furiously and then, looking straight at Marion, he almost spat out the words, 'Any further widening of the price differential would be disastrous.'

Barry was surprised by the silence in the room, by the heads nodding around the table, but most of all by Marion's response. 'I agree. The growth in the market is levelling off, and in those circumstances market share is vital. Even a fall to 47 per cent – that was your guess, I think, Barry, if we all stay as we are – even that would be disastrous. I think it's time we put the pressure back on the competition.'

To everyone's surprise, and before anyone else could speak, Marion was on her feet, and taking a pen she wrote in large thick letters on a flip chart – PRICE REDUCTION TO £9.50.

Walter was the first to comment. He was completely behind Marion, he said. The energy levels in the room were rising fast, and Walter was getting quite excited by the turn of events.

Back in 1998 Walter had persuaded the board to approve a sixth production unit (they were standard machines producing 120,000 kilograms per annum) based on sales projections of 690,000 kilograms in 1999 and 720,000 kilograms in 2000. Things had started out well – the sixth machine had come on stream with impressive speed, helping Ambient to record sales in 1999. Walter had been something of a hero, with a handsome performance bonus to show for it. But for most of 2000, the machine had stood idle. Walter had managed to switch production to it as he took out each of the older machines for overhaul and maintenance, but that had not taken long. Now the additional staff he had taken on were going to be as idle as the machine, unless sales rose again. He faced the prospect of dismissing staff newly taken on with dismay – not least because his sister-in-law's son was among the newer recruits and would almost certainly be one of the first to go. He liked what he was hearing from Marion.

Marion and Barry were now standing side by side at the flip chart, drawing upward sloping curves with the sort of enthusiasm that the board had not seen since the launch of Ambo 5. At £9.50, market share would go back to 52 per cent, and with a strong sales effort behind the price cut the market might well grow by more than the projected 6 per cent. The price cut should stimulate growth of just over 8 per cent (to 1,360,000 kilograms) with Ambo 5 accounting for 710,000 kilograms.

Faith tapped out the new figures on her calculator, and with Marion, Barry and now Walter standing around the flip chart, they barely noticed the MD getting up to leave. 'Thank you for your thoughts,' he said. 'I suggest we meet again at 3 o'clock this afternoon. Is that OK with everyone?'

Just like the boss, they thought. No clue to what he was thinking, and no support for their new-found enthusiasm. They separated, each wondering what would happen when they regathered at 3 pm.

CASE QUESTIONS

1. Consider, and comment on, the views of each board member.
2. Comment on the figures provided by the two board members shown in Tables 14.1, 14.2 and 14.3. How useful were these in the pricing decision?
3. Comment on the way in which the board discussed the issues, and prepared their plans for 2001.
4. If you were employed as a consultant to the board, what proposals would you make for 2001 pricing, and for any other marketing issues?

If you would like to e-mail your answers or any other comments on this case study to INSIGHT at customer.service@insight-mp.com, we will gladly critique your report and send you our own thoughts.

15

Promotion strategies

'P-p-p-pick up a
Penguin'

Club biscuits once 'owned' the UK market for the break-time chocolate biscuit until one year they chose to pull back on advertising and regard the money saved as extra profit. They were after all the brand leader. What harm could one year do? It was their bad luck (or marketing myopia?) that this decision coincided with a massive campaign behind the Penguin biscuit, with Derek Nimmo's famous stuttering tag line. Penguin never looked back and Club never regained their position.

Promotion for a major brand must be a long-term activity. Consistency of spend is everything, hard as it might be for financial directors to understand. But this isn't the only story for promotion, and it is a subject that extends well beyond the realm of seven-figure TV advertising campaigns.

The key for any promotional strategy is its objective – know what you intend to achieve and you will avoid most of the pitfalls of wasted activity and overspent budgets that make new government offices look like well-forecast bargains.

THE PURPOSE OF PROMOTION

You might engage in a promotional activity in order to:

- grow the total size of the market;
- grow your own sales volume; √
- increase market share; √
- support a sales drive;
- improve distribution; √
- attack a competitor's offer;
- develop awareness of your product, or brand, or company; √
- influence the customer's needs and desires; √
- affect the customer's perceptions of your proposition;
- overcome prejudices;
- gain trial for your product or service;
- increase frequency of usage;
- reinforce existing behaviour;
- establish a unique link between your proposition and the customer's needs;
- establish or build credibility;
- dispel rumours of your imminent decline;
- demonstrate a social or political awareness;
- affect the customer's disposition to buy your product;
- inform customers of a change to your proposition;
- inform customers of a change in the market environment.

This far from exhaustive list represents just some of the things that the marketer might desire from promotion, but the discipline is not to be too greedy – a promotional activity that tries too much will end up achieving very little. Each one of these aims is unique, and will require a unique treatment.

The campaign and the communication

The promotional campaign might have a wider set of objectives than any individual communication or activity within that campaign. The campaign might include a variety of media, each used for its character and merit in effecting a particular response – TV for awareness and developing desire, press for disseminating information, the sales offer for stimulating purchase, etc. The individual communication will require a more focused objective.

The promotional objectives

Be pedantic about your promotional objectives. Write them down for the whole campaign, and for each specific communication and activity, using the following construction:

> **This** promotional activity... (define the medium and method)
> **will**, or is intended to... (state the intended effect, the planned response from the customer or the market, to include a verb – gain, build, achieve, win, convert, dispel, etc)
> **with** the target audience... (specified)
> **to** the following timings... (specified)
> **with** the following results... (specified – impact on sales, share, profits, etc).

An example for a new brand of lager might read as follows:

> This £3 million TV campaign of 30-second commercials placed at prime time will gain trial for Hogshead lager among men aged 18 to 25 living in the Granada TV area, between 1 May and 30 June, resulting in a 160 per cent increase in sales over the period (£x revenue) and a prompted brand recognition rate of 90 per cent among the target audience. It will also support the trade-based promotional campaign intended to gain initial distribution.

The importance of this apparent pedantry cannot be overemphasized, for the following reasons:

- When you brief an external agency they must know what they are seeking to achieve on your behalf.
- When you ask your own business for the money to pay for the activity you must be able to demonstrate the return on the investment.
- If you want to measure the effectiveness of the activity then you must know what you set out to achieve.
- Lazy objectives lead to lazy activities with confused messages and confused customers.

● Promotion, perhaps more than any other part of the marketing mix, is prone to a subjective 'that feels good' syndrome, whereas it needs discipline as much as any other area of marketing. For many businesses this will be the single largest marketing expenditure – it deserves to be managed professionally.

The first golden rule of promotion

The most important thing to remember about any form of communication, whether it be a one-to-one conversation or a £5 million TV campaign, is that the message received is more important than the message sent. Without great clarity on what message you want the customer to hear, the message sent can be constructed with horrible inappropriateness. Laziness over promotional objectives is the prime sin. A promotion strategy to increase awareness for your product may sound straightforward enough – but what kind of awareness, by whom and to what purpose? Let's suppose you want to increase awareness for British beef. You couldn't do better than the last 10 years of scandal and tragedy, and of course you couldn't do worse in attempting to market your product. Promotion is more than building awareness – it must be awareness to a purpose.

The marketer must recognize that the message received is hugely bound up with customers' existing perceptions of your company, brand or product, and much less with what you actually say. High-profile rostrum-thumpers such as Ian Paisley or Arthur Scargill rarely make conversion with their audience. Perceptions are set for or against them before they start and they speak largely if not exclusively to an existing band of supporters. The same can apply to a product. Adverts on the Continent extolling the delights of British beef are almost entirely misplaced while there is still any climate of mistrust. Worse than failing to achieve their intended response, they risk setting off a larger wave of cynicism and disbelief.

When a company is aware of a poor image for its product, it will need to do more than just tell people how great it is. Humour is a favourite tack, and there have been many adverts that appear to knock the advertiser as a means of changing people's perceptions.

A recent TV ad for a Skoda car has a car park attendant apologizing to a worried Skoda car owner for the vandalism done to his car – some little devil has stuck a Skoda badge on the front. Humour, recognition of the current perceptions and a clever point about how things have changed, yet some (not you, of course) are still behind the times.

Skoda – beyond a joke

The single-minded proposition

We will encounter this most important notion of the _single-minded proposition_ again in Chapter 16 when discussing the development of a brand. The idea recognizes a fundamental truth about the human ability to receive and process information, that while the brain's ability to comprehend and interpret is enormously impressive, it reaches overload surprisingly quickly. A single communication should not attempt to say too much. Most people can only take in a few items of information at a time, and can handle even fewer concepts. Most promotional media can only hope to keep the customer's attention for a few seconds – perhaps 30 in the case of the average TV advert, maybe more for a piece of magazine 'advertorial' and substantially less for an Internet Web site passing under the surfer's temporary gaze. With this in mind, saying one thing but saying it clearly and memorably, and saying it so as to elicit the intended response is a very good idea indeed.

The single-minded proposition is just that, and ideally it will also be the single most motivating and differentiating thing that you can say about your brand or your product. Perhaps there is much that can be said about your offer, but take care not to try too much. Over the course of a promotional campaign it may be possible to build up a series of individual single-minded propositions, but each specific activity within the campaign should aim to tackle just one at a time.

Kyocera, the office equipment manufacturer recently ran a series of press adverts for their Ecosys printer range with a strong central theme and a series of individual messages, one per advert. The campaign was designed to establish a clear link between Kyocera's unique capabilities (based on their technology) and a single-minded identification of the customer's needs – business efficiency and environmental concern. Each advert identified a different aspect of the technology, but used a consistent tag line throughout: 'because business demands efficiency and the earth needs attention.'

Kyocera – saving the earth

The effective communication

The proposition is only the start. An effective communication must achieve the following:

- It must reach the target audience.
- It must penetrate their attention, through a combination of timeliness, relevance and simplicity.
- It must communicate the intended message.
- It must *bond* the message to the brand name.

Many high-cost adverts fail this test, sometimes on all four points – the cost of an advert does not guarantee its effectiveness:

- *Reaching?* The brilliant Web site with every latest interactive technique is entirely wasted if nobody can find it.
- *Penetrating?* The TV remote control has consigned many TV ads to the 'mute' dustbin by their failure to come up to the same standard as the programmes during which they are shown.
- *Intended?* I once saw an advert for cigars that showed a dinner-jacket-clad man sitting opposite an admiring companion, the source of her admiration clearly being the cigar on which he puffed. The tag line implied that as well as the more obvious things, your choice of cigar was one of the ways that you demonstrated your concern for your loved ones. Unfortunately this particular advert had the government health warning pointing out that passive smoking can cause cancer – so much for love and attention.
- *Bonding?* One of the perils of *not* being the brand leader is that your advertising often gets mistaken for the number one in the market. For many years when I was working on the Dulux paint brand I would receive congratulations (or sometimes criticism) from friends and relatives on our latest advert, only to discover that they had just seen one of Crown's, the long-time number two player.

The second golden rule of promotion

Telling people stuff is not enough – you want to know what they think about what you tell them, and you want them to do something positive about it. Good promotional activities engage the customer in a 'conversation' by eliciting a response. Chapter 18 looks at the way in which the Internet allows promotional messages to become dialogues with customers, an example of how the e-revolution is enhancing the marketer's work.

Different media are better or worse for eliciting a response, and will promote different kinds of response. Choosing the right medium takes us back to the clarity of our promotional objectives. TV may be great for awareness, and it may well stimulate response through purchasing behaviour, but what if you seek a different kind of response? The next section discusses the pros and cons of the different media across a range of concerns including the ability to target the message and gain the intended reaction.

THE MEDIA CHOICE – PROS AND CONS

Each medium has its own strengths and disadvantages depending of course on your intended outcome. The following lists compare the pros and cons of the main media choices, taking into consideration issues such as cost, planning, targeting, technical limitations, speed, impact, response, etc.

TV

The strengths are:

- You control the message.
- Close targeting is possible through slot bookings.
- There is huge impact with good recall.
- It builds high awareness quickly.
- There is good impact on perceptions and latent needs.
- There is high branding opportunity.
- It builds credibility.
- There is the opportunity to build over time whether by reinforcement through repeats or the development of a theme.
- Regional targeting and flexibility are possible.

The disadvantages are:

- There is the cost – not only of buying space but also production.
- There are occasional problems with placement associations.
- It is increasingly impersonal given the development of other more direct media.
- It is still largely a national medium – few TV adverts travel well, as shown by the popularity of TV programmes that find 'Johnny foreigner' ads so hysterical!

The ability to book specific slot times for TV adverts provides a high degree of targeting and minimizes the old problem of unplanned and embarrassing placement associations. There are still occasional problems, as with the advert for slimming products that ran adjacent to a breaking news story on a dreadful famine in East Africa.

The cost of TV still makes it the medium for the big players, and production costs are such that small campaigns are rarely cost-efficient. Cutting production costs leaves you with an ad that, unless it captures some kind of cult following, will be first victim to the remote control zapper.

TV ads have to be better-made than the programmes they sit next to: they have to be funnier, stranger, more arresting, or they just have to find some means to engage our attention. The 'what on earth is this an advert for?' technique is one angle, the running story is another – witness the Gold Blend saga of next-door neighbours or the 'Nicole? Papa?' soap.

Radio

The strengths are:

- It has local tailoring.
- It has the ability to 'talk' to people in their home.
- The low cost allows for high frequency.
- It is an 'immediate' medium, good for prompting action – a favoured medium for retailers.

The disadvantages are:

- Sometimes the audience size will be quite low.
- Lack of visuals is a problem for many propositions, though a creative agency should be able to 'paint pictures' with words and sounds.
- There are problems for national campaigns.

National press

The strengths are:

- It gives the ability to react quickly to events and developments in the market.
- Messages can build over a run of days – tease campaigns of the 'what's coming tomorrow?' variety abound.
- It is good for making offers, particularly time-related ones.
- Promotional offers can be made for the advertiser by the newspaper itself – holidays, flights, train tickets, etc.

The disadvantages are:

- It is costly.
- There may be problems of placement associations.

EasyJet make very effective use of 'buy now' ads for their low-cost European air fares. The placement in a daily paper gives the ad an immediacy and sense of urgency, and at least in EasyJet's early days the 'association' with the big-name papers was important in helping to build credibility for a new business taking on the big boys.

Special interest press

The strengths are:

- It is highly targeted.
- You can enter into more complex messages – particularly with inserts rather than ads in the magazine itself.
- You are among 'friends' and can be more informal with your approach.

The disadvantages are:

- Everyone else is there – overload.
- There are high production costs relative to the audience reached when compared to more mass media.

Kodak – 'our real advert is on pages...'

Kodak once ran a one-page ad in a leading photography magazine that consisted simply of a plain yellow page with the text, 'Our real advert is on page 5, 12, 28 and 37'. On each of these pages was a beautiful photograph as part of an article, with reference to the film used – Kodak, of course. This was a clever way to maximize impact on a slim budget with almost no production costs – usually a high part of the spend for a company like Kodak.

The use of the 'advertorial' is common in many magazines – adverts dressed up to look like articles. The credibility of the magazine can suffer if it makes too much use of this technique, and so opportunities are not always easy to come by.

Trade press

The strengths are:

- There is good targeting.
- It can build a market presence through regular use.
- It is good for reinforcing the single-minded proposition – 'leave it to Lonza', etc.
- It is also good for more complex messages – readers will accept more text in trade press than in other magazines.
- It is good for new entrants.

The disadvantages are:

- It has low impact.
- It is a slow burn, and takes time to generate awareness.
- There is the danger of overload – your immediate competitors will probably use the same media.
- Advertising claims can sometimes cause problems for sales-people confronted by 'local' issues for which the advertising is not wholly relevant.

● There are small target audiences, which mean small production budgets, which in turn may equate with dull, 'home-made, cut-and-paste' ads.

Posters

The strengths are:

● They are good for visual messages.
● They are good for tease campaigns (remember Sid?), 'surprises' or shock tactics – Benetton, fcuk, etc.
● Local targeting is possible – even down to specific streets.
● A continuous presence is possible.

The disadvantages are:

● There are high production costs for the audience reached.
● They need great care to manage placement.
● Bonding the brand to the message is not always easy.
● There are problems with defacement!

A DIY brand with a small budget for a new product launch was able to use posters very effectively. The product was a fairly complex wood-treatment product – not an impulse buy, and one where reputation and dependability would be important. Posters were placed on the main routes to major DIY stores so that consumers would see them just before arriving at the store. In store, the consumers were faced with a bewildering choice of options, but the last thing sown in their mind *outside* the store was an image of this manufacturer's product, and the association helped build a sense of credibility and trust.

The problem with bonding the message to the brand finds posters, ironically, a popular medium for non-supplier-specific campaigns. Trade and manufacturer associations will often use posters to promote the market rather than any particular supplier. British beef, pure wool and milk have all had the poster treatment. The UK bed manufacturers often use posters to tell us to replace our beds more frequently, for health reasons, of course, using posters almost as a public service medium.

Internet

(A much fuller discussion of the Internet and promotion will be found in Chapter 18.) The strengths are:

- It has a huge potential for interactive exchange – promotion becomes communication, and then becomes a trading exchange.
- It can build huge demand – but be careful that you can respond.
- It is essential for a modern image.
- It is great for updating messages or materials.
- Small players can look as good as the big guys – opportunities for the Davids to take on the Goliaths (but see the cautions in Chapter 18).
- There is the opportunity to provide large amounts of information to those who want to search.
- Customers' use can be monitored.
- Getting established is easy (but it is also easy to be incredibly dull!).

The disadvantages are:

- It is not 'free' – people still have to know where to find you, which involves expenditure on more traditional media – posters in particular have enjoyed a boom from the dotcom brigade.
- Many sites are clearly amateur, uninspiring and ultimately frustrating.
- It requires a substantial back-up of people and logistics to deal with the responses.

Yes, the Victoria' Secret Web site in the USA *did* get 250,000 hits *an hour* just before Christmas 1999 (Victoria' Secret is a lingerie retailer), but when it crashed for three days due to the overload, lost sales were estimated in the millions of dollars.

A Web site is much more than a promotional vehicle (see Chapter 18), but when used on that level the following tips may be helpful:

- The Web site design must hook people within four seconds or most visitors will leave – get an expert to help with the design. This is not a job for the youngest member of the marketing team just because he or she happens to be 'Internet literate'.

- For those customers searching for something specific, the 'two clicks and you're there' rule is a good one.
- Content and design must be changed regularly if you want people to keep returning – old Web sites can get 'tired' very quickly.
- The use of banners on other people's sites can be very wearing if transfer is not fast and if it doesn't take you to precisely where you want to get.
- Aim to generate a response – and then handle that response immediately.
- Use the medium to develop an understanding of what people are looking for (see Chapter 18 on CRM – customer relationship management).
- Monitor usage and conversion rates.

Direct mail

The strengths are:

- With good databases, it is highly targetable, even personalized.
- It has a very controllable message and an ability to go well beyond the single-minded proposition.
- It provides an opportunity to establish dialogue with customers.
- It is relatively easy to measure effectiveness.
- It has a relatively low cost of start-up.

The disadvantages are:

- It is identified with junk mail.
- There are low hit rates – usually well below 1.5 per cent.
- It is dependent on the quality of mailing lists.

Most people hate junk mail, so we are pleasantly surprised if something of genuine interest lands on our doormat. The secret to direct mail is being relevant, and the quality of the database is everything. This is a medium that alongside the Internet perhaps has the biggest potential for growth as databases improve with the advent of CRM (see Chapter 18).

Telemarketing

The strengths are:

- There is a relatively low-cost start-up.
- There is the opportunity to engage in a conversation with the customer.
- There is the opportunity to do research on real customer needs and perceptions.
- It is easy to start up without competitors knowing, and easy to close down without the market knowing you have 'withdrawn'.

The disadvantages are:

- It is probably regarded as the most intrusive of all media.
- There is the danger of creating strong antipathy (and a place on the next TV exposé of 'cowboy' sales techniques).
- It has a low hit rate.

Some of the potential benefits of telemarketing, the extended conversation and the opportunity for research, are only achievable if the staff engaged on the job are sufficiently briefed and trained and, most importantly, allowed the time to engage in such pursuits. The strict time-bound and result-based regimes of many telemarketing operations may work actively against this aim. If this is a purpose of your exercise then careful selection and briefing of the agency or staff providing the service will be required.

Exhibitions

The strengths are:

- There is direct contact with customers and potential customers.
- They are good for trade relations.
- They are a good platform for new product launches.
- They are a shop window.
- They establish presence and credibility.
- They afford opportunities for customer entertaining.
- They generate sales leads.

The disadvantages are:

- There is a high cost (or the risk of looking tacky).
- There are high demands on staff time.
- Your competitors will usually be present (and might outshine you or out-entertain you).
- Once started, it is difficult to pull out without incurring negative comment – 'I see so and so can't afford to be here this year.'

Sponsorship and celebrity endorsement

The strengths are:

- They have a high profile.
- They provide the opportunity to link strong values and perceptions to your own proposition, so enhancing your own product's perception.
- With the right vehicle, they provide an opportunity to substantiate your proposition.
- There are entertainment opportunities.
- Success builds success.
- There is the opportunity for a unique position or statement.

The disadvantages are:

- Failure breeds contempt!
- The wrong associations can be embarrassing, and not all eventualities can be planned for, eg Pepsi and Michael Jackson.
- There are complex targeting issues.
- They can build opponents as well as supporters, particularly where sports teams are sponsored. It might be supposed that not many Manchester City supporters own Sharp appliances and few will now sign up for Vodafone contracts (see below).
- They need a long-term commitment – withdrawal can be difficult, with negative PR.

Aprilia, the Italian motor-scooter manufacturer, secured the Spice Girls to endorse its product, and was outraged when Gerri Halliwell promptly left the group, leaving Aprilia with a highly embarrassing set of non-usable images and materials. **And then there were four...**

In February 2000, Manchester United signed a £30 million, four-year sponsorship deal with Vodafone. This came after 18 years with Sharp and a good deal of talk from observers about how Vodafone will aim to extract a whole lot more value in their four years than Sharp did in their 18. Vodafone will certainly plan to 'leverage' the deal well beyond the use of hospitality boxes. The deal illustrates how sponsorship can be used beyond simple promotion, taking it into the realm of the other Ps in the marketing mix. Manchester United is the product and Vodafone the distributor, quite literally. The Manchester United Web site gets 75 million hits a month, and access will soon be available through mobile phones.

Sponsorship of broadcast media, such as The Equitable Life Assurance Society's sponsorship of the TV comedy *Frasier* on Channel 4, allows for targeting of specific audiences – great if your target segment corresponds closely with the audience for the show. But beware, TV shows can lose their appeal and 'go off', and the sponsor needs to be fast on its feet to remove its connection before it suffers the same fate. The message can only be very simple, and has more to do with the association than the message itself, calling for very careful selection.

Media relations and product placement

(This includes such things as DIY products used on TV home improvement programmes, or retailers providing items for fashion magazines.) The strengths are:

- The costs are low.
- They can build credibility over time.
- They have a high profile.
- They can turn on sales very fast.

The disadvantages are:

- There is low control of the message – with occasional surprises if your product is slated!
- They are prone to short-term bursts of enthusiasm.

Why Delia is the supermarkets' darling

UK supermarkets now try to find out in advance what products Delia Smith will be using on her cookery programmes as she only has to mention a new type of cream or some little-known vegetable for the shelves to be emptied of these things the following day. Delia once famously exhausted the UK supply of sun-dried tomatoes as that humble vegetable was rocketed to superstar status through her programme.

'Product placement' is an art. Philips once scored a coup by having a number of their highest-tech products 'placed' in the latest Bond movie. Endorsements by fictional (or long-dead) characters sometimes seem to be more powerful (and more believable?) than those by the real and the living.

A specific type of product placement, not restricted to media relations, is having your product associated with another that is in turn promoting itself. Soap powders might feature particular washing machine manufacturers in their advertising, Little Chef might place Bird's custard on their menu and the Dulux dog might be used by Heineken to demonstrate how its beer really does reach the parts other beers cannot reach (the dog was shown doing the painting for its owner while he relaxed with beer in hand).

Nor is this just for consumer brands. Rockwell Automation has promoted its name to investors and customers alike as a supplier to Nestlé, associating itself with Nestlé's success in the ice-cream market. 'Rockwell Automation is helping Nestlé scoop the market in ice-cream with perfect flavour and consistency' runs the ad, placed in the share price section of the _Financial Times_.

PR

The strengths are:

- This is the subtle approach – not being seen to promote.
- It is good for managing the big issues and the top-level messages.

The disadvantages are:

- It needs very professional management – amateur attempts can lead to big problems.
- It is hard to measure its impact or effectiveness – it is often a matter of 'faith' (and much easier to measure its failings!).

Sales promotion

The strengths are:

- It is highly targeted.
- It has measurable impact.
- Increased sales during the activity can reduce the sort of cash-flow problems associated with most other promotional activities.
- It builds distributor commitment.

The disadvantages are:

- There can be forecasting problems, eg Hoover's famous débâcle with the airline tickets (see Chapter 5).

- It might have only a short-term effect – when the promotion stops, so can the sales.
- It can become established as the norm.
- It can devalue the brand, particularly if price is always the vehicle.

There's nothing wrong with pinching a good idea

Brake Bros, a leading food supplier to the catering industry, introduced a 'buy one, get one free' offer in the first quarter of 2000. This was a relatively unusual form of promotion in the catering trade and they were pleasantly surprised by winning 2,000 new accounts. They didn't allow it to go to their heads, however; 'our challenge now is to make those regular customers' was their wise reaction.

The role of the sales force in promotion

In many business-to-business environments, the face-to-face contact provided by the sales force is a hugely valuable part of the promotional activity, allowing genuine dialogue and feedback beyond those experienced in any of the other media. Unfortunately the costs are high and, as sales forces reduce in size, the time given to genuine promotion rather than selling can grow very small; some salespeople might even resent the imposition of the task. The trend towards smaller sales teams, a trend that e-commerce will do little to reverse, has seriously reduced the ability of many business-to-business operations to promote themselves in the market. Some are even finding that their growth aspirations are restricted by the size of the sales team.

The instant sales force – just add Innovex

Nowhere has the impact of a sales force been more important in recent years than in the pharmaceutical market, evidenced by the great care taken with selection and training, but nowhere does the cost of such sales teams hit harder on the bottom line.

The launch of a new drug is a phenomenally expensive exercise; perhaps $1 billion goes on promotion costs in the first two years, and a significant slug of that is the sales force. The drug companies have looked for ways to reduce this cost and a popular option has been the idea of the contract sales force. Companies like Innovex will provide a bespoke sales team to the drug company, making it possible to create the ideal team for the promotional period and then to disband the team at no cost at the end.

SELECTING AND BRIEFING AN AGENCY

The huge number of agencies available to help with every conceivable form of promotion can be rather overwhelming when you are faced with the need to select just one. Too many large agencies behave as if they are from a superior species to mere business folk, while too many one-man bands feel that their own business experience and a fancy logo are sufficient to warrant charging you for their help, yet it is precisely with some of these smaller agencies that the real gold dust can be found. So how to make the right choice – is it reputation, size, personal chemistry, experience?

Selecting the right agency starts well before reaching for the telephone directory. It starts with an absolute clarity about your own promotional objectives. You will need to brief the agency, so start by preparing that brief. Once completed, the sort of agency best placed to help will already be that much clearer.

The briefing

The agency will need to know (and if they say they don't, then perhaps they are not the agency for you):

- the key characteristics of your company, brand and product;
- the market performance;
- the market dynamics;
- the main competitors;
- the main trends in the market;
- market segmentation;
- any previous promotional activity and its impact;
- any restrictions on your ability to promote – financial, legal, moral, etc;
- the target market, segment, customers;
- the purpose of the promotional activity – the desired outcome, the target audience, the timings, the specific results required;
- your single-minded proposition – unless you are engaging their help to determine one for you;
- supporting evidence for this proposition;
- the desired brand positioning;
- the preferred media;
- timings and budgets.

Agencies that show too much concern with the last of these points before understanding your purpose and objectives may be helping you with your selection process more than they think.

Once the brief is complete, select the agencies from which you wish to have a response. Don't go for too many. First, the briefing process is time-consuming. Second, receiving the agency proposals will be even more time-consuming. Third, it is unfair on the agency to ask them to put in a significant amount of work if they are one of a large number under consideration.

Getting to the short list of agencies to brief will be a combination of references from colleagues, perhaps ruling out those used by the competition, and an assessment of their track record of success in similar areas. This last is not a question of 'advertising awards' and the like; rather it is an assessment of how successful the clients of the agency have been.

Some 'rules' on briefing the agency are:

1. Take the time to give a full briefing.
2. Give the agency a written copy of the brief.
3. Be very clear on objectives, timings and budgets.
4. Agencies should welcome your creative thoughts, but try to leave the final creative process to the experts.
5. Ask for the agency's questions.
6. Encourage a critical assessment from the agency.
7. Give the agency as much information as possible on your selection process – timing, criteria, competitors, etc. Help them to do a good job; this is not an obstacle course you are setting them.
8. Determine when you want their response, and in what format.
9. Be very clear on how you wish them to respond; is it just ideas, or do you want a full campaign proposal?

Some 'rules' on receiving their proposals are:

1. Allow them the time they require.
2. Start by restating the objectives of the activity, or ask the agency to do so.
3. Use those objectives as your test – try not to be swayed by the flood of exciting creative ideas. The important question is whether the ideas will achieve your objective.
4. Demand full costings of design, production and placement.

When you finally award the work, do so in writing and repeat the crucial elements of objectives, mechanics, timings and costs. Some marketing people would encourage the involvement of professional purchasing people in the agreement of contracts, etc. This is fine, provided that your own purchasing people understand the objectives and that you don't allow them to 'steal' the relationship.

BUDGETS

How much to spend is the toughest question of them all. Undoubtedly, three of the biggest sins of business-to-business promotional campaigns are budget, budget and budget.

On the one hand we recall Henry Ford's comment on advertising expenditure, that half of the money is wasted, but unfortunately you can never be certain which half. On the other hand, we see marketing plans with expansive vision strangled at birth by parsimonious promotional budgets.

There are various ways to arrive at the right sum: a percentage of sales revenue, a percentage of profit, benchmarking based on competitors' spend, last year's expenditure plus or minus a percentage dreamt up by the finance department. All are used frequently, but none of them is remotely satisfactory.

Perhaps the percentage of sales or profit approach is OK if you have a long experience of the relationship between spend and performance, but times change. Not only that, but such measures have a way of self-perpetuating themselves with a deadly circular logic. Who is to say that what the competitors do is right, and what does that have to do with your own objectives in any case? Last year's expenditure plus or minus doesn't even deserve a comment.

There is only one basis on which to determine the budget. Promotion is one of the four Ps in the marketing mix. The marketing mix is how you plan to achieve your marketing objectives, and to be certain of success the elements must be in balance. The promotional spend must be adequate for the particular job in hand. Expect the costs to be higher for the introduction of something new than they are for a boost to an old favourite. Each circumstance is unique, and the application of simplistic formulas is unlikely to work. If after presenting your marketing plan you find that the promotional budget is cut, then you must seriously consider changing the other elements of the mix, or the objectives of the plan.

None of this says that you shouldn't seek creative ways to stretch a budget; we saw in the section on special interest press how Kodak made clever use of a tight budget. Nor does it suggest that we shouldn't continually review the impact of our expenditure with a view to changing it as required.

Tracking

It is important to track the effectiveness of what for many businesses will be one of their highest single expenditures. This is not just about looking at the impact on sales; there are often too many competing variables to be confident of pinning growth on a promotional campaign. For a £5 million TV campaign it will be worth spending the additional £80,000 to measure the campaign's impact on customer perceptions and attitudes. A typical tracking study would look at levels of awareness (often called the *cut-through* of the medium), what perceptions are formed of the brand or product, what promises are seen to be made, what level of belief or confidence exists that they will be upheld, and what disposition the audience has to make a purchase. Only with such information (and the sales statistics!) can you go to your finance director and properly justify your expenditure.

16

Branding

Two or three hundred years ago, branding was something you did to a cow. A brand declared rights of property and ownership, and meant, particularly in remote Scottish glens, 'keep your hands off'. It is a nice irony that this meaning has now been turned on its head – the 21st century brand most determinedly declares 'get your hands on'!

Branding is a big subject, a very big subject, and this chapter will content itself with trying to answer three broad questions:

1. What defines a brand?
2. What are the purpose and benefit of brands and branding?
3. How should a brand be managed?

DEFINING A BRAND – THE HISTORY

We might learn something about the definition and purpose of brands by looking at their historical development. The history of branding is more than of academic interest; it explains the development of a concept through learning to match the circumstances of its times so that it now sits at the heart of modern marketing. Its evolution does not guarantee the brand its future; the brand has no God-given right to exist and, as the following will show, what we understand today by a brand has not been with us all that long.

Who knows, our descendants may look back in 100 years' time and say: 'The 20th century, wasn't that when they had those things called brands?' Above all else, the brand is something to be managed by the marketer, protected, nurtured, amended and changed. Few marketers will have the task of creating a brand from scratch; most will inherit one, for better or worse. Inheriting a brand is like inheriting a grand stately home, a major responsibility as well as a great luxury.

Trade marks

The history tour starts in 1876 with the UK's first registered trade mark, the red triangle still used today by Bass the brewers. Brands had existed before that, but this marked their official recognition. So why now? The explosive rise of urban populations during the Industrial Revolution meant that by the close of the 19th century only a tiny fraction of people still bought direct from the original producer. The age of mass production and mass distribution had arrived. Where their parents would have made bargains with artisans to 'make to order', or shopped at local stores for goods that were finished on the spot, late-19th-century consumers had to put their trust in an intermediary, or indeed a string of intermediaries. The late-Victorian tippler never met the man who brewed his ale, but the red triangle told him that he was as safe with it as if the brewer had been his neighbour. The brand as we know it today began its life as a simple mark of authenticity.

There's only one ENO

ENO's Fruit Salt carried the following caution in 1903 – 'Examine the bottle and capsule and see that they are marked "ENO's Fruit Salt", otherwise you have been imposed upon by a WORTHLESS imitation.'

The 19th-century legacy

Brands were trade marks, and trade marks were brands. The honour roll of 19th-century consumer brands that are still with us is remarkable when we consider the huge changes in all other walks of life. Anchor butter, Avon cosmetics, Bassett's Liquorice Allsorts, Baxter's soup, Beecham's pills, Bird's custard, Bovril, Brooke Bond tea, Cadbury's, Clark's shoes, Coca-Cola, Colman's mustard, Fyffe's bananas, Heinz (even the 57 varieties go back that far), Horlicks, Hovis, Jacob's biscuits, Johnson's baby powder, Kellogg's, Kodak, McVitie's, Omega watches, Parker pens, Pear's soap, Robertson's Golden Shred marmalade, Rowntree's Fruit Pastilles, Schweppes (strictly speaking, late-18th-century), Slazenger tennis rackets, Tate & Lyle sugar, Wrigley's chewing gum, Yale locks: they all started life over 100 years ago.

The names, or trade marks, have survived, as have products that are still identifiable with their originals, but as for what the brands meant or stood for, time has marched on.

By 1911 Kellogg's was already spending $1 million in the USA on advertising the familiar red signature, one of the world's most consistent claims to authenticity. Mass production had seen the rise of trade mark brands, and soon it spurred the rise of imitators. The very fact that trade marks existed made them worth stealing! A new need to protect their property arose and the brand owners started to look beyond simple statements of authenticity. They were turning their brands into promises. The promise might be for a better taste, purer ingredients, a longer life, a better physique, and to begin with these promises could sometimes get out of hand.

Dr J Collis Browne's Chlorodyne was advertised in 1902 as:

> The most wonderful and valuable remedy ever discovered. Chlorodyne is the best remedy known for *coughs, colds, consumption, bronchitis, asthma*. Chlorodyne effectually checks and arrests those too often fatal diseases – *diphtheria, fever, croup, ague*. Chlorodyne acts like a charm in *diarrhea* [sic] and is the only specific in *cholera* and *dysentery*. Chlorodyne effectually cuts short all attacks of *epilepsy, hysteria, palpitation* and *spasms*. Chlorodyne is the only palliative in *neuralgia, rheumatism, gout, cancer, toothache, meningitis*, and etc. Caution – Beware of *Piracy* and *Imitation*.

They just don't write them like that anymore

(Collis Browne is still available today and is said to be good for treating diarrhoea.)

This period is rich with examples of products and advertisements that tried to 'hit' on every front at once. Carter's Extra Concentrated Lemonade offered 'lemonade in a moment' but not only that, it was also a 'prophylactic against cholera' and, to top it all, in case anybody thought the notion of 'cost in use' (see Chapter 13) was a new one, the tag line was 'goes farthest – therefore cheapest'.

The unique selling proposition (USP)

As consumers grew more 'brand-literate', so the promises had to moderate, and advertisers began to latch on to rather more single-minded claims as a means to give direction to the brands in their charge. In the 1940s, Rosser Reeves led the way with USPs, and brands became very single-minded. USPs gave brands competitive advantage and some USPs remain to this day. Volvo still 'owns' safety as a proposition in the car market, so much so that it has to try that much harder whenever it wants any message other than safety to be heard.

Campaigns like 'Birds Eye – the modern way to cook', or 'Chew Wrigley's – freshen your taste!' might seem rather tame and innocent today, but at the time they were seen by many as aggressive and intrusive. The USP gave critics and competitors alike something to shoot at, and this was its drawback. If all your eggs were put in that one basket, what happened if someone came along with a better product? You might claim best performance, but new technology could outflank you.

The brand image

By the 1950s people in advertising like David Ogilvy were working to go beyond simple promises; they wanted to build 'brand image'. If a brand could acquire an image, a personality even, then that would enhance its protection against competitors. This was not simply the trick of a clever copywriter (though many of today's famous novelists had their writing apprenticeships in the post-war advertising agencies); this was marketing as defined by the marketing model (see Chapter 3). A brand needed credibility to build its image (company capability) and it needed customers who would value that image (market needs). Only then would big advertising budgets bear fruit.

ICI, as one of the world's largest chemical companies, had credibility as a paint manufacturer, but it recognized that the new DIY paint buyers wanted more than technology in a tin. People wanted to turn their houses into homes, and that meant the warmth of family life. The old English sheepdog (or Dulux dog, as most people have come to call it) was added to ICI's paint brand to give it that warm family feeling, and a brand *personality* was born.

Making a house into a home

Brands were becoming more complex, multi-faceted, eliciting emotional responses, and as a result they were able to command premiums for longer. The brand was a route to not only competitive advantage but also long-term security.

The 'T plan'

In the 1960s the J Walter Thompson agency was working with its 'T plan', an intellectual concept that a brand was a synthesis of *knowledge*, *beliefs*, and *emotional projections*. In other words, a brand was something that you knew about, that you might be able to state 'facts' about that you believed to be true, and that engendered feelings and emotions that went well beyond the product or its USP. It was these emotional projections that were most important. Volvo might 'own' safety as its USP, but the emotional projections were even more important – this was safety with a purpose, protecting your family. In the end it is this emotional projection or what we might call 'emotional charge' that gives Volvo its brand value, not the statistics about safety records or crash tests.

DEFINING A BRAND – THE 'EMOTIONAL CHARGE'

Take a quick look at the four pictures on the next page; don't take too long over any of them, a few seconds, and then turn the page.

(Left) **Figure 16.1**
The Pope

(Right) **Figure 16.2**
Coca-Cola logo

(Left) **Figure 16.3**
Virgin logo

(Right) **Figure 16.4**
Mercedes logo

If you took the time, you could probably now fill a whole side of A4 with the various facts, pieces of knowledge, ideas, thoughts, beliefs, promises, expectations and emotions that just a few seconds exposed to four well-known 'brand images' have communicated to you.

Is the Pope a brand image? He isn't designed to be such in practice, of course, but the Pope carries a different order of emotional promise and expectation from Coca-Cola. I mean no sacrilege by the comparison, but want to make the simple point that some brands carry more 'emotional charge' than others. The reasons are numerous, but might be summarized into two factors: 1) what brands do about their own image; and 2) how consumers interact with them.

Brand activity

Some brands clearly do more about building their image than others. This isn't just a question of money; it is about consistency and use of heritage.

Fairy Liquid held a children's competition to celebrate the millennium asking kids to redesign its famous 'Bizzy' logo, the baby with the towelling nappy. Unsurprisingly the winning images were very space-age and appeared on 'limited edition' bottles. As a means of reinforcing a part of the brand heritage and emotional charge at minimal cost, while creating new interest, this was a marketing and branding *tour de force*.

Heritage doesn't mean nothing changes

Sponsorship and PR are part of the plan for raising the 'emotional charge' of a brand. The link between cigarette brands and sporting events (a historical oddity of the 70s and 80s) was always more than an awareness campaign. While few were moved to believe that cigarettes were good for you as a result of the emotional projection, many were 'relaxed' in their habit by the good associations. Virgin is all the more powerful as a brand just because Sir Richard Branson kept trying to take a balloon around the world.

Consumer interaction

Some brands call on the consumer's emotional responses more than others. The reasons are numerous and complex, and depend most importantly on the individual consumer's perceptions. The following are some of the factors involved:

- the price paid;

- the frequency of purchase;
- the risk involved in the purchase;
- the risk involved in use;
- the conspicuousness of the purchase;
- the importance of consistency;
- the utility of the product or service;
- the tangibility of performance;
- the number of brands competing for attention.

The factors don't work in isolation and nor do they always work in the same direction – just because an item is low priced, regularly purchased and has a utilitarian purpose doesn't mean that it can't have an emotional charge. Toilet paper is a case in point; the Andrex brand spends a lot, and does so consistently, to build emotional responses that go beyond these factors. The Andrex puppies exude messages of softness, warmth, care and responsibility (at the same time as helping communicate messages about the length of the roll!) – a subtle blend with a strong appeal.

It is the job of a brand to create and maintain loyalty, and the more complex the relationship the consumer has with the brand the greater the chance of success. Loyalty to a make of car is an excellent example. You are considering a new Mercedes. It is a high-price item, purchased rarely. Buying the wrong car is a big mistake, driving the wrong car is a big mistake, plenty of people will draw conclusions about you from the car you drive, your father had one and it was great, you will use it every day for important business calls, you can feel its performance beneath your foot and, after all, there is only one Mercedes.

Perhaps, but for other people the price is outrageous, they don't care what people think, it's only for a run-around, they never go above 30 miles per hour and, for them, a car is just a car.

People and their different priorities – it's what brands are made for. A brand can develop a high level of loyalty and emotional charge in the group of people at whom it is targeted. In so doing it may even antagonize those for whom it is not intended. Ever seen a TV ad that just makes you want to scream? Chances are you weren't in the target audience. 'Alcopops' in the 1990s rekindled some of the latent outrage against marketing and advertising folk that had been quiet for some time, while teenagers took to the stuff like fishes. Brands and segmentation go together and a consumer brand in particular must tune in to the social values of its consumers.

We have spoken a lot here about consumer brands. Does the same apply to brands in the business-to-business or service sphere? The answer is yes, but with different emphasis on different factors. If a consumer brand must tune into the social values, so must a business-to-business or service brand tune into the commercial environment of the time.

Intel captured the loyalty of PC manufacturers for a variety of reasons but mainly because of their ability to supply chips of ever-reducing size and ever-increasing speed. This is what mattered to equipment manufacturers in pursuit of a constant stream of new product development. There are signs now that costs are becoming more important; this is a market approaching maturity already! Intel is genuinely threatened for the first time by lower-price suppliers and the question is, will Intel's current brand values be right for the next decade?

DHL works hard to create its brand value around reliability and speed. The emotional charge for DHL comes from the business community's need to do things fast, globally. A brand that facilitates that is a hero brand. And then there is e-mail. There is less need for such heroics – huge documents can be sent in seconds with no need for planes, boats and trains. The brand must change into something other than a specialist emergency service.

Times change – will Intel and DHL?

Types of emotional charge

Table 16.1 defines four types of emotional charge, describes the main issues raised by that charge and looks at the role of the brand against each.

This table is not intended to pigeon-hole particular brands, only to help express a concept. Of course there are crossovers between the levels and brands that work on more than one – that is their strength. There are many consumers who would fail to tell Kellogg's cornflakes from a retailer's own label in a blind test, yet would gain genuine satisfaction from pouring their favourite breakfast cereal from a reassuringly genuine Kellogg's box.

Let's consider each of these levels of emotional charge, starting at the lowest level and rising in intensity, illustrated by examples from an fmcg, business-to-business and service industry.

Table 16.1 *Brands and 'emotional charge'*

Emotional Charge	The Main Issues	The Role of the Brand	Examples
A Social Expression	personal ego, conformity/ nonconformity	to facilitate conspicuity	Rolex watches
A Satisfaction	personal fulfilment, pleasure in use	to win a premium price	Janet Reger Cadbury's
A Promise	performance in use	to influence choice	Crest toothpaste Fairy Liquid
A Guarantee	authenticity	to make choice easy	Kellogg's

The brand as a guarantee of authenticity

Brands as we know them may have started life back in the 19th century as marks of authenticity but the notion is far from a dead one. It only takes an unstable market for the earliest forces behind branding to resurface.

Keeping ahead (when all around are losing theirs)

In the days of the USSR, Borjomi sparkling mineral water from the Caucasus in Georgia was said to be the third-best-known brand in the Union; the Volga car and Aeroflot took the top spots. By 1996, after a decade or more of the kind of free enterprise that encouraged the rise of piracy and gangsterism, as much as 90 per cent of what went under the Borjomi label was said to be counterfeit! Then came the advertising campaign, reminding consumers of the distinctive packaging of the real Borjomi ('beware imitations'), and the not insignificant financial crisis of 1998 that killed off many of the poorly financed counterfeiters. By 2000 the claim is that 90 per cent of Borjomi sold is genuine. Who knows for sure whether it is 90 per cent or only 50 per cent, but what is certain from the company's revitalized fortunes is that branding as a mark of authenticity has worked.

The value of a strong trade mark or logo is clear when there are many players in the market and customers simply want an easy choice that they can trust. This is the home of the USP:

● fmcg – Kellogg's and the famous 'If it doesn't say Kellogg's on the pack, it isn't Kellogg's inside the pack';

- business-to-business – Hewlett-Packard replacement ink cart-ridges will work, and won't wreck those expensive printers you've just had installed;
- service – Citizens Advice Bureau advice will be genuine.

Of course, the Rolex logo or the Lacoste label is proof of authenticity just as much as the Kellogg's signature, but here lies one of the ironies of branding: if authenticity was all it was about, who would ever _knowingly_ buy an imitation Rolex watch or a fake Lacoste shirt? That people do (though few would admit to it) only shows that some brands work on much higher levels of emotional charge and that some people are prepared to lie, even to themselves, to reach those levels.

The brand as a promise of performance in use

If a brand makes a promise of performance then it must be able to prove it. Often the proof is in the longevity of the brand, but this can be a problem, as Coca-Cola found when they tried to launch a new formulation. New Coke was a flop for a host of reasons but one was undoubtedly the fact that many consumers felt a promise had been broken.

The higher the price tag or the risk involved in the purchase, the more important is the promise. Some products give long lists of their features as proof – computer hardware comes to mind – but good brands can achieve the same end more effectively. While a motor car will quote fuel consumption figures and torque ratios, the evidence of performance is promoted by more intangible imagery, references and associations. Condoms may print statistical evidence of their testing procedures on the packet, but for most people it is a matter of trusting in a particular brand name. When Durex started to market their more exotic range (the pursuit of satisfaction in use, not just performance), some consumers questioned for a moment whether the brand still retained its absolute trustworthiness and reliability.

Consider these:

- fmcg – Fairy Liquid's famous comparison tests, or the Duracell battery in the Christmas toy that goes on, and on, and on…;

- business-to-business – a brand such as Lycra promises performance on two levels, as a high performance raw material for clothing manufacture and as an aid to sales of that clothing through its strong consumer franchise;
- service – Andersen Consulting or Ernst & Young have brands that are able to promise performance through the 'honour roll' of their client list.

The brand as satisfaction – pleasure or fulfilment

One of the best examples of a brand acting as an aid to satisfaction is the label on a bottle of wine. Simply seeing the bottle, if we recognize the name and think well of it, can convince us that the taste will be, and is, good. Try it for yourself in an open and then a blind test and just see if it isn't true, and if you disagree with me then at least you will have enjoyed the enquiry.

There is plenty of hard evidence that headache sufferers will feel better treated or soothed by taking a brand of analgesic that they have heard of rather than an unknown generic. Placebos masquerading as well-known brands have been shown to be more effective than placebos in plain white boxes.

Can a washing powder be elevated to the level of satisfaction or fulfilment? The marketers of Persil believe so and have for many years advertised the product as something more than just clean clothes. The inference of the message is a clean family, putting the washer into the role of protector and carer. If this doesn't quite put washing on a par with eating chocolate or watching movies, injecting that element of pride into using the brand certainly raises it above the level of plain drudgery.

These are examples of the brand as satisfaction:

- fmcg – Dulux paint, not just colour for your walls but a means of 'transforming your home', or Dunlop golf balls – just hitting them makes you feel better about your golf, or Cadbury's Flake, a simple product that has achieved levels of sensuality rarely seen in confectionery;
- business-to-business – 'Nobody ever got fired for buying IBM', a famous phrase that makes plain that commercial buyers buy on more than product performance, not to mention the question of job security;

- service – INSIGHT Marketing and People: it is not unusual in the training business to have people ring you and say that they want their team to go through one of your courses because 10 years ago *they* went on it and they still remember the good time they had, and the amount they learnt, and the great trainers, and the use it has been...

The brand as a social expression – ego, conformity/nonconformity

Sometimes this is just plain conspicuous consumption – driving a Jaguar, wearing a Barbour jacket and carrying those green plastic bags from Harrods even when shopping in Waitrose.

Sometimes it is about confidence, and the need to have your decisions justified. Seeing other people wearing the designer jeans you just bought can upset some people but for most it says – whew, you did the right thing. Social expression can be about conformity or nonconformity, and brands can fit either of these positions. Drinking Pimm's on ice in an East End pub can set you apart from the crowd, while Hofmeister lager will make you one of the lads (for the reverse scenario, substitute Henley Regatta).

Hofmeister was launched successfully in the UK, targeted at young working-class males, a closed shop where beer is concerned and group conformity is the key. Hofmeister used George the bear, a 'dude', to gain it street credibility, and of course those that don't see the appeal of George just aren't in the target segment.

George the 'dude'

The subtext of many car advertisements is more about reassuring you that you have in fact *already* made the right decision *and* it will be respected by your peers than it is about trying to influence you in the first place.

Consider these brands:

- fmcg – Rolex, Hofmeister, Rémy Martin;
- business-to-business – Gore-Tex allows the manufacturer to position its product on the right level, passing on the boast of superiority to its own consumers, and allowing the consumer to be in with 'those in the know';
- service - American Express is said to say something about the user, and saying that is saying it all.

It might seem from looking at these examples that a brand would always want to appeal at the highest level of emotional charge, but this is not always the wisest ambition. For one thing, sustaining a brand image at the level of social expression is an expensive activity and requires a continuity of credibility over a long period of time. Maintaining such customer loyalty to the brand, for that is what we are discussing, is not an easy business.

DEFINING A BRAND – LOYALTY

Let's consider two particular variables that customers might weigh when making a purchasing decision: the risk involved in that purchase, and the amount of money spent. By risk we mean the significance of the decision to the purchaser, and by money spent we mean expenditure in relation to the purchaser's total expenditure over a period of time. These variables will help to determine customers' expectations from their purchase, and also help to define the level and type of loyalty that they may exhibit towards any particular brand offer.

In many business-to-business environments, professional purchasing organizations are starting to use a matrix based on just these two variables in order to position and manage their suppliers (see Figure 13.3). Based on their position in the matrix, suppliers and their products are expected to perform in certain ways, and suppliers seeking to build a credible and relevant brand image must understand these expectations and position their own brand accordingly. The process is of course circular (see Figure 16.5); customers' expectations from a brand will define how that brand will appear, their changing expectations will cause the brand (if it is 'alive') to evolve, and the changes to the brand will in turn influence the customers' expectations. The marketer can jump into this process at any point, to act or to react, though as we can see from experience, reacting is usually a lower-risk activity.

When people talk of brands or products being 'before their time', they are generally referring to a brand that acted before reacting – it forced its definition on the market rather than evolving with the market.

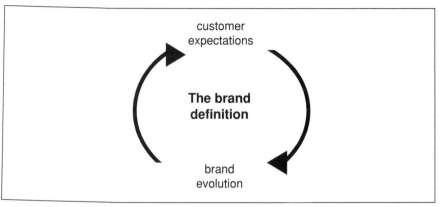

Figure 16.5   *Brands and customer expectations*

Back in the 1970s, Levi Strauss attempted to move into the formal menswear market with the Levi name sown into off-the-peg suits – Levi Tailored Classics. The market research warned them against it. 'People are not ready for such a big step – why not try separates first?' it said, but Levi went ahead and paid the price of forcing a brand into territory that was not yet ready. Of course, from time to time such 'action' will work and we will hail a revolutionary new concept or a breakthrough brand (Amazon.com perhaps) – from time to time.

Levi Strauss – a bridge too far

An understanding of customers' expectations from a brand is but a precursor for something larger: an understanding of the kind of customer loyalty that we might expect that brand to secure. Let's go back to those two variables, risk and spend, and see what light they might shed on this vital issue of brand definition. Chapter 13 discussed these variables in a business-to-business context when looking at the role of price, so we will consider them here in a consumer situation, seeking to understand their impact on customer loyalty and so the branding responses required. I have relabelled the matrix accordingly, as shown in Figure 16.6, and suggested some items that I would put in the matrix, based on my own perceptions.

You may disagree with my positioning. Perhaps for you baked beans are a vital purchase and getting the wrong brand is a minor disaster – perhaps you have children… This is the whole point about understanding consumer expectations, branding and loyalty. Different groups of consumers have different expectations, and if we wish a brand to be relevant then we have to be targeting the right groups; branding and segmentation are almost inseparable.

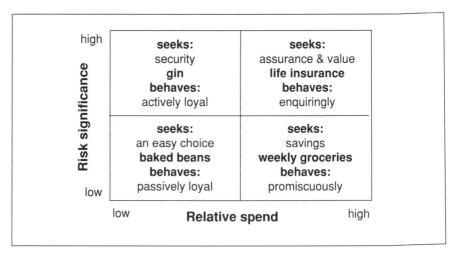

Figure 16.6 *The customer expectation matrix*

Rather than using my examples, position some of your own purchases on the matrix and then ask yourself some questions:

● Do you go about purchasing these items in the same way, or differently?
● What do you expect from a product or service positioned in each box?
● What 'value' are you seeking?
● How loyal would you be to a brand in each box?

The answers will demonstrate how brand values must be positioned depending on consumers' expectations, and that those expectations depend on how consumers position you in their 'mental map', in this case represented by the matrix in Figure 16.6. There are plenty more 'mental maps' that might be appropriate in considering consumers' expectations (see Chapter 11 on perceptual mapping) and how they impact on brand loyalty; I choose this one only as an example.

Table 16.2 takes the items from the matrix and, based on the value sought by consumers and their likely purchasing behaviour, adds a comment on the possible branding approach. The good brand acts appropriately for the value sought and the purchasing behaviour. A pension plan that says 'Tick this box, you're covered' probably won't fly.

Table 16.2 *Expectations, loyalty and branding*

Item	The Consumer Seeks ...	The Consumer Behaves ...	Possible Branding Approach
Gin	security	actively loyal	retain loyalty – 'confidence' 'It's got to be Gordon's'
Baked Beans	an easy choice	passively loyal	make loyalty easy 'Beanz meanz Heinz'
Life Insurance	assurance and value	enquiringly	earn loyalty – 'trust' 'Because life's complicated enough'
Weekly Groceries	savings	promiscuously	'lock in' loyalty supermarket loyalty cards

Rather than pigeon-holing brands, what we see from this analysis is why and how brands can, and do, act to influence consumer expectations, as illustrated in Figure 16.5. The shopper for baked beans may be looking for an easy choice, but the brand activity of Heinz does more than simply respond to this need; it also helps to raise the significance of the purchase (indicated by moving it northwards on the 'customer expectation matrix' shown in Figure 16.6). And as the purchase moves northward on that 'mental map', so does the potential for raising the emotional charge of the brand.

THE BENEFITS OF BRANDING

It will be clear by now that brands are hugely valuable properties (towards the end of this chapter we will look at some of the ways by which businesses seek to quantify that value) and this next section on the benefits of branding may seem to go without saying. We should look, however, a little more closely at three specific benefits:

1. branding and profitability;
2. branding and loyalty;
3. branding and risk management.

Branding and profitability

Strong brands tend to be more profitable than weak ones. Research by PIMS (Profit Impact of Market Strategies) shows that, in the UK food market, the number one food brand in any particular sector has an average profit margin of 18 per cent while the number two brand has an average of only 4 per cent. These are averages; many number two brands run at a loss. In the UK canned food market, Nestlé were clearly the number two player with their Crosse & Blackwell brand, and they chose to pull out entirely, because the game was not worth the candle – Heinz had won.

Table 16.3 shows the average return on investment (ROI) assessed across 3,000 businesses looking at how they stood based on market share (brand strength) and quality.

Table 16.3   *PIMS research on brands and ROI*

	Low Quality	Medium Quality	High Quality
High Market Share	21.00	25.00	38.00
Medium Market Share	14.00	20.00	27.00
Low Market Share	7.00	13.00	20.00

These figures alone are by no means conclusive but they suggest some truths that other pieces of evidence would give backing to: investing in brands to gain market share is as rewarding as investing in the product to improve quality, and if a good-quality product also has a good brand standing, then it will be far more likely to return good profits.

Strong brands tend to return good profits for a variety of reasons:

● Top brands command premium prices (emotion pays more than logic).
● Good brands win customer loyalty, and loyal customers will cost less to retain and service.
● A strong brand gives negotiating power.

- High market share gives you presence in the market, which brings knowledge, and that allows vision, which facilitates an ability to change (famous cases to the contrary apart!).
- A good brand provides the vehicle for evidencing a unique match between company capabilities and market needs – the strong brand is an expression of competitive advantage.
- Strong brands give high-value 'surrounds' to their product or service 'core' (see Chapter 12).
- Good profits resulting from all of the above can be reinvested in improvements to the brand – the 'virtuous circle'.

Branding and loyalty

We have already defined brands as, in part, tools for building and retaining customer loyalty. The value of such loyalty should not be lightly dismissed – many businesses would love the kind of loyalty that brands bring, instead of the methods that they have to use in the absence of strong brands:

- Loyalty does not result from monopoly. Watch how customers will jump ship, almost regardless of the relative merits of the new offer, when a new player enters the field previously held by a monopoly – British Gas and their industrial customers, British Telecom and the new wave of providers, IBM and the PC story.
- Loyalty does not result from bribery. Retailer loyalty cards, credit card membership reward schemes and air miles are bribery, and when the bribe is withdrawn or the novelty wears off, the customer looks elsewhere.
- Loyalty does not result from discounting. Many studies have shown that when consumers buy a 'cheaper' product on a price basis, they still yearn to buy the higher-priced, big brand name alternative, but money won out this time – just wait until they win the lottery…

Loyalty results from the relationship between the supplier and the customer, whether experienced directly or through the product or service. Chapter 19 will look at this in much more detail, particularly in the business-to-business and service environment. When looking at the costs of branding, and the investment is long-term as well as short, you should also consider the costs of winning loyalty through the kind of alternatives shown above. What will it cost to keep competitors out through the maintenance of an effective monopoly, to lock customers in through rebates or rewards, or to keep them through continual price discounting (for once started it rarely stops)?

Branding and risk management – the brand 'halo'

The Ansoff matrix (Figure 8.5) showed how risk increased as a business moved from a growth strategy based on penetration into one based on market extension, or the yet more risky territory of new product development, or beyond that, diversification. The moral of the matrix is not that you should avoid growth strategies based on anything but penetration, but that you should aim to reduce the risks of other strategies by whatever means are appropriate: market research, pilot trials, joint ventures, etc. A key means of reducing the risks involved in such growth strategies is branding.

Virgin's halo (that's around the brand – it's not St Richard... yet)

Virgin have diversified their business activities more often, and at a faster pace, than almost any other company in business history, and yet they handsomely beat Ansoff's forecasted 15 per cent success rate. The answer is in the way they do their market research (thoroughly), the way they work with experts (particularly suppliers) and the way they use their brand. Each new Virgin activity benefits from the success of the ones that went before. People wanted to buy Virgin's PEPs (personal equity plans) because they had been impressed by the way Virgin ran their airline, or they liked the Virgin cola, or they liked Richard Branson. Virgin has enjoyed the effects and benefits of the 'brand halo'.

The brand halo works as it sounds – providing a prefabricated protective surround to the new venture, and so easing its way, even when the new venture might be as unconnected from the previous ones as cola is from airlines or mobile phones from cinemas. The halo also allows the marketer to infuse the new venture with the brand values (hopefully saintly) of the existing ones. The ability to transfer brand values in this way is of huge importance, but it must be done well, and it must be appropriate to the circumstances. The section below on brand management will look at this in more detail in 'Branding the product, or branding the company?'.

BRAND MANAGEMENT

Job titles breed like rabbits in marketing circles, and those titles often have a tendency to aspire to more than is actually involved; some CVs can look quite spectacular after the owner has been in the profession for only a few years! Few titles are more coveted than 'brand manager', especially in the fmcg world, and the responsibilities are indeed broad and onerous. For the world's leading brands, the management task takes place in the boardroom.

The tools and processes used by brand managers are in practice those used by marketers as described in this book; they must conduct market and brand audits, segment the market and manage the marketing mix. In the fmcg world doubtless more attention will be given to promotion, and much time will be spent at those infamous agency lunches (though more like agency tea-breaks these days), but in the main it is a matter of degree and emphasis, not an entirely different job. There are however a few aspects of the brand manager's task that deserve a little more attention here:

- brand positioning;
- brand extension;
- brands and generics;
- branding the product, or branding the company?;
- global or local?;
- valuing the brand.

Brand positioning

Above all else brand managers must recognize that their brand _must_ change over time because the environment in which it exists changes over time. Those that don't change, despite their dominance at a particular moment, will come crashing down as their relevance disappears. It is too depressing to consider the long list of dead, dying, or much reduced brands that might have survived and prospered had they read the runes a little better – Dunns the tailor, Treetops fruit squashes, Tootal shirts, Spangles, Magicote paint. I list these in particular, not because they were any worse than others, but because they died when others in the same line of business prospered. Why?

The 1960s and 70s was a boom period for concentrated fruit squash drinks, and Treetops was a leading brand with an eye-catching bottle design (I recall that the bottle tops in particular were eagerly collected for use in innumerable 'Blue Peteresque' ways). Today most of us will happily pay more for a 250-millilitre bottle of flavoured mineral water than for a litre of squash that might make 20 pints. We will even pay a huge premium to have that same squash (though not Treetops) in a small cardboard box, ready diluted.

The Treetops brand values were about economy and thrift. Today the values of convenience and social expression have grown more significant in this market; some brands managed the transition, while some did not. A brand is the sum of its associations, and the value of those associations will change over time. Not only must brand managers be able to position their brand to occupy a space where its values will be relevant, they must also be able to reposition that brand when required – perhaps one of the most challenging tasks in the marketer's book.

A complete understanding of market segmentation is a vital starting place for brand positioning, and we will take the ideas discussed in Chapter 11 and build on them here (also see the section on repositioning in Chapter 12).

Positioning is the task of finding the relevant space in the target customer's mental or perceptual map, as discussed previously (and in Chapter 11), and cementing your brand's values there. The initial way to do this is through manipulating the elements of the marketing mix and, as a result of this targeted 'package', beginning to influence the shape and boundaries of the customer's expectations and perceptions (see Figure 16.5). Positioning can lead into some very subjective territory and it may be helpful to look for some common means of discussing within your business such issues as customer perceptions. Matrices such as that shown in Figure 16.6 can provide some terms of reference, as can the axis of perceptual maps, as can the notion of describing your brand as a personality.

Identify the brand personality and the personality gap

Start by understanding the brand's 'personality' as it is perceived today. The idea of a brand personality is a convenient way of describing its essence, its appeal, its presence. Since we are talking of personalities, it is appropriate to use a technique that encourages the analogy. Ask a group of people, ideally a focus group of customers and potential customers, to say 'who' your brand would be if it were:

- a movie star;
- a comedian;
- a news-reader;
- a politician;
- a sports person;
- a writer;
- a TV 'personality';
- a game show host;
- etc.

You might even ask:

- Is it male or female?
- How old is it?
- What are its politics?
- What religion does it follow?
- Is it married with kids, or single?
- How's its health?
- How does it respond to stress and crisis?
- etc.

You can take this exercise further and go beyond the limits of human personality. What would your brand be if it were:

- a newspaper?
- a novel?
- a television programme?
- a building?
- a restaurant?
- an animal?
- a country?
- a style of government?
- etc.

With the help of a professional market researcher (experienced in brand positioning) to pose the questions and assess the answers, you will be able to construct a personality profile of your brand. This will be a genuine personality as perceived by your customers, not a wish list as defined in your marketing plan. Now for some questions:

- Is it what you want the brand to be today?
- Is it consistent with how you wish the brand to be positioned (you want a young liberally minded female, and they see a crusty old male)?
- Is this brand personality suitable for communicating and evidencing the match between your offer and the customers' needs?

The gap that emerges between the perceived personality and the personality you wish for your brand represents the positioning or repositioning task ahead. The same exercise could be repeated, making a comparison between the perceived personality and your own vision for the brand's future; will the brand be up to the job, will it require a major facelift, or must it be repositioned?

Brand repositioning

New brands require positioning, existing ones might need repositioning, but which is the harder task? You might suppose that the history and heritage that gave strength to the existing brand might provide a foundation on which to work, so making the task easier, but in fact it is precisely this history that makes the task of repositioning so hard – so hard in fact that many brands die before their owners can even start to think about repositioning.

We can see the problem more clearly if we continue our analogy between brands and people, and note that people's personalities exist in a frame of reference – their family, their place of work, their community. If people want to change their personality they may try as hard as they might but their family and friends will still see the old 'them' shining through. The frustration grows so strong that if they really want to make the change, the answer is usually to leave home. This is what repositioning a brand involves: changing the frame of reference, leaving home.

Predictor, a self-use pregnancy testing kit, found that its personality was not entirely suited to its growth aspirations. The product was well thought of, reliable and responsible, but it suffered from some negative associated images – unpleasant surprises, let-downs, unwanted pregnancies. The purchasing context for the product was often negative; it was something you bought when trouble was looming. While that might have been a base on which to position the brand – a promise of performance in use – it wasn't where Predictor wanted to be. They wanted the brand to have a more upbeat emotional charge, and so a more prominent place in the customer's mind: personal fulfilment. A combination of a packaging redesign and an advertising campaign demonstrating the joy, private and public, of discovering your dreams come true put the brand on to this new level.

Predictor – looking for the right emotion

Ribena was once identified as the drink you were given when you had a cold. It came in large bottles with a suitably medicinal-looking label, was bought in the chemist's and was 'administered' by a parent in careful measures of dilution – a great place for a brand offering a guarantee of authenticity or a promise of performance in use, but the prospects for future growth were limited. Ribena has been one of the most dramatic and successful brand and product make-overs of recent times, moving from a health drink to perhaps the leading exponent of the art of convenience on the move. The marketing mix was transformed – the product went into a Tetra Pak and an explosive variety of flavours and types from low-calorie strawberry to multi-pack orange, the place became the petrol forecourt and motorway service station, the price bore no resemblance to that of its undiluted parent, and the promotion made fun and convenience the message, in place of runny noses and warm beds.

Ribena – a revolution in the marketing mix

The story makes it sound easy, even obvious, but imagine the howls of protest within the company. Picture the upheaval in changing capabilities. Listen to the sales team protesting to their new customers… And before all that even began, imagine the thought process that considered such a leap!

Lego spent much of the last 20 years of the 20th century slowly slipping out of style, culminating in a loss in 1998. But at the same time, the signs of repositioning were to be seen. Lego's aim is to reposition their brand to become the main brand for families with kids, not the main brand for toy bricks, not even toys, but the main brand for families with kids – quite an aspiration! The Legoland theme parks had been taking them out of plastic bricks and into family entertainment, with marked success. Now, licensing deals to use Star Wars characters and Winnie the Pooh are revitalizing the traditional brand, as are Lego lifestyle kids' clothing and watches. New ranges such as Mindstorms, Technic and Mybot combine bricks with technology (the curse of the 80s and 90s), Mybot taking the Lego brand into computer stores as well as traditional toyshops. The success of this repositioning can be seen in the business results, and in the new perceptions that this generation of kids have of this old timer, now reborn.

Lego – no longer just a toy

What is nice about each of these examples is that repositioning was achieved, but the old products were not killed, and nor were their values lost. Predictor still brings sober and reliable news, Ribena is still good for colds and kids still play with the simplest Lego bricks. When Woolworths finally decided to leave behind its 'five and dime' variety store heritage with a dramatic restyling and repositioning programme, it left behind some of its more traditional and most loyal customers. Losing the little old lady who came in to buy a quarter of sweets and a quarter of bacon was a painful transition, for both parties.

Brand extension

It is reckoned that as many as two out of three new product launches are examples of brand extension – taking a known brand into a new product line, often in a completely new market. The reason is clear: to reduce the risk of NPD and diversification (see the Ansoff matrix in Chapter 8) by using the halo effect of the brand.

Will Virgin over extend?

Virgin has managed this process time after time, from record label to airline to financial services to cola to mobile phones and a host more. It is not always successful, as Virgin's foray into clothing has shown, but the Ansoff matrix suggests a 15 per cent success rate for such diversification, and Virgin does a whole lot better than that! Some commentators warn of the risks of brand extension, the danger of a problem with one use of the brand reflecting badly on the others. It is an important question, particularly when a company takes its brand into uncharted territory. Would you find yourself worrying about the reliability of the jet engine on a Virgin Atlantic aircraft while sitting impatiently on a broken-down Virgin train?

Transferring the brand values – JCB

Cosmopolitan has taken its brand into yoghurts and flavoured mineral waters, while JCB has taken its famous 'yellow digger' brand into clothing, toys and hardware. The halo effect only works of course if the existing brand values can be transferred to the new product. For JCB, durability, functionality and a rugged outdoor quality were all values and images that could be transferred to a range of clothing. In such a case the brand had value in the new market and brand extension was a sensible strategy. This will not always be so straightforward, and we wait with interest to see how Philip Morris will extend the Marlboro brand into the new ventures currently under consideration – how will the Marlboro brand values translate for instance to hotels? Some brand extensions come naturally, and some are forced for reasons of growth targets – dangerous ground for the marketer.

Is becoming the generic a good thing?

Some would regard it as a strength of a brand that it becomes the generic name for a product or service – to 'hoover' the carpet, to 'sell-otape' a package, to 'FedEx' this to Sydney. Al Ries (1998) in his book, *The 22 Immutable Laws of Branding*, makes 'owning a word' in this way one of the 22.

But how often have you hoovered the carpet with a Dyson, sell-otaped with Scotch Tape, or FedEx-ed that package by DHL? How often have you ordered a Coke in a café and been served a Pepsi without comment, from you or the staff?

Awareness through use of your brand name as the generic is a great thing, but we have seen that branding is about more than simple awareness; it is about associations. If customers will happily associate other people's products with your brand name, then where does this leave the personality of the brand? Becoming the generic is good provided that you really *do* own the word, and continue to retain that ownership. That takes massive and continuous investment, continued vigilance, continuing evolution, and a refusal to rest on your laurels.

Hoover owned the word, without any doubt, but in the 1990s they lost their unquestioned ownership of the UK market to Dyson. Hoover owned the word because they owned the match in people's minds between the product and what people wanted the product to do for them. This is of course what any good brand should be, the evidence and communication of a match between product capability and customer needs, but Hoover rested on their laurels. They failed to spot a potential update to the match, even when it was placed under their nose (see Chapter 1). When Dyson identified that users of vacuum cleaners wanted something better – better suction and less messy disposal – he invented the bag-less cleaner and the 'cyclone system', so stealing a march on Hoover who were more concerned with preserving their lucrative market for bags.

Dyson – the brand coup of the 1990s

Owning the word relies on owning the match – brands cannot survive for long in the ether of image without substance. Big names can decline fast when they fail to realize this need for real substance – a great heritage is not enough.

Branding the product, or branding the company?

Should the brand be applied to the product (Persil), to the company (Yamaha), or to both (Cadbury's Flake)? They can all work, but for reasons that suit their particular circumstances, and most importantly because they are managed that way. This is an important choice, for once made it will influence the operation, the management structure and the investment strategy of the whole company.

Yamaha sell boats, pianos, hi-fi, motor cycles and electronic organs, among a long list of other things, all branded as Yamaha. They have been able to take their company name, with all its associations, and apply it as a brand across a wide range of products. They benefit from huge economies of scale, and enjoy the halo effect as success in one area rubs off on another. So why doesn't everyone do this? Why does Unilever have 1,600 different product brands world-wide?

How would you feel about receiving as a gift a nice box of Boeing chocolates? Not *too* bad? So how about flying to Australia on a Cadbury 747? Some associations work, and some don't (unless somebody makes them work). It all comes back to a brand being the sum of its values and associations. If a corporation has a very clear set of values and associations, and those can be applied universally to a range of products, then the corporate branding strategy can work – with huge economies of scale and brand halo benefits. Virgin is a case in point.

Corporate brands need corporate values – Virgin has them in abundance	Virgin's corporate values are around challenging the status quo, constructively, as the consumer's champion. They love to take on the 'establishment' in whatever market they place themselves, and this value is personified in Richard Branson, entrepreneur, adventurer and friend of the consumer. There is always a new twist to any Virgin venture – not just selling PEPs (personal equity plans) but taking out the intermediary, not just flying aircraft but getting you to the airport on a limo-bike. Hotels with 'standby' tariffs, mobile phones with attitude and bridal shops for brides (not just the bride's mother), these are all applications of the corporate brand values – championing the customer in style. (Perhaps the exception is the Virgin rail operation where the values are either absent or sit a little uneasily, maybe explaining some of the public's disenchantment with that particular venture.)
A Japanese effort of 'Will'	In Japan a new brand name has been created, Will, to be used as an umbrella brand for a range of products from a number of companies, including a Toyota car, a

National Panasonic PC and an Asahi beer. Each product will retain its own company name, but will have the values and associations of Will superimposed: an intriguing attempt to create a ready-made corporate brand overnight.

Unilever have announced their intention to reduce that staggering list of 1,600 brands world-wide down to 400, still a large number, but it's a start. Individual product branding can get out of hand and, once the brands start to breed, profits can fly out of the window.

Unilever's focus

Nestlé have reduced the number of manufacturer brands in their portfolio with startling rigour. As they have acquired companies and their brands, they have removed such well-known names as Rowntree from the Kit-Kat or Mackintosh from the Quality Street, replacing them with the increasingly universal Nestlé. Is this a good thing?

Nestlé Kit-Kat – whatever next?

The arguments for and against might seem to represent the quantitative versus the qualitative, the ascendancy of the accountant over the marketer, possibly even the internal versus the external, but there is more to it than that. Arguments 'for' are certainly in the realm of economies of scale, but also include the power of a consistent message and the benefits of the halo effect. Arguments 'against' include the short-term damage to a hard-earned consumer franchise and many 'what if' scenarios, not least of which is 'What if Nestlé become identified with a food scare?'.

Recent surveys in the UK have shown that many consumer brands are trusted more than the police or the royal family, but also, and of greater relevance to us, they are trusted more than the big corporate concerns, their owners. Among those brands winning high levels of trust were Pepsi, Mars and St Michael (product brands), while among the less trusted were Shell, Microsoft and Sky (corporate brands). It would seem that when a brand's values become mixed with those of the corporate owner, and that corporate owner has high-profile problems, then brand problems can result. Shell's tussles with environmental groups on issues to do with exploration and drilling have an impact on how we see their product at the pump. Sky's arguments with the Manchester United supporters' club can have an impact on their image quite out of proportion to the scale of the particular dispute. Companies that appear to the media, or to the government, to be growing too powerful, such as Microsoft, can have consequent problems with their brand image in the eyes of the consumer.

Peter Doyle has developed a matrix (Figure 16.7) that considers how feasible a corporate brand strategy might be, and where a product brand strategy might be better. The matrix asks how uniform the target markets for products in the portfolio are, and how uniform across these products the differential advantage of the company is.

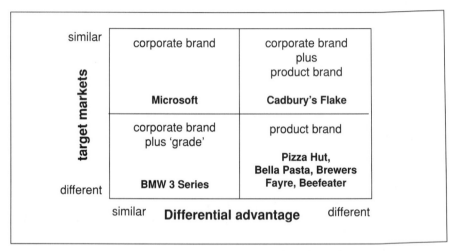

Figure 16.7 *Corporate or product branding*

The greater the similarity of market and differential advantage the more scope there is for a corporate brand with all its benefits. Where there is no similarity, the greater is the need for unique product brands. Of the two factors it is the uniformity, or otherwise, of the differential advantage that seems to make the most important impact on the decision. Cadbury's is chocolate, but Flake has a very different personality to Dairy Milk. If you think of brands as personalities then it points out the problems of forcing different products under the umbrella of a single brand name. In some cases there would be no point at all.

On my high street there are four restaurants owned by Whitbread (as well as a Hogshead pub, also Whitbread), which (and it shows my age) I still associate primarily with beer. The restaurants go under four different brands – Pizza Hut, Beefeater, Brewers Fayre and Bella Pasta – and most of their clientele would not know the link. Why should they? What advantage would Whitbread gain from that? A quick walk down the high street demonstrates the hugely different clientele in each restaurant (but the relative uniformity in each individual case), a credit to Whitbread's ability to link segmentation with branding. There would only be room for one Whitbread-branded restaurant in the town and then even that would be mistaken for a pub by the likes of me! Whitbread practise market segmentation and they use product branding as a means to position their products within the resultant segments.

Whitbread – textbook branding on the high street

As well as corporate brands and product brands there are instances of both combined – Nestlé Kit-Kat, Ford Mondeo, ICI Dulux. Where company brands are used alongside product brands then it is important to understand which part of the dual branding brings what values.

ICI Dulux has long enjoyed a 'double whammy', as it were. Ask people to imagine that they live by the coast and hate painting. What brand of paint would they use on the outside of the house, ICI or Dulux? Most would say ICI, as the circumstances of the task make their thoughts lean towards the technical strengths of an ICI-made product. Ask those same people to imagine that they love DIY and are painting their bedroom. If asked to choose between ICI and Dulux, the Dulux values win through every time.

Painting your house? ICI or Dulux?

Some corporate brands, whether used solus or twinned with a product brand, can actually limit the company's potential.

Ford always found it hard to move into the higher-priced luxury end of the car market and in the end found it easier to buy Jaguar in order to achieve their ends. The high emotional charge of car brands makes them a particularly interesting case in this debate. Toyota chose to launch their new quality car under the Lexus brand and Honda chose to create the Acura brand, because the target markets were sufficiently different from their current ones and their intended differential advantage was very different (remembering that small things count for a lot in people's perceptual mapping of cars!).

Who'd buy a Jaguar if it was called a Ford?

The halo effect of a corporate brand can be good or bad, saintly or devilish. Some brands can be overextended – used across too many products or varieties of product – and so suffer the problems of credibility. There are now so many variants of Holiday Inn (from Crowne Plaza all the way down to Express) that the brand is in danger of losing its own definition and integrity – what does it mean to you?

Global or local brands?

The 18th 'immutable law' of branding, according to Al Ries, is that all brands should be global brands, and he cites Heineken as an example of a brand that knows no borders. Good example, and if you can do it the benefits are enormous, but where does that leave positioning? Brand positioning is based on market segmentation and in very few markets indeed do we find that 'the world' is a useful segment. The genius of Heineken's 'refreshes the parts other beers cannot reach' campaign was that it provided a humorous means to knock the competition (without ever having to mention them by name) but more importantly carved out a memorable position focused on refreshment – a unique match that *could* work globally (although in the event the ads were not used globally).

Would you sell vodka in France in the same way you would sell it in Poland? You would maybe want to play up the Polish heritage in a way that would make little sense back home in Poland.

'Some brands are born global, some have globality thrust upon them.'

In 1999 ICI Paints sold its Autocolor brand to long-time rival PPG. Autocolor was the paint brand for the car refinish market, the 'you bend 'em, we mend 'em' business, as insiders were wont to call it. Some observers were surprised: the business was a success and a technical jewel in the ICI crown, but as a global brand it was a non-starter. John McAdam, executive VP for coatings at ICI, was clear about the sale: 'Technical markets are global... if you are not in the top three – forget it.'

In the decorative paint market, ICI owns the Dulux brand. Nearly 20 years ago when ICI bought, in quick succession, Valentine, one of France's leading paint brands, and Glidden, owners of some of the USA's top brands, the plan was set for a process of 'Duluxization' – a truly global brand. No more, because as John McAdam points out, 'Decorative markets are different from technical ones because you can be number one in the UK and be nowhere in Italy'. Instead, the policy is to use local brands where they have strengths and resonances, and to build a portfolio of strong brands that now includes Cuprinol, Hammerite, Polyfilla and Polycell. John McAdam concedes: 'We thought we could apply a UK solution to the US, without doing regional research.'

We find some of the same elements as in the debate over corporate or product brands: the economies of scale that global brands can bring (though never forget the staggering costs of their upkeep) versus the need to recognize local differences. Global brands can stand local variation of course – Kentucky Fried Chicken is essentially the same brand in Japan as in the USA, but without the coleslaw – the Japanese don't go for coleslaw. Global brands with local customization can turn over time into quite distinct brands, without assiduous management. It is a difficult line for brand managers to follow – they must be ever vigilant for variations that might actually change the brand's personality and values, while not becoming seen as the 'Gestapo' of the business. Remember that brands must evolve and that the 'thought police' approach can only bring stagnation.

Care is required at both ends of the spectrum. Perhaps the greatest care should be taken to avoid corporate egos getting into the brand's driving seat. Brands, global or otherwise, may be managed by the boardroom, but they should be driven by the market. National and cultural differences are still huge despite the ever-shrinking globe, and there is still positive advantage in tailoring a brand to find a unique match with a local need – it's called finding a competitive edge. It's also called marketing, and perhaps tomorrow's winners will be those that have the time and the resources to do it.

Valuing the brand

In 1985 Reckitt & Colman bought Airwick from Ciba-Geigy, with a good chunk of the payment being for 'goodwill', the accountants' term for the value of such apparently indefinable things as Airwick's customers and their brand. In fact 'goodwill' makes these items quite definable, placing an actual market value on them. Normal practice would have been for Reckitt & Colman to pay the money but see no increase in the net assets shown on the balance sheet – not a new problem, but Reckitt & Colman had a new solution: they decided to capitalize the value of the brand.

In 1987 Grand Met bought Heublein, owners of the Smirnoff brand. Grand Met announced that they would include £588 million on their balance sheet for acquired brands.

These two moves were unusual, but not revolutionary. Reckitt & Colman and Grand Met were only valuing acquired brands as part of the complexity of acquisitions and valuations. The real revolution came in 1988.

In 1988, RHM decided to value all their brands, not just newly acquired ones, and many companies have followed their example since then. What this means for brand managers is that they now have an additional responsibility: not only to improve the subjective value of their brands (ever a task, but not always easy to measure), but also to improve their value as measured by the accountants. Given this responsibility, they should know something about how the accountants will go about it – not that there is any one agreed method.

The task was relatively easy when a company was buying a brand as part of an acquisition – what they paid was what they thought it was worth, so the market decided. But what if you already own the brands? Two methods stand out from the crowd. The *existing use method* attempts to value the brand based on the price premium it receives over its generic competition, plus a calculation for the level of recognition the brand has in the market and the esteem in which customers hold it. The *earnings multiple system* calculates something called *brand earnings*, largely based on the cash flow provided by the brand, and multiplies that by a multiple based on *brand strength*. Brand strength is a combination of factors including market share, global presence, investment and any brand protection measures taken.

It can be seen that the methods still allow a lot of room for subjective analysis, but as the practice becomes more common so do the standards used for this analysis, and brand managers have an additional, increasingly quantitative target to meet.

The 'how to' of brand valuation need not detain us longer, but we should consider the important question for the brand manager, 'What does it do for me?'. Brand valuation is a discipline that forces the brand manager to focus on some rather important issues:

- What actually represents strength and value in our business – is it the brands?
- What is the relative importance of our brands compared to, let's say, our physical assets?
- If a brand has a value, then it can be sold. What will be best for the business, selling a brand or continuing to invest in it?

- Valuing brands helps puts a price on licensing and royalties.
- The value of a brand is not based solely on today's receipts, but as for any investment also on tomorrow's potential. The practice of valuing brands forces the business to regard those brands as investments over time, making quite clear the brand manager's responsibility to build and sustain that investment consistently. This is a great argument the next time the boss asks for a cut in the advertising budget!

SUMMARY OF A 'GOOD BRAND'

This is, as will be quite clear by now, an impossible task; circumstances make the brand what it must be, and the brand helps create the circumstances. The following list can only be a summary of some of the points discussed but it may be helpful to use as a checklist for your own brand. How well does your own brand 'score' against these criteria of success?

A good brand:

- communicates and evidences a unique match between the company's capabilities and the customer's needs;
- communicates a clear 'emotional charge';
- maintains its relevance over time by evolving in response to changing customer expectations and perceptions;
- makes people want to get their hands on it;
- is demanded by customers, at a premium, because it represents excellent value;
- increases the profitability of the business;
- wins, builds and retains customer loyalty;
- provides a protective 'halo' for growth strategies;
- provides a barrier to entry for new entrants or substitutes;
- is uniquely positioned in the market and in the customer's perceptions;
- has a unique, recognizable and memorable 'personality';
- is an investment of increasing value that others will want to own;
- is managed and supported consistently over time;
- works in all parts of the marketing mix whether applied to the product, place, price, or promotion;

- has a dominant market share?
- improves the health of the market?

The last two points in particular are entirely down to circumstances. Many a great brand has a tiny market share (or perhaps has a larger share of a highly specialized segment?), and some brands set out to disrupt markets and to reshape them for their own competitive advantage. All is fair in love and branding.

17

Place strategies

Place is without question the most poorly named of the four Ps in the traditional marketing mix. In order to have something starting with the letter P, we end up with a term that severely misrepresents and underestimates this significant part of the marketer's concern. There is a suggestion in 'place' that we are dealing only with where the product is sold to the final customer – the buyer's office, the show-room, the retailer. On that basis too many marketers abandon this part of the mix to the sales force, for surely they are responsible for managing this end of things?

Place is not just about *where* the product or service is sold. The real concern is with the whole enterprise of getting it to market – order reception, logistics, the *channels of supply* – and with supporting the product or service throughout its journey; before the sale, during the sale and after the sale. Of all the elements of the marketing mix, place probably requires the involvement and co-ordination of the widest range of functions within a business – distribution, supply chain, sales and customer service – and these are all the proper concern of the marketer.

It is only when we appreciate the range of activities that managing place involves, not least the number of 'internal' functions that must be pointed in the customer's direction, that we can properly understand some of the problems confronting the marketer. Take for instance one of the most traditional 'obstacles', the sales force.

Tales abound of conflicts between sales and marketing; as with nations it seems it is always the closest neighbours who fail to get on with each other. Is it because sales feel they are the poor cousin to marketing? Is it because sales feel that they are there to pick up the pieces of marketing's mistakes? Is it because salespeople are dyed in the wool cynics? The truth of the matter is that marketing gets the sales force it deserves. How the product is sold into the market is marketing's responsibility, and if they choose to shirk it then they must learn to put up with the result.

Rather than P for place we might prefer C for *channels of supply*, or even C for *convenience* as suggested by Philip Kotler, and we will return to this notion in Chapter 19. There we will explore how the marketer must manage not only the 'hard stuff' like logistics, but also the 'soft stuff' like the relationships throughout the channels. Logistics don't just happen; they require dialogue, agreement, collaboration and, above all, trust.

CHANNELS OF SUPPLY

'Channel manager' is a job title much on the increase as the importance of this aspect of the marketing mix comes ever more to the fore. Why the increase in importance? Place always mattered; it is simply that as products, prices and promotions grow more uniform between competitors so it is that companies start to see place as their best opportunity for competitive advantage. Not only that, but it is within place that some of the biggest cost reductions are to be made through the efficiencies and disciplines of supply chain management. It is also here that the impact of the e-revolution is perhaps most dramatic.

Most businesses are faced with a variety of routes to market or channels of supply, and an early task within the management of place is to make your choices and determine your priorities. Figure 17.1 shows just some of the choices.

Should we supply direct to the end user? Should we work through wholesalers, or distributors, or agents? Only once that is clear can the channel manager get down to the task of managing the channel.

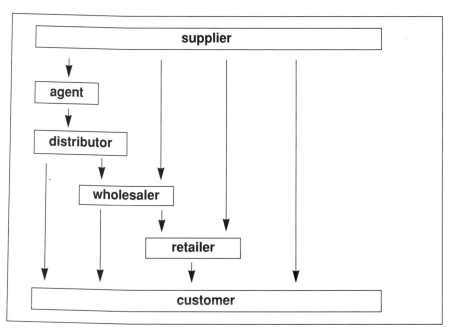

Figure 17.1 *The routes to market*

There has been a lot of controversy recently over banks closing rural branches. The banks argue that new channels such as the Internet not only forced them into this decision but also provide the consumer with adequate alternatives. They are also looking at other alternatives. Lloyds TSB has an arrangement that allows Post Office branches to carry out some simple banking tasks on its behalf, and Barclays is piloting a similar idea in Cornwall. The Post Office, particularly in rural sub-post offices, is suffering a significant loss of business as over-the-counter payments of social security benefits come to an end. Perhaps there is a potential win–win outcome for banks, Post Office and consumer alike?

A bank in a Post Office – why not?

Here are three examples that illustrate some novel choices when looking at routes to market or *channels of supply*.

Fantastic Fireworks, based in Luton, has a turnover of around £1.5 million, with about £800,000 from managed firework displays and £500,000 from what they lightly call 'mail order'. The remaining £200,000 comes from sales through temporary sales sites based on farms. This arrangement suits both parties fine: the farmer gets a 20 per cent commission on a sale or return product at a time of year when other sources of income are slim, and Fantastic Fireworks gets a safe and instant sales network for the short pre-5 November season.

Fantastic Fireworks

Somerfield supply their competition	Somerfield, the supermarket group, have recently started a delivery service to some of their competitors – small independent grocery shops, particularly in rural areas. They will deliver their total range of products at wholesale prices, including their own-label lines. The service helps utilize an asset that was not being 'sweated' as much as the operational people would have liked, and helps extend the Somerfield brand presence into new areas.
Farmers' markets	Farmers' markets are growing in popularity with farmers and consumers alike. Consumers get to talk directly to the supplier and can enjoy the experience of sorting their potatoes from the earth in which they were grown or carrying away their Brussels sprouts still attached to the stalk. The farmers get to sell at prices hitherto undreamt of, learn a lot about what consumers really want (as opposed to what wholesalers and retailers tell them they want) and by all accounts enjoy themselves into the bargain!

The channel audit – the market map

To help in the task of choosing the best routes to market we must start with the same *market map* discussed in Chapter 11 and shown in Figure 17.2.

This map lays out the various routes to market, or the channels of supply. At this point the map should aim to trace all the possible routes, current *and* potential, so that we don't get trapped in a 'Well, we've always done it that way' syndrome – all too easy in this particular neck of the marketing woods.

One of the hardest things for the marketer to get to grips with is the dynamics within these channels, for they are too often the carefully protected 'territory' of the sales force. Their complexity is often embellished with anecdotal stories, usually designed to terrify the uninitiated, and the power of channel players can sometimes be magnified to a point that not even the players themselves would recognize.

Getting to grips with the dynamics is one thing; seeking to change them is quite another (that's why they kept you out, to stop you meddling in *their* business!). You have what you inherit: agents with contracts written 30 years ago, distributors who know more about the market than you do (and want to keep it that way), wholesalers who extract margins for doing, well, not very much from what you

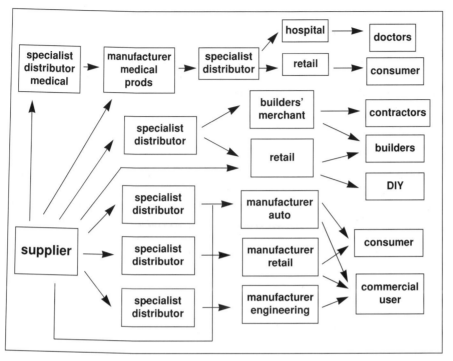

Figure 17.2 *The market map*

can see, and salespeople who might have done your product justice a decade ago, but no more. Try taking that on and see the vested interests rise against you.

You must start with information, an audit of the channels to market. This is where sales and marketing can come together to work as a collaborative team. Channel managers might be people with sales backgrounds brought into marketing, or marketers put into sales management roles – the boundaries start to blur at this point, and a good thing too.

The audit follows much the same path as we examined in the segmentation process, looking for 'hot spots' or points of leverage. These are the points in the market map where the real decisions that affect your success in the market are made: to buy or not to buy. Is the hot spot at the final consumer, or is it somewhere in the channel? In other words, are you engaged in *push* or *pull* marketing?

Push or pull?

Nike spend millions on persuading us to buy their shoes, and we respond in droves, going eagerly to the retailer expecting to find them on prominent display. If we don't see them we probably go somewhere else. We might even complain to the store. This is pull marketing. The supplier is targeting customers right at the end of the chain and pulling them into the channel of supply, the retailer. The retailer doesn't need much persuading to stock the products, nor does the wholesaler or the distributor; the shoes will sell themselves. And in a remote country or territory where Nike have no physical presence, finding an agent will be child's play; everyone will be fighting for the nomination.

The supplier of an unbranded adhesive used in the manufacture of a wide range of things from silicon chips to packaging materials sells its products through specialist distributors, each focused on a particular market. The users of those silicon chips, whether Compaq or the users of Compaq PCs, are not too concerned whose adhesive was used, provided it works, and the further they are from the adhesives supplier the less they care. When this adhesives supplier calls on the specialist distributor it has a problem – why should it be *its* adhesive? The distributor shows it a competitor's product, at a lower price, it is told, or in a more convenient pack size, or the competitor is doing a better job in helping the distributor sell the product to the silicon chip manufacturer. This is push marketing. The supplier has to persuade the channel to accept its product, and it has to push it down the line with incentives and rewards.

Ford play the game at both ends – large-scale advertising campaigns to pull us into the showroom and dealerships incentivized to get us walking out with one of Ford's products. In reality most businesses will combine both push and pull, the differences being in the balance – branded fmcg is more pull than push and a lot of business-to-business is predominantly push.

Can the adhesives supplier redress the balance and develop more 'pull'? The task of developing a brand and promoting it to end users is a significant one, a long haul, and in this circumstance perhaps of less value compared with other options. Pull strategies are not just about promotion and branding. The supplier could develop relationships with the silicon chip manufacturers to find out more about their needs and use that knowledge to help the distributor make the sale, perhaps even working on its behalf. It could go further down the chain to the PC manufacturer and see if there were any positive implications from the choice of the bonding technology used for the chips, so helping the silicon chip manufacturer make its sale, and so helping the distributor with its sale. And even the consumer – if the bonding technology was part of the balance between size and speed, understanding the consumer's preferences might just give it something to take back through the channel.

The balance is of great importance because it will impact on your strength in the market, influence the cost structure of your business and determine your reward. It will also determine how you view your customers and how you manage them. Table 17.1 indicates some of the differences, admittedly in a rather black and white fashion, but designed to help you find your own particular shade of grey.

Table 17.1 *Push or pull strategies*

	Strength	Cost Structure	Reward	Customers
Pull	suppliers own the market	investment in promotion	higher margins	channel partners
	able to 'select' channel partners		security through the brand	
Push	dominant channel players own the market	investment in sales effort	lower margins	customers
	fight for customers	discounts and rebates	margin is 'shared' with distributors	

We should say more about the issue of reward. Think of it from the distributor's point of view. You present it with an unbranded, non-supported product, with no knowledge of the market to give direction, and ask it to sell it for you. Who will need to make the investment? Who will be taking the risk? Who will expect a good reward? Distributors and wholesalers need good margins for such propositions and the supplier will need to 'share' the total margin in the channel with the channel players.

Or, perhaps you present it with a gold-plated certainty: a big brand name, a promotional campaign about to break, a high level of demand, a knowledge of the market that allows you to direct its effort, and you ask it to take the orders and deliver the product. You are making the investment and taking the risk, and you will expect the reward. You may even be in a position to select your distributors, a position of strength indeed.

What all this starts to make clear is just how you should regard the players in the channel: are they customers, or are they part of your distribution network? We are still talking in very black and white terms here, and the real world is coloured with every imaginable shade of grey, but let's continue with the two rather extreme situations discussed above. For the unbranded, unsupported case, the distributor is a customer, to be won, persuaded, cajoled and rewarded for taking on the next step in the chain. In the second case, the gold-plated one, the distributor is a means to an end, an extension of the supplier's own distribution network, an extension of its own sales team – a *channel partner*, to be managed and rewarded for its service.

It may seem that so far I have painted a rather glowing picture of the pull strategy and a life of toil and frustration for the push strategy; perhaps we should redress the balance a little. Sure, pull is great, if you can do it. We are back with company capabilities: do you have brands with strong customer franchises, the money for major promotional activity, the knowledge of the market to know what hot buttons to press, the capacity to handle demand, the resources to talk with the players downstream? The cost structures of a company pursuing a pull strategy can be frightening – the up-front investment is huge and, in a new market with a new product, we know the risks involved.

A pull strategy might suggest to you that you don't need distributors: if there is such a great demand then let's cut out the intermediary. Capabilities again. Do you have the systems to cope with the flood of orders from big and small, do you have the physical capability – the warehouses, the fleets of vehicles – and will these costs be justified by the extra margin you get from cutting out that intermediary? Specialists can often work more efficiently and effectively than generalists, and a good specialist distributor should be able to operate at lower costs than you *and* earn a living. If you can work with your distributors as if they are true extensions of your own distribution network, if they really are channel partners, then why not enjoy the benefits of a sales and logistics operation working at a lower cost than you could achieve, and providing a more appropriate capability? The answer may well depend on how manageable these 'partners' really are, of which more below. Of course, the world is changing fast with regard to this debate. The Internet, e-commerce and other manifestations of the e-revolution are starting to change some of the rules. We will come back to this issue in Chapter 18, 'Marketing and the e-revolution'.

The push strategy requires its own set of capabilities – the ability to find good distributors, just for one. As Russia emerged from the Soviet Union and began opening its doors for business, suppliers from the rest of the world found that they had a problem. In the old days the government handled the buying and the distributing. Once you understood the rules, life was relatively simple: one contact, one order, and you were supplying the USSR! With the fall of the Soviet Union these buying committees started to disappear, and in their place was – nothing. Finding a good distributor was hard work, particularly as so many of the crop that did appear were financially unstable or worse.

We will say more about choosing and managing distributors later in the chapter but for now we should go back to our channel audit and the challenge of identifying and selecting the right channels. Already we have helped our task by considering the notion of push or pull. This gives a strong direction to the sort of channel we are looking for, and the options of course are enormous – let's just consider some of them.

CHANNEL MANAGEMENT

Considering the options

We might start with the simplest of all, direct supply. Build a Web site, install an order reception system, get to know the mailing options, and you have an instant channel to market. Such is the dream of many, and in too many cases such is the underestimation of the task. Beautiful Web sites are easy; it is the infrastructure behind them that determines your success or failure. EasyJet and Dell are two famous examples of direct supply through the Internet, and they have both invested heavily in the systems to make this happen.

At the other extreme we might have a channel to market such as that shown in Figure 17.3, with a whole host of players between you and the end consumer.

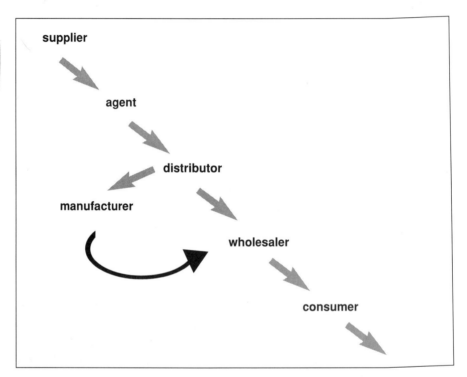

Figure 17.3 *The channel to market*

They all play their part in adding value, or if they don't and only add costs, then they should be removed from the channel (see the section below on value in the channel). Agents will have specialist knowledge and an understanding of the 'rules' of the territory or market, they will have local contacts and they will charge for that value added, usually through some form of commission. Distributors will handle large volumes delivered from the supplier and 'break bulk'. They may also do something to the product – repackaging, dosing with additives, or testing its application. In a business-to-business market the product may now pass to a manufacturer as a 'raw material' or component, coming back into the wholesale/retail channel in its new form. Wholesalers take the product to the local level, providing a sales force, credit terms, delivery, customer service, etc. Retailers handle the consumer, the enquiries, the complaints and the after-sales service.

Alternative channels might include licensing or franchising. Let's consider licensing first. For a fee or a royalty you pass your technology, expertise, intellectual property or brand name to another business, allowing it to manage the channel of supply in its own territory or market. This is an attractive option for markets or territories where you have no ability to reach customers, or perhaps where you have very little interest in reaching them but are pleased of the income. But beware – licensing has a nasty way of coming back to bite you. Today's lack of ability or interest may all change tomorrow, and then what of your 10-year contract that allows someone else to reap the reward in return for your easy life? And is licensing the easy life in any case? Licences need to be supported and managed. Your product or your name is in the hands of the licensee, and so is your reputation. Take care not to regard licensing as the easy way to handle non-core markets.

Franchising is another option for channel management – setting other people up in business with your formula, but it differs from licensing in that you perhaps retain a greater control over essential elements of the mix. Many McDonald's outlets are franchised, but they are obliged to buy their materials through tightly regulated channels, and they are obliged to maintain very strict operational and management standards. The speed with which a new idea can penetrate the market is phenomenal with the use of franchising, and if cash flow would be likely to impede your progress then this can be a very attractive option.

Channel selection and priorities – value in the channel

Having mapped out the existing and potential channels, and taking into account the options discussed above, we must now look at their relative merits. A good start is to assess which channels add most value, or to look from the negative position and assess which channels add most costs. The precise definition of value, and to whom it is added, will of course depend on your own marketing objectives, but might include things such as speed to market, ability and willingness to invest, expertise and capability.

For each channel under consideration, work through the route from supplier to end consumer, noting against each point in the chain the function performed, a definition of the value added and, if possible, a quantitative estimate of that value. Table 17.2 shows this analysis in a typical chain for a consumer product exported from the UK to Eastern Europe. As the final product is not changed at each stage it is possible to note the price at which each point in the chain sells, and the margin that each point makes. The price achieved at each point represents only a very crude assessment of the value added, assuming as it does that the customer in each case is happy to pay that price and by so doing recognizes that value has been added.

Table 17.2 *Value in the channel*

	Function	Value Added	Price	Margin
Supplier	the product	the great idea	£10.00	10%
Agent	expert knowledge	the ability to trade	(commission)	5%
Distributor	breaks bulk	?	£12.50	20%
Wholesaler	sales effort	service to local independents	£14.40	13%
Retailer	customer service	promotion, advice and after-sales service	£21.60	33%

Having done this analysis we can use it to answer some simple questions:

- Does each channel player add value to its immediate customer?
- Does each channel player add value to the final consumer?
- Do any channel players add more cost than value?
- Is the channel player's reward justified for the value added?

- Does each channel player add value to your business?
- Are there alternative channels – e-commerce, licensing, franchise, etc?
- Are any of the channel players dispensable?
- Could you take on any of the functions?
- Do you have the appropriate capabilities?
- Could you take on any of the functions at a lower cost than the existing channel player?
- What impact can you have on the activities of the channel player?
- What impact can you have on the reward received by the channel player?

In the analysis from Table 17.2 it is not clear what value the distributor adds. How significant is the break bulk activity? This would be deserving of further enquiry, as it may be possible to re-engineer the supply channel straight to the wholesaler, freeing up to £2.50 per item to pay for the costs of this direct supply, or to invest in market development, or to take as additional profit.

There are more specific questions to ask, depending on the circumstances. Let's suppose that you are supporting a major promotional campaign in the market, a significant attempt at a pull strategy; does the share of reward in the channel represent a just return for your and others' efforts? Perhaps the retailer's margin represents a reward from an earlier period where a greater 'push' was required in the market – should that margin now be reduced?

Utility and manageability in the channel

The analysis performed on the channel will help us to assess channel players on two broad bases – their utility and their manageability. Where we are considering a number of alternative channels this simplification will be an important aid to our decision, otherwise confused by a whole range of competing circumstantial issues.

Consider their 'utility' – do they perform a valuable role for you and the customer, and will they continue to do so in the future? (As always with marketing, the future role is more significant than the current, raising one of the problems between sales and marketing in this area – their different planning horizons.) Consider also their manageability – are you able to influence their activities and their rewards? Will they work to your agenda?

Some care should be taken with how we think about the second of these two issues – the *manageability* of distribution channels. There must be a very clear difference between influencing channels and behaving anti-competitively. The UK car market has been under close inspection because it is believed that car manufacturers 'manage' the channels unfairly, particularly with regard to the prices at which distributors can or may sell – leading to an estimated £1,100 excess charge per car sold to the consumer.

As an example let's consider the channels available to a major supplier of paint to the professional decorator market in the UK. There are five main options, shown in Table 17.3, together with their share of the current market, a comment on their future share and an assessment of their utility and manageability.

We might plot these different channels on a four-box matrix, Figure 17.4, based on their relative utility and manageability. The matrix might start to indicate those channels that offer the greatest prospects for development to our own agenda (top left), those that will require the most effort to 'manage' towards our agenda but be worth the effort (top right), and those that we may choose to manage with a lower order of priority (bottom left) or perhaps not at all (bottom right).

As with the 'Boston box' or the 'DPM', described in Chapter 12, we have *wildcat* or *problem child* channels like the emergent retailers and to a lesser extent the newly aggressive builders' merchants. These are relatively new players with potentially high future utility but, because of their newness and their nature, relatively low current manageability. Should the paint supplier chase and encourage these 'wildcat' channels?

Put yourself in the shoes of this supplier. Here are some *fors* and *againsts* chasing the retail channel. You might like to consider what else you would want to know before making your judgement, and then what additional steps you would take after making your decision, whichever it might be.

These are the points for:

- There are some very strong and significant players here.
- Their trading practices *may* be the way of the future.
- Should they make a serious entrance they will gain share quickly.

Table 17.3 *Channel options and priorities in the professional decorator market*

Channel Option	% Share of Current Market	Future Trends	Utility	Manageability
Supplier-owned Chain of Decorator Merchants	12%	stable	very high, unlikely to see a significant increase in market presence	high – although issues abound over allowing the chain to operate as a genuine merchant, not a supplier's 'puppet'
Competitor-owned Chains of Decorator Merchants	40%	stable	almost zero!	almost zero!
Traditional Independent Decorator	26%	in slow decline, under threat of faster decline if new entrants come in from the retail sector	declining utility as customers begin to regard them increasingly as behind the times, particularly for price and service	moderate – good relationships as a result of a long trading history
Builders' Merchants	11%	fast growth	aggressive price and service propositions are increasing their significance in customers' eyes	low – trying to forge a new style of operation in the market
Retail Outlets	11%	prospect of major growth should a big player make a serious entrance	significant, if they succeed in establishing a presence in this highly traditional market	very low – new entrants likely to want to create their own position, independently of suppliers

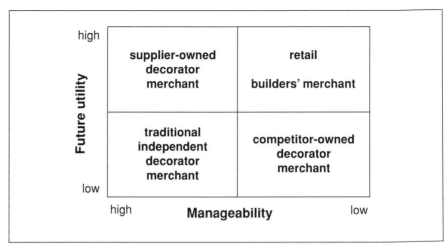

Figure 17.4   *Channel options and priorities*

- We need to be in partnership with them before this happens, not attempting to forge partnership after they have made their move.
- We must certainly not be seen as impeding their progress.

These are the points against:

- Our existing customers will be very displeased.
- Our own decorator merchant chain will be affected – we will be supporting our own competitors.
- The sales force will not support the move.
- The risk of failure by the retail sector in entering this conservative market is high, with the consequent waste of our resource in supporting them and the unnecessary bad PR with existing customers.

MANAGING DISTRIBUTORS

Imagine you left the management of place entirely in the hands of your own sales force, to do as they wished. Can you imagine anything worse? Most certainly. Imagine leaving the management of place in the hands of someone else's sales force. When you make significant use of distributors you are handing chunks of responsibility over to a third party, and you should want to know what is going on, and to be in control. If you are operating principally in push mode, with the distributor seen as a valued customer, then 'managing' that distributor takes on a different connotation, though one of no less importance, from managing a *channel partner* in a pull scenario. The tone of voice will need to be more subtle, your expectations will be modified, the balance of power in any negotiation will be rather different, but the motivation remains the same – to learn as much about your customers as possible and to retain control over the sale of your product or service. Remembering these points of difference, let's look at some of the ways of managing distributors.

Selection

The best way is to start by selecting your distributors carefully – easier said than done if you have inherited your predecessor's selection, or you are in a market with precious little choice. Whether you have a real choice or not, there will be value in trying to identify a list of qualities that would define the perfect distributor. These can be used in any selection process, but they can also be used in assessing existing distributor performance, forming the basis for improvement plans, the core of any management process.

The list might include any of the following:

- their market knowledge and experience;
- their market coverage;
- track record and reputation;
- their commitment to, and enthusiasm for, your product;
- low (or no) competitor involvement;
- the size, quality and reputation of their sales force;
- the frequency of sales calls;
- their product knowledge, application knowledge, etc;
- the quality of their customer service;
- their costs of operation;
- their willingness to discuss costs of operation;
- inventory control – whether they will hold stock and manage it effectively;
- their manageability – whether they will work to your agenda;
- whether they will share information on their customers;
- whether they are open to suggestions for improvement;

- whether you can develop shared business plans;
- the quality of relationships;
- their expectations for reward.

The real world operates over and above all these points, and the balance of power between the two parties is a constant theme, whether witnessed in regular negotiations or experienced through working relationships. Nowhere will it be more felt than in the area of monitoring and improving performance.

Performance improvement plans

Unless you have the world's perfect distributor there will always be areas for improvement, and unless you are the perfect supplier the same will apply to your own operations. An indication of a good relationship will be your ability to discuss things openly and constructively, and the existence of a performance improvement process. The way in which you go about this process will have much to do with the success of the relationship; as with sales teams, marketers tend to get the distributors they deserve.

The ideal scenario is a two-way process as a regular feature of the relationship, not an occasional response to emergency and crisis (rarely the best environment for collaboration and improvement!). Both sides should list their aspirations against a number of issues and then compare notes. Where are the likely points of conflict? What actions are required to reduce or avoid that conflict? There are probably two parts to the table – issues between your two businesses, and issues in the market-place. You may end up with a table that looks something like that in Table 17.4 (an example only, not an attempt at a full list).

If we look at just one of these issues we can see the kind of differences that may appear in 'managing' a distributor between a strongly *push* and a strongly *pull* scenario.

Range and stockholding

In a push scenario, the supplier's aspirations are usually for greater stock commitments from the distributor, breadth and depth, while the distributor's may be just the reverse! The actions to resolve these differences may lie in the area of incentives or 'deals', or perhaps

Table 17.4 *Performance improvement planning*

Our Relationship	Supplier's Aspirations	Distributor's Aspirations	Potential Conflict?	Actions to Reduce/Avoid Conflict
Range and Stockholding				
Prices and Discounting				
Margins and Shared Costs				
Terms and Conditions				
Training Programmes				
Complaint Procedures				
Market Issues	**Supplier's Aspirations**	**Distributor's Aspirations**	**Potential Conflict?**	**Actions to Reduce/Avoid Conflict**
Customer Selection				
Sales Effort and Targets				
Prices and Discounting				
Promotion				
Customer Service Package				
Supplier's Support Package				
Complaint Procedures				

some form of vendor-owned and managed stock. Consignment stock (where stock is held on the distributor's premises but remains the property of the supplier until it is drawn to be sold) is one of the means of persuading reluctant distributors to take on new ranges, but there are significant drawbacks.

First off, it is almost always enormously costly to the supplier – ask any accountant. Second, it is notoriously hard to manage and control; staunch opponents of consignment stock will sometimes refer to it as 'lost' stock! The third drawback is the impact that such arrangements can have on the distributor's 'energies' behind your products. The supplier wants its products pushed, but filling the distributor's warehouse with supplier-owned stock is not perhaps the best way to give the distributor an incentive to work hard.

In a pull scenario the supplier will be much more able to influence the distributor's range and stockholding through market information and sales forecasts. Details of a specific promotional campaign, for instance, can be used to 'instruct' the distributor to build stock.

The pull scenario might look much the more attractive for managing the distributor, but don't forget that the supplier must be involved in a whole range of activities and investments to initiate this pull, activities and investments that the push strategy supplier is not required to undertake.

Training

A key ingredient of any supplier's support package will be the provision of training. At the very least this will be product training for distributor staff, but there is scope to go much further. Distributors will often look to their best suppliers for help in providing training for their own staff – what better way to cement relationships between the two teams than joint training? Sales training provided to both supplier and distributor sales teams can be used to explore relevant issues within the market, and can be as useful as a joint planning session as it is valuable as training. Some care is required however to ensure that the supplier is not seen to take too dominant a role, with accusations for instance of 'brainwashing'. The use of an independent trainer, rather than the supplier delivering the training itself, will often help to avoid these problems.

One of the best examples that I have seen of using training to cement relationships and develop channel partner capabilities involves PPG, a supplier of refinish paint to the car repair market. Many of their customers are independent spray shops, small businesses with huge training needs but precious few resources to hand. PPG deliver a programme of training on a range of 'running a small business' issues, which customers pay to participate in (a subsidized rate, but enough for them to appreciate the value), including how to raise their own prices in the market-place – an issue of some interest to the supplying company!

Why not train your customers to put *their* prices up? PPG do

Joint business planning

If a distributor is a true channel partner then this will be evidenced by the desire on both sides to develop a joint business plan. Many suppliers see distributor business plans simply as a range of sales targets to be imposed and then achieved, and are surprised when distributors fail to get excited by such treatment! A genuine channel partnership plan may look something like the following (loosely based on a real example from the UK agrochemical market):

- a joint statement of intent – what both parties seek from the relationship and what their expectations are;
- the values and aspirations of the supplier and the distributor;
- a SWOT analysis of the target market, with strengths and weaknesses of both parties;
- an identification of customers and target customers – and also key accounts where appropriate;
- a statement on the needs and aspirations of the target customers;
- the value chain analysis (see Chapter 20);
- the sales proposition;
- the support package – supplier responsibilities, distributor responsibilities, budgets, the customer service package, training programmes;
- specific sales targets;
- the 'service level agreement' (see section on customer service below);
- action lists – who, what, when;
- key performance indicators and review criteria.

Such plans not only take time to develop, but they require high levels of trust and collaboration. Don't expect them to come easily, and certainly not of their own accord. The marketer's role in making such plans happen will bring them into very close collaboration with their sales colleagues, a collaboration that can only be of benefit to all concerned.

LOGISTICS AND SUPPLY CHAIN MANAGEMENT

Being able to deliver, on time and in full, is just one of the things you have to be able to do these days, just to be on the page. But it isn't so very long ago that measures such as OTIF (on time in full) were used to express the competitive advantage of one supplier over another. This is the story of logistics in the marketing mix, a continuous effort to improve, a few blissful months every now and then of genuine competitive advantage, and then everyone else catches up and it's back to being just one of life's givens. Of course, get logistics wrong and everyone knows about it.

Logistics has long been one of the less glamorous areas of marketing, but one where the greatest damage can be done very quickly through disregard, carelessness, or lack of discipline. The logistics experts are the unsung heroes of the supplier's offer, yet there is increasing evidence that in most markets, from fmcg through business-to-business and service, being easy to do business with is seen to be of vital importance. How many times would you go back to a mail-order firm that sent you the wrong things? How long would you stay with a bank or credit card company that put other people's charges on your monthly statement?

As markets mature, as they become more and more competitive, and as the need for competitive advantage increases (just when it is becoming hardest to achieve), so issues of supplier reliability are raised to new levels of importance. In such markets it is becoming the supplier's ability to forecast accurately and to 'deliver' with speed that is increasingly dividing the winners from the losers. In the past the competitive battleground has so often been one of market share, with the strongest brands winning through; in the future we will also see the battle of the supply chains. The rise of *supply chain management* as an activity within most large businesses is witness to this, and an excellent example of how internal operations are being focused on to the customer and the market-place. Figure 17.5 illus-

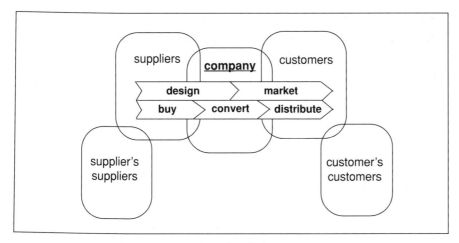

Figure 17.5 *Supply chain management*

trates how this external focus is taken back into the operational functions of the business and beyond to purchasing and into the supplier's suppliers.

The dialogue between marketers and operations can only be a productive one in this respect. The objectives of the manufacturing plant or the purchasing department can be defined by reference to measures of customer satisfaction as well as internal measures of operational efficiency. The plant can still aim to maximize its occupacity (a measure of its efficient use of its total capacity), not because greater occupacity is simply a 'good thing' but because of the understanding of the benefits that can accrue to customers through reduced costs, and the potential for competitive advantage. Such an approach will help to remove those conflicts of interest between operations and marketing as both focus on the same ends. Terms such as 'appropriate occupacity' will help determine the path that operations must take between the huge efficiencies of uniformity (an old-fashioned plant manager's holy grail) and the market's needs for variation and flexibility (an old-fashioned marketer's holy grail).

By understanding the supply chain, marketers can set themselves two targets – to improve the efficiency of the chain in order to drive out costs, and to improve the effectiveness of the chain in supplying the customer. Within logistics and the supply chain lie both routes to competitive advantage, lower costs and greater differentiation.

Mapping the supply chain

Any business that is seeking to reduce costs through supply chain efficiency, or improve service to customers through supply chain effectiveness, will benefit from regular reviews of that supply chain. A hugely valuable exercise is to map out the chain from start to finish, and a very low-tech but highly effective way to do it is to plaster a blank wall with Post-it notes. For every step that is carried out write a separate note and find yourself a *large* wall, because things can get surprisingly complicated. Start with the customer's order, in all its varieties, whether received through the sales rep or a telephone call, the faxed order, the electronic order, the standing order, and follow it back into the organization and out again to the final delivery to the customer, and then beyond to the invoice and final receipt of payment.

Aim to follow the chain back into production and then beyond that into your own purchasing activity. Involve the experts in this exercise – customer service, internal sales, distribution, supply chain, master schedulers, purchasing, salespeople, credit controllers – all will add their own Post-its to the chain. By keeping it visual in this way you will begin to appreciate the complexity of what might have seemed to you just a straightforward order and dispatch system, and the need for close interfunctional relations to ensure its smooth operation. You might also be pleasantly surprised by the evidence of the capability within your organization to achieve what now looks like something of a minor miracle every time you deliver an order!

Once you have plastered the wall with yellow squares, place large black crosses on those points that cause problems – the credit check that takes three days, the bottleneck in the packaging department, the high level of errors in the invoicing office. Place large red crosses on those points in the chain that are absolutely vital hand-over points from one function to another – sales pass the order to the factory, the warehouse hands responsibility to the transport company, etc. Stand back and note where you need to look for improvements (black crosses), and where you need to ensure the absolute reliability of the process (red crosses). Think of it as a relay race, each runner passing a baton to the next, and look out for the places where the baton might just get dropped.

This may all sound rather archaic in an age of high tech and software packages, but there is still no better way *really* to understand the dynamics of the supply chain. Of course, it is not just the problem spots that you are seeking out. Chase down those unnecessary links and those backwaters of inactivity and delay, and hound them into extinction. The aim should be to seek means to shorten the chain, speed the process, debug the system and allow the customer as close access as possible to your own systems.

How would it be if you allowed the customer to place the order direct on your factory – chaos, or a route to competitive advantage? The marketer's interest in the supply chain should be around making this possible – providing customers with such close access to your supply chain that they are effectively locked into the relationship simply because it is so easy for them to do business with you. (Chapter 18 will look more closely at the way IT contributes to this goal through the software packages behind the customer relationship management (CRM) revolution.)

CUSTOMER SERVICE

Good customer service wins every time, and that's why it's worth the marketer's time. There are many reasons for providing good customer service, but I want to highlight three in particular:

1. Good customer service means a point of differentiation in an increasingly uniform world – it is a part of the surround to your product core, the value in your value price, the substance behind your promotion and the glue for your place strategies.
2. Satisfied customers are loyal customers. Good customer service makes a major contribution to customer retention.
3. Of all your investments, good customer service will be one of the most cost-effective.

And what makes good customer service such a certainty as a winning strategy is that, unlike so many of the levers to be pulled by the marketer, this one is entirely within your control.

Just consider the following. Good news about your service can travel fast, but not nearly so fast as bad news. Here is an example of an increasingly common style of complaint about bad service, made to a major corporation:

I would be grateful if you will settle my problem as a priority and keep me informed of your actions either by fax or e-mail (not by post as this is too slow). If I don't hear from you within two days I will contact your HQ in the US. I will also inform dedicated mailing lists on the Internet and the consumer watchdogs here and in the States. I will ensure that the maximum number of people get to hear about the way your company treats its customers. I run my own company and would never dream of treating my customers like this.

The interesting aspect is not the complaint itself but the intention to do something about poor service, to 'get even'.

The Internet is mightier than the sword

A recent news story concerned a young man whose wedding had been ruined by a bout of food poisoning among the guests at the reception. He had received no help from the hotel concerned in trying to explain the outbreak, deal with the problem, or take any interest whatever. He was not looking for an admission of guilt, simply a dialogue, but the hotel chose to wash its hands of the whole affair. The young man discovered that the hotel chain had not yet registered an Internet site using its own name, so he registered one with its name and posted a series of articles on his plight for anyone who might be thinking of using the chain to read. Vindictive, or simply the power of the Internet being greater than the sword?

Customer service and differentiation

Some people buy Heinz baked beans in Fortnum & Mason, knowing full well that they are paying a premium. The premium is for the environment, the experience, the prestige and the impeccable service. Some of these people are one-off tourists, but plenty go back week after week.

Some professional buyers will pay a premium to a supplier that manages its stock for it, or provides quality assurance checks, or contributes to forecasts, or will break bulk, help out with emergency deliveries, or provide expert technicians to work problems through on the customer's premises. With such service, who would want to bother about changing supplier?

Some hard-nosed businesspeople will pay a premium for a photo-copier that comes with a 'no questions asked' guarantee to have the copier replaced. Xerox gained nearly five market share percentage points when it introduced such a guarantee.

Customer service and customer retention

Good service retains customers, and countless studies have shown the huge (and obvious?) financial benefits for a business in retaining customers compared to the costs involved in regaining lost customers. For many businesses, retaining customers (and growing those customers' businesses) may be the single best thing they can do to their bottom line – better than reducing costs, better than winning new customers. In a mature market, investing in retention through customer service is a good investment, as it is, too, in high-growth markets where the continual addition of new customers can lead suppliers to be cavalier about losing their older ones. Nowhere is this more true than at present in the telephone services market. Companies that have only been around for three or four years are now losing the customers that their revolutionary approach won for them in the early days of their existence, and yet they still focus on a 'hunter' mentality sales drive, with woefully inadequate customer service provision. It is the customer service propositions of the 'old dinosaurs' like BT that are helping to win them back their prodigal children.

Bad service loses customers. Consider the following statistics of reasons for a business-to-business customer to change its supplier (measured across a broad range of industries and markets):

- changes in its own personnel (often the outgoing supplier's excuse, but rarely the sole truth) – 10 per cent;
- a competitor's offer (the costs involved in changing often outweigh the benefits of an apparently 'better' offer) – 10 per cent;
- dissatisfaction with the product (getting a supplier to improve its product is often easier than changing supplier) – 15 per cent;
- poor customer service, often expressed as 'indifference' shown by the supplier or a member of the supplier's staff – 65 per cent.

It is interesting to note the use of the word 'indifference' in relation to service. Few customers expect 100 per cent perfection. To err is human ('but to really foul things up requires a computer', Farmer's Almanac, 1978), it is said. What really gets to customers is the supplier's failure to act in response to a problem, or even to recognize that anything has occurred. Too many suppliers are afraid that any recognition of a problem will imply an admission of guilt, so let's keep quiet and hope it goes away (and as we see, the customer often does).

When customers 'snap'

Of course, when there are no competitors, or demand far exceeds supply, bad service doesn't matter, or so many businesses have thought. All seems well as the sales graph points skyward, and then the market starts to level out, or a new player arrives on the scene. Now comes the frantic pursuit of customer loyalty schemes, and the price-cutting exercises that turn customer retention into an expensive activity. Worse follows as customers that seemed entirely happy suddenly 'snap' and go elsewhere. Of course, the truth is that they were probably far from happy, but had no alternative but to stay with their existing supplier. They were on the *low competition* curve shown in Figure 17.6.

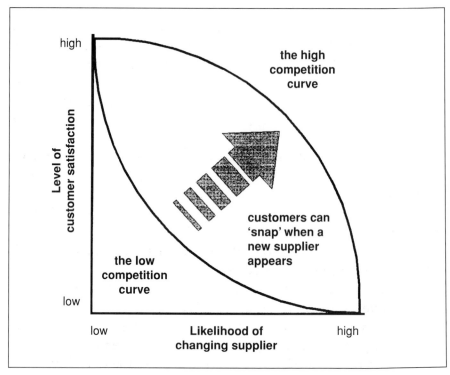

Figure 17.6 *When customers 'snap'*

When customers have only a few alternatives their level of satisfaction must be very low indeed to warrant the effort involved in changing supplier. When choice is wide and easy to take up, the competition curve can 'snap' like a piece of high-tension wire and the smallest dissatisfaction can see them on their way. If BT lost many of their customers as a result of such a 'snap' when new players were allowed into the market, then they now appear to have learnt the lesson well with regard to customer service.

Developing a customer service strategy

Of first importance, and it may sound rather obvious, the business should have a customer service strategy – good customer service doesn't just happen. Start by determining what benefits the business wants from providing good service – growth, customer retention, reputation, customer satisfaction, etc. Then define the levels of service required; some businesses will go as far as agreeing this with their customers through SLAs (service level agreements). Finally, determine how that service will be delivered.

Good customer service will come from two sources, with a great debate as to which is the more important – good staff and good systems. The right mix must in the end depend on the market needs and the supplier's capabilities. Strictly applied 'formulas' for customer service delivered through tightly managed call centres will suit some strategies, while others will demand the personal attention of empowered staff.

The debate is sometimes blurred because the call centre approach is seen as the lowest-cost option by large businesses with long customer lists. This finds it seized on eagerly as the _right_ solution, where other methods might be more appropriate. We are back to the bad habits of letting an internal focus drive what the customer gets. Before going down the call centre route, make sure that this really does give you a competitive edge.

There is another issue that comes in at this point, and that is the role of systems way beyond just providing service. The e-revolution has seen a rush of new software packages designed to harvest information from every customer interaction, and to use that information to help determine the shape of the whole customer offer. This is the world of CRM, to be discussed in Chapter 18. With this in mind, the call centre may not simply be a low-cost means of delivering service; it may be the engine of your future marketing strategy.

Good service based on good staff

Good people = good service = good profits. Marriott have the figures to prove it

The Marriott hotel group realizes that their own staff are at the heart of any customer service strategy, and if staff turnover gets too high then they start to have customer service problems. Marriott found a correlation between reducing staff turnover and increasing customer retention. A 10 per cent reduction in staff turnover at a particular hotel would lead to a 1 to 3 per cent decrease in lost customers, and that translates to an increase in revenue across the chain of between $50 million and $100 million. Marriott consider their investment in customer service through staff retention a sound one.

This is a very different view of 'staff as an asset' from that propounded by Henry Ford when discussing the manufacture of the Model T. The car required 7,882 different operations but only 949 needed 'strong, able bodied, and practically physically perfect men'. Of the rest, 'ordinary physical strength' was OK for 3,338 operations and the rest were fine for 'women or older children'. Displaying his passion for the nitty-gritty, he noted that '670 could be filled by legless men, 2,637 by one-legged men, 2 by armless men, 715 by one-armed men and 10 by blind men'.

Good service based on good systems

A 'good' system is one designed for the benefit of customers, which can be changed as customers' needs change, delivers value to the customer and enhances the supplier's ability to improve that value over time. In a small business that might mean no more than regular meetings of the staff concerned to discuss better ways of handling their customers. In a large business this will call for the new technologies and software packages that are behind the CRM revolution. This is in turn a part of the whole e-business revolution, to be discussed in the next chapter.

Part V

Marketing And The Future

18

Marketing and the e-revolution

Does the e-revolution change the rules of marketing? Is the Internet establishing some new principles, or is it simply shifting the balance between the options in the traditional marketing mix? Will the complex software behind initiatives such as customer relationship management (CRM) put the IT department in the driving seat and leave the marketer simply to implement its findings?

Opinions fly around like confetti on the subject, many of the more bullish driven by the IT industry with its eye on software sales and consultancy projects. I have no wish to add to the litter, but rather to set the marketer's mind thinking. Many businesses have yet to appreciate the potential of the e-revolution, while others are at the point of believing that it turns everything upside down. Whichever the view, the result is a great deal of inertia – either there is no vision, or else the vision is so frightening that it is too daunting to know where to start.

That there are huge opportunities there is no doubt. That there are hurdles to cross that are scarcely yet imagined there is also no doubt. For those thrilled by the prospect of rewriting the marketing 'rule book' there are some cautionary doubts on just how revolutionary all this really is. For those scared witless by the constant refrain of 'You're doomed!' if you don't get on board, there is some comfort in realizing that getting on board doesn't have to change your life.

Perhaps the most important observation to make is that the kind of professional marketing practices described in this book are not negated by the e-revolution. Certainly many aspects of the marketer's work will be enhanced, some quite significantly, but the basic disciplines will still apply. Indeed, many of the tales of woe that result from early forays by companies into this 'brave new world' can be seen to have their cause in some shortfall, not of technology, but in marketing thinking or planning.

Big ambitions and growing pains in e-retailing

Online shopping has been a headache for many an e-retailer.

Slick Web sites don't make the money without slick logistics. Toys 'R' Us and Victoria's Secret learn the hard way

Toys 'R' Us in the USA saw some of their customers considering legal action when they didn't get their purchases delivered in time for Christmas 1999. The retailer was forced to offer a $100 gift voucher as compensation, an expensive rearguard action, but the cost to its reputation and the cost of lost sales was much greater.

Victoria's Secret, the US retailer of lingerie, scored a massive initial success with their pre-Christmas 1999 Web site, said to be receiving 250,000 hits an hour. With 1.5 per cent of these hits turning into sales at an average of $80 a time the prospect was looking good for a very happy Christmas, until the system broke under the load. On these numbers, a three-day crash might have cost the retailer anything up to $7.2 million in lost sales.

Some e-retailers have been guilty of creating demand that couldn't be met through their current supply chain systems. Whether by inadequate forecasting or creaking logistics, the result is a blow to consumer confidence that slows down the adoption of this new channel to market.

Sure, these are short-term teething problems, but the marketer should take care not to put the blame simply on the technology. All too often the fault lies in thinking that traditional marketing disciplines no longer apply. If we go right back to the marketing model from Chapter 3, the e-revolution may provide the vehicle for some unique propositions that meet emerging customer needs, but the matching process requires the appropriate capabilities to be in place.

A recent advert from Bull, one of the big players in the e-revolution, promoted the need for their system networks with the following 'sad tale': 'The success of John's virtual store exceeded all his expectations. It also exceeded the capabilities of his company.'

The ups and downs of e-commerce

On the same day in February 2000 the *Financial Times* carried two items on high-profile uses of e-commerce in managing place strategies.

British Airways announced that e-commerce would save them £440 million by 2002, through its application to ticketing and other management systems. In 1999 only 1 per cent of BA's revenue came through the e-commerce channel, and they target over 50 per cent by 2004. Online sales will grow from £45 million to £700 million, with an investment of £90 million to make it all happen.

On the same day the *FT* also carried the story that Hershey, the US chocolate manufacturer, was issuing a profit warning owing to a disastrous period of trading since October 1999. A new computer system designed to revolutionize customer order processing was blamed. Hershey had seen their market share 'whittled away by its inability to get customers the right amount of chocolate'. The disaster struck at the worst time possible – the Hallowe'en and Christmas boom periods – and the Hershey share price tumbled from $53 to $38.

BA plan to ride the revolution while Hershey paper over the cracks

Doubtless Hershey's problems are temporary, but let nobody underestimate the pain involved in getting to some of the promised savings through the use of IT in *place*. If that pain is suffered by the supplier, then that is one thing, but inflicting it on the customer is quite another. Once customers start to suspect that they may be getting a poorer service as the supplier pursues a cost-saving strategy, then that will open the door wide to a supplier that can promise improved levels of service.

Before identifying the marketing steps, we need to know some terms:

- *e-commerce:* computer-to-computer transactions between supplier and customer, whether providing information, placing orders, invoicing or giving after-sales support, etc;
- *e-business:* a much broader canvas – using the information gathered from customer transactions to drive other business systems

including forecasting and production planning, distribution, promotional planning, product development, etc;

- *customer relationship management (CRM):* techniques for harvesting information about customers, which can be used to design new propositions.

STEPS TOWARDS THE REVOLUTION

We might identify five stages through which a marketer might choose to make use of the e-revolution:

1. as an opportunity for promotion;
2. as an opportunity for trade – e-commerce;
3. as an opportunity for information and knowledge – CRM;
4. as an opportunity for locking the customer into your supply chain;
5. as an opportunity for customization or individualization.

As ever, the purpose is competitive advantage, whether by reducing suppliers' costs or by differentiating their offer. These are the same choices noted by Michael Porter and discussed in Chapter 8, only, as we will see, perhaps the e-revolution does offer the supplier the chance of pursuing both routes without falling foul of the 'inbetweeny' syndrome.

Opportunities for promotion

'And the great thing about advertising on the Web is that it's free!' Such notions have set the pulse of many a small business running fast – the idea that they can at last take on the big boys in the area of promotion. Certainly the Internet has given smaller players the ability to represent themselves using the same style and format as the multinationals, but a Web site alone doesn't make Davids out of every small business – and the Goliaths still have some big muscles.

Let's be clear, promotion through the Web isn't free, at least no more so than fly-posting is free. As Chapter 15 makes clear, for a promotional message to work it has to reach its audience. A great name for your Web site is not enough – people still have to know about it and be able to find you. Sure, if you're Ford, or the BBC, or British Airways, your customers have a pretty good chance of finding you just by using your name – but what if you are small and relatively unknown, or new? Here's a 'great' idea for a domain name for a US-based home cleaning service – www.SpruceSpringclean.com (maids in America?), but without a great deal of traditional promotion, who's going to hear of it? One of the ironies of the boom in the electronic medium for promotion is that traditional advertising media have enjoyed a parallel boom. When the search provider AskJeeves.com was launched it was promoted by a campaign using TV, press and posters no less costly than a traditional pre-Internet-era campaign. You still need money to get yourself heard.

Web promoters rely heavily on the ability of customers to find them. If you are in a rarefied line of trade such as organically grown vegetarian sausages then perhaps there is a good chance that your sort of customer will seek you out, but what of the rest of us? Just having your Web site on the Net is not enough. If you want to be listed higher than the thousand or so in response to a customer's search, then you will have to consider paying the search engine provider handsomely for the privilege.

Having sounded this caution, there is no doubt that the Internet has changed the way that companies should think of promotion in the marketing mix. Word of mouth has become word of e-mail and some suppliers can take advantage of the undoubted 'jungle drums' syndrome, where enthusiasts will help disseminate your message like no number of dinner parties ever could. Placing your message is certainly easier and yes, the costs _are_ potentially lower, but it is more than this that promises to make the medium a truly revolutionary one for the marketer. It is the way that what was once simply 'promotion' can now become 'communication' – two-way. Philip Kotler in his book, _Kotler on Marketing_ (1999), has challenged the use of the four Ps as being too much about what the supplier does to the market, suggesting four Cs in their stead (more of this in Chapter 19). P for promotion becomes C for communication, and this is the very point about the Internet. Direct mailers have always had a golden rule – whatever else you do ensure that you encourage a response – and they have tiny hit rates for all their efforts. The Internet as a response medium for promoters (or communicators as we should call them now) is potentially just phenomenal.

Given this potential it is sad to see how badly so many companies use the medium. Constructing the Web site is too often a job for the most junior member of the team, or the IT department, whose grasp of htmls and the like might be fine but who have little experience in the business of marketing.

Just as it isn't free, Internet promotion isn't as simple as some might suggest. Advertising has always been a job for the professionals, but the Internet has made a lot of marketers believe that they can go it alone. The sheer dreadfulness of so many Web sites is testimony to that – hard to find, hard to navigate, heavy on hype and low on genuine help, initially enticing but ultimately frustrating. Not many pass the two simple tests of a good site: two clicks and you're where you want to be, and managing to hold customers' attention for those crucial three or four seconds before they decide to surf somewhere else.

Frighteningly, only about 40 per cent of enquiries through company Web sites are answered at present. Remember that this is communication – that's like putting the phone down on a customer half-way through the conversation, 6 times out of 10!

The Internet may reduce the costs of promotion, but do not imagine that they are somehow removed altogether – there will be a different set of costs related to your ability to respond to consumers, and to match the promise of your Web site with the reality of your service.

Opportunities for trade

For the consumer the new age of home shopping is ushered in – but is this really such a new thing? At the start of the last century, Harrods telegraphic address was 'Everything – London' and the telegraph ushered in a new era of home shopping. Some people who still don't know how to switch a computer on (and lose no sleep over their 'loss') have been indulging in home shopping for years – through catalogues and 'snail mail'. It is a thoroughly 19th-century phenomenon! What online shopping changes is the speed, volume and range of possibilities, but not the principle.

Dixons, the UK retail chain, refers to its use of the Internet as 'Martini retailing' – 'any time, any place, anywhere'. But it is not just a question of 'have Web site, will prosper'. Traditional retailers are starting to team up with the new e-tailers to combine their different capabilities in pursuit of what they call a 'clicks and mortar' strategy.

E-commerce has raised the profile of place (once the ugly duckling of the marketing mix) to a new order of prominence. E-commerce-based place strategies now offer significant opportunities for competitive advantage. Here are just four avenues that you could pursue:

1. reducing the cost of getting products and services to market;
2. differentiating the offer through the ease of purchase for the customer;
3. differentiating the offer through the customer's ability to access your supply chain;
4. differentiating the offer through the ability to customize.

If e-commerce were only about cost reduction then it would be of passing interest, and certainly only a fraction of the issue it really is. The opportunity to differentiate the offer is simply staggering, and for many still the most underestimated part of the equation. E-commerce even promises to help the marketer escape the peril of the 'inbetweeny', as discussed in Chapter 8, stuck between chasing the goals of lowest-cost supplier and of differentiated supplier in pursuit of competitive advantage. In this regard then, perhaps the e-revolution is starting to bend some of the rules of marketing.

It must be said, however, that the longer companies delay their involvement, the less likely they are to gain competitive advantage as they simply find themselves playing a continual game of catch-up with those already versed in the channel and with the demands of their customers (that refrain of 'You're doomed!' again).

It is not only the opportunity that changes, but also the capabilities required. Tesco was caught out by the massive response to its home shopping service, leading to long lead times (often a week ahead) for deliveries. What this highlights is the need to have the supply chain infrastructure in place ready to cope with this new channel. The supermarkets are still exploring the different logistical options: Sainsbury's is developing specialized picking centres, while Tesco uses existing stores and an army of 'personal shoppers'. At present the logistical constraints of the old systems and channels are restricting the growth of the new, slowing down further the development of new capabilities. This gives an opportunity to new entrants who can of course benefit from the learning experience of the trailblazers. The winners in the electronic trading contest will not be the suppliers with the fanciest Web sites (important though this 'front end' is), but the ones with the best supply chain – the best expediters.

Trading by e-commerce may be a means to competitive advantage for some, while for others it is already a question of avoiding disadvantage. Purchasing organizations are realizing that trading by e-commerce has the potential to save them millions in transactional costs, and in many businesses it is the purchasing department, not the sales or marketing folk, that is most active in pursuing the opportunities. For many a supplier in a business-to-business environment, the time is coming closer when the ability to trade by e-commerce is a prerequisite. A popular use of the channel is the online auction, where suppliers are asked to bid for business within a short time frame and in immediate competition with other suppliers. This calls for new skills for the supplier and unfortunately many of these will be gained the hard way.

E-commerce is not just for the dotcom brigade – United Technologies show the way for the 'old economy'

An evangelist for the technique is United Technologies (Otis elevators and Sikorsky helicopters among others), which regularly determines contracts worth millions through online auctions. Suppliers to UT are virtually obliged to use e-commerce one way or another. The head of purchasing at UT, Kent Brittan, has argued strongly that e-commerce has huge benefits for large industrial companies in what might be regarded as the 'old economy', just as much if not more than for the 'new economy'. He also sounds a warning: 'Some of our suppliers didn't think we could do it. They are no longer with us.'

The death of the distributor?

One of the predictions made in the early days of the e-revolution was the demise of the distributor – all business could now be direct. In reality we are seeing quite the reverse. Traditional distribution channels are still required to move products, but they must take on board the systems required to link them into the suppliers' e-business network. And we are seeing the emergence of a new kind of intermediary, the businesses that survive on pennies and fractions of pennies from each consumer purchase by 'working in the *clickstream*'.

Let's imagine I want to buy a toy, one of those hyped bits of merchandise spun off from a movie. I get on to the Internet (click) and find myself a search engine (click). The toy's name takes me to a list of possibilities. I choose a site (click) and find myself in a film buffs' heaven with reviews of every film imaginable. After a little bit of browsing (click, click) I find mine (click), and take an advertising link (click) to a Web retailer selling my toy at a bargain price. I place the order (click), to receive a package just a few days later. My transaction has given the toy manufacturer its reward, a retailer a discounted margin, the mail service its due but, on top of that, a host of intermediaries their penny or less for entertaining me or routeing me on my way. Each 'click' is a mini transaction, with commissions paid for referrals, and provided the volume is there such intermediaries can thrive on fractions of a penny per transaction while the Web retailer fights it out on price and worries about its overheads. In Chapter 17 we suggested an analysis of value provided by each step in the channel and the need to provide the reward accordingly. This notion is just as applicable in the new electronic channel, but the economics are quite revolutionary.

The idea that new technology will reshape traditional forms of business is of course not new. If we trace the history of retailing in the USA we will see a series of technological changes that reshaped that industry. The telegraph and the railway heralded the rise of the mail-order business and the department store, which threatened the livelihood of many a local merchant. The car raised the possibility of the discount store, and the humble bar code played its part in the development of specialist discounters (or 'category killers') and hugely efficient chains such as Wal-Mart.

Web retailers will continue the process, but this time there is a twist. The Internet will not only speed the pace of change, but it raises the potentially revolutionary idea (and so for some a particularly worrying, even suspect idea) that the new players will not need the backing of huge amounts of capital in order to make a significant dent in the big boys' armour. Have Web site, will trade?

Opportunities for information and knowledge – CRM

Time after time with the e-revolution we find ourselves saying that the concept is not new but the application is revolutionary. Nowhere is this more true than in the area of customer information. The salesperson is trained to build relationships with customers, and through those relationships to develop knowledge about needs and desires. The theory goes that this knowledge is transferred to the people within the supplier company in a position to do something with it – the R & D department, production, distribution and the marketers. We all know how often such knowledge stays locked in the salesperson's head, or is lost in a string of miscommunications, or is simply ignored by the head office folk who clearly know better.

CRM seeks to use a variety of different systems and software packages to harvest this kind of information, not just from the face-to-face transactions but now from the host of electronic transactions. Once e-commerce becomes a two-way communication and not simply an advertising medium, then the information starts to build. Every interaction with customers has the potential to provide information about their needs, their buying behaviour, their perceptions, their concerns and their frustrations.

The Internet allows various techniques to be used. Analysis of customer clickstreams as they work their way around your site and into your system can reveal how they go about making their choices – do they look for information first, and do they check for alternatives?

The 'virtual sales assistant' is a technique that allows customers to ask questions, and in so doing reveal much about their interests, certainties, doubts and priorities. Some sites allow customers to interrogate 'virtual customers', to seek 'opinions' of the product or service, and through this interaction customers display a whole range of concerns, attitudes and perceptions. This is no different in principle from utilizing the traditional skills of the salesperson. We might equate the analysis of the clickstream with the salesperson's ability to read body language, only now we see the potential for harvesting these observations on a massive scale and using them to modify the proposition. (It is an irony that marketers will now happily listen to what the salespeople have to say, provided that those salespeople remain reliably virtual!)

Such information is kept in what is referred to increasingly as the *data warehouse* and at this point the amount of information could be mind-boggling. Without sophisticated analysis techniques such as *data mining* we would soon be pining for 'old-fashioned' market researchers with their clipboards. Data mining involves a range of techniques for identifying patterns of behaviour from sales information and other transactional histories. The concept of 'signalling', or trying to recognize customer intentions from their transactional behaviour, is one such – perhaps a willingness to pay more for speed, or a desire to set a specification.

The rise of the call centre has been helped by the ability of systems to provide a 'single view' of the customer on-screen. Sales of CRM-related software to call centres are predicted to increase sixfold between 1999 and 2003, and many businesses are now calling in the experts to run their call centres for them – 24 per cent of the telecommunication industry's call centres are already outsourced, as are 20 per cent of financial service's and 16 per cent in the fmcg sector. Simply installing a new system will do nothing for the supplier or the customer. This mode of doing business requires trained staff, clear objectives and genuine value for the customer – elements of the equation all too often ignored by companies that think they can hand the responsibility of all this over to the IT experts.

Analysis of the information opens up a raft of possibilities, from redesigning your supply chain to suit customers' purchasing behaviour to allowing them to customize your offer or even design it to their own specification. At this point we are certainly in rule-changing territory as notions of pull or push place strategies are replaced by supplier–customer collaboration and the management of customer relationships – CRM.

Of course, concerns abound as to how such relationship management will be used. How many of us would want our bank to analyse our behaviour in this way, even if they did do so in order to provide us with a better service? Boots are big users of various CRM techniques, but they make it clear that they would never seek to use them for individual customer selling – health care is too sensitive an issue to be seen to be prying. They aim to aggregate the information to identify trends and to customize their offer, but not to individualize it.

CRM – marketing's baby, or IT's toy?

The huge variety of competing IT providers, software packages and CRM consultants demonstrates and perpetuates the breadth of definitions behind this concept. For some, CRM is about call centres, while for others it is about field sales force data management tools, etc. In some ways CRM is a product of the IT suppliers' pressure on the market – 'Just plug this in and you're set' – and it is fair to say that many marketers have not yet begun to integrate it into their own planning. In many cases the business CRM strategy is not owned by marketers, largely because it is not understood by them. The folk from IT, from supply chain and from MIS (management information systems) have stolen a march, and it is for the marketer to get involved.

For CRM to become integrated into the marketing planning processes there will be a need for a cross-functional collaboration. Marketing cannot 'run' CRM on its own any more than IT can (though too often it is thought by IT that it should). Once such a collaboration is under way, then CRM has the potential to reshape the whole business, and in so doing to break down many of the barriers between internal functions that prevent a truly market-orientated business focus.

Understanding customer profitability

As well as mining information on customer needs and aspirations, CRM allows a more detailed analysis of customer profitability. Understanding where the best returns come from has always been vital to any proper segmentation strategy as you aim to target your limited resources, but CRM raises the stakes. The irony of CRM is that as well as providing information it becomes all the more important to act on that knowledge.

Consider the following scenario. You know that some customers will pay more than others and you attempt to segment on that basis. Unfortunately it is not easy to target these different segments with discrete offers and over time your price becomes uniform to all. In effect you are now seen by some customers as expensive and others as cheap and they are all less than satisfied. A competitor armed with a CRM strategy, with the knowledge it provides on customer profitability, and with the ability it gives to target individual customers, now proceeds to pick off your dissatisfied customers.

What CRM gives the competitor in this scenario is an enhanced ability to use skimming and penetration pricing strategies (see Chapter 13). At the risk of yet more cries of 'You're doomed!', this is a case of get in first before you're got.

Opportunities for locking the customer into your supply chain

By understanding the way that customers make their purchases, the supplier can design its supply chain to maximize customers' ease of access. Again, not a new concept: car hire firms, hotels and theme parks, to name but three, have long been good at making it very easy for customers to spend their money. The e-revolution allows one further step, however: not just ease of doing business, but doing it inside the supplier's own supply chain – direct to the factory, distribution depot and service providers. Once inside, and if the experience is good, customers will find it very easy to stay doing business that way – the supplier will have achieved *lock-in*, a concept further explored in Chapter 20.

It is at this point in the e-revolution that suppliers' capabilities will have to change most dramatically. So many of the operational systems in place in traditional businesses are designed to keep the customer out, relying on internal data to drive them, and craving uniformity, not the variations of individual customer demands. The supplier of a highly standardized product with low costs does not have to become a supplier of complex menu choices, but perhaps it does need to be able to deal with the different purchasing behaviours of its customers – a standardized, lowest-cost product but a flexible, differentiated supply chain?

Opportunities for customization or individualization

Perhaps the most exciting application of the new technology for the marketer is in using the information harvested by CRM systems to drive the design of the offer itself. Once more the concept is not new, but the application is potentially revolutionary. The practice of segmenting a market is based on information about customers' needs, attitudes and behaviours. The purpose of segmentation is to design specific marketing mixes, or propositions, to meet those needs. Segmentation then aims to customize the offer to a specific group of people.

CRM can be used in the same way, though with access to much more detailed information and the ability to analyse it in more sophisticated ways. Taking it one step further, however, CRM offers the potential of segmenting down to an individual customer level. Of course, you may not need to do this, nor want to; traditional segmentation may provide coherent enough customer needs and allow you the economies of scale of an offer customized to that level. But would individualization give you competitive advantage? Suppliers of products with a standard core but a variety of possible add-ons have much to gain in this way – witness Dell and their online 'configurator', allowing customers to design their very own Dell.

I hate the whole business of buying a car. For some it is a joy but for me it is just one long series of compromises and frustrations. I make my choice only to find that the model I want can't have the type of seat I want and the one that has the seat I want won't take off the boy racer spoilers... The car manufacturer that allows me to talk directly to the factory and design my own car will have my undying loyalty.

The problems with making such a notion reality are of course many and complex, but the challenge is on. Firstly, current manufacturing systems will stand in the way of such 'interference' from customers. Secondly, the supply chain logistics could easily be frozen solid by such 'infinite variety'. Thirdly, and for now perhaps the biggest issue, in many markets there will just not be enough takers to make such a proposition economical. Of course, once customers wake up to what they can get from a supplier, and once the demand starts to build, then manufacturing and supply chain systems that cannot oblige will leave their owners looking like dinosaurs. Competitors that *can* oblige will start to siphon off the customers prepared to pay for such a service, most likely the high-margin end of the business, and the dinosaurs will find themselves in a potentially vicious circle of decline.

Looked at from the other perspective, the supplier that offers such choice will be the supplier that builds the most detailed knowledge of customer requirements and motivations. This knowledge will be used to drive better-value propositions and so start a virtuous circle of growth.

As has been said before, in this respect the e-revolution hastens the battle of the supply chain in place of the battle of the market share.

Building loyalty

Whether used to provide more convenient means of trading, to lock the customer into the supply chain, or to individualize the offer, the e-revolution will have a significant impact on customer loyalty. Loyalty is not the same as getting repeat orders. So-called 'loyalty schemes' such as points cards from petrol stations will bring repeat orders, but they won't bring loyalty to the supplier. Remove the scheme and the customer moves on; the loyalty was to the scheme, not the supplier. In this sense, repeat orders are being bought, and the same applies to discounts and rebate schemes. Loyalty cannot be bought in this way; it must be earned through the provision of genuine value, as perceived by the customer.

Research has shown for instance that many business-to-business customers value very highly things that make it easier to do business with a supplier – e-commerce for one. Individual consumers may be prepared to put up with a good deal of hassle if it results in them getting 'a bargain' (though probably only those with plenty of time on their hands, or perhaps those that enjoy the chase), but most professional buyers will not.

If the e-revolution makes doing business easier, and if the knowledge provided by CRM makes suppliers able to smooth further the path to their door, then we will see suppliers able to build the kind of loyalty only previously anticipated for the manufacturer of the proverbial perfect mousetrap. The next chapter will look further at this question of customer loyalty, with a particular focus on the importance of relationships.

MAKING IT HAPPEN

The hurdles standing in the way of any business intent on harnessing the e-revolution are many and varied, but let's consider just four.

The first is to do with the business's own history. A long experience of what we might call 'transactional marketing' – the one-way traffic of 'Take it or leave it, that's what we have to offer' – will not provide the most fertile ground for harnessing the full potential of the e-revolution. No longer can the supplier just tell the market what it will be getting; it must now be able to respond to the signals coming from the market, signals that its competitors will be picking up and using to improve their offer.

The second hurdle will often be the existing supply chain, especially if designed for a 'We decide what the market is getting' kind of operation. Only if definitions of supply chain efficiency include 'responsiveness' and 'flexibility' will the supplier be pointing its logistics in the right direction to cope with the coming tide.

The third hurdle will be found in the kind of thinking that sees all of this as just the old techniques of mass marketing warmed over. Certainly the Internet gives suppliers access to larger markets than ever before, but its value will soon be exhausted if it is seen simply as a new form of promotion. It is the potential for building relationships with customers based on close knowledge of their needs and speedy provision of relevant solutions that gives the medium its truly revolutionary edge.

The final hurdle to be discussed here lies squarely with the marketing department itself. The truth of the matter is that many marketers have still not grasped the potential of the e-revolution and view it as more the domain of the IT expert than as any substantial part of their marketing mix. If marketing is about forging a unique match between market needs and company capabilities, then this is an area where too many marketers are shirking their responsibility for developing and influencing a key capability.

It is reckoned that as many as two-thirds of potential e-commerce purchases entered into by consumers are abandoned before they complete the process. This is down to uncertainty on the consumers' part, doubts about the process, fears of ordering the wrong thing, worries about security, and a host of other discomforts. Marketing is clearly not doing its job of making it easy for customers to do business with the supplier. Solutions such as 'click to chat' buttons are an advance but there is a long way to go before buying through the Web is as easy and as painless as promised. Marketers cannot expect the IT department to come up with these solutions; the responsibility rests squarely on their own shoulders.

Where the e-revolution has been seen to falter or stall, or has been used inappropriately, or has failed to bring the expected profits, the fault can often be found with the poor application of traditional marketing skills and disciplines. We started this chapter by asking whether the rules of marketing were about to be changed. We have seen some signs that this may be so, but what is abundantly clear is that the e-revolution as a tool of marketing will not work if it is not used with the same rigour and discipline as any other tool.

Before commencing a major research project, or starting an advertising campaign, or launching a new product, the marketer will ask some straight questions – what is the purpose of this activity, and what return do I expect from my investment? Why should the e-commerce strategy or plans for using the Internet be any less clear on these two questions? If your decision to be involved is simply to keep up with the competition, then you are already missing out on the real purpose of this revolution. If you see it as enhancing your proposition and so providing a source of competitive advantage, then you will have some clear objectives, a coherent plan and a firm proposal for recouping your investment. If not, then you will fail, not because of the complexities of a new technology, but because of poor marketing.

19

Relationship marketing and key account management

The core of this book has been written around the marketing mix, the famous four Ps – product, price, place and promotion. Each P has its own range of options and strategies but marketing success depends on establishing the correct balance between these strategies – the mix is always more important than any single element.

The notion of the marketing mix is a very powerful one but, like any tool, its lazy application can lead us into some difficulties. We have already noted some potential weaknesses of the four-P approach: place for one (not to mention the perils of alliteration). In seeking four words each starting with the letter P, we find that place is not named to represent properly its full scope. Why only four Ps? We have already seen in Chapter 11 that many involved in the marketing of services consider the seven Ps, adding people, processes and physical evidence.

These are relatively minor complaints, but there is a third and more serious problem waiting to trip up the unthinking marketer. The idea of the marketing mix was in part an attempt to escape from the limitations of a 'make and sell' business philosophy. It introduced the idea that customers were influenced by more than the hard facts of a product and so encouraged a greater spirit of enquiry into the dynamics of the market-place, its segments and its customers. The language used was not particularly revolutionary and suited the predominantly manufacturing-based economy of the time. The outcome has been that many still regard the mix as a set of things that we do _to_ the market.

Philip Kotler in his book, _Kotler on Marketing_ (1999), has suggested an alternative to the four Ps – the four Cs, with the intention of reminding us that marketing is something that we must do _with_ the market. The four Cs encourage us to look at the market through our customers' eyes. It is not that the four Ps do not, if understood properly, but perhaps the choice of words makes it easier for those who still retain a predominantly inward focus to use them and tell themselves that they are in fact practising professional marketing:

- _Product_ becomes customer value, reminding us that not only is everything in the eye of the beholder but that successful products must provide genuine value to the customer (see Chapters 12 and 20).
- _Price_ becomes cost to the customer, reminding us that price is simply a marker and that the full costs in use are of much greater significance in most purchases (see Chapter 13).
- _Place_ becomes convenience, a much better term that encourages us to remember why we consider routes to market in the first place – to make it easy for our customers to get hold of our offer (see Chapter 17).
- _Promotion_ becomes communication, perhaps the most important change of emphasis, recognizing that good promotion should aim to develop into a dialogue with the customer, an aim much facilitated by the e-revolution (see Chapters 17 and 18).

Cynics might say that this is mere semantics, but the true marketer will recognize the important differences in tone. It is much the same issue that can be raised with regard to segmentation. Segmentation is a pillar of modern marketing practice, but it too can be applied lazily. We have already noted that a segment never bought anything; only people do that. Segmentation, in its attempt to place individuals into groups for which appropriate marketing mixes can be developed, can run the risk of homogenizing the market, so losing the insights into individual needs that can provide the sparks and perhaps the greatest opportunities for competitive advantage.

Let's consider milk – marketed variously as a refreshing drink, a source of health and nutrition, a cooking ingredient, an additive to tea, fun and plenty more besides. These are potential segments – but do they go far enough? If we take the health and nutrition segment – is that a homogeneous group, or do different people seek different health benefits from milk? Some may consider it principally as an aid to healthy bones while others look at it more holistically, and yet we should remember that there are many cultures that consider milk only as an aid to growth for infants and that adult consumption is seen as a health *problem*, the cause of flatulence and diarrhoea. Clearly then, we must look at micro-segments, and the closer the magnifying glass gets, the closer we get to real individuals. At such a point, we are entering the territory of relationship marketing.

Relationship marketing places great importance on the depth and breadth of relationships formed with customers. For obvious reasons this has been much more the preserve of business-to-business operations where direct contact is both possible and necessary. The rise of CRM (customer relationship management, discussed in Chapter 18) has attempted to raise the importance of individual customer relationships for all suppliers, fmcg as well as business-to-business, but CRM still suffers from some aspects of the 'This is a new technology that allows us to do something to the market' syndrome. Much of the resistance from individual consumers to the attempt by companies to forge closer relationships through e-commerce stems from a feeling that businesses are trying to do something *to* us rather than *with* or *for* us. E-commerce can be seen by some as an invasion of privacy rather than a conduit for collaboration. The relationship can be rather one-sided, at best an attempt to buy loyalty and at worse an attempt to infiltrate.

Relationship marketing sees customer contacts as opportunities for collaboration, not simply as a selling or a promotional activity. In some cases it will go beyond that, aiming to integrate the outcome of those collaborative relationships into the operation of the business. This is a three-stage process:

1. Close relationships with customers allow for much better understanding of their perceptions and needs.
2. This understanding is shared by a wide group of people in the supplier company, as the nature of the relationship is necessarily a broad one on both sides.
3. Armed with this understanding, the business is able to organize itself to respond to the needs of its customers, replacing vertical silos based on functions or products with customer-focused structures.

Picking up this last point, company structure is important to the marketer but too many marketers believe that sort of thing to be somebody else's business. Figure 19.1 shows a traditional silo structure, with all the problems of aligning internally focused functions and activities towards the market and the customer.

What then is the right structure? This must of course depend on circumstances. No precise blueprint will help you, and in any case one thing is for sure – it will never be perfect! Let's say you want to be a customer-focused business and you have only two customers – sounds easy? But what if one of those customers has a strongly centralized organization dominated by purchasing and supply chain

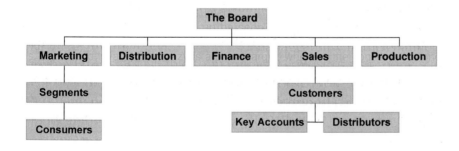

Figure 19.1 *The silo structure*

management, and the other customer is a loose federation of regional sites each focused on a particular technology? Unless you divide into two businesses, then however you structure yourself you are likely to be wrong at least half the time!

Figure 19.2 shows not so much a structure as an intention, with service functions providing the core, operating in support of those parts of the business with direct customer contact. The 'contact' may be with markets, with segments, or with customers – perhaps your key accounts, which brings us to this important part of relationship marketing.

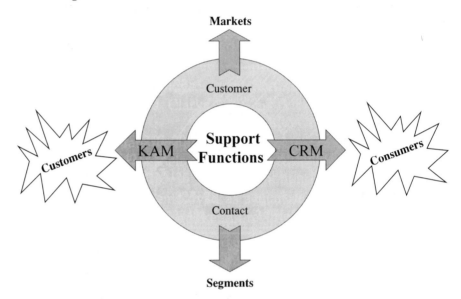

Figure 19.2 *The market-focused structure*

KEY ACCOUNT MANAGEMENT

Two factors will limit the extent to which you will take the notion of relationship marketing – the number of customers with which you can build truly collaborative relationships, and the number of individual customer needs that you can cope with before pulling yourself apart at the seams! Key account management (KAM) is the process by which you manage the extent of your aim to be driven by your customers. By selecting a small number of key accounts, the appropriate resources can be applied to develop the relationships, and the organization can cope with the resultant rise in activity levels. Having too many key accounts will result either in no effect at all, or worse, the splintering of your capabilities.

Identifying key accounts

Using a modified version of the directional policy matrix described in Chapter 12, you can identify your key accounts as being those customers that are attractive to you, and that regard you in a similar light. This mutuality is important, as we will see when looking at the development of the relationship itself. Figure 19.3 shows the matrix. The process for completing such a matrix is described at length in the book, *Key Account Management* (Cheverton, 1999).

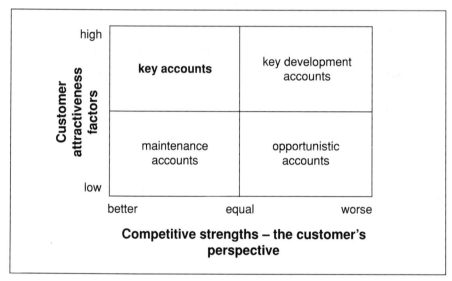

Figure 19.3 *Identifying key accounts*

The elements that determine how attractive customers are to you will depend on your own priorities, but should be focused as much on the future as possible. Customers' perspectives will be based on whatever criteria they use to measure and select suppliers – their vendor ratings – and will be unique to each customer.

A one-line definition of a key account might be: a customer that will help you get your business to where you want it to be in the future. In this sense your key accounts are investments in that future. Those identified as key development accounts will require an even greater investment, as you are currently judged less well than your competition. Maintenance accounts are not unimportant – they are the cash cows of the portfolio and it is from here that you will get the revenue to finance your investment and from here that you will have to take the resources required. When we speak of resources we are talking principally of people's time, and nowhere will that be more visible than in the effort taken to build relationships.

Building the relationship – its significance

Why is the relationship so important? If we go right back to the marketing model from Chapter 3, we will recall the need to identify the market opportunity and match that with appropriate capabilities. This applies just as much with an individual customer, and the kind of relationship built at what we will call the partnership stage of KAM (see Figure 19.8) provides the means by which you can first identify the opportunities and then ensure that the right capabilities are developed.

In increasingly competitive markets it becomes less and less reasonable to expect an individual salesperson to develop the depth and breadth of relationships required with a key customer. There are many reasons for this, not least the shortage of bona fide superheroes to carry out such tasks, but in particular the complexity of the customer's decision-making process and its search for key suppliers.

Penetrating the customer's decision-making process

Let's consider the example of a food flavours supplier selling to a top-brand food manufacturer. The supplier has a particular capability for developing novel flavours and what it wants more than anything else is early access to new product developments so that it can get its ingredients listed. If we consider how new ideas for such products emerge from a typical fmcg company, it might look something like the diagram in Figure 19.4.

Typically, a new idea sees the light of day in the marketing department and develops by working its way through a series of other departments – first to market research for an early evaluation of interest, then on to R & D to be certain it can be made, then manufac-

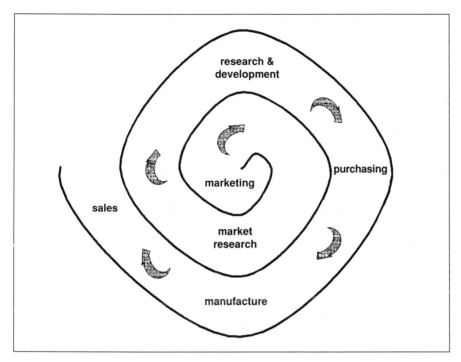

Figure 19.4 _The opportunity 'snail'_

turing to prepare for scale-up, purchasing to source the materials on a large scale and finally to the sales force to sell it into the market. The development may not be entirely linear, with plenty of overlaps and backward loops, but it is a reasonably accurate picture of many new product developments.

Now let's consider the supplier and its contacts. If its relationship is primarily with the purchasing people, not untypical, there are some pros and cons for the supplier. The pros are:

- If an idea has reached this point in the snail then it is probably a genuine requirement, not a speculative one, and an order could be on its way soon.
- You will be discussing real details, not 'wild blue yonder' forecasts.

The cons are:

- The conversation is going to be about price – perhaps not the supplier's strongest suit.

- It may be too late; another supplier may already be preferred and talking with you is just a ruse to get the price down.
- You may not have enough time to develop whatever is required.
- You probably only get to hear about existing product opportunities, not those all-important new ones.

Perhaps the supplier has managed to penetrate further into the customer's 'snail' and has a relationship with the R & D people; now there is a different list of pros and cons. The pros are:

- The conversations are about technical ability – your strong suit.
- You have time to develop your proposition.
- If you get specified by the R & D folk it will be hard for purchasing to pressure you on price.

The con is that this new product still may not see the light of day – this could be a risky investment of your time and effort.

Clearly the supplier should want to get to these R & D folk, but that requires a deeper relationship than the classic 'bow tie' seen in Figure 19.6.

And what if it penetrates even further, to the marketing people? The pros are:

- Being in at the start gives you plenty of time to get your act together.
- You can head off the competition before they even hear of the opportunity.
- The conversations are about the future and collaboration.
- The customer is taking you into its confidence.
- This will not be about price.

The cons are:

- Marketing have 100 great ideas and only three or four turn into real successes – this could eat up your resources in speculative trials.
- Perhaps the customer's R & D folk don't have much time for their own marketing people. You could be seen by your prime contact as collaborating with the internal enemy!

The downsides are not to be ignored, but if they can be managed the upsides are overwhelming. Consider the customer's ambitions. The snail is necessarily a slow process and most fmcg companies seek to increase their speed to market. In pursuit of this they will attempt to modify the snail, to break down its linear nature, perhaps talking of process re-engineering, supply chain management or matrix management as they do so. Whatever the terminology used, they require suppliers who will help them, suppliers with the ability to manage complex relationships across functions, businesses and even continents. Such suppliers will be regarded as key suppliers and this is the true significance of the key account relationship: the achievement of key supplier status.

Building the relationship – the key account relationship development mode

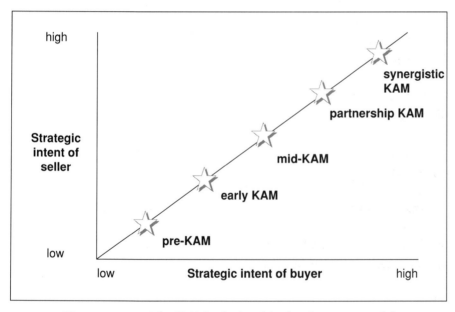

Figure 19.5 *The KAM relationship development model*

(adapted from a model developed by Millman, A F and Wilson, K J (1994)

This model (Figure 19.5), first developed by Professor Tony Millman and Dr Kevin Wilson in 1994, was further researched and developed at Cranfield University School of Management by Professor Malcolm McDonald, Tony Millman and Beth Rogers. Their findings were published in 1996 in a research report, 'Key account management: learning from supplier and customer perspectives'.

The model describes the developing relationship between supplier and customer, from pre-KAM, through early and mid-KAM, on to partnership KAM and then synergistic KAM. We will look at just three of these stages – early, mid and partnership.

For a relationship to develop along this path it is clear that both sides must want it to do so. Chances are that the supplier's strategic intent (the level of its belief that an improved relationship will bring business improvements worth the effort) will be ahead of the customer's; patience is often required, but suppliers that demonstrate a concern for the customer's needs and evidence their ability to provide valuable solutions will see the relationship deepen and broaden over time.

Early KAM

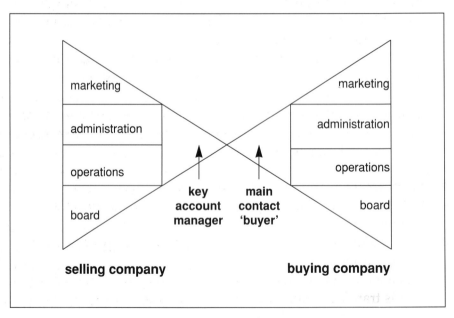

Figure 19.6 *Early KAM*

(adapted from McDonald, M, Millman, A F and Rogers, B (1996) Key account management: learning from supplier and customer perspectives, Cranfield University School of Management)

Some possible characteristics of this stage might include:

- The principal contact is between two people – salesperson and buyer.
- The relationship may be competitive, each seeking to gain advantage.
- At worst, the relationship may be confrontational.
- The buyer may see any attempt to gain access to other contacts as a threat to his or her position and power.
- Price discussions dominate – the buyer focuses on costs.
- The supplier focuses on increased volume.
- Suppliers are judged on unspecified performance criteria.
- The customer is still assessing alternative suppliers.
- Disputes can lead to long-term breaks in supply.

This is probably the most typical sales relationship, the classic 'bow tie', and it is a dangerous stage. It is all too easy, and apparently attractive, just to stay here. The salesperson is in full control of the relationship with no distractions from badly informed colleagues – and gets all the praise for success! This is the stage that promises 'a place in the limelight' at the next sales conference.

Moreover, the buyer may also be quite happy with this state of affairs – he or she is secure, knows all that goes on with the supplier and can keep all the carefully guarded secrets.

The buyer as gatekeeper, matched with the salesperson as super-star, makes for a relationship with a built-in resistance to change, but the downsides of staying here are many:

- Expertise on both sides is seriously underutilized.
- Seller and buyer are expected to be all-round experts – an unlikely scenario.
- Information flow is restricted as buyer and seller jockey for negotiating position.
- When information does flow, it is littered with 'Chinese whispers' as it is translated along the chain – expert to non-expert, to non-expert, to expert… and back.
- Projects and activities are held up by the sales/purchasing bottleneck.
- There is over-reliance on one relationship, and if it breaks (buyers

retire, salespeople get promoted) then the whole thing must start again. The future is permanently at risk.

● Salespeople become 'kingpins' who cannot be moved on for fear of losing the business (rewrite that last point's comment – salespeople retire, buyers get promoted).

A major limitation of this kind of relationship is the way that it denies the supplier full access to the customer's internal processes, and to its market. A salesperson might have very little knowledge of what happens to the product once it is bought, still less how the customer operates in its own market. These are serious gaps if the supplier is to understand how it may best help the customer.

Sometimes the denial of access will be deliberate. In the retail industry it is not unusual for buyers to limit a supplier's access to contacts and valuable information. It is a matter of power, and ownership of the market. In the past, major brands often dominated relationships as a result of their consumer knowledge and huge advertising budgets. Increasingly, the retailer's enhanced knowledge of consumer behaviour through, for instance, electronic point of sale and loyalty cards, is shifting the balance. Knowledge is undeniably power, and why should it be shared with suppliers? Many purchasing organizations are becoming increasingly concerned about the leakage of valuable information to suppliers, with no tangible return.

Having said all of this, there are advantages to this kind of relationship – it is simple, it is relatively low-cost, it is controllable – and if it gets you what you want there may be no need to go beyond it. But take care with such certainty; be sure it is not just complacency.

Mid-KAM

Some possible characteristics of this stage might include:

● Principal contacts start to facilitate other contacts, through a mutual desire to increase understanding of the customer's processes and markets.
● There is an increase in time spent in meetings.
● There is a focus on reporting those meetings, action minutes, etc.
● Increased trust and openness develop.

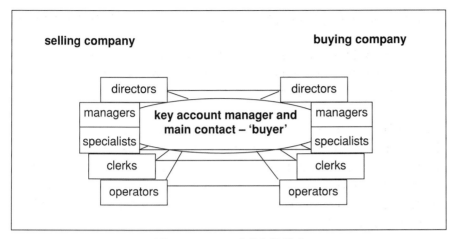

Figure 19.7 _Mid-KAM_

(adapted from McDonald, M, Millman, A F and Rogers, B (1996) Key account management: learning from supplier and customer perspectives, Cranfield University School of Management)

- Links are informal, and are still facilitated through the sales-person and buyer.
- It is perhaps at this stage that the greatest chance for 'mishaps' occurs – expect set-backs.
- This is a lot of work for both seller and buyer!

This is the transition stage between the classic 'bow tie' and the 'diamond' of the partnership KAM stage. It is a stage full of sensitivity and, if the supplier is wise, slow, measured steps forward.

Noting that the buyer is quite likely to feel threatened by any increase in contacts beyond his or her own control, the key account manager must ensure that all these new contacts are cleared with the buyer, and arranged through him- or herself. The key account manager will almost certainly have to be involved in putting the contacts together, attending the first meetings, and perhaps more. Ideally, the buyer will also be involved in these meetings but, if not, their outcomes will certainly have to be reported to him or her in full.

Add to this activity a briefing and coaching role, and we can see the biggest problem of this stage – the potential overload of activities for the key account manager. The question raised when looking at this stage is how many key accounts an individual key account manager can have responsibility for, if the accounts are passing through this stage. Add to this the fact that the mid-KAM stage can go on for many months, perhaps even years, and we must think seriously about how many customers can be classified as KAs.

One possible result of this period of hard labour is that it can be all too easy to throw in the towel. It can be seen as just too much effort, not worth the candle; and after all, the resultant benefits of moving towards partnership KAM are unlikely to flow for some time. The temptation to go back to the relative comforts of the 'bow tie' will be strong. Resist!

Partnership KAM

Some possible characteristics of this stage might include:

- Key supplier status is awarded.
- Relationships are based on trust.

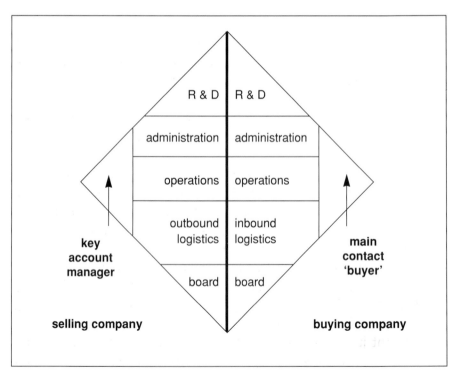

Figure 19.8 *Partnership KAM*

(adapted from McDonald, M, Millman, A F and Rogers, B (1996) Key account management: learning from supplier and customer perspectives, Cranfield University School of Management)

- Information is shared.
- Access to people is facilitated.
- Pricing is stable.
- The customer gets new ideas first.
- Continuous improvement is expected.
- There are clear 'vendor ratings' and 'performance measures'.
- There are possible contractual arrangements.
- Value is sought through integrated business processes.
- Value is sought through focus on the customer's markets.
- 'Step-outs' are permitted.
- The key account manager's role is one of co-ordination and orchestration.
- The supplier's main contact, while perhaps still the commercial buyer, is now focused on developing the supplier's capabilities rather than challenging them.
- The supplier's total organization is focused on customer satisfaction through 'supply chain management'.

This is where the benefits should start to flow. With the proper deployment of expertise on both sides, the more open and honest transfer of information and the resultant improvement in customer understanding, the supplier has the potential to move towards significant competitive advantage. By taking the right actions, it may even secure key supplier status, with its attendant increase in long-term security.

If a major downside to the 'bow tie' of early KAM is the denial of access to the customer's internal processes and to its market, the main advantage of the 'diamond' relationship is in seeing those conduits of understanding opening up. At this point of the KAM journey, the path to providing genuine solutions to the customer's problems changes from a rutted track to a metalled road.

But watch out. As contacts proliferate, so does the speed of activity and the risk of saying and doing the wrong things. People without experience of sales will be put in front of customers, and some of them might just panic at the prospect. The key account manager's role will already have changed through the mid-KAM stage from 'super salesperson' to 'super coach'; it must now move on to 'super co-ordinator'.

If it doesn't, then the potential for losing control is great, resulting in well-meaning but misdirected individuals charting their own quite separate courses. Without clarity of objectives and shared under-standing of what the customer values, you could just be about to race down some blind alleys. Your very enthusiastic IT expert, working with an equally keen customer counterpart, might see this new metalled road as an opportunity to try some unaccustomed speed.

Some things to watch out for

The hardest part of the journey will almost certainly be the transition from 'bow tie' to 'diamond'. Working through the transitional mid-KAM stage can be very hard work indeed. At times, it will seem more effort than it is worth, to both sides. This will call for all the patience, understanding and resolve that you can muster. It will call on every skill and tool within your grasp, and some that are beyond your reach. At this point, you will need friends and allies. This, let it be understood very clearly, is not a task for loners:

- Don't expect your journey to be one-way; there will be U-turns and side alleys.
- Remember that the strategic intent must be mutual and, even then, don't expect the customer to make it easy for you. You will have to lead a lot of the way, and while stamina and persistence will be two valuable assets, so will subtlety and finesse. You will know you are getting there when the customer starts to pull.
- Remember, buyers have a lot of power when they are the only point of contact. Your efforts to develop broader contacts might be for the good of their company, but they might not see it as good for them! You are about to threaten their control.
- To sell, or not to sell? If the customer sees your 'selling' activity as a pushy concern for satisfying your own needs, then don't be surprised if you come up against obstacles. If it perceives your activity as seeking solutions to its problems, then the doors will start to open.
- Some customers will demand that the key account manager should not be a salesperson at all, but a business and relationship manager.
- Some customers might not like being called 'accounts' – so this is a word for internal use, not for your business card (in the end, you can call them whatever makes them feel good!).

- Don't let your organization loose on theirs without direction and control – chaos can be the only outcome, quickly followed by a rapid raising of the customer's drawbridge.
- Don't allow the commercially 'innocent' members of your team to be taken for a ride by the customer – brief them first, and above all train them. This goes for everyone, including the boss (actually, especially the boss…).
- Don't describe this journey, internally, as an initiative – many companies have had 'initiative overload' and your own team will steer clear of this latest 'seven-day wonder'.
- One sure killer of progress from early to mid- and partnership KAM is the unrealistic tightening of travel budgets – strong relationships require personal contact.
- Be careful how you present your intentions to the customer: being told that you wish to be more 'intimate' may concern them, confuse them, or worse!
- Take care if you are the first to use the word 'partnership'. Try to hear it on the customer's lips first.
- Perhaps your customer will use 'partnership' as a trap. 'Let's work in partnership,' they say, meaning, 'You tell us your cost breakdowns, and then we'll take you to the cleaners.'

From hunters to farmers

Key account management and relationship marketing are vital activities in mature markets where competition is tough and the customer's decision processes are complex. But what about times of rapid growth – might all this just slow you down?

There is a time to hunt and a time to farm; the marketer's task is to know when to make the transition.

With the opening up of the telecommunications market in the 1990s, the appearance of new players such as MCI WorldCom and Mercury saw a frenzy of hunting, and quite rightly so, as the opportunities were there to be seized by the most energetic. Within just a few years however the easy targets were gone and the original players such as BT were starting to win back their lost customers. The time for farming had arrived, with a new focus on customer retention and growth rather than just new customer acquisition.

Hunting is easy in the telecoms jungle, but for how long?

377

KAM and the marketer

Throughout this description of the developing relationship, it may have seemed that not only has the salesperson been replaced by the key account manager but the marketer has also been missing – not so! Key account management is not a sales initiative; it is a business initiative, and calls on the participation of all functions if partnership KAM relationships are to be formed and if the outcome of those relationships is to be used to drive the business.

For relationship marketing and KAM to succeed, suppliers will have to move away from structures based on functions working in vertical silos (as shown in Figure 19.1) and towards more fluid structures where all activities are focused on building customer satisfaction. This is not the place to describe such changes (*Key Account Management* by Peter Cheverton (1999) goes into full details) other than to say that the role of the marketer is crucial in such customer-focused organizations, as is the role of the marketing plan. Individual customer plans must be subsets of segment plans, which are in turn subsets of the marketing plan, as shown in Figure 19.9.

Without segmentation, the selection of key accounts will tend to suffer from 'sizeism'. The basis of identifying key accounts shown in

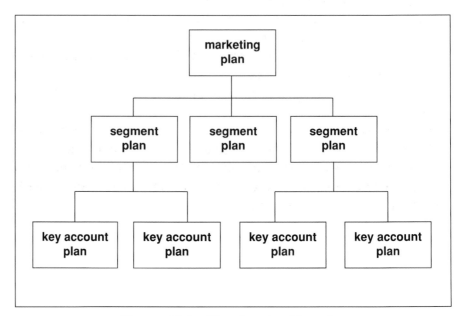

Figure 19.9 *The planning hierarchy*

Figure 19.3 called for a comparison of the factors that made customers attractive and of the customer's assessment of you as a supplier. Without segmentation, most markets are too large and diverse for this process to be workable – what seems attractive in one part of the market is not so important in another – and so the scale of business becomes the only truly comparable factor, hence 'sizeism'. The 20 per cent of customers that represent 80 per cent of the business will be the key accounts. This is often true for now, but in fast-changing market-places is often not the best indication of the future.

We opened this chapter with a warning of the potential misapplication of traditional marketing models such as the marketing mix, often criticized as too short-term, too tactical, too 'transactional'. Relationship marketing seeks to ensure that this is not the case, attempting to align the whole business towards its customers through a focus on the relationship between supplier and customer.

Challenges include:

- rigorous identification of those customers that really are key accounts;
- the need to move away from transactional selling to relationship management;
- basing relationships on trust and value;
- putting the focus on the future and the longer-term – aiming to maximize the lifetime value of customers and market segments;
- changing internal organization and attitudes in order to align the business towards the customer;
- The need to develop cross-business processes.

What some call key account management others might call relationship marketing. In reality the two point in very similar directions. C Gronroos calls relationship marketing 'the mutual exchange and fulfilment of promises' – grand words but not a bad basis for partnership key account management.

20

Delivering value – making relationship marketing work

Marketers talk a great deal about adding value, and there usually follows a frantic pursuit of new ideas to help gain competitive advantage, but so often a vital ingredient of the equation is left out. Adding value to what? The answer is adding value to the customer's desired experience, and that experience may extend well beyond what the supplier has been used to regarding as its product's 'arena'.

Ask any salesperson and he or she will tell you that customers don't buy features; they buy benefits. Customers are not interested in the facts about a product so much as what it will do for them. But are today's customers even more demanding than that, seeking solutions, perhaps even *experiences*?

In Chapter 13 we explored the differences between price, cost and value, finding that value is without doubt the most important measure for supplier and customer alike, though the hardest to pin down. Value could be a measure of what a product will do for you (its benefit), or how it solves a problem, or how it enhances an experience. Finding ways to pin down this value and its definition, to identify and quantify value (because only then can a price be put on it) is the goal of the modern marketer.

Chapter 19 argued the importance of broad and deep customer relationships as a means to understanding customers' needs and their perception of value. In this chapter we will look at the tools that can be used to analyse the information secured through those relationships, in order to 'pin down' value – in essence, making relationship marketing work.

Traditional sales practice (much simplified) seeks to identify a set of benefits and present them to customers as efficiently as possible. Traditional marketing practice (even more simplified!) seeks to segment markets so that packages of benefits can be presented to customers in the same efficient way.

If success is possible in your market by these means (and you are 100 per cent certain of that), then perhaps you might decide to go no further, for the capabilities required to deliver more than this are significant. If competitive advantage can be attained through packages of benefits, then your market must be quite a simple one, and the way to work in simple markets is to keep it simple yourself. Ambitions to 'delight' or 'excite' your customers beyond their real needs is one of the faster ways to penury, but then, do you know their real needs? Who is to say that their _real_ needs are not just hiding below the surface, those famous _latent_ needs?

As ever, marketers have a choice as to how 'sophisticated' they feel they need to be in pursuit of competitive advantage. Table 20.1 summarizes four levels of this 'sophistication', or more properly four different ways to secure a unique match between your capabilities and the customer's needs.

Let's take as an example a company that sells fertilizer to farmers, and at the first stage that means all farmers:

1. Stage 1 – 'Take it, because that's what I'm offering, and I know you want it...' You regard your customers as essentially the same, and you deliver a standard product or service – you probably talk 'features'.

    Your product is fertilizer, in three bag sizes, and it contains the magic ingredient 'Oomph'.
2. Stage 2 – 'It's all in the presentation...' You uncover customer needs that allow you to present those features as relevant

Table 20.1 *Beyond benefits?*

The Offer	Stage 1 features	Stage 2 benefits	Stage 3 solutions	Stage 4 total business experience
Customers	all	segmentation	key accounts by type	individual key accounts
Marketing Approach	sales-led marketing	traditional four Ps marketing	traditional marketing in transition	relationship marketing
Sales Approach	traditional 1:1	enhanced 1:1	key account management	partnership account management
Competitive Advantage	first, largest, best known, perhaps none	ability to communicate benefits	quality of solutions	quality of relationships
Supplier Organization and Focus	sales focus	marketing focus	customer focus	value chain focus

'benefits'. The product or service may remain much the same, perhaps with some minor cosmetic changes, but you are starting to recognize your customers as being different from one another, often expressed through some kind of customer segmentation.

You have segmented your market, perhaps by crop types, and so now you have to address yourself to wheat farmers. The magic ingredient 'Oomph' is still there, but a reformulation – 'Oomph Plus' – has made it particularly beneficial to wheat growers.

3. Stage 3 – 'Tailored just for you…' You uncover a deeper set of needs that force you to make more substantial changes to your product or service, recognizing the increasing individuality of the customer. This allows you to present your offer as a tailored solution. This is usually done only for a small group of customers – your key accounts, perhaps even types of key account.

You have identified a trend towards minimal use of chemicals, and have developed some low-application formulations of your product, still containing 'Oomph', but the real trick now is the application rate.

Based on this trend, and your ability to meet the need, you have identi-fied a key account 'type' – large farm, keen to minimize chemical use, wheat production for human consumption, likes high-tech solutions, 'early adopter'.

4. Stage 4 – 'Managing the customer's total business experience…' You uncover a breadth of needs that allows you to understand the customer's values and aspirations in full. This is not just with regard to your offer – you understand its 'total business experi-ence'. Your tailored solutions are now designed to have a posi-tive impact at all levels of this business experience, before, during and after the use of your particular product or service. Indeed, your customer regards you as more than a simple supplier of a product or service. You now add value at many (why not all?) points of its business experience – you have achieved the status of key supplier.

    Many of your farmers, you discover, regard fertilizer application as a very low-grade task in the great scheme of things. It takes a lot of time, time that they could use for doing other things, only all these new hi-tech fertilizers make it difficult to pass the job on to a jobbing contractor. Your offer has now been transformed. You no longer talk about 'Oomph' or 'Oomph Plus'. Indeed, you rarely mention the product at all, for your business now is in providing a managed fertil-izer application service for key farmers. You charge by results (a percen-tage of farm profits), not by volume of material, and you are continually developing formulations to reduce the volumes required. Indeed, your joint aspiration is to move to a stage where you can use more environ-mentally friendly alternatives and be rid of 'Oomph' for good.

The key to success here, in moving from stage to stage, is the ever-improving understanding of what your customer wants. Features tend to be supplier-focused; benefits begin to consider the customer; solutions are about meeting requirements; but addressing the total business experience requires you to go beyond this, beyond expecta-tions to anticipating the customer's needs.

At its best, you understand the customer's aspirations, not just with regard to your products as a supplier, but with regard to its total business, and so you have an opportunity to enhance its total busi-ness experience. For the farmer in our example, the TBE is being able to forget about the fertilizer issue altogether, and spend time on more profitable, or more challenging, or perhaps just more interesting activities – it all depends on the farmer.

TBE in the oil supply industry – BP lead the way

Another example of a supplier going beyond benefits and enhancing the customer's TBE is found in the oil supply industry. BP, among others, has identified that it has a certain expertise in managing fluid supplies on a customer's site. For key accounts, it will offer to manage the customer's total 'fluid requirements'. This will almost certainly involve taking responsibility for the supply of products outside its own portfolio, perhaps in some cases even working with a competitor's products. As with the fertilizer example, the focus moves to reducing the volumes of product required and improving efficiencies of use. The focus is squarely on providing value rather than lowest prices. Indeed, the price of the product becomes almost irrelevant as the services are charged for in more creative, more *holistic* ways.

THE CUSTOMER'S 'TOTAL BUSINESS EXPERIENCE'

In the bad old days, sometimes we would tell our customers what they needed, and sometimes we were lucky and we got it right. Then, *sometimes* wasn't enough, and we realized that we had to learn to ask, and some of us are still learning. But now we hit on some problems:

- What if our customers don't know what they need?
- What if things are changing around them so fast that they can't see a clear way forward?
- What if the things they keep telling us they want are just, well, what they think they *should* be saying? Everyone wants a lower price, a better product and slicker service.

When Alexander Graham Bell invented the telephone, he toured the USA, showing it off to what he hoped would be interested businessmen. After one such session, he was approached by an apparent enthusiast. 'Mr Bell, I really like your new toy. It's my daughter's birthday party tomorrow, and I would be very grateful if you would come along to show it.'

Well, the great man was incensed. 'It is not a toy!' he exploded. 'Don't you realize that this will revolutionize communications, and your business. Just think, with one of these you can talk to a customer 300 miles away.'

The businessman thought for a moment, and then answered, 'But Mr Bell, I don't have any customers 300 miles away.'

Telling them isn't enough. But sometimes, even *asking* your customer isn't enough. Who knew that they needed Post-it notes before they were invented, or the Internet, or a telephone? The job of the marketer is to identify and understand what their customers *might* want, based on their *latent* needs, to aim to provide it and to sell them the vision. And how do you gain this new *insight*?

Benchmarking?

Useful, but why should we think that everyone else has seen the light? And anyway, we want competitive advantage, not a 'me too' solution.

Market research?

Of course, but asking traditional questions will get traditional answers. Yes, of course they want a lower price, a better product and slicker service: hardly an *insight*. My own company once commissioned a piece of research to see why training managers chose particular training suppliers. The answers seemed very worthy – value for money, value for time, leading edge and all the rest – except that we knew that wasn't the truth, at least not the truth that went to the root of their desired experience. The truth of the matter was that many training managers chose the supplier least likely to make them look foolish. See it from their standpoint. They arrange an event and commit people's time – it is their reputation that is on the line if the trainer turns out to be an embarrassment. How did we know that? Because we focused on what training managers wanted from the total experience of doing business with us – their TBE. We got customer-intimate, and it helped that we had all seen life from the customer side of the desk. This is what you must do for your customers if you are to match their total business experience.

So, don't do market research? None of this is arguing against market research. Research is vital if we are to understand our customers and their needs. What this argues for is the *kind* of research required. In the relationship marketing environment, when dealing with sophisticated purchasing organizations that talk of supply chains and value, and when you seek to go beyond benefits to solutions and enhancements to TBE, you need to research into customers' motivations, aspirations and values. And beyond that, you need to uncover the things that they don't even know themselves.

Remember, customers are lazy. This is not a prejudiced remark – suppliers are probably even lazier, that is, they seek the simplest solution to a problem. For a customer, the simplest solution to many a problem is to ask the supplier. 'The supplier,' said one of my customers once, 'is the soft underbelly of the market; they'll do anything to get the order.'

Certainly buyers might assume that, and their requests and demands are often made in that light. Is the buyer that demands you provide consignment stock really wanting consignment stock? Perhaps the company wants to reduce its working capital, and consignment stock seems a much easier option than installing EDI and efficient response ordering – easier for it, but not for the supplier and, in the end, not the optimal solution for either.

Customers may find it difficult to articulate their desired *total business experience*; they may even lie to save themselves time, money, or effort. It is the supplier's responsibility to understand their customers well enough to be able to articulate that experience for them, and to argue for the appropriate activities to meet it, not just the simplest.

The following case study looks at one company that has been remarkably successful in identifying its customers' requirements by first understanding the customers' customers – the end consumers. And based on that understanding, it has been able to add value to its customers well beyond simple product benefits, and secure a handsome reward in return.

The NutraSweet case study

NutraSweet brand sweetener, generally known as aspartame, is a high-intensity sweetener used in a wide range of food and drinks around the world. The fact that it has a brand name is perhaps the most important point, as NutraSweet aims to create consumer demand for the 'invisible' raw material used in well-known brands such as Coca-Cola or CareFree (chewing gum). Its aim is to create value for the end consumer and, most importantly, also for the 'carrier' product.

In a market where consumers had all sorts of doubts about artificial sweeteners, from taste to health concerns, NutraSweet created strong consumer demand that resulted in a pull for its product even through massive 'carrier' brands such as Coke. How did it do it?

The strategy was clear from the start – NutraSweet had to have a strong consumer franchise. Just being a superior product would not be enough, as without consumer awareness the carrier product would gain virtually all the credit and reward, and any reward that there was would be slight and short-lived. One tactic in this campaign was the 'gumball' promotion. Millions of these sweets were made with NutraSweet's product and mailed direct to US households. This was an unashamed assault on the taste-buds of the end consumer. At the same time it made use of a clear brand logo, the NutraSweet 'swirl' stamped on the packaging of a range of low-calorie products.

Consumer awareness was only the start, of course. To be sustainable, such a strategy also had to mean something to the 'carrier', NutraSweet's immediate customers. Here a range of activities was in place. First, a clear patent for aspartame allowed it to negotiate long-term deals with market leaders in the food and drinks industry. The patent expired in December 1992 and many in the industry had expected this to signal a move towards commodity status for aspartame. Instead, both Coca-Cola (1991) and PepsiCo (1992) signed long-term partnership deals with NutraSweet – actions far from the expected hunt for the lowest-priced alternative. Both Coca-Cola and PepsiCo seemed to feel that it would be a competitive disadvantage to be without the NutraSweet brand, a validation of NutraSweet's consumer-focused strategy.

Second, NutraSweet sought to collaborate with its direct customers in promoting the 'carrier' products, gaining in return the application of its logo to the packaging.

Third, experience in the food as well as the drinks market allowed NutraSweet to improve its product, in particular extending its shelf life, something that had been an early limitation. Such improvements allowed broader applications and experience that led to further improvements, and so the virtuous circle continued.

Fourth, as well as attending to its customers' requirements regarding end consumers, NutraSweet also attended to its customers' own business requirements. As volumes increased so economies of scale became apparent, and these were shared with customers through steadily lowering prices. This was important, as some customers might have become uncomfortable that NutraSweet had some kind of hold on them, through its consumer franchise, which might tempt it to exploit its position. Steadily reducing prices put paid to any such thoughts.

Perhaps the most value that NutraSweet brought to its customers and to the end consumers was in recognizing that the full potential in the low-calorie market had not yet been realized. NutraSweet was able to identify with the end users' desired total business experience – they wanted low-calorie food and drink that didn't taste strange and that was safe (saccharin had been the cause of a number of consumer 'scares'). NutraSweet tasted like sugar, felt like sugar in the mouth and had no consumer health scares. As for the food and drink manufacturers, where their desired total business experience was double-digit growth, then NutraSweet contributed significantly. Diet drinks grew dramatically while others saw more sluggish performances.

So, the secrets of NutraSweet's success? Firstly, a good product with unique competitive advantage. Secondly, a strong consumer franchise, important for a supplier a few steps down the chain from the end consumer. Thirdly, working in partnership with its customers, all focused on the end consumer. Fourthly, and most important of all perhaps, identifying what both consumers and manufacturers really wanted, their desired total business experience, and delivering it.

POSITIVE IMPACT ANALYSIS (PIA)

This is a tool intended to open up your understanding of your market in the same way that NutraSweet understood its market. The purpose of PIA is to give insight, and to help you prioritize your actions based on those insights. It aims to answer the following question: what set of activities within your own organization will result in a positive impact being made on the customer's total business experience?

Let's consider an example. You travel by air, business class, transatlantic, London to New York. Why do you travel business class? Is it because of the champagne? Unlikely. Is it because of the wider seat? Perhaps, but surely that's not the whole story. Perhaps you are doing it because you believe you will arrive in better shape to do your job. You are a businessperson, and your desired total business experience is to 'do the deal'. Flying business class increases your chances.

This is important to realize (if you are in the airline business) for two reasons.

If people are paying for an increased likelihood of 'doing the deal', not just for a wider seat, then they will probably be prepared to pay more – they perceive greater value.

If your customers want to 'do the deal', then enhancing their TBE will take more than a good flight. It will involve getting them to the airport, checking them in with ease, speeding them through security, speeding them through immigration in the USA, collecting their luggage, providing them with facilities on arrival to shower, to send e-mails or to get a presentation printed, getting them met, getting them to their next destination, and making sure that they don't come down with a cold the next day – one they are convinced they caught on your plane! We know the experience sought, and we have some clues already as to how we might be able to make a positive impact on it.

Value chain analysis

The next thing to do, having identified the desired TBE for this particular market segment, is to list out all the activities that your customers currently have to go through to do business with you and to achieve their TBE. We might call it a process chain, or better, a value chain.

The customers' value chain for a flight consists of the following typical activities:

- route enquiry;
- ticket purchase;
- receive tickets;
- drive to airport;
- park in long-stay;
- shuttle bus to terminal;
- check in and luggage;
- security;
- passport;
- waiting;
- boarding;
- safety procedures;
- take-off;
- watch a movie, play games;
- read, talk, work;
- meals and drinks;
- sleep;
- meals and drinks;
- landing;
- disembark;
- passport and immigration;
- luggage;
- customs;
- into the terminal;
- find taxi;
- check in to hotel;
- business meetings;
- reconfirm flights;
- recommence the process...

So far so good – we know what our customers are up against. The next stage is to try to understand all the things that could go wrong at each stage, or what it is that could make each stage a burden or a frustration, because after that we aim to identify the range of activities that could have a positive impact on the TBE. Table 20.2 lists the potential problems, and some possible actions for positive impact.

Table 20.2 *The value chain – problems and possible activities*

Customer Activity	Problems	Positive Impact
route enquiry	confusing alternatives, no personal incentive	corporate client service, 'air miles' packages
ticket purchase	frustrating admin	electronic commerce
receive tickets	worry of not receiving	no ticket – electronic ticketing
drive to airport	time, getting lost	limo door to door
park in long-stay	time and hassle	no need, given the above
shuttle bus to terminal	time and more hassle	no need, given the above
check in and luggage	queue, debates over cabin baggage	completed in limo
security	time	fast track
passport	time	fast track
waiting	time, lack of business facilities	deliver direct to business lounge with IT and secretarial services
boarding	a rush for locker space	larger lockers, wardrobes
safety procedures	fine, but you didn't listen – heard it all before	cartoon video, personalized briefings?
take-off	long waits on the tarmac	fast-track arrangement with air traffic control?
watch a movie, play games	great, but caught a cold from the guy next to you	new air-conditioning
read, talk, work	couldn't, because of noisy neighbours	design seating so that it can be closed off from neighbours
meals and drinks	OK, but the choice and timing are so limiting	offer a buffet rather than a served meal

Table 20.2 (contd)

sleep	couldn't, because the seat was too small	put beds in business class
meals and drinks	you usually have an earlier breakfast	have a buffet option
landing	never-ending circling and circling	fast-track arrangement with air traffic control?
disembark	a tedious wait – so close but yet so far	psychology …
passport and immigration	big delays	fast-track arrangement, schedule to arrive at less busy times
luggage	worry of non-arrival	on arrival, limo service handles collection
customs	time	check on departure, not arrival?
into the terminal	tired, can't send your e-mails	arrival lounges with showers, business services
find taxi	huge hassle	on arrival, limo
check in to hotel	tired and emotional	check-in handled by limo
business meetings	lots of admin, no support	associate hotels provide support
reconfirm flights	plain nuisance	not required
start over …	etc	…

Not all of the ideas for positive impact will work, nor should we seek to do them all. Remember that this stage of the process is a brainstorming one – expanding our horizons before narrowing in on our choice of activities.

Always try to map out the value chain from as early in the customers' process as possible to as late as possible. In many cases it will be both convenient and illuminating to divide the value chain into three sections: the before, the during and the after – Figure 20.1.

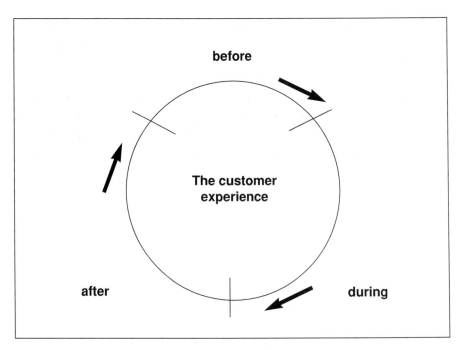

Figure 20.1   *The value chain as 'before, during and after'*

Portraying the chain as a circle rather than a linear table is perhaps more helpful, as it reminds us that we are not in a one-deal operation; we want customers to return and head round the cycle again and again.

'Before' relates to all the activities that occur before customers are directly involved with purchasing and using your product or service. This will include their generation of ideas, identification of needs, selection process, vendor ratings, trials, supplier negotiations and purchase. 'During' includes all the activities from purchase through to use, whether that be final consumption or an intermediate use. The 'after' section of the value chain includes all those activities for customers in their own market – the customers' customers.

The purpose of this split will become clear as you enter the steps in the customers' chain around the circle, and then add those activities that you already carry out to add value to the customers' experience. There is a good chance that you will have a very full picture of the 'late before' (they are talking to you and thinking of placing an order) through to the 'mid-during' (they have taken your product and started to use it). You probably have a much hazier picture of the 'early before', the 'late during' and, most likely of all, the 'after'. It is in this white space that many of the opportunities for competitive advantage lie.

Very often a supplier will have exhausted most of the value-creating ideas in the 'during' stage. This is, after all, where it has most contact with and knowledge of its customers. Exploration of the before and the after can often pay dividends in such circumstances.

We saw in the NutraSweet case study how significant value was when added through an understanding of what went on in the 'after' section of the customers' chain. Other examples of this strategy would include DuPont's use of brands such as Teflon and Lycra, or Intel with its ubiquitous 'Intel inside' stickers.

In the airline example we can see how, if we regard the flight itself as the 'during', there are not too many opportunities left for value enhancement, though some airlines are starting to put beds into first and business class while others say that they will fight back on price, so making the prospect of a bed seem a very expensive luxury indeed. Perhaps the best opportunities lie in the 'before' and the 'after'? Many of the options listed in Table 20.2 are already in place, such as limo pick-ups from home and fast-track arrivals, while others are still thoughts, for example fast-track air traffic control. This last idea caused a good deal of controversy when it was suggested that the air traffic controllers might sell a fast-track service to the highest bidders, one of the ideas raised in the discussion of privatizing parts of the UK air traffic control system.

The before–during–after split reminds us of two more important issues, the market chain (see Chapter 3) and the opportunity snail (see Chapter 19).

Value chain analysis and the market chain

Chapter 3 introduced the idea of the market chain, taking account of suppliers' suppliers, and customers' customers, right through to the end consumer. As your marketing approach moves towards solutions and beyond, the significance of the chain will increase. From the example in Chapter 3, an agrochemical supplier to farmers, it was at the supermarket/consumer interface that most market _noise_ was generated, and solutions for farmers must take account of that noise. In pursuit of value, each part of the chain will be looking for the impact it can have on solutions for the final consumer – the greater the impact, the greater the share of the reward in the chain. For a supplier some way back in the chain to the final consumer, the more it can understand the experiences sought by each step in the chain the more chance it will have of securing a greater share of the value in the chain. Figure 20.2 shows how you might need to consider a series of value chains, each starting off in the after stage of the one before. As you get further from your own customer so the circles may become hazier – and that spells an opportunity to gain competitive advantage, provided you have the capabilities.

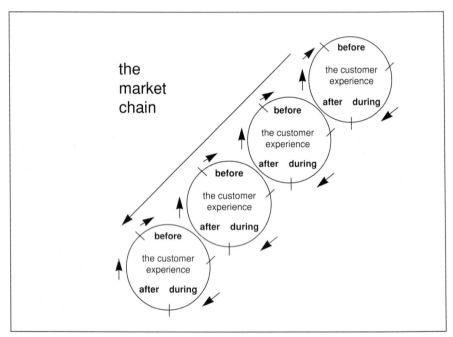

Figure 20.2   *Value chain analysis in the market chain*

Suppliers to the retail industry talk of *category management*, the idea that they should base their propositions on a combination of the retailer's perception of value received and the consumers', all of which is considered on the broad canvas of the market, not simply the suppliers' own products. This calls for an understanding of at least two separate value chains and the dynamics of the market besides.

A food supplier like Kraft combines its knowledge of the consumer with its knowledge of the retailer to deliver a high-value proposition to both. In the US, Kraft has segmented its consumers into six broad types based on their shopping behaviour. It has then designed specific ranges of products to appeal to these six types in different ways. Working with the retailer, it assesses what balance of these six types shop in each of the retailer's stores, and plans the store's range and layout accordingly. By looking beyond its immediate customer (the retailer), Kraft is able to add value to that customer *and* to the final consumer offer.

Kraft – delivering value to customers and consumers

Value chain analysis and the opportunity snail

In Chapter 19 we looked at the idea of the 'opportunity snail', a representation of how an idea develops in a business and how the practice of relationship marketing seeks to penetrate into that process. Our example of a food flavours supplier selling to an fmcg company placed marketing at the centre, moving out through R & D, manufacturing, purchasing and sales. We observed that if the supplier could gain access to the marketing people, then it would enhance its opportunities to add value, gain competitive advantage and be regarded as a strategic supplier. The problem was gaining access – why should marketing people want to see a raw materials supplier?

If we turn to the idea of the value chain we may see an answer to this question. Perhaps the best way to gain access to the marketing people at the *early before* stage is to demonstrate your value to them at the *late after* stage – this is, after all, a circle.

If the flavours supplier gains an understanding of consumer preferences by focusing on the after stage of its customer's chain, and if it can demonstrate this expertise, perhaps through research reports, then it might be invited into a dialogue to discuss future trends – the beginning of the opportunity snail.

SCREENING AND SELECTING POSITIVE IMPACT ACTIVITIES

We now have a range of *possible* activities that *might* make a positive impact on the customer's TBE. Of course, no supplier could work on all these at once, and in any case no customer is likely to want them all at once. The next step is to screen these possibles, selecting the priority actions. The following is a suggested checklist to be applied to each possible action:

- Does it add value to the total business experience sought?
- Does it remove the problem?
- Does it reduce the problem?
- What value does the customer put on this?
- Does it impact on the customer's core values (Weirsema's value drivers, for instance)?
- What does it cost the customer – time, money, other?
- Would the customer pay for it as part of a service?
- What will it cost you to provide?
- Can you charge enough to cover cost, or make a premium?
- Can you secure your fair share of the value added to the market?
- Do you have the capability?
- Can you work with a partner to bring the capability?
- Does it give you sustainable competitive advantage?
- Does it enhance your service to other customer groups, segments, markets?
- Does it help you avoid competitive disadvantage?
- Does it give you 'lock-in' – in other words, is this something that will tie your customer to you and is difficult for your competitors to replicate?

Enhancing the total business experience

Going back to our airline example and the search for added-value ideas, a particular favourite of mine is a service from Virgin Atlantic where visitors to Walt Disney World in Orlando can check their luggage in at the park, so allowing them a proper last day to their holiday rather than the traditional slog to the airport and check-in three hours before the flight.

Why this particular service? Because Virgin has identified the desired total experience sought by a particular segment of the market, the family on holiday. This group wants to squeeze the most holiday time out of the week or the fortnight.

For business travellers, a different segment of the market, there is a different total business experience sought. These travellers may be focused on completing business deals, and anything the flight does to assist them – reduced waiting times, space to work, office space on arrival – will be regarded as adding value.

'Lock-in'

This is a matter of huge importance. Any supplier can do things that are of value to customers, but whether they bring sustainable competitive advantage is another matter. Extended credit is certainly of value to customers, but it is very easy for a competitor to match or even surpass. Such added value is short-lived, the competitive advantage is not sustainable and, worst of all, it can start a process that will spiral out of control as competing suppliers vie to improve the last offer.

Sustainable competitive advantage comes from activities that encourage loyalty, and that competitors are not able to match without costly effort. Buying loyalty rarely works. Frequent flyer miles are said to be about loyalty, but it is very often false loyalty; customers go elsewhere as soon as the scheme is stopped. Worse, everyone can do them.

The secret of 'lock-in' is finding an activity or service that customers value and would rather not perform themselves, which the competitor doesn't offer and which doesn't involve handing the supplier too much power. It is a delicate balance – 'lock-in' implies supplier power, and suppliers should tread carefully. The airline that offers to manage its corporate clients' full business travel arrangements must take great care not to abuse its position – London to Moscow via New York (the airline has no direct flight) is not value; it is an outrage!

The lock-in that got them locked out – Apple

Perhaps the most famous example of a misplaced attempt at lock-in was that of Apple. Apple had a truly splendid operating system but wanted to hang on to it and use its strength to sell its own machines; you could only have it if you bought an Apple computer. This effectively restricted the value that consumers could receive, and when Microsoft allowed MS-DOS to be put on any machine you liked, they won the day.

Lock-in can be unpopular if used for too obviously selfish ends. Much of the complaint against the development of genetically modified seeds is that they are designed to resist the effects of the suppliers' own pesticides, a clear attempt to lock the customer in to the purchase of those pesticides. Somewhere along the line the intention to help farmers improve their yield becomes confused with other more selfish intentions if the marketing is not handled well. The notorious 'terminator gene' that would prevent the crop from producing new seed was a step too far, particularly when considering the sale to Third-World countries, and that particular attempt at lock-in was withdrawn.

Gaining advantage or avoiding disadvantage?

The PIA process will help to identify those activities that will add most value to your customer's business. Some of these things may be unique to you – we might call them differentiators – and they provide a real source of competitive advantage.

It will also help identify another type of activity, which we might call the 'givens'. These are the things that must be in place for business to be carried on. While it is the differentiators that will gain you competitive advantage, it is by attending to the givens that you will avoid suffering competitive disadvantage. More than this, customers will be loath to listen to your ideas for adding value if they feel that you are letting them down on the everyday front. Failure to attend to givens leads to a perpetual round of 'catch-up' and fire-fighting that can quickly sap a supplier's energy and dull a customer's enthusiasm.

Does an automatic telling machine outside a bank give it competitive advantage? Probably not. Does the absence of such a money machine cause it to suffer competitive disadvantage? Probably so: the ATM has become a given.

Some hints on using positive impact analysis

- Involve a cross-functional team – each member will see a different aspect of the customer relationship and value chain, and so the different opportunities.
- Use PIA as a means of uncovering gaps in your knowledge and so as a spur to further research.
- If possible, involve the customer (but take care not to build unrealistic expectations).

- Be open-minded about the need to work with partners.
- Repeat the exercise regularly, backed up by market research, customer surveys, customer involvement, etc.
- Don't stop at considering the customer's value chain – include the customer's customers and beyond, all the way to the consumer. Go beyond your customer.

ADDING VALUE BY REMOVING FEATURES

It is easy to get into the mindset that to add value you must do more, and that differentiation is the only route to take. Always remember that the marketer has choices; there is rarely only one route to success. Michael Porter spelt out the two routes to competitive advantage – differentiation and lowest-cost supplier – and warned against the perils of being an 'inbetweeny'. This model fits into what we might call the 'either or' school of thought, followed since the 1960s by those folk concerned that variety, far from being the spice of life, can be the fast road to bankruptcy. Several factors in more recent times – the focus on supply chain management and the e-revolution stand out in particular – have allowed some to follow what we might call the 'this and' school of thought, looking at the prospect for a lowest-cost supplier with a genuinely differentiated offer.

Understanding the customer's value chain allows us to ask the vital question – what elements of the experience with the supplier are valued most (some perhaps hugely so) and what parts are valued least (perhaps not at all)? If elements of the experience are not valued at all, then they can only represent unnecessary costs in customers' eyes, so why not remove them? The result is a stripped-down offer that truly meets customers' value perceptions, and one with lower costs to boot. If those lower costs are then passed on to customers through a lower price, then their perception of value received will be even greater – folk might even start to talk of 'bargains'! (The debate over what constitutes a bargain is a long one – is it the receipt of extras that you didn't really want but are nice to get if they are 'free', or is it about getting what you really want for a great price? Horses for courses, but for now I am following the latter line.)

399

Formule 1 – where less is proving to be more

Let's look at this approach with a real example – the Formule 1 hotel chain, which delivers a dramatically stripped-down product for a very good price. Figure 20.3 shows what we might call the value curves for three hotels, a typical one-star, a typical two-star and Formule 1.

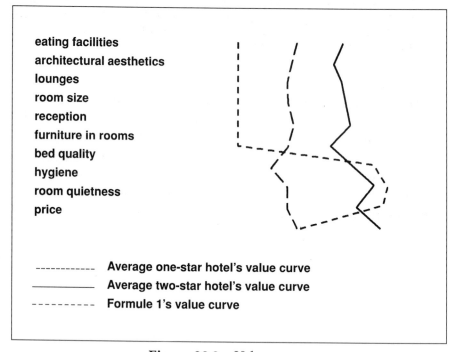

eating facilities
architectural aesthetics
lounges
room size
reception
furniture in rooms
bed quality
hygiene
room quietness
price

\- - - - - - - - - - -   **Average one-star hotel's value curve**
_____   **Average two-star hotel's value curve**
\- - - - - - - - -   **Formule 1's value curve**

Figure 20.3 *Value curves*

Measured against the whole range of features of a hotel, the two-star's enhanced facilities command a price premium because there are customers out there who value those things. Their operating costs, assuming a similar scale of business, are doubtless higher and the secret to their success in competition with the one-star is in gaining a sufficient premium to outweigh those costs – a typical differentiation strategy.

What Formule 1 aims to do is strip out all those features that it believes its customers do not want and so do not value. For those features that really are valued – the bed, the cleanliness and the low noise level – Formule 1 aims to go one better than the typical two-star hotel. This approach makes the hotel a very low-cost operator indeed – low cost position, minimal staff and huge space efficiencies being just some of the reasons. This low cost can be passed on to the customer in a price barely different from a one-star hotel. Sometimes less truly is more.

The key to this strategy lies of course in that word – sometimes. It is the specific segment of the market that Formule 1 targets that makes this the appropriate offer, the right marketing mix. For the business traveller who is constantly on the move, out with the client all evening and up with the lark in the morning, and who simply needs a good sleep at night, this is the ideal pitch. Motel 6, a US chain with a similar approach, has even gone as far as placing a poster above the bed that says, 'When you're asleep, our rooms look as good as anyone's!'

Other hotels have tried to copy aspects of this approach; Ramada International advertises itself as 'everything except excess', with a photograph of a fancy sterling silver food dome at a $$$$ price next to one of a simple catering plate ring at a $$ price, but this is only a part of the story. The no-frills approach must drive down costs so that customers can see the value of their abstinence in a low price, and they must receive what they really value in spades.

The real secret lies in observing some basic disciplines of marketing – a good basis for segmentation, thorough market research on the chosen segment, looking into the needs, attitudes, perceptions and behaviours of target customers, an excellent understanding of their concept of value, and good targeting. After that the resultant offer of a good clean bed in a quiet room and the ruthless eradication of unnecessary costs is simply a matter of implementation.

21

Getting further help

The opportunities for developing your marketing knowledge expertise and professionalism are huge, so I will focus on just four:

- training opportunities;
- professional qualifications;
- application tools;
- further reading.

TRAINING OPPORTUNITIES

This book was born out of a training event (Key Marketing Strategies) that has grown in reputation and stature over the last 20 years. Originally designed to 'introduce marketing to ICI', Key Marketing Strategies is now delivered by INSIGHT Marketing and People both as an open event to delegates from all backgrounds – business-to-business, fmcg and service – and as an in-house event for international clients in a wide range of markets, including telecommunications, speciality chemicals, fmcg, pharmaceuticals, financial services and IT.

Key Marketing Strategies is a three-day event and is delivered in the UK as an open event at venues such as Corpus Christi College, Cambridge, three or four times a year. If you would like details on dates and venues, including those for outside the UK, please contact INSIGHT Marketing and People Ltd, PO Box 997, Wexham Road, Slough, Berks SL2 5JJ, UK (tel: +44 (0)1753 877750; fax: +44 (0)1753 877342; e-mail: customer.service@insight-mp.com).

You will find full details on the objectives and content of the event on the CD ROM that accompanies this book.

PROFESSIONAL QUALIFICATIONS

Key Marketing Strategies can be the gateway to the Chartered Institute of Marketing's Postgraduate Diploma in Marketing (DipM). INSIGHT is an accredited CIM Study Centre and, for a graduate, attendance at Key Marketing Strategies and its follow-up event, Marketing for Competitive Advantage, gives exemption from up to two years' study and allows direct entry to the final four CIM examinations for the Diploma in Marketing.

For details of how you can enter the fast track to this highly regarded professional qualification please contact INSIGHT as shown above.

APPLICATION TOOLS

The CD ROM attached to this book contains a number of tools to help you apply the concepts to your own business:

- The INSIGHT Marketing Planning Proforma gives you a template to help prepare your own marketing plan.
- The INSIGHT Directional Policy Matrix allows you to plot your own markets, segments, products or customers as described in this book.
- The main models and diagrams used in this book are provided as a PowerPoint presentation, to help you prepare your own internal presentations.

If you wish, INSIGHT is able to critique your plans, or provide other consultancy services.

Further reading and references

The list of books on marketing is huge, so this list is only a very small sample of those that will help you to develop your understanding and application beyond this title.

Barrett, N (1997) *Advertising on the Internet*, Kogan Page, London

Bird, D (2000) *Commonsense Direct Marketing*, Kogan Page, London

Cheverton, P (1999) *Key Account Management: The route to profitable key supplier status*, Kogan Page, London

Kotler, P (1999) *Kotler on Marketing*, Free Press

McDonald, M (1999) *Marketing Plans: How to prepare them, how to use them*, Butterworth Heinemann, Oxford

Payne, A *et al* (1995) *Relationship Marketing For Competitive Advantage*, Butterworth Heinemann, Oxford

Porter, M (1980) *Competitive Strategy*, New York Free Press, New York

Ries, A (1998) *The 22 Immutable Laws of Branding*, HarperCollins, New York

Treacy, M and Weirsema, F (1995) *The Discipline of Market Leaders*, HarperCollins, London

Index